O9-ABG-856

Visual Perception
Physiology, Psychology and Ecology

Visual Perception Physiology, Psychology and Ecology

VICKI BRUCE and PATRICK R. GREEN

Department of Psychology
University of Nottingham
Nottingham, U.K.

 LAWRENCE ERLBAUM ASSOCIATES, PUBLISHERS
London   Hillsdale, New Jersey

Copyright © 1985 by Lawrence Erlbaum Associates Ltd.
All rights reserved. No part of this book may be reproduced in
any form, by photostat, microform, retrieval system, or any other
means, without the prior written permission of the publisher.

Lawrence Erlbaum Associates Ltd., Publishers
Chancery House
319 City Road
London EC1V 1LJ

British Library Cataloguing in Publication Data

Bruce, Vicki
   Visual perception: physiology, psychology
   and ecology
   1. Visual perception
   I. Title   II. Green, Patrick
   152.1'4   BF241

   ISBN 0–86377–012–6
   ISBN 0–86377–013–4 Pbk

Typeset by Multiplex Techniques Ltd, Orpington.
Printed and bound by A. Wheaton & Co. Ltd., Exeter.

104120

To Michael
and
To the memory of Rodney Green

Contents

Preface

Our primary aim in writing this book has been to present a wide range of recent evidence and theoretical developments in the field of visual perception to an advanced undergraduate readership. The material covered is drawn from three areas: the neurophysiological analysis of vision, the "computational" accounts of vision which have grown out of traditional experimental approaches and artificial intelligence, and work on vision which shares at least some of J. J. Gibson's "ecological" framework.

In the first part of the book we discuss the evolution of different types of eye, the neurophysiological organisation of visual pathways, particularly in mammals, and contrasting theoretical interpretations of single unit responses in visual systems.

We turn in the second part to psychological and computational models of the interpretation of information in retinal images, discussing perceptual organisation, the perception of depth and of movement, and pattern and object recognition. The contribution of David Marr's work to these problems is emphasised.

In the third part we discuss how extended patterns of light can provide information for the control of action and to specify events; topics covered are the visual guidance of animal and human locomotion, theories of the control of action, the role of vision in animal social behaviour and human event perception.

We have assumed that our readers will have some prior knowledge of basic neurophysiology (for Part I of the book) and experimental psychology (for Parts II and III), such as might have been gained from an introductory psychology course.

Our choice of topics differs in some respects from that of most textbooks of visual perception. Some topics are excluded. In particular, we do not discuss sensory physiology and psychophysics in as much detail as other texts. We do include material on animal perception which would usually be found in an ethology text, and consider in detail research on human and animal reactions to patterns of optic flow. Our choice of topics is governed by a consistent theoretical outlook. We have been committed to the value of an ecological approach in its *wider* sense; that espoused by David Marr as much as by James Gibson, who both argued for the need to consider the structure of the world in which an animal or person lives and perceives. It is this commitment which has guided the overall plan of the book.

We have attempted to go beyond exposition of theoretical and empirical developments in each of our three areas, to discuss promising issues for further research, and to present an analysis and critique of the theories we discuss. We have been most speculative about future possibilities for the ecological approach in Chapters 12 and 13, and we address global theoretical issues most fully in Chapter 14. Our final conclusion is that an ecological perspective offers valuable insights, but that a "direct" theory of perception is not adequate.

These are exciting times in the study of visual perception, and we believe that there is much to be gained by cross-fertilisation between research areas. There are real and important issues dividing different theoretical camps, which must continue to be debated vigorously, but it is also worthwhile to mark out some potential common ground.

Although the readers we have in mind are advanced psychology students, we have designed the book to also be useful to zoology students specialising in neurophysiology and in animal behaviour, and particularly to students in the increasingly popular courses which combine zoology and psychology. We hope that research workers may also find the book useful; although it will surely be superficial in their areas of primary interest, it may be helpful in approaching the literature in adjoining areas.

Our manuscript has been improved considerably as a result of critical comments from a number of people. Our colleague Alan Dodds read the entire manuscript, and Robin Stevens read parts. A number of anonymous reviewers furnished further comments. We would like to thank all these people most sincerely. They spotted blunders, and suggested ways of making points more clearly, which would not have occurred to us alone; any remaining errors are, of course, our own. Mike Burton helped us with our own, and other people's, mathematical reasoning. He was also one of several people who introduced us to the mysteries of word-processing; Chris Blunsdon, Roger Henry and Anne Lomax are the others.

Roger Boulton-Somerville (WIDES Advertising and Design) drew all those figures not otherwise acknowledged, and thus contributed enormously to the text. Sam Grainger took many photographs, and E. Hildreth, D. H. Hubel, Fergus Campbell, John Frisby and Paul Ekman all provided photographs for us to use. Penny Radcliffe typed endless letters and helped in many other ways when we ourselves were flagging. Mike Forster and Rohays Perry encouraged us to see this project through, and gave us editorial help.

I
THE PHYSIOLOGICAL BASIS OF VISUAL PERCEPTION

1 Light and Eyes

All organisms, whether bacteria, oak trees or whales, must be adapted to their environments if they are to survive and reproduce. The structure and physiology of organisms are not fixed at the start of life; to some extent, adjustments to changes in the environment can occur so as to "fine-tune" the organism's adaptation. One way of achieving this is through the regulation of growth processes, as when plants grow so that their leaves face the strongest available light. Another way, which is much more rapid and is only available to animals, is movement of the body by contraction of muscles.

If the movement of an animal's body is to adapt it to its environment, it must be regulated, or guided, by the environment. Thus the swimming movements of a fish's body, tail and fins are regulated so as to bring it into contact with food and to avoid obstacles; the movement of a person's throat, tongue and lips in speaking are regulated by the speech of other people, linguistic rules and so on.

In order for its movement to be regulated by the environment, an animal must be able to detect structures and events in its surroundings. We call this ability *perception*, and it in turn requires that an animal be sensitive to at least one form of energy which can provide information about the environment. One source of information is provided by chemical substances diffusing through air or water. Another is mechanical energy, whether pressure on the body surface, forces on the limbs and muscles or waves of sound pressure in air or water. Further information sources, to which some animals are sensitive but people probably are not, are electric and magnetic fields.

An animal sensitive to diffusing chemicals can detect the presence of nearby food or predators, but often cannot pinpoint their exact location, and cannot detect the layout of its inanimate surroundings. Pressure on the skin and mechanical forces on the limbs can provide information about the environment in immediate contact with an animal, while sound can provide information about more distant animals but not usually about distant inanimate structures.

Sensitivity to diffusing chemicals and to mechanical energy gives an animal considerable perceptual abilities, but leaves it unable to obtain information rapidly about either its inanimate world or about silent animals at a distance from itself (there are a few exceptions, however; see Chapter 9, p. 207). The form of energy that can provide these kinds of information is *light*, and consequently most animals have some ability to perceive their surroundings through vision. We will begin our discussion of visual perception in animals and people by considering first the physical nature of light and then how the environment structures the light that reaches an observer.

LIGHT AND THE INFORMATION IT CARRIES

Light is one form of *electromagnetic radiation*; a mode of propagation of energy through space which includes radio waves, radiant heat, gamma rays and X-rays. One way in which we can picture the nature of electromagnetic radiation is as a pattern of waves propagated through an imaginary medium. It therefore has a velocity, 3×10^{-8} m/sec in a vacuum, and a wavelength, which ranges from hundreds of metres in the case of radio waves to 10^{-12} or 10^{-13} m in the case of cosmic rays. Only a very small part of this range is visible; for human beings, radiation with wavelengths between 400 and 700 nanometres (1 nm = 10^{-9} m) can be seen (Fig. 1.1).

For some purposes, however, the model of electromagnetic radiation as a wave does not work and we must picture it differently, as a stream of tiny particles called *photons* travelling in a straight line at the speed of light. Each photon consists of a quantum of energy (the shorter the wavelength of the light the larger the energy quantum), which is given up as it strikes another particle. We need these two conceptions of the nature of electromagnetic radiation because nothing in our experience is analogous to the actual nature of it and we must make do with two imperfect analogies at the same time.

These problems are of no concern in understanding how light is propagated around the environment. For these purposes we can think of light as made up of rays, which vary in both their intensity and their wavelength. Rays are emitted from light sources and would, in a vacuum, travel in a straight line without attenuation. A vacuum is not a congenial environment for

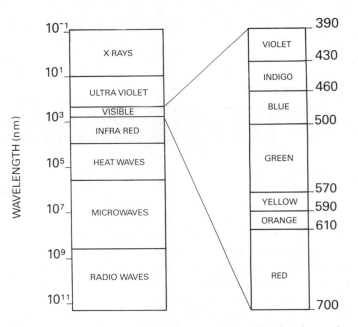

FIG.1.1.   The spectrum of electromagnetic radiation. Wavelengths are given in nanometres (1 nm = 10^{-9} m). The visible part of the spectrum is shown on the right, with the colours of different wavelengths of light.

animals, however, and the fate of light rays travelling through natural habitats is more complex.

First, as light passes through a medium, even a transparent one such as air or water, it undergoes *absorption*, as photons collide with particles of matter, give up their energy and disappear. Absorption is much stronger in water than in air and even in the clearest oceans there is no detectable sunlight below about 1000 metres. Longer wavelengths are absorbed more strongly, so that available light becomes progressively bluer in deeper water.

Secondly, light is *diffracted* as it passes through a transparent or translucent medium. Its energy is not absorbed, but rather rays are scattered on striking small particles of matter. Diffraction of sunlight by the atmosphere is the reason why the sky is blue; light of shorter wavelengths is scattered more and so a greater proportion of light reaching the ground is blue. Without an atmosphere, the sky would be completely dark, as it is on the moon.

Thirdly, the velocity of light falls when it passes through a transparent medium; the greater the optical density of the medium, the greater the decrease. As a result, when rays of light pass from a medium of one optical density to a medium of a different density, they are bent, or *refracted*, unless they strike the boundary between the two media perpendicularly. Refraction occurs, for example, at the boundary between air and water or between air and glass, and we will consider it in more detail when we describe the structure of eyes.

Finally, when light strikes an opaque surface, some of its energy is absorbed and some of it is *reflected*. A matt black surface absorbs most of the light falling on it and reflects little, while a silvery surface does the opposite. The way surfaces reflect light varies in two important ways. First, a surface may reflect some wavelengths more strongly than others, so that the proportions of wavelengths in the reflected light differ from those in the incident light. A leaf, for example, absorbs more (and hence reflects less) red light than light of other wavelengths. Note that surfaces do not reflect single wavelengths and absorb all others; they reflect a mixture of wavelengths that differs from the mixture in the light striking them.

Secondly, the *texture* of a surface determines how coherently it reflects light. A perfectly smooth surface such as a mirror reflects light uniformly, but most natural surfaces have a rougher texture, made up of a mosaic of tiny reflecting surfaces set at different angles. Light striking such a surface is therefore reflected in an incoherent way (see Fig. 1.2).

Now that we have described the nature of light and the processes governing its travel through space, we turn to ask how it carries information for animals about their environments. A useful concept in understanding this is the *ambient optic array*, a term coined by Gibson (1966). Imagine an environment illuminated by sunlight and therefore filled with rays of light travelling between surfaces. At any point, light will converge from all directions, and we can imagine the point surrounded by a sphere divided into tiny solid angles. The intensity of light and the mixture of wavelengths will vary from one solid angle to another, and this spatial pattern of light is the optic array. Light carries information because the structure of the

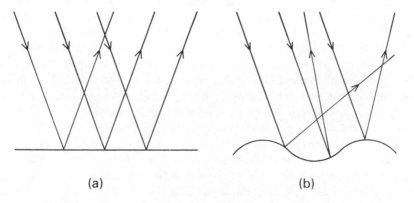

(a)   (b)

FIG.1.2.   Regular reflection of rays of light from a polished surface such as a mirror (a) and irregular reflection from a textured surface (b).

optic array is determined by the nature and position of the surfaces from which it has been reflected.

Figure 1.3 illustrates the relationship between environment and optic array. At a point just above the ground, there is a simple pattern in the array, with light in the upper part coming directly from the sun or scattered by the atmosphere, and light in the lower part having been reflected from the surface of the ground. The array is therefore divided into two segments differing in the intensity and mixture of wavelengths of light arriving through them. The boundary between these two areas specifies the horizon.

Each of these two segments can be further subdivided, and finer levels of spatial pattern in the optic array carry further information. The upper segment contains a region in which light of very high intensity arrives from the sun, and its position relative to the horizon specifies time of day. The pattern of light intensities and wavelengths in the lower segment will not be uniform unless the surface is smooth and mirror-like; the rays of light in the array reflected from a natural, textured surface will differ in intensity and wavelength from point to point in the array. In other words, there will be a fine structure in the optic array, characteristic of the surface from which the light has been reflected. A sandy surface and a stony surface, for example, would give different patterns of fine structure in the optic array.

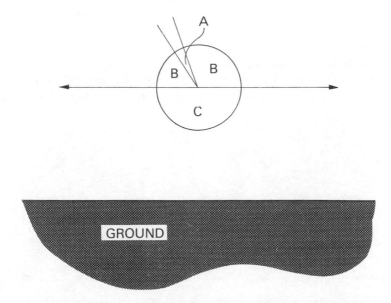

FIG.1.3. Section through the optic array at a point above the ground in an open environment. In angle A incident light arrives directly from the sun, in angles B it has been scattered by the atmosphere and in angle C it has been reflected from the ground. The arrows point to the distant horizon.

If we add objects to this simple environment (Fig. 1.4) we get an optic array with a more complex spatial pattern. It is divided into many segments, containing light reflected from different surfaces, and differing in the average intensities and mixtures of wavelengths of light passing through them. The boundaries between these segments of the optic array provide information about the three-dimensional structure of objects in the world. Again, at a finer level of detail, each segment of the array will be patterned in a way determined by the texture of the surface that its light is reflected from. At this level, the optic array can carry information about further properties of objects and terrain.

So far, we have considered how a static optic array provides information about the world. Most natural environments contain movement, however, and most animals need to detect it. Any movement in the environment will be specified by a change in the spatial pattern of the optic array. Some movement in nature is slow, such as the daily movement of the sun across the sky. The optic array in Figure 1.3 will change with the movement of the sun, not only in the position of the segment of rays arriving from the sun but also in the pattern of wavelengths from different parts of the sky.

Rapid movement, such as that of other animals, will be specified in short-term fluctuations in the spatial pattern of the optic array. If one of the objects in Figure 1.4 moves, the boundaries of some segments in the optic array will move relative to the others. This spatiotemporal pattern in the optic array can carry further information about the direction, speed and form of movement involved.

We have been looking at simple optic arrays in daylight in open terrestrial environments, but the same principles apply in any illuminated environment. At night, the moon and stars illuminate the world in the same way as does

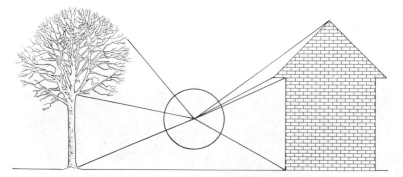

FIG.1.4.   Section through the optic array at a point above the ground in an environment containing objects. The optic array is divided into segments through which light arrives after reflection from different surfaces. Each segment has a different fine structure (not shown) corresponding to the texture of each surface.

the sun, though with light that is many orders of magnitude less intense. In water, however, there are some differences. First, refraction of light at the water surface means that the segment of the optic array specifying "sky" is of a narrower angle than on land. Second, light is absorbed and scattered much more by water than by air, so that information about distant objects is not specified in the pattern of intensities and wavelengths in the optic array. Third, in deep water, light from below is not reflected from the substrate but scattered upwards (Fig. 1.5).

These examples all illustrate one important point; the spatial and temporal *pattern* of light converging on a point in a land or water environment provides information about the structure of the environment and events occurring in it. The speed of light ensures that, effectively, events in the environment are represented in the optic array instantaneously. Only in deep oceans and completely dark caves is no information at all available in light, although the phenomenon of *bioluminescence*—the emission of light by organisms—means that even in these habitats light may carry information about the biological surroundings.

Up to this point we have considered a point just above the ground, or in open water, and asked what sort of information is available in the optic array converging on that point. Now, we must put an animal at the centre of this optic array and ask how it can detect the information available in it. If it is to detect any information at all, it must first have some kind of structure sensitive to light energy, and our next topic is the evolution of such structures among animals. How do different kinds of light-sensitive structures allow light energy to influence the activity of animals' nervous systems, and what scope do these structures have for detecting the fundamental

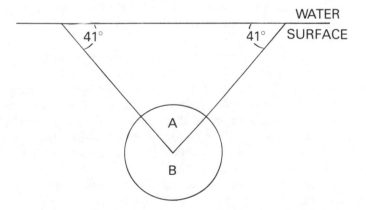

FIG.1.5. Section through the optic array at a point below the water surface. Because light rays from the sky and sun are refracted at the air-water boundary, they are "compressed" into an angle (A) of 98°. Incident light in angle B has been scattered by water or reflected from underwater objects.

information-carrying features of optic arrays; spatial pattern and changes in spatial patterns?

THE EVOLUTION OF LIGHT-SENSITIVE STRUCTURES

Many biological molecules absorb electromagnetic radiation in the visible part of the spectrum, changing in chemical structure as they do so. Various biochemical mechanisms have evolved which couple such changes to other processes. One such mechanism is photosynthesis, in which absorption of light by chlorophyll molecules powers the biochemical synthesis of sugars by plants. Animals, on the other hand, have concentrated on harnessing the absorption of light by light-sensitive molecules to the mechanisms which make them move.

In single-celled animals, absorption of light can modulate processes of locomotion directly through biochemical pathways. *Amoeba* moves by a streaming motion of the cytoplasm to form extensions of the cell called pseudopods. If a pseudopod extends into bright light, streaming stops and is diverted in a different direction, so that the animal remains in dimly lit areas. *Amoeba* possesses no known pigment molecules specialised for light sensitivity, and presumably light has some direct effect on the enzymes involved in making the cytoplasm stream. Thus, the animal can avoid bright light despite having no specialised light-sensitive structures.

Other protozoa do have pigment molecules with the specific function of detecting light. One example is the ciliate *Stentor coeruleus*, which responds to an increase in light intensity with a reversal of the waves of ciliary beat which propel it through the water. Capture of light by a blue pigment causes a change in the membrane potential of the cell, which in turn affects ciliary beat (Wood, 1976).

Other protozoans, such as the flagellate *Euglena*, have more elaborate light-sensitive structures, in which pigment is concentrated into an eyespot, but *Stentor* illustrates the basic principles of *transduction* of light energy which operate in more complex animals. First, when a pigment molecule absorbs light, its chemical structure changes. This, in turn, is coupled to an alteration in the structure of the cell membrane, so that the membrane's permeability to ions is modified, which in turn leads to a change in the electrical potential across the membrane.

In a single cell, this change in membrane potential need travel only a short distance to influence processes that move the animal about. In a many-celled animal, however, some cells are specialised for generating movement and some for detection of light and other external energy. These are separated by distances too great for electrotonic spread of a change in membrane potential, and information is instead transmitted by neurons with long processes, or axons, along which action potentials are propagated.

In many invertebrates, particularly those with translucent bodies, the motor- and interneurons, which generate patterns of muscle contraction, contain pigment and are directly sensitive to light. This sensitivity is the basis of the diffuse "dermal" light sense of various molluscs, echinoids and crustacea, which do not possess photoreceptor cells but nevertheless are sensitive to light, and particularly to a sudden dimming of light caused by an animal passing overhead (Millott, 1968).

Most animals sensitive to light possess *photoreceptor* cells, specialised for the transduction of light into a receptor potential. Photoreceptor cells may be scattered over the skin, as in earthworms, or may be concentrated into patches called *eyespots*, such as those along the mantle edge of some bivalve molluscs.

Recall that it is the spatial pattern of light in the optic array which provides information about the environment. To what extent can an animal with single receptor cells or patches of cells in eyespots detect spatial pattern? The answer is that it cannot, since a single receptor cell samples the *total* light reaching it from all directions. It can, however, detect changes over time in total intensity, and invertebrates with a dermal light sense or simple eyespots probably do no more than this. For an aquatic animal, a sudden reduction in light intensity is likely to mean a potential predator is passing overhead, and clams and jellyfish respond to such dimming with defensive responses.

If any spatial pattern in the optic array is to be detected, an animal must have a *number* of photoreceptors and each must be sensitive to light in a narrow segment of the array. In practice, any photoreceptor cell has some such directional sensitivity. The way pigment is arranged in the cell makes it more sensitive to light from some directions than from others, and further directional sensitivity is achieved in simple eyespots by screening the receptor cells with a layer of dark pigment.

An animal with eyespots distributed over its body, each screened by pigment, therefore has some ability to detect spatial pattern in the light reaching it (see Fig. 1.6). It would, for example, be able to use the pattern of activity in its eyespots to maintain its swimming orientation by keeping the source of greatest light intensity above it, or to orient defensive responses according to the rough direction of approach of a predator.

The evolution of greater complexity in eyes can be thought of as the invention of various ways of improving directional sensitivity. One simple way of doing this is to sink a patch of receptor cells into the skin to make an "eye-cup" or *ocellus* (Fig. 1.7). Many invertebrates possess eye-cups, particularly coelenterates, flatworms, molluscs and annelid worms. Eye-cups vary in the detail of their structure; some are open to the water, others are filled with gelatinous material, while many contain a crystalline lens.

The receptor cells in an eye-cup are clearly sensitive to light from a narrower angle than if they were on the surface of the skin, and the presence of a refractile lens further helps to reject light rays at a large angle from the axis. An animal with eye-cups distributed over its body can, because of this greater directional sensitivity, detect finer spatial pattern in the optic array than can the animal in Figure 1.6 with its eye-spots. Some molluscs have rows of regularly spaced eye-cups along the body—examples are the marine gastropod *Corolla* and some bivalves with eye-cups along the mantle edge—

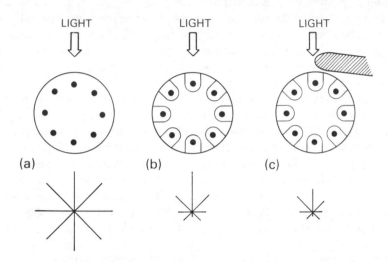

FIG.1.6. A hypothetical transparent disc-shaped animal with patches of photoreceptor cells around its edge. The lengths of the bars in the lower diagram represent the intensities of light falling on each patch. In (a) each patch is sensitive to light through 360° and so each receives the same amount of light. In (b) and (c), screening of the patches by pigment reduces the angle through which they are sensitive to light. The amounts of light striking each receptor now differ, and the pattern of differences captures information available in the optic array specifying the direction of the water surface (b) or an overhead object (c).

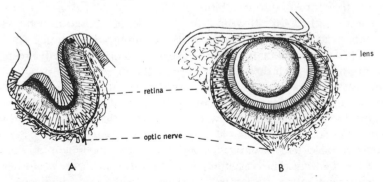

FIG.1.7. Examples of eye-cups, from the limpet *Patella* (A) and the snail *Murex* (B). Reproduced from Barnes, (1968) by permission of the publishers.

and these animals are potentially able to detect nearby moving objects through successive dimming of light in adjacent eye-cups.

Because the angles through which eye-cups are sensitive to light are wide, and overlap a good deal, the degree of directional sensitivity achieved by an animal with many eye-cups is not great. Further directional sensitivity requires the possession of a true *eye*. The eye-cups of molluscs appear to be miniature eyes, but their function differs from that of eyes in a crucial way. A true eye forms an *image* on a layer of photoreceptor cells. When an image is formed, all light rays reaching the eye from one point in space are brought together at one point in the image, so that each receptor cell in the eye is struck by light coming from a different narrow segment of the optic array.

In most mollusc eye-cups possessing a lens, the image lies some distance behind the layer of photoreceptors (Land, 1968) and so spatial pattern in the optic array is not mapped on to the array of receptors in a single eye-cup. Instead, following the principle illustrated in Figure 1.6, it is mapped onto the array of eye-cups over the body. In a sense, it is the whole animal that is an eye. To build a true eye requires *both* concentration of photoreceptor cells into one part of the body *and* some apparatus for forming an image on them. We describe the two basic structural plans of eyes; the compound and the single-chambered eye.

The Compound Eye

A compound eye can be constructed by continuing the process of making eye-cups more directionally sensitive, while at the same time making them smaller and grouping them all together into a single structure. Eyes of this kind have evolved in some bivalve molluscs (e.g. *Arca*) and in the marine annelid *Branchioma*, but the most elaborate eyes based on this principle are those of crustaceans and insects. A compound eye is made up of a number of *ommatidia*; each one is a small, elongated eye-cup with a crystalline cone at the tip and the light-sensitive *rhabdom* below it. Transparent cuticle—the cornea—covers the whole array of ommatidia (Fig. 1.8a).

Compound eyes vary in several ways around this basic plan. The number of ommatidia varies greatly, and the structure of the cone differs in the eyes of different insect groups, some eyes not having a cone at all. A particularly important kind of variability in the compound eye is the degree of optical isolation between adjacent ommatidia. This is greatest in the *apposition* type of eye, characteristic of some crustaceans and of diurnal insects, in which the rhabdoms and cones touch and there is absorptive screening pigment between the ommatidia. These two features reduce the amount of light that can reach a rhabdom from cones other than that above it and so keeps the angle of acceptance of light of each ommatidium low.

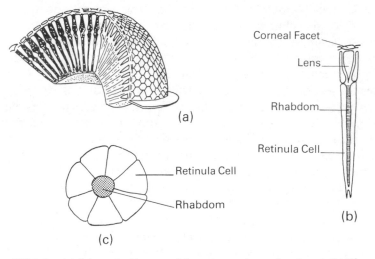

FIG.1.8. (a) Schematic diagram of the compound eye of an insect. (b) The structure of a single ommatidium. (c) Cross section through an ommatidium, showing the rhabdom made up from overlapping folds of retinula cell membrane. Adapted from Wigglesworth (1964).

At the other extreme is the *superposition* eye, which has less pigment between ommatidia and a clear space between the layer of cones and the layer of rhabdoms, so that there is more opportunity for light to reach a rhabdom from neighbouring cones. The difference in structure between apposition and superposition eyes reflects an important difference in the means by which they form an image on the layer of rhabdoms. In the apposition eye, light striking the cone of an ommatidium from outside its narrow angle of acceptance does not reach the rhabdom, but is either reflected or absorbed. This mechanism yields an image in bright light, but has the disadvantage that, in dim light, each ommatidium cannot gather sufficient light to stimulate the receptors.

The superposition eye forms an image in a different way, according to optical principles described by Land (1980). For our purposes, the important point is that light rays from one point in space striking *many* adjacent cones of a superposition eye are brought to a focus on the same rhabdom, so that each rhabdom gathers light over a wide area of the eye without necessarily losing directional sensitivity. Superposition eyes can therefore provide vision in dimmer light than can apposition eyes, and accordingly are commonly found in nocturnal insects.

So far, we have seen how the structure of a compound eye ensures that each rhabdom samples a small segment of the optic array. How do the rhabdoms transduce the light striking them into electrical changes in nerve cells which can ultimately modulate behaviour? Figures 1.8b and 1.8c show the structure of a typical rhabdom, made up of between six and eight *retinula cells* arranged like the slices of an orange. The inner membrane of each retinula cell is folded into a tubular structure called the *rhabdomere*.

The rhabdomeres contain molecules of *rhodopsin* pigment. The rhodopsins are a family of light-sensitive molecules, each made up of opsin (a protein) and retinaldehyde linked together. The shape of the molecule changes when it absorbs light, and this change is coupled to an increase in membrane conductance and consequently a wave of depolarisation. The size of this *receptor potential* is proportional to the logarithm of the intensity of light striking the cell.

Most diurnal insects and crustaceans possess more than one type of retinula cell, each type having a pigment with a different relationship between wavelength of light and the probability of absorption, or *absorption spectrum*. Commonly, there are three types of pigment, with peak absorption at different points in the range of wavelengths from yellow through blue to ultraviolet. As we will see later, possession of two or more pigments with different absorption spectra makes colour vision possible.

The response of single retinula cells does not depend only upon the wavelength and intensity of light striking them; they are also sensitive to the *plane of polarisation* of light. Unpolarised light is made up of waves vibrating in all planes around the direction of propagation. If light is absorbed or diffracted in such a way that some planes of vibration are represented more than others, the light is said to be polarised. One piece of information that the plane of polarisation of light from the sky can provide is the position of the sun, even when completely blocked by cloud, and bees make use of this information in navigating.

Single-Chambered Eyes

The second basic structural plan for eyes is that of the single-chambered eye, which can be derived by enlargement and modification of a *single* eye-cup rather than by massing eye-cups together. Figure 1.9 shows three devices—a pinhole camera, a concave mirror and a convex lens—which can form an image, and all three designs can be achieved by modifying an eye-cup in different ways.

A pinhole camera can be made from an eye-cup by nearly closing off its opening, and the cephalopod *Nautilus* possesses an eye of this kind. The design has not been a popular one in the animal kingdom because the aperture of a pinhole camera must be small to form an image and so can admit only small amounts of light.

A concave mirror can be made by coating the back of an eye-cup with reflecting material and moving the photoreceptors forward to the image plane. The eyes of the scallop *Pecten* are arranged in this way, with a silvery

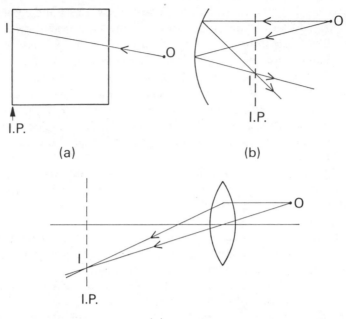

(a)   (b)

(c)

FIG.1.9. The optics of image formation. An image is formed when rays of light arriving at one point I in the *image plane* (IP) all come from the same point O in space. In the pinhole camera (a) this occurs because the aperture is so small that each point in the image plane is illuminated by light arriving through a narrow cone. A concave mirror (b) reflects light in such a way that all rays striking it from one point are brought to a focus at the same point in the image plane. A convex lens (c) achieves the same result by refraction of light.

layer of guanine crystals at the back of the eye forming an image at the level of the retina (Land, 1968). This is also a rare tactic, and only one other animal, the deep-sea ostracod crustacean *Gigantocypris*, is known to adopt it.

By far the most evolutionarily successful type of single-chambered eye uses a convex lens, as a camera does, and is found in the vertebrates and the cephalopod molluscs (octopus and squid). This type of eye has evolved by the enlargement of the eye-cup so that the image formed by the lens falls on the receptor cells and not behind them. Intermediates on the evolutionary route from eye-cup to single-chambered eye can be seen in gastropod molluscs such as *Pterotrachea* and in the alciopid annelids.

For the moment, we only outline the basic structure of the vertebrate eye, before looking at it in detail in the next section. Figure 1.10 shows the important components of this kind of eye—the cornea, iris, lens and retina— and also the remarkable degree of convergent evolution of the eye in two unrelated groups of animals, the cephalopods and the vertebrates (a convergence so close that dilation of the pupil of the eye signals sexual arousal in cuttlefish just as in people).

The structure of the retina, the mat of photoreceptors at the back of the eye, does differ in the two groups. Cephalopod photoreceptors are built on the same rhabdomeric plan as those of the arthropods, but vertebrate receptors are of the *ciliary* type (see Fig. 1.11). Like a rhabdomeric cell, a ciliary cell has densely packed layers of membrane containing light-sensitive pigment, but these are in an outer segment rather than on one side of the cell.

There are two types of ciliary receptor, the rods and the cones, and they have differently shaped outer segments (Fig. 1.11). Rods and cones are packed into the retina with their long axes parallel to the direction of incident light, and a layer of absorptive pigment behind, which reduces internal

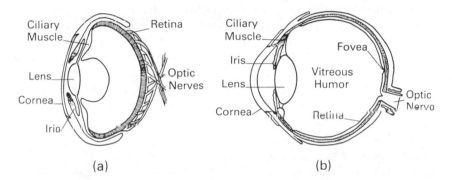

FIG.1.10. Section through (a) an octopus eye and (b) a human eye. (a) Adapted from Barnes (1968). (b) Adapted from Walls (1942).

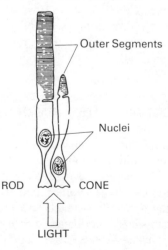

FIG.1.11. Structure of rod and cone in the vertebrate retina. The outer segments contain folded layers of membrane packed with light-sensitive pigment. Adapted from Uttal (1981).

reflection. Whereas receptors in the cephalopod eye are arranged sensibly, facing the light from the lens, the vertebrate retina is "inverted"; that is, the rods and cones are in the layer of the retina furthest from the lens, with their outer segments pointing away from it, so that light must pass through a layer of cells to reach them.

Transduction in rods and cones begins with the same effect of light on rhodopsin as in the retinula cells of insects; the retinaldehyde part of the molecule changes in shape and detaches from the opsin part. This change is coupled to changes in membrane structure which reduce the sodium conductance of the membrane and cause a wave of hyperpolarisation (in contrast to the depolarisation of a rhabdomeric receptor).

Conclusions

The pattern of evolution of light-sensitive structures in animals, as we have outlined it, is summarised in Figure 1.12, and the interested reader will find further details in Land (1981). The central theme in this pattern is increasing directional sensitivity of photoreceptors and therefore increasing ability to detect spatial pattern and movement in the optic array. At one extreme, a jellyfish can detect dimming of the total light reaching it in order to escape from an overhead predator, while at the other a hawk can spot a mouse running through grass hundreds of feet below.

As we have seen, increased directional sensitivity has been achieved in a variety of ways, through the evolution of two quite differently constructed eyes, and the modification of each type to form an image in more than one way. It would be mistaken to attempt to rank these different types of eye in order of merit, and in particular to see the vertebrate eye as an evolutionary pinnacle. As Kirschfeld (1976) has shown, the eyes of vertebrates and insects achieve comparable directional sensitivity, but the two designs are most appropriate for large and small animals respectively. We see here an example of diverse biological solutions to the common problem of image formation.

THE ADAPTIVE RADIATION OF THE VERTEBRATE EYE

In the remainder of this chapter we examine in more detail the workings of the vertebrate eye and particularly the differences between the eyes of different species. In the course of evolution, many variations on the basic single-chambered plan have evolved and, to some extent, these variations are related to the demands of each species' environment and way of life. This kind of evolutionary modification of a basic structure is called *adaptive radiation*.

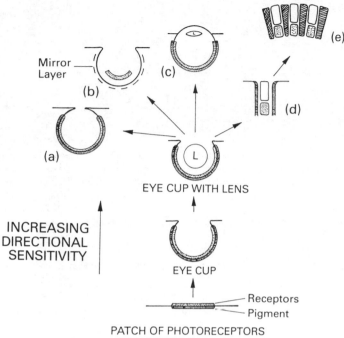

FIG.1.12, Schematic diagram of the evolution of different types of eye. (a) "Pinhole" eye of *Nautilus*; (b) Reflecting eye of *Pecten*; (c) Single-chambered eye; (d) Single ommatidium; (e) Compound eye.

Focusing the Image

The fundamental job of a single-chambered eye is to map the spatial pattern in the optic array onto the retina by forming an image; all light rays striking the eye from one point in space are brought to a focus at one point on the retina. What influences how efficiently vertebrate eyes do this?

The ability of a person or animal to detect fine spatial pattern is expressed as their *visual acuity*. This can be measured by the use of a *grating*; a pattern of parallel vertical dark bars on a bright background, separated by a regular space equal to their width. As the bars are made narrower and more closely spaced, there comes a point when an observer is no longer able to *resolve* the grating; that is, to distinguish it from a uniform field of the same average brightness. Since the spacing of the bars at which this happens will depend on how far the observer is from the grating, we do not measure spacing as a distance but as a *visual angle*; the angle which the space subtends at the eye. Figure 1.13 shows how size, distance and visual angle are related. Under optimal lighting conditions, the minimum bar spacing which a person can resolve is about 0.5 min of arc.

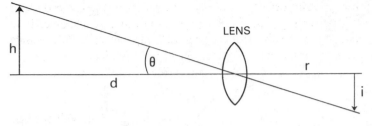

$$\tan \theta = {}^h\!/_d = {}^i\!/_r$$

FIG.1.13. The formula relating visual angle θ subtended by an object to its height h, and its distance from a lens d, and also to the height i of its image on a projection plane at a distance r from the lens. For small visual angles, the retinal surface approximates to a projection plane, and r is the diameter of the eye and i the height of the retinal image. For larger visual angles, the curvature of the retina is significant, and the relationship $\tan \theta = i/r$ does not hold.

Visual acuity is limited by several processes. The first is the efficiency with which the optical apparatus of the eye maps the spatial pattern of the optic array on to the retina. The second is the efficiency with which receptor cells convert that pattern into a pattern of electrical activity; and the third is the extent to which information available in the pattern of receptor cell activity is detected by the neural apparatus of retina and brain.

For the moment, our concern is with the first of these processes, and the important consideration is how sharply the eye focuses an image on the retina. As an image becomes more blurred, spatial pattern in the optic array is smoothed out in the pattern of light at the retina and the detection of fine differences is compromised.

Before considering how the eyes of different species achieve optimal focusing, we need to explain in more detail the optical principles governing the formation of an image by a single-chambered eye. An image is formed because light is bent, or refracted, at the boundary between two transparent media of different optical densities, such as air and glass. The degree of bending of light is determined by the difference in refractive index of the two media. In a convex lens, the two air–glass boundaries are curved in such a way that parallel rays of light are bent through a greater angle the greater their distance from the axis (Fig. 1.9 c). Rays of light from one point on an object at optical infinity, arriving at the lens in parallel, therefore converge to the focal plane of the lens. The distance of the focal plane from the centre of the lens is its focal length, f.

The greater the degree to which a lens bends parallel light rays to converge at the focus, the shorter its focal length. A convenient measure of a lens' performance is its *power*, defined as the reciprocal of its focal length (power is measured in dioptres if focal length is measured in metres).

An image of an object at infinity is therefore formed at a distance f from the lens, and we say that the *image plane* lies at this distance. If the object is brought closer to the lens, the relationship between its distance u from the lens and the distance v of the image plane is given by:

$$\frac{1}{f} = \frac{1}{u} + \frac{1}{v}$$

As the object comes nearer to the lens, the image plane will therefore move further back from it, so that the image formed on a surface located in the focal plane will be blurred. In a camera, the image is kept focused on the film as object distance varies by changing the distance between the lens and the film. As we shall see, the vertebrate eye solves the problem in a different way.

In a vertebrate eye, there are four refracting surfaces as light passes from medium to cornea to aqueous humour to lens to vitreous humour. The refracting power of each surface is determined both by its curvature (a fatter lens is more powerful) and by the difference in refractive indices (RIs) of the media on either side of it. For an animal living in air, there is a large difference in RI between the medium (RI = 1) and the cornea (RI = 1.376 in the human eye), and this surface has considerable refracting power. Accordingly, the eyes of land vertebrates have a flattened lens contributing little to the total refracting power of the eye (in the human eye, the front surface of the cornea provides 49 out of a total of 59 dioptres).

For aquatic vertebrates, however, none of the refracting surfaces have such a large difference in RIs, as the RI of water is similar to that of the cornea. A strongly curved surface is therefore needed somewhere, and it is provided by a near-spherical lens, not only in aquatic vertebrates but also in squid and octopus. Also, the lens of a fish eye is of a higher refractive index than that of the human eye.

Now, if the power of the lens–cornea combination, and its distance from the retina, are both fixed, then a sharply focused image will only be formed of objects lying at a certain range of distances from the eye. This range is called the *depth of field*, and is the distance over which the object can move to and from the eye without the image plane falling outside the layer of retinal receptors. For a human eye focused at infinity, this range is from about 6 metres to infinity. We can, however, focus on objects less than 6 metres from the eye, and the reason is that the optics of the eye can be adjusted by a process called *accommodation*.

Vertebrate eyes can accommodate in either of two ways. One way is to move the lens backwards and forwards to keep the image plane on the retina, and this method is used by fish, amphibians and snakes. The second method, used by other reptiles and by birds and mammals, is to alter the power of the lens by changing its shape. In the human eye, contraction of the *ciliary muscles* attached to the lens causes it to thicken, increasing its curvature and therefore its power, so that nearby objects are brought into focus. When the ciliary muscles are fully relaxed, the lens takes on a flattened shape and the eye is focused at infinity.

In this way, the power of the human lens can be adjusted over a range of up to 15 dioptres, a figure which falls with age. The ability to accommodate over a wide range is clearly useful to primates, animals which characteristically examine the detail of objects at close range. The ability of other vertebrates to accommodate does not always need to be as great, and this is true particularly of fish and other aquatic animals. Because light is scattered and absorbed by water, there is no need for the eye to focus on distant objects, and it can be somewhat myopic (unable to bring an object at infinity into focus) without missing out on any information available in the optic array.

In contrast, the need for accommodation is especially great for animals which live both on land and in water, and need to achieve acuity in two media of different refractive index. Diving birds, seals, and amphibious fish and turtles show a fascinating variety of adaptations in eye structure and function to solve this problem.

The problem can be overcome by brute force, as in otters, cormorants and turtles, which possess a highly flexible lens and powerful ciliary muscles, allowing accommodation of up to 50 dioptres. Another tactic, used in the eyes of penguins and the flying fish *Cypselurus*, is to flatten the cornea so that it has little or no refractive power in air or water, and rely largely on the lens for refraction.

Still another solution is to divide the eye into separate image-forming systems with different optical properties. Such eyes are found in the 'four-eyed' fish *Anableps*, which swims at the surface with the upper part of the eye, adapted for vision in air, above the surface, and the lower part, adapted for vision in water, below it. Finally, a fourth solution is found in the eyes of seals, which have a spherical lens suitable for underwater vision, but a narrow slit pupil which closes in air to form small apertures which act as pinhole cameras, so that the lens no longer forms the image. More details of these and other adaptations of the eye in amphibious animals are given by Sivak (1978).

Even when an eye is optimally focused, there is a certain degree of blur in the image caused by optical imperfections in the eye. For several reasons, lenses do not bring light rays to a focus in the ideal way we have described so far. First, parallel rays may be brought to a slightly different focus depending on how far from the axis they strike the lens (spherical and comatic aberration) or depending on their orientation relative to the lens (astigmatic aberration). The refractive index of a medium varies with the wavelength of light, so that different wavelengths are brought to a focus in slightly different planes (chromatic aberration). Finally, scattering of light in the fluids of the eye and in the retinal layers overlying the receptors further blurs the image.

A boundary between two segments of the optic array differing in intensity is therefore spread out on the retina to some extent, even with optimal focus. Given the figure for the acuity of the human eye mentioned earlier, however, the impact of these aberrations is not great, at least in optimal conditions. One way in which some sources of aberration, particularly spherical aberration, can be reduced is by constricting the pupil so that light only enters the lens through a narrow aperture. This means of reducing aberration, however, is not available in dim light.

Vision in Bright and Dim Light

If an eye is optimally focused, the spatial pattern in the optic array is transformed into a pattern of light intensity on the retina, with a minimum degree of blur. The second constraint on an animal's or a person's visual acuity now comes into play; the efficiency with which this pattern of light on the retina is transformed into a pattern of electrical activity in receptor cells.

One factor which will influence this efficiency will clearly be the density of packing of receptor cells in the retina. The more densely receptors are packed, the finer the details of a pattern of light intensities that can be transformed into differences in electrical activity. If acuity were limited by receptor spacing and not by optical factors, the minimum spacing for a grating to be resolved would be equal to the average distance between adjacent receptors. The difference in acuity between people and falcons is the result of a difference in receptor packing. The photoreceptors in the falcon's eye are packed three times more densely than in the human eye, and the falcon can resolve a grating with a spacing of 0.2 min of arc, as compared with the figure for a human observer of 0.5 min (Fox, Lehmkule, & Westendorff, 1976).

A second factor, which we need to dwell on at more length, is the intensity of light striking the retina. It makes a difference to the detectability of a spatial difference in light intensity on the retina whether two neighbouring cells are being struck by 5 and 10 photons per second or by 5000 and 10,000.

The reason is that, even under constant illumination, the rate at which photons strike a receptor fluctuates around an average value. If light intensity is high, so that the average rates of photon flux striking two adjacent receptors are also high, then the difference between the two rates will be large relative to the fluctuation in each.

As the light reaching the eye becomes dimmer, the difference in photon flux at adjacent receptors eventually becomes comparable to the extent of fluctuation, and so is detectable only if the two rates of flux are averaged over a period of time. Now, if this difference is caused by a moving boundary in the optic array, the difference in photon flux may not be present in any part of the retina long enough to be detected. As light becomes dimmer, the maximum speed of movement in the optic array which can be detected will fall.

One solution to this problem would be to increase the cross-sectional area of receptor cells so that each sampled a larger segment of the optic array and so received a larger flux of photons. Alternatively, the outputs of neighbouring receptors could be "pooled" by connection to one interneuron, so that they effectively acted as a single receptor. Either solution would increase the *sensitivity* of the eye, but, as we discussed above, they would both decrease its *acuity*. The design of a vertebrate eye is therefore subject to a trade-off between sensitivity and acuity; what are the implications of this constraint for the evolution of vertebrate eyes?

Many vertebrate species use only part of the daily cycle for their activities, being either nocturnal or diurnal. Nocturnal animals need eyes with high sensitivity in dim moon- and starlight, and this is true also of deep-sea fish. Diurnal animals, on the other hand, can have eyes with high acuity. Even so, it is unusual for a species' vision to operate in a very narrow band of light intensities. Most diurnal animals have some sensitivity to dim light, presumably for use in nocturnal emergencies such as an attack by a predator, and most nocturnal animals need some day-time vision, strict specialisation only being found in deep-sea fish and bats living in dark caves by day. Most species therefore need vision in a *range* of light intensities.

The most striking way in which the vertebrate eye is adapted for vision in a range of light intensities is in the structure of the retina. We noted earlier the two kinds of vertebrate photoreceptor—rods and cones—and saw that a rod has a deeper stack of pigment-filled layers of folded membrane in its outer segment than has a cone. A photon passing through a rod therefore stands a lower chance of coming out the other end than one passing through a cone, and so the membrane potential of a rod will be influenced by levels of light too low to affect a cone.

It is therefore not surprising that there is a correlation between the ratio of rods to cones in an animal's retina and its ecology. Diurnal animals have a higher proportion of cones than do nocturnal animals, though pure-cone retinas are rare, found mostly in lizards and snakes. Pure-rod retinas are also rare, found only in animals—deep-sea fish and bats—which never leave dark habitats.

A further adaptation of the retina in animals active in dim light is the presence of a silvery *tapetum* behind the retina, which reflects light back through it and so gives the rods a second bite at the stream of photons, though at the cost of increasing blur through imperfect reflection. The glow of a cat's eyes in the dark is caused by reflection of light by a tapetum behind its retina.

A possibility exploited by a few nocturnal animals is to use infra-red (IR) radiation, which can provide information about the environment in the absence of visible light, subject to some limitations. First, IR is rapidly absorbed by water, and therefore only potentially useful on land. Secondly, the IR radiation emitted by a warm-blooded animal would screen any radiation it detected, and so we would only expect sensitivity to IR in cold-blooded animals. Thirdly, it could only be used to detect objects differing in temperature from the rest of the environment.

The one group of vertebrates which do detect information carried by IR radiation are a group of snakes, the pit vipers, which hunt for small birds and mammals at night. The cornea and lens of the vertebrate eye are opaque to IR, and so a different kind of sensory organ is required. These snakes have specialised organs alongside the eyes, acting as pinhole cameras to form an IR image of their surroundings, which enable them to detect the location of nearby warm-blooded animals.

So, a retina containing only rods or only cones adapts an animal for vision in a narrow range of light intensities. How is retinal structure adapted for vision over a wider range? Imagine that we start with an animal which is basically diurnal but needs to be equipped with some night vision. We add rods to the pure-cone retina, scattering them about evenly among the cones. We discover, though, that to capture much light at night, we need a great many rods. In the human eye, for example, there are 120 million rods as opposed to only 7 million cones.

Now, if we have added the rods evenly over the retina, we would find the distances between the cones are now much larger than when we started and that acuity in daytime vision is reduced. The way out of this problem in many vertebrate eyes is to divide the retina into two regions. One small area is rich in cones, with little or no pooling of the outputs of adjacent receptors, while the other, larger, area is rich in rods, with considerable pooling of outputs. The cone-rich region provides high-acuity vision in bright light, whilst the rod-rich area provides high-sensitivity vision in dim light.

This pattern is found especially in birds and in primates, where the cone-rich area is usually circular, and sometimes contains a pit-like depression in the retina, called a *fovea*. The cone-rich area of the human eye is called the *macula lutea*, and it contains a fovea. There are only cones in the centre of the fovea, and their proportion and density of packing decrease further out into the retina. At more than about 10° from the centre, outside the macula, there are few cones, and the peripheral part of the retina contains almost all rods.

There are other ways in which vertebrate eyes are adapted to operate over a range of light intensities. One is movement of cells containing pigment, and sometimes also the receptor cells, in the retina. These *retinomotor* responses are found in fish, and in some reptiles and birds, and act to screen the rods with pigment in bright light and to expose them in dim light.

A second mechanism, rare in fish but more common in birds and especially mammals, is dilation and constriction of the pupil by the muscular tissue of the iris. In diurnal mammals, the pupil is usually round, and its function is to reduce the aperture of the lens in bright light and so reduce blur of the retinal image due to spherical and other optical aberrations. In dim light, when sensitivity and not acuity is at a premium, the pupil opens to admit more light. Mammals active in both day and night often have a slit pupil, which, for mechanical reasons, can close more completely than a round one. A cat's eye has a retina adapted for nocturnal vision and a slit pupil which allows it to operate in the daytime.

A third process, known as *adaptation*, occurs in the retinas of many animals to adjust the sensitivity of photoreceptors and interneurons to varying intensities of light. In the human eye, the iris does not play a major role in regulating the intensity of light reaching the retina, and so adaptation is the main means by which sensitivity is adjusted. We can see over a range of approximately 7 log units of light intensity (a 10^7-fold range), but at any one time, our vision is effective over a range of only one or two log units, and this range can shift upwards (light adaptation) or downwards (dark adaptation). We return to adaptation in the next chapter.

To conclude, vertebrate eyes are subject to the basic physical constraint that greater sensitivity in dim light can only be won at the cost of reduced acuity. Different species strike different bargains between these two factors, depending upon their ecology, but many manage to operate over a range of light intensities. Humans are an example of a basically diurnal species with acute *photopic* (bright light) vision and some degree of low acuity *scotopic* (dim light) vision. We are fairly adaptable, though not as much as cats!

Sampling the Optic Array

An animal with simple eye-cups distributed over its body can detect light reaching it from any direction, and therefore, at any instant, it samples the entire optic array. As soon as an animal's photoreceptors are concentrated into a pair of compound or single-chambered eyes at the front of the body, constraints arise on how the optic array can be sampled.

Some insects, such as the dragonfly, have large compound eyes wrapped almost completely around the head and so can gather light from almost the entire optic array without moving. The angle through which light striking a single vertebrate eye is focused onto the retina can be as great as 200°, and so the same opportunity exists for nearly panoramic vision. This is achieved by placing the eyes *laterally*, on either side of the head with their axes perpendicular to the body.

All vertebrate groups include species having laterally placed eyes. By and large, the arrangement is characteristic of animals especially vulnerable to predation, such as fish living in open water, ground-living birds such as quail and chickens, and grazing mammals such as rabbits and horses. The dominant consideration in the arrangement of these animals' eyes is the need to detect predators approaching from any direction.

In other species, however, there are other demands on eye structure and position which reduce the angle through which light reaching the eye is focused on the retina. First, animals with a small, cone-rich area in the retina can sample only a small segment of the optic array at any instant, under photopic conditions. Second, some species need to make the image at the retina larger in order to increase acuity. This is particularly true of predatory birds needing to spot prey from a considerable height; such birds have a deeper eye than that of ground-living birds. Just as in a telephoto lens, however, increased magnification is achieved at the cost of a reduced field of view.

Third, animals with laterally placed eyes have only a small degree of *binocular overlap*—that segment of the optic array which is sampled by both eyes. For reasons which we will discuss in Chapter 6, binocular overlap can contribute to the perception of depth, and the eyes of some species are swung forward from the lateral position in order to take advantage of this possibility. The greatest extent of binocular overlap is found in primates, which have their eyes at the front of the head with parallel axes. The human eye, for example, accepts light through an angle of about 150°, but binocular overlap means that the angle for two eyes is not much greater.

Many birds have an arrangement of eyes which compromises between binocular and lateral placement, with some degree of overlap of the angles of admission of light of the eyes. Examples are hummingbirds and various birds of prey, which often have two cone-rich areas in each retina, one corresponding to an area of acute monocular vision, and one corresponding to the area of overlap between the two eyes.

If, for one or more of these reasons, an animal has less than panoramic vision, it can only sample the entire optic array over time, by moving its eyes. In some vertebrates, such as frogs, the eyes cannot move relative to the body to any appreciable extent. For such animals, sampling the optic array through eye movement would mean moving the whole body, which would clash with other concurrent demands on body movement. Consequently, animals with immobile eyes usually have them laterally placed to allow panoramic vision.

One means of moving the eyes is available when the head can move relative to the body, and most birds use head movement to scan through the optic array. Birds of prey, in particular, can rotate their heads through large angles. A second means comes with the ability to move the eyes relative to the head. Most vertebrates can do this to some extent, although few can move their eyes through large angles. The chameleon is an animal with strikingly mobile eyes; its angle of vision is small, and, as it searches for prey, its two laterally placed eyes swivel about quite independently, giving a distinctly creepy impression!

The chameleon apart, the eyes of primates make the largest, most rapid and most precisely controlled eye movements. The human eye is held in position by a dynamic balance between three pairs of antagonistic muscles, and instability in this balance causes a continuous small-amplitude *tremor*. As a result, the image on the retina is in constant motion, any point on it moving by about the distance between two adjacent foveal cones in 0.1 sec.

Sampling of the optic array is achieved by three kinds of eye movement. First, rapid and intermittent jumps of eye position called *saccades* are made in order to fixate an object with foveal vision. As a person reads or looks at a picture, their eyes make several saccades each second to scan the page or screen.

Once an object is fixated, *pursuit* movements keep it in foveal vision as it moves, or as the observer moves. If the distance of an object from the observer changes, *convergence* movements keep it fixated by the foveas of both eyes. As an object comes closer, convergence movements turn the directions of gaze of both eyes towards the nose. If an object comes within a few inches of the face, further convergence is impossible and "double vision" occurs (we say more about convergence and stereoscopic vision in Chapter 6). Whereas saccades are sudden, intermittent changes of eye position, both pursuit and convergence are smooth, continuous eye movements.

In conclusion, the human eye at any instant samples a relatively large segment of the optic array (the *peripheral* field) with low acuity, and a much smaller segment (the *central,* or foveal field) with high acuity. Smooth and saccadic eye movements shift this high-acuity segment about rapidly, so that acute vision over a wide angle is achieved. Further details of human eye movements, their anatomical and neural mechanisms, and models of their control may be found in Carpenter (1977).

This highly specialised way in which we sample the optic array makes it difficult for us to appreciate the different ways in which other animals do so. We are used to detecting what another person is looking at from the direction in which their eyes are pointing, but this direction may mean something quite different in other species. A horse, sheep or rabbit does not need to look straight at something in order to see it, while the angle of a bird's head may be related to what it is looking at in quite a different way depending on whether it is fixating monocularly or binocularly. It is only when watching animals such as cats and apes looking that we are on familiar ground!

Detecting Colour

A vertebrate eye maps not only the pattern of light intensities in the optic array onto the retina but also the pattern of different mixtures of wavelengths of light in different parts of the optic array. We have already seen that the mixture of wavelengths in a segment of the optic array can carry information about the kind of surface the light was reflected from. The intensities of light reflected from a leaf and from an insect resting on it might be equal, but if they reflected different mixtures of wavelengths it would pay a bird searching for food to be able to detect this difference.

The ability to detect differences in mixtures of wavelengths is called colour vision. It is important, however, to stress that our perception of colour is not determined simply by the proportions of wavelengths reflected from a surface, but by complex interactions between this factor and light intensity. Even so, differential sensitivity of photoreceptors to wavelength is necessary before the more complex processes of colour perception can operate.

A retina containing receptor cells with only one pigment type could not detect differences in the mixtures of wavelengths in adjacent regions of the optic array. This is because the response of each cell is determined by both intensity and wavelength and a particular level of response could be caused by any combination of the two. In order to detect wavelength differences independently of intensity differences, at least two sets of receptor cells are needed, each with a different wavelength-receptor potential relationship.

We have already seen that the retinula cells of insects usually fall into three groups, each with different pigments. In any one vertebrate species, all rods in the retina contain the same pigment type, and so animals with pure-rod retinas cannot detect wavelength and intensity differences independently. This need not be a handicap; for deep-sea fish, the spectrum of available light is narrow, and such fish usually have a pure-rod retina in which the peak of the absorption spectrum of the pigment matches the blue light available.

Species capable of colour vision may have cones with a pigment different from that in the rods, or they may have two or three types of cone, each with different pigments and therefore with different wavelength sensitivities. The cones of birds and some reptiles additionally contain coloured oil droplets through which light must pass to reach the outer segment, and these coloured filters will further differentiate the wavelength sensitivities of cones.

Coloured oil droplets in bird and reptile cones may have two further functions. The droplets are always red, orange or yellow, and Walls (1942) argues that they act to screen out short wavelength light and thereby improve acuity in two ways; by reducing chromatic aberration and by filtering out light scattered from the sky in the same way as a skylight filter on a camera does. He suggests that the yellow pigmentation of the lens in the human eye and of the macula lutea may have similar functions. Alternatively, Kirschfeld (1982) proposes that the function of such pigments is to screen short wavelength light which damages receptor cells through photooxidation.

The presence of different pigments in different cone types is the most common basis for vertebrate colour vision. Some fish and turtle species have cones large enough for direct recording with a microelectrode, and this method reveals three types of cone with different wavelength sensitivities. The evidence is less direct in the case of the primate retina, but we know that it contains three different types of cone opsin, with peak absorption at 445, 535 and 570 nm (Fig. 1.14), and presumably cones containing these pigments have corresponding peaks in their sensitivity spectra. In photopic conditions, we are able to distinguish colours because of this differential sensitivity of cones, while in scotopic conditions, when only rods are stimulated, we have no colour vision.

We have given only a brief introduction to the topic of colour vision in this chapter; the reader wishing to follow the subject further will find a

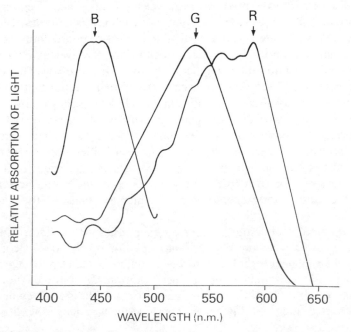

FIG.1.14.   The absorption spectra of the pigments from individual blue-, green- and red-sensitive cones from the retina of a rhesus monkey. Adapted from Marks, Dobelle, & MacNichol (1964).

detailed treatment of the chemistry of visual pigments and of the transduction process in Davson (1977), and a review of recent work on human colour vision in Mollon (1982).

Conclusions

We have followed the workings of the vertebrate eye from the entry of light through the cornea to the formation of a pattern of excitation in the receptor cells of the retina. We have seen how the eye is adapted in different ways in different species to maximise the amount of information in the optic array captured in this pattern of excitation, and that the extent to which this can be achieved is constrained by various factors, especially the amount of available light. A more detailed account of the adaptive radiation of the vertebrate eye is given in Walls' (1942) classic work.

The reason why the spatial pattern of the optic array is captured in the pattern of retinal activity is that each receptor is stimulated by light from a narrow segment of the array. This in turn happens because the optics of the eye form an image on the retina. The same thing happens in a camera, where the light striking each light-sensitive grain in the film comes from a narrow segment of the optic array, and so the camera is a useful analogy for understanding the optics of the eye.

It is important to realise, however, that the analogy between camera and eye has serious limitations. First, there are differences in quality between retinal images and images formed by cameras. Judged by the same standards as a camera, even the most sophisticated eye forms an image of extremely poor quality, and would be put to shame by an Instamatic camera. As well as the optical aberrations causing blur which we have already mentioned, there are aberrations of lens and cornea causing distortion of the image. Together with the curvature of the retina, these mean that images of straight lines are curved and metrical relations in the image do not correspond to those in the world.

In addition, the movements of the eye consist not just of a series of fixations, during which the image is static, but of smooth movements and tremor, causing the image to move continually; a camera which moved in this way would produce blurred pictures. The image also has a yellowish cast, particularly in the macular region, and it contains shadows of the blood vessels overlying the layer of receptor cells in the retina.

In principle, as these factors cause predictable distortions of the retinal image, it would be possible to correct for them and to recover the right metrical relations, colours and other properties of the image (although any pattern lost through blurring could not be recovered). To think in terms of "cleaning up" the retinal image to the point where it resembles a photograph implies, however, that the role of the eye is to take a snapshot of the world at each fixation and to send a stream of pictures to the brain to be examined there.

This conception of the eye's role betrays a second, more serious, limitation to the analogy between camera and eye. The purpose of a camera is to produce a picture to be viewed by people, but the purpose of the eye and brain is to extract the information from the changing optic array needed to guide an animal's or a person's actions, or to specify objects or events of importance. Although this could be achieved by first converting the retinal image into a neural "image" of photograph-like quality and then extracting information from this second image, such a process seems implausible on grounds of economy; it would be wasteful.

Blurring apart, the imperfections of the retinal image do not result in the loss of any information about spatial pattern and changes in spatial pattern in the optic array, and a more plausible design for a visual system would involve the extraction of important variables of pattern directly from the pattern of electrical activity in rods and cones, without first correcting distortions. As we show in Chapters 2 and 3, the extraction of information about pattern begins in the retina itself, and the optic nerve does not transmit a stream of pictures to the brain, as a television camera does to a television set, but instead it transmits *information* about the pattern of light reaching the eyes.

2 The Neurophysiology of Vision

Information is available to animals, in the spatial and temporal pattern of the optic array, to specify the structure of their surroundings and events occurring in them. Compound and single-chambered eyes map this spatio-temporal pattern onto an array of light-sensitive receptor cells, so transforming it into a pattern of electrical activity in these cells. This pattern of receptor cell activity must in its turn be transformed so that information needed to guide the animal's actions is made available.

These further transformations take place in the central nervous system, and one way of studying them is to record the electrical activity of single nerve cells in retina, optic nerve and brain in response to stimulation by light. The ultimate aim of this approach is to understand how information important to an animal is detected by networks of nerve cells and represented in patterns of neural activity. For all but the simplest animals, this is a distant goal indeed, and our knowledge does not yet extend beyond the first stages of neural transformation of patterns of light. In this chapter we will describe these early stages first in a simple invertebrate nervous system and then in the visual system of mammals.

THE RETINA OF THE HORSESHOE CRAB

The horseshoe crab *Limulus* has two compound eyes placed laterally on its shell, each made up of several hundred ommatidia. Each of these contains 10 or more retinula cells arranged radially around the dendrite of an eccentric cell (Fig. 2.1). The axons of the eccentric and retinula cells form a bundle,

33

LIGHT

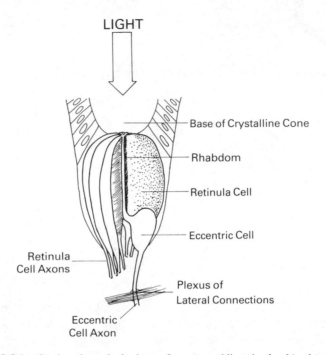

FIG.2.1. Section through the base of an ommatidium in the *Limulus* eye. Retinula cells are packed like the slices of an orange around the dendrite of the eccentric cell, and their inner edges make up the light-sensitive rhabdom. Adapted from Ratliff, Hartline, & Lange (1966).

the optic nerve, which runs to the brain. What information passes down the axons making up the optic nerve when light falls on the eye?

The first step in answering this question was taken by Hartline and Graham (1932), who recorded the activity of single axons in the optic nerve while shining a spot of light onto the corresponding ommatidia. They established that impulses pass down an axon at a rate roughly proportional to the logarithm of the intensity of light falling on its ommatidium. We saw in Chapter 1 that transduction of light by a rhabdomeric receptor generates a depolarisation of the membrane proportional to the logarithm of light intensity, and so this result is just what we would expect.

What is the significance of this *logarithmic* coding of light intensity by impulse frequency in an optic nerve axon? The intensity of light falling on *Limulus'* eye varies by a factor of about 10^6 or 10^7, from dim light in deep water to bright light in shallow water under a clear sky. Linear coding would require the same range of impulse frequencies and therefore, since the maximum rate at which impulses can pass down an axon is about 1000 sec^{-1}, the dimmest light would be coded by a frequency of one impulse every several thousand seconds.

Such slow rates of impulse transmission would make it impossible to follow changes in light intensity, and logarithmic coding solves the problem by compressing the range of intensities into a 6 or 7-fold range of impulse frequencies. Logarithmic coding of stimulus intensity is a common feature of many sensory systems, wherever a wide band of physical intensity must be coded by a narrow band of impulse rates.

So far, it seems that the pattern of light intensity over the eye of *Limulus* is reproduced faithfully in the pattern of activity of optic nerve axons, each one reporting light intensity in one part of the optic array. In fact, things are by no means so simple, and both the temporal and the spatial pattern of light undergo transformation in the retina.

Transformation of Temporal Pattern

Impulse frequency in a receptor cell axon does not follow changes in light intensity in a simple way, but shows the phenomenon called "adaptation," which was mentioned in the last chapter. At the onset of light, impulse rate rises rapidly to a peak and then falls, after a second or so, to a steady level maintained while the light is on (Fig. 2.2a). Both the peak rate and the steady level are related logarithmically to the intensity of light (Fig. 2.2b). This process is called *light-adaptation*, and it means that a high impulse rate signals a sudden *increase* in light intensity and not a steady bright light.

Second, if a receptor is adapted to light and then left in darkness, its sensitivity to light gradually rises; the impulse rate generated in response to a test flash of light increases rapidly over the first few minutes in darkness,

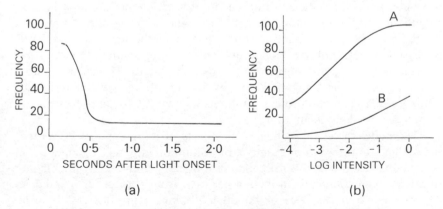

(a)   (b)

FIG.2.2. (a) The response of a single ommatidium to light. The frequency of discharge of impulses rises rapidly to a peak and then falls to a steady level within 0.5 sec. (b) The peak response (A) and the steady response (B) of a single ommatidium to a flash of light at different light intensities. Note the logarithmic relationship between intensity and response. Adapted from Hartline & Graham (1932).

and then more gradually to reach a maximum after about an hour. This process of *dark-adaptation* is the much slower converse of light-adaptation. It means that the activity of an axon does not signal absolute light intensity but intensity *relative to* the degree of dark-adaptation of the receptor.

The effect of these two processes is that the output of a photoreceptor is quite stable over a wide range of light intensities, but that this stability can be disturbed by a sudden change in intensity. The temporal pattern of the output is therefore a transformation of the temporal pattern of the input; slow changes in light intensity are filtered out while rapid ones are not. This means that the pattern of optic nerve activity will not carry information about gradual changes in the environment such as diurnal fluctuation in light level or gradual changes in turbidity of water, but it will carry information about events such as the shadow of an animal swimming overhead.

Transformation of Spatial Pattern

In their first experiments, Hartline and Graham used spots of light small enough to illuminate only one ommatidium at a time. What happens when, as in real life, light falls on all the ommatidia of the eye? Is the pattern of activity in the optic nerve simply the sum of the responses of individual photoreceptors to light, or do the signals from ommatidia interact with one another?

In a classical experiment, summarised in Figure 2.3a, Hartline, Wagner, and Ratliff (1956) demonstrated that the outputs of ommatidia do indeed interact with one another, through a process of *lateral inhibition* between neighbouring photoreceptors. Each cell inhibits the firing rate of those in a roughly circular area around it. The strength of the inhibition rises with increasing intensity of light falling on the inhibiting ommatidium, and falls with increasing distance between the ommatidia. Lateral inhibition is mutual, each photoreceptor being inhibited by its neighbours, which it in turn inhibits. Also, each photoreceptor inhibits its own activity, a process in part responsible for light-adaptation.

This model successfully predicts the effects of more complex patterns of light falling on the eye. For example, the inhibition imposed on ommatidium A by illumination of another ommatidium B, can be reduced by illumination of a third ommatidium C on the far side of B from A (Figs. 2.3b and 2.3c). The neuroanatomical basis of lateral inhibition is in collateral branches spreading sideways from each receptor cell axon in a layer just below the ommatidia, making inhibitory synaptic contacts with other nearby cells (Purple & Dodge, 1965).

Just as adaptation in receptors causes a transformation of the temporal pattern of light at the eye, so lateral inhibition causes a transformation of its spatial pattern. If the whole eye is evenly and diffusely illuminated, excitation of receptor cells by light will be largely cancelled by inhibition from neighbouring cells. The activity of optic nerve axons will therefore be low and will vary little with changes in light level.

Consider next what happens if there is a sharp boundary between a brightly and a dimly lit area of the eye. The output of those ommatidia lying just inside the bright area will be less inhibited, as their neighbours to the dim side are less active, while the output of those just across the boundary

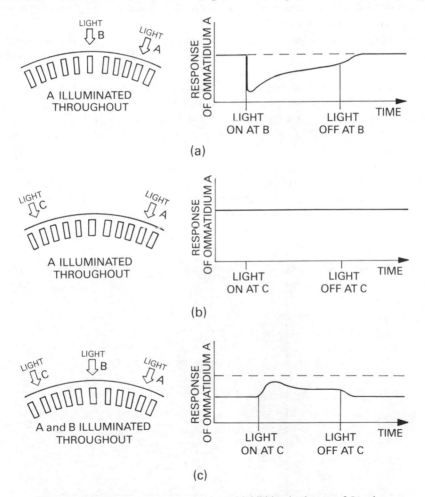

FIG.2.3. Experiments demonstrating lateral inhibition in the eye of *Limulus*. (a) Light falling on ommatidium B inhibits the response of ommatidium A to light. (b) Ommatidium C is too far from A for it to inhibit A's response. (c) Even so, light falling on C causes an inhibition of B's response and therefore lifts the inhibition imposed by B on A.

will be more inhibited, as their neighbours are more active. The result is shown in Figure 2.4; a steeper gradient in impulse rate at the boundary than would occur without lateral inhibition.

Just as adaptation transforms temporal pattern to give prominence to rapid changes in light intensity, so lateral inhibition gives prominence to rapid *spatial* changes in light intensity. Shallow gradients of intensity over the eye are smoothed out in the pattern of optic nerve activity, while steep gradients are maintained. The optic nerve will therefore carry information about some features of the crab's environment but not all. Are these features the important ones in organising the animal's actions?

The optic nerve will carry information about any aspect of the environment specified by sharp boundaries in the optic array. For example, one such boundary will be that between the bright disc of light reaching the animal direct from the sky and the dimmer ring around it scattered through the water. As a result of lateral inhibition, this boundary will be prominent in the pattern of optic nerve activity, and detection of its position could be useful to the animal in keeping upright as it moves around an uneven seafloor.

Sharp boundaries in the optic array will also be caused by the shadows of animals swimming overhead. As a shadow moves over the crab's eye, lateral inhibition will generate steep gradients in the responses of ommatidia. Responses will be further increased at the trailing edge of the shadow by a burst of impulses in response to light onset. Again, information specifying an

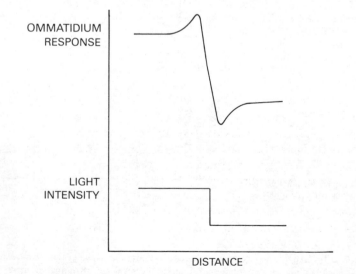

FIG.2.4. The responses of a row of ommatidia to a dark–light boundary falling on the eye. Note the sharpening of the response at the boundary caused by lateral inhibition.

THE VERTEBRATE RETINA   39

event of significance to the animal—a potential predator passing overhead—is made prominent in the pattern of optic nerve activity and can be used to organise defensive responses.

To conclude, there is a complex relationship between the spatiotemporal pattern of light falling on the eye of *Limulus* and the pattern of activity in the optic nerve. Transformations of pattern occur in the retina which filter out information about slow changes over space and time, and pass on information about rapid changes. These rapid changes specify events in the environment which are significant to the animal, and the challenge for physiological research is now to explore the further transformations which occur between the optic nerve and the pattern of commands to limb muscles.

THE VERTEBRATE RETINA

In Chapter 1, we described the vertebrate retina simply as a carpet of rods and cones covering the back of the eye. In addition, however, there is a layer of nerve cells between the photoreceptors and the vitreous humour filling the eye. It contains four classes of cell in addition to the rods and cones; *horizontal, bipolar, amacrine* and *ganglion* cells.

By detailed electron microscopy, Dowling (1968) established how these classes of neuron connect synaptically, and Figure 2.5 summarises his findings.

Receptors synapse in the *outer plexiform layer* with both horizontal cells and bipolar cells, and bipolars synapse in the *inner plexiform layer* with both amacrine and ganglion cells. Some ganglion cells receive input directly from bipolars, while others are driven only by amacrines. The axons of ganglion cells run over the surface of the retina to the blindspot, where they form a bundle, the optic nerve, which runs to the brain. This pattern of synaptic connectivity is common to frogs, monkeys and other vertebrates, but there are important differences between species in the proportions of different types of synapse; a point we will return to later.

Although the vertebrate retina is more complex than that of *Limulus*, there is a basic similarity in structure. In both cases, there are nerve cell pathways running in two directions at right angles to one another; a receptor-brain pathway and a lateral pathway. The first pathway is represented in the *Limulus* retina by the axons of receptor cells, but in the vertebrate retina it consists of a series of cells linking the receptors through the bipolars and amacrines to the ganglion cells.

Whereas in *Limulus* each eccentric cell axon runs from one photoreceptor unit, the outputs of a number of vertebrate photoreceptors are pooled at the level of connections to the bipolars. The number of receptors pooled reflects the trade-off between acuity and sensitivity discussed in Chapter 1.

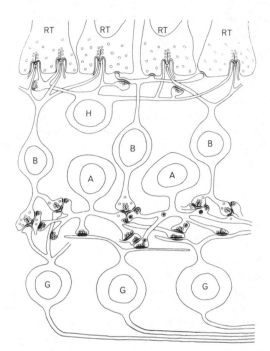

FIG.2.5. The structure of the vertebrate retina. RT—receptor terminals; H—horizontal cells; B—bipolar cells; A—amacrine cells; G—ganglion cells. Reproduced from Dowling (1968) with permission of the author and publishers.

In a primate eye, for example, each bipolar cell in the fovea connects to one or two cones, whereas in the periphery, a bipolar may connect to many rods. The ganglion cell axons leading from the fovea therefore have the potential to carry information about fine detail in the pattern of receptor excitation, whereas those leading from the periphery sacrifice this potential in order to achieve greater sensitivity to dim light.

The lateral pathway is also simpler in the retina of *Limulus*, and consists of the collaterals of receptor cell axons. In vertebrates, it is made up of two systems, the processes of horizontal cells ramifying in the outer plexiform layer and the processes of amacrine cells in the inner plexiform layer. The anatomy of the vertebrate retina therefore suggests that transformations of spatial pattern similar to those in *Limulus* are carried out, but also hints that these patterns are likely to be more complex.

THE OUTPUT OF THE RETINA

The first step in analysing the transformations of pattern taking place in the vertebrate retina is to establish the relationship between its input and its output; the pattern of light falling on it and the rate at which ganglion cells fire impulses. The first experiments of this kind were just like Hartline's on the *Limulus* retina, using small spots of light as stimuli. These demonstrated that each ganglion cell has a *receptive field*; a region of the retina, usually roughly circular, in which stimulation affects the ganglion cell's firing rate.

Concentric Receptive Fields

There are many different kinds of ganglion cell field, but one type is probably common to all vertebrates. It is the *concentric* field, first discovered by Kuffler (1953) in a study of the responses of cat ganglion cells. Kuffler found that the effects of a spot of light on a cell with a concentric field depend on whether the light falls in a small circular area in the centre of the field or in the ring-shaped area surrounding the centre.

Some cells respond with a burst of impulses to either the onset of a spot of light in the centre of the field, or to the offset of a spot of light in the surround; this is called a *centre-on* response. Other cells show the converse, *centre-off* response; offset of a spot of light in the centre of the field or onset in the surround causes a burst of impulses (Fig. 2.6).

Enroth-Cugell and Robson (1966) found that both these categories of ganglion cell can in turn be divided into two sub-groups differing in their responses to sinusoidal gratings. Like the gratings described in the last chapter used to measure visual acuity, a sinusoidal grating is made up of

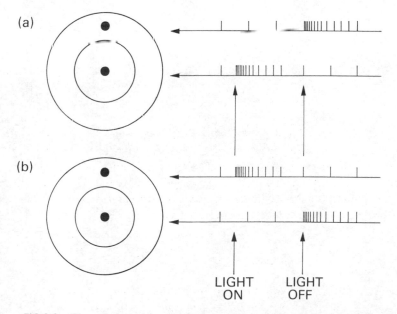

FIG.2.6.   The responses of cat retinal ganglion cells to spots of light. A centre-on cell (a) responds with a burst of impulses to the onset of a spot of light in the centre of its field or to the offset of a spot of light in the surround area. A centre-off cell (b) responds in the opposite fashion.

parallel bright and dark bars. Their edges have a blurred appearance, however, as the brightness of the pattern varies sinusoidally with distance rather than changing sharply at the boundaries of the bars.

Figure 2.7 shows a sinusoidal grating; the intensity of light reflected from it along a horizontal line follows a sine wave, in just the same way as the sound pressure near a vibrating tuning fork varies sinusoidally with time. A grating is described by the parameters of: *frequency*, expressed as cycles per degree of visual angle; *contrast*, expressed as the ratio of maximum to minimum intensity in the pattern; and *phase*, expressed in degrees, of the pattern relative to a fixed point.

Enroth-Cugell and Robson exposed an area of retina to a diffuse field of light alternating at regular intervals with a sinusoidal grating of the same average light intensity. What responses would be expected at onset and offset of the grating by cells with concentric receptive fields?

Figure 2.8 shows the distribution of light intensity over the receptive field of an on-centre cell when it is illuminated by a grating of wavelength equal

FIG.2.7. A sinusoidal grating. The brightness of the pattern varies sinusoidally along its horizontal axis. Photograph courtesy of Fergus Campbell, University of Cambridge.

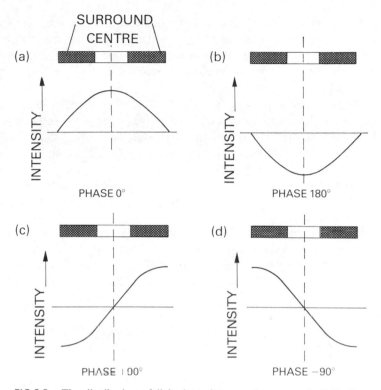

FIG.2.8. The distribution of light intensity over the concentric field of a
retinal ganglion cell when a grating is projected onto it and the phase of the
grating is varied. In (c) and (d), there is no change in total intensity in either
centre or surround when the grating replaces diffuse light of the same average
intensity; these are the null positions of the grating for an X cell.

to twice the field diameter. In the first case, where the peak of the distribution
falls on the centre of the field, a burst of impulses will occur at the onset of
the grating, because the centre becomes brighter than the surround. If the
phase of the grating relative to the centre of the field is shifted by 180°,
there will be a response to grating offset, when the centre is no longer
dimmer than the surround. If the phase is shifted by 90° in either direction,
however, there is no net change of light intensity over either the centre or
the surround at grating onset or offset.

If the response of a ganglion cell is determined by the difference between
light intensity in centre and surround, we would therefore expect to find two
null positions as the phase of the grating relative to the field centre is changed
through a full 360°. At these positions, in both on- and off-centre cells,
there will be no response to onset or offset of a grating.

Enroth-Cugell and Robson found that some ganglion cells, which they
called *X cells*, behave in exactly this way. They are said to have a *linear*

response, as it is a linear function of the difference between the intensities of light falling in the two areas. Others, called Y *cells*, behave differently, however. With these, no null position of a grating can be found, and the cell responds with a burst of impulses to on- and offset of the grating whatever its phase.

A further distinction between X and Y cells is in their response to moving gratings. As a sinusoidal pattern of light moves over an X cell's field, the cell's impulse rate rises and falls with the peaks and troughs of the pattern. The response of Y cells, on the other hand, shows a constant elevation to a drifting grating, with a modulation in phase with the grating superimposed on it. This test also shows that the response of a Y cell to the pattern of light in its receptive field is *non-linear*; it cannot be predicted by algebraic summation of excitatory and inhibitory influences from centre and surround.

X and Y cells differ in other ways besides linearity of response. First, an X cell gives a *sustained* response to a stationary grating, continuing to fire impulses while the grating is present. A Y cell, in contrast, gives a *transient* burst of impulses to the onset of such a stimulus. In order to evoke a sustained response from a Y cell, it must be stimulated with a moving grating.

Second, in any part of the retina the centres of Y cell fields are larger than those of nearby X cell fields (the fields of both types increase in size from the centre of the fovea outwards, reflecting the greater pooling of receptor outputs in the periphery of the retina). Third, X and Y cells have different distributions over the retina. Most cells in the central part of the retina are X type, while in the periphery Y cells are more common. Finally, Y cells have faster-conducting axons than X cells.

All these conclusions apply to the retinal ganglion cells of cats, but it is likely that all vertebrates possess retinal ganglion cells with concentrically organised fields. They have been found in retinal ganglion cells of species as diverse as frogs (Gaze & Jacobson, 1963), ground squirrels (Michael, 1968a) and monkeys (de Monasterio, 1978a). It is less clear how general the distinction between X and Y cells is in other species, although it is firmly established in monkeys (de Monasterio, 1978a).

Clearly, the rate at which a cell with a concentric field fires impulses does not signal the intensity of light falling in its field. Instead, it signals the degree of *contrast* between the centre and surround regions of the field. Just as in the horseshoe crab, the pattern of activity in the optic nerve will therefore give prominence to spatial change in light intensity. As they have transient responses, Y cells will also signal changes over time in spatial pattern, suggesting that they have some role in carrying information about movement.

Non-Concentric Receptive Fields

Concentric receptive fields are by no means the only kind possessed by the retinal ganglion cells of vertebrates. In addition to X and Y cells, the optic nerve of the cat contains a poorly defined class of W cells, which all have slowly-conducting axons but a variety of types of field.

Cleland and Levick (1974) and Stone and Fukuda (1974) found two relatively common types of W cell, together with other rarer types. The first, called "on-off" cells or "local edge detectors," respond with a burst of impulses both when a spot of light moves into the field centre and when it moves out again. Cells of the second group give no response to a stationary spot of light but respond strongly to one moving through the field. Many such cells show *direction selectivity* (or preference), giving their maximum response to a spot moving in a particular direction across the field and no response to movement in the opposite direction.

W cells are less common in the monkey than in the cat (de Monasterio, 1978b), but cells with similar responses are common in other vertebrates. Direction selective, on-off and "uniformity detector" cells make up a substantial proportion of the retinal output of frogs (Lettvin, Maturana, McCulloch, & Pitts, 1959), pigeons (Maturana & Frenk, 1963), grey and ground squirrels (Cooper & Robson, 1966; Michael, 1968b), and rabbits (Barlow & Hill, 1963; Levick, 1967).

At one time it seemed that there was a clear distinction between the simple concentric fields found in cats by Kuffler (1953) and the more elaborate fields found in frogs by Lettvin et al. (1959), suggesting that more complex transformations are carried out in the retinas of simpler vertebrates. This distinction has become greatly blurred, however, with the discovery of non-concentric fields in cats, squirrels and other mammals, and the explanation of some apparently elaborate fields in simpler terms of concentric organisation (e.g. Gaze & Jacobson, 1963).

Even so, it appears that the *proportions* of different field types vary between species. In cats and monkeys the large majority of ganglion cells have concentrically organised fields and there are few on-off, directionally selective and other W cells. In squirrels, rabbits, pigeons and cold-blooded vertebrates, on the other hand, a greater proportion of cells have non-concentric fields. Although caution is needed in interpreting such data, because electrodes are selective in the types of axon from which they record impulses, it does seem that the information provided by the retina of a cat or monkey to the brain is a less complex transformation of the optic array than that provided in other vertebrates. Perhaps this is because greater flexibility and scope for learning is possible when the input to the brain is less highly transformed.

Wavelength-Selective Retinal Ganglion Cells

The retinal ganglion cell responses we have described so far only carry information about the spatial and temporal pattern of light intensity on the retina, and none about the pattern of wavelengths of light. As we saw in Chapter 1, wavelength and intensity differences cannot be detected separately if all the photoreceptors in the retina contain a single pigment type. For colour vision to be possible, there must be receptors with differing peak spectral sensitivities.

In primates and other animals with three cone types, some ganglion cells, not surprisingly, respond differently to light of different wavelengths over a wide range of intensities. The simplest kind of wavelength selective cell is one with an *opponent-colour* response; light of one wavelength anywhere in the cell's field excites it, while light of another wavelength inhibits it. Such a cell responds strongly to wavelengths to which the cones providing its excitatory input are sensitive, and the inhibitory component sharpens its wavelength selectivity (Fig. 2.9). Cells of this kind have been found among the monkey's W cells (de Monasterio, 1978b).

A more complex kind of wavelength-selective cell combines opponent-colour responses with concentric organisation; the centre and surround parts of the field have different wavelength sensitivities. Cells of this kind have been found in the ground squirrel (Michael, 1968c) and monkey, where X cells all have superimposed opponent-colour responses (Wiesel & Hubel, 1966; de Monasterio, 1978a). The fields of monkey X cells fall into four classes. The most common are the two kinds of red–green opponent fields, in which either the centre of the field is most sensitive to red light and the surround to green light, or vice versa. Less common are the two kinds of blue–yellow opponent fields, in which either the centre is most sensitive to blue light and the surround to yellow light, or vice versa.

Finally, a more complex type of field still is the "dual-opponent" field, which has opposite antagonistic organisations in each part of the field. For example, red light might be excitatory and green light inhibitory in the centre, while green is excitatory and red inhibitory in the surround. No mammalian retinal ganglion cells have been found with such fields, but they have been found in the goldfish (Daw, 1968). Note that a dual-opponent cell would respond strongly to a simultaneous difference in wavelength between centre and surround, whereas an opponent-colour cell would not.

RETINAL MECHANISMS

How is it that retinal ganglion cells have such complex responses to the pattern of light falling on the retina? We can think of photoreceptors as

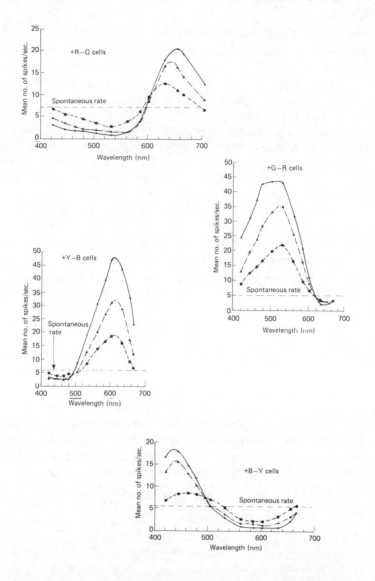

FIG.2.9.   The relationship between wavelength of light and response for four different classes of opponent-colour cell in the monkey, each at three different levels of light intensity. The dashed lines show the cell's spontaneous firing rate in the absence of light stimulation (+ R − G—excited by red light and inhibited by green; + G − R—excited by green and inhibited by red; + Y − B—excited by yellow and inhibited by blue; + B − Y—excited by blue and inhibited by yellow). Note that in all cases the cross-over wavelength between excitation and inhibition is independent of light intensity. Reproduced from De Valois, Abramov, & Jacobs (1966), with the permission of the author and publishers.

measuring light intensity in each small part of the retina, and of these measurements being combined and transformed in the network of retinal cells and their synaptic connections. Here we discuss briefly the ways in which the wiring pattern of the retina organises two kinds of ganglion cell receptive fields; concentric and direction-selective.

Before tackling this problem, it is important to emphasise that it is an over-simplification to see receptors as simply measuring light intensity. Even before receptor signals pass to horizontal and bipolar cells, transformation of the input pattern occurs, as the hyperpolarisation of rods and cones in response to light is not a simple function of intensity. Instead, receptors show adaptation in the same way as the photoreceptors of *Limulus*.

Normann and Werblin (1974) made intracellular recordings from rods and cones of the amphibian *Necturus*, and found that cones respond to light with a hyperpolarisation proportional to the logarithm of light intensity over an intensity range of 3.5 log units. The centre of this range continually shifts, however, to match the current background illumination. Figure 2.10 shows the intensity-response curves for cones adapted to three different background intensities.

Note that the cell's response does not signal absolute light intensity but intensity relative to the current level of adaptation. The situation is rather different in rods, in which the operating range does not shift far above the dark-adapted level.

Even at this early stage receptors respond to changes in light intensity over time and not to absolute levels. Diurnal animals are active in a wide range of light levels, and, through adaptation, cones achieve maximum sensitivity to changes in intensity at whatever the current background light level may be. Rods do not work in this way because they are specialised for detecting a narrow range of dim light intensities.

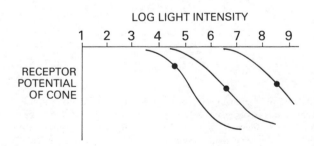

FIG.2.10.   The relationship between log light intensity and receptor potential of a cone. The circles mark the light level around which each curve was obtained and to which the receptors were adapted. Adapted from Normann & Werblin (1974).

Concentric Fields

What processes in the retina bridge the gap between the responses of rods and cones and those of ganglion cells with concentric receptive fields? The response of an X cell can be described by the model shown in Figure 2.11 (Enroth-Cugell & Robson, 1966). The output of the cell is determined by the algebraic sum of a centre and a surround component. Each component sums the total light falling in a circular area, and the contribution of each part of the area is weighted according to its distance from the centre, according to a Gaussian relationship. The curve obtained by taking the difference of the two Gaussians describes the antagonistic organisation of the field. Light falling in the outer part of the field has the opposite effect on the output to light falling in the inner part of the field.

What neural mechanisms perform this computation on the pattern of receptor signals over the retina? Dowling and Werblin (1969) made intracellular recordings from the retinal neurons of *Necturus*, and found that bipolar cells have concentric fields. The linear spatial summation necessary to establish centre-surround organisation therefore occurs in the outer plexiform

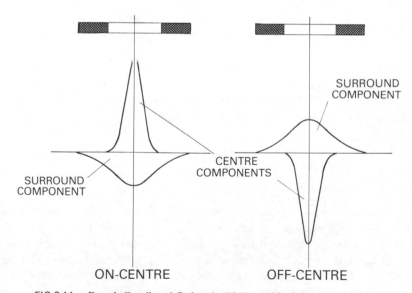

ON-CENTRE   OFF-CENTRE

FIG.2.11.   Enroth-Cugell and Robson's (1966) model of the organisation of X cell fields. The strength of the centre component depends on the light falling in the centre of the field and the strength of the surround component on light falling throughout the field. In both cases, the contribution of light intensity is weighted by a Gaussian function. The response of the cell is determined by the difference between the two components.

layer; the centre component is generated by the summed input of a group of neighbouring receptors to a bipolar cell, and the surround component by the input from a wider circle of receptors, mediated by horizontal cells. The two inputs act in an opposing way to generate a sustained slow potential in the bipolar cell. In *Necturus*, some ganglion cells are driven directly by bipolars, and therefore have concentric fields comparable to those of mammalian X cells.

Y cells share the basic concentric organisation of X cells, but have additional non-linear responses. Hochstein and Shapley (1976) showed that a further component added to the model in Figure 2.11 accounts for these non-linearities. Small subunits of the receptive field, distributed throughout it, respond in the same way as the centre of the field to either onset or offset of light. The responses of these units are not, however, summed together linearly with the responses of the centre and surround. Instead, a non-linear *rectification* takes place; in an on-centre cell, the response of the subunits adds to that of the centre at light onset but does not subtract from that of the surround at light offset (and vice versa in an off-centre cell). The result is that there is a response to light onset and offset whatever its spatial pattern.

This non-linear rectification probably occurs at synapses in the inner plexiform layer between bipolar, amacrine and ganglion cells. In *Necturus*, some ganglion cells do not synapse directly with bipolars but only with amacrine cells, and Dowling and Werblin (1969) suggest that these ganglion cells respond to changes in contrast. Victor and Shapley (1979) argue that the subunits of Y cell fields are bipolar cell responses, which are rectified at synapses with amacrine cells and then pooled by amacrines which in turn drive Y ganglion cells.

Direction–Selective Fields

How does the neural wiring of the retina give rise to ganglion cells sensitive to the movement of a spot of light in a particular direction? A model of the neural organisation involved was developed by Barlow and Levick (1965) from detailed analysis of direction-selective receptive fields in the rabbit (see Fig. 2.12). They argue that such fields contain adjacent excitatory and inhibitory regions; movement of a stimulus in one direction will cause first an excitatory effect on the ganglion cell and then an inhibitory effect, so that the cell responds. Movement in the opposite direction, however, causes first an inhibition with a long time course, blocking the later excitation; this is the null direction in which movement gives no response.

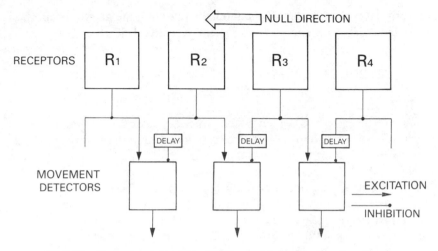

FIG.2.12. Barlow and Levick's (1965) model of directionally selective ganglion cells. If receptor R_1 is stimulated and then receptor R_2, the signal from R_1 arrives ahead of inhibition from R_2 and the cell responds. With movement in the opposite direction, inhibition from R_2 coincides with the signal from R_1 and there is no response.

The physiological basis of this field organisation has been elucidated in the pigeon; Holden (1977) argued that the excitatory and inhibitory parts of the field are units with on–off responses which converge to a single amacrine cell, and Mariani (1982) has discovered a class of pigeon amacrine cell with long processes separating two regions of dendritic spread. It is likely that such cells exert the inhibitory influence on a ganglion cell's activity which Barlow and Levick's model requires. Such a model gives further support to the idea that non-linearities in ganglion cell fields are mediated by amacrine cells in the inner plexiform layer.

We mentioned earlier the differences between species in the kinds of fields their retinal ganglion cells possess, and concluded that the differences are probably quantitative. In cats and monkeys, the large majority of cells have concentric organisation, whereas in rabbits, squirrels and non-mammals, cells with more complex receptive fields, such as direction-selective cells, are more common. If our picture of retinal wiring is correct, we would expect to find corresponding differences in retinal structure.

Dowling (1968) provides evidence of such differences, between frogs and monkeys, in the structure of the inner plexiform layer. Frogs have few direct bipolar–ganglion cell synapses, and many amacrine–amacrine and amacrine–ganglion cell synapses, whereas the opposite is true of the monkey. This suggests that more complex processes are taking place in the frog inner plexiform layer than in that of the monkey, reflecting the greater proportion of ganglion cells with complex, non-linear receptive fields.

BEYOND THE RETINA: THE MAMMALIAN VISUAL CORTEX

So far, we have been considering the processes taking place in the retina which transform a pattern of light intensity into a pattern of activity in optic nerve axons. Elaborate transformations of spatial and temporal pattern occur in both the simple retina of the horseshoe crab and the more complex vertebrate retina. In some vertebrate species, it has been possible to take physiological analysis further by recording from cells in the brain.

The first step in tackling the brain is to determine where the fibres of the optic nerve project. Whatever animal is studied, their projection is always orderly, with axons maintaining the same topographic relationship to each other as that of their receptive fields on the retina. In frogs and toads, for example, the retinal ganglion cells project to the optic tectum, in which cells are arranged in four *retinotopic maps* (Lettvin et al., 1959). Each map is made up of a layer of cells which each respond to stimulation in one small part of the visual field. The topography of this map corresponds to that of the retina.

Fish, reptiles and birds also have this relatively simple projection of retina to optic tectum. In mammals, however, the situation is more complex, as pathways to the cerebral cortex are also involved. We will first sketch out the structure of the mammalian visual pathway and then go on to look in more detail at responses of cells in it to light stimulation.

The Mammalian Visual Pathway

The primary visual pathway of mammals begins with the projection of X cells, most Y cells and a few W cells from the retina to the dorsal part of the two *lateral geniculate nuclei* (LGN) of the thalamus. There is a second projection, of some Y cells and most W cells, to the *superior colliculi*, which are paired structures in the midbrain homologous to the optic tectum of non-mammals. In addition, some W cell axons run to various structures such as the hypothalamus, tegmentum and ventral LGN, but little is known of these pathways. There are therefore two main pathways from eye to brain; the evolutionarily older route from retina to midbrain and a new projection to the thalamus. The second of these is the beginning of the primary visual pathway (Figure 2.13).

Optic nerve fibres terminate at synapses with LGN cells, which are arranged in layers, or laminae. Each lamina contains a retinotopic map of half of the visual field, those in the right LGN having maps of the left side of the visual field and those in the left LGN maps of the right side. In animals with laterally placed eyes, this is because there is complete crossing over of the optic nerves at the optic chiasm to run to opposite sides of the brain. In animals with binocular overlap, there is a partial crossing over, or decussation, of the optic nerves at the chiasm. The fibres of ganglion cells in the left halves of each retina (carrying information about the right half of the visual field) run to the left LGN, and conversely for fibres from the right halves of each retina, as illustrated in Figure 2.13. In the monkey, the LGN contains six laminae, three of which receive input from one eye and three from the other eye.

LGN cells have much the same X and Y type receptive fields as retinal ganglion cells. Each LGN cell is thought to be driven by one or more retinal ganglion cells of the same receptive field type. The output of the LGN projects to the occipital lobe of the cerebral cortex—the highly folded sheet of nerve cells that forms the outer layer of the cerebral hemispheres. In the monkey, all the fibres from the LGN run to a region of the cortex in area 17 called the striate or visual cortex, whereas in the cat things are more complex. X cells from the LGN project only to area 17 of the cortex, while Y and probably W cells have branching axons and project not only to area 17 but also to the adjacent areas 18 and 19 and the suprasylvian gyrus.

Receptive Fields in the Visual Cortex

The first recordings from single cells in the striate cortex of cats and monkeys were made by Hubel and Wiesel (1959, 1962, 1968). They found a class of cortical cells with concentric fields, in the layer of the cortex where input fibres from the LGN terminate, but in other layers cells had quite different receptive fields. These fields can be divided into two main categories, called *simple* and *complex*.

Cells with simple receptive fields are similar to those with concentric fields in having excitatory and inhibitory areas which can be mapped out using spots of light, but the shapes of these areas are quite different. In all cases, the boundaries between excitatory and inhibitory areas are straight lines. In some cells, there is a single line dividing two antagonistic areas, while in others there are two boundaries separating a central excitatory area from flanking inhibitory ones, or vice versa (see Fig. 2.14).

From a knowledge of these areas, the response of the cell to stimuli more complex than spots of light can be predicted. Cell (a) in Fig. 2.14 will respond most strongly to an edge lying along the boundary of its two zones, with brighter light to the left, while cell (b) will respond most strongly to an edge the opposite way around. For cell (c), the strongest response will be to a bright "slit" on a dark background, covering its excitatory region, while for cell (d) it will be to a dark bar on a bright background.

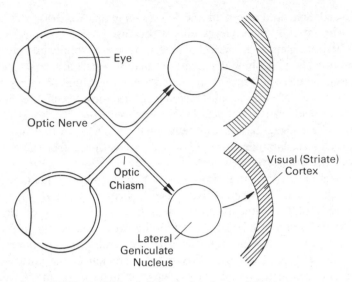

FIG.2.13.   The primary visual pathway of a primate.

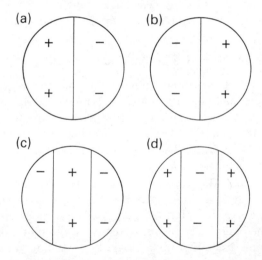

FIG.2.14.   Examples of four kinds of simple cortical cell fields (+ + excitatory region; − − inhibitory region).

Simple cells, like X cells, perform a linear spatial summation of light intensity in their fields and their responses can be predicted from the contrast, orientation and position of a stimulus falling in the receptive field. *Orientation preference* is a particularly important feature of simple cells; as would be predicted from their receptive fields, their maximum response is to a bar or edge oriented at a particular angle to the visual axis. This preference is quite a narrow one, and turning the stimulus through more than about 20° from the preferred angle greatly reduces the cell's firing rate (Fig. 2.15).

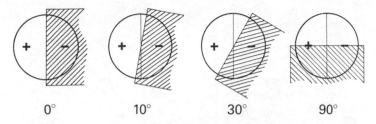

0°   10°   30°   90°

FIG.2.15.   The orientation preference of a cortical simple cell. A light–dark
edge falling on the vertical boundary between excitatory and inhibitory areas
evokes the maximum response. As the edge is rotated, less of the excitatory
and more of the inhibitory area is illuminated, and the response is reduced.

For complex cells, the optimal stimulus is also a bar or an edge with a
particular orientation, but falling anywhere within the cell's receptive field.
The field of a complex cell cannot be marked out into excitatory and
inhibitory regions using spots of light, and so there is no region in which
the stimulus has to fall to cause a response. Like Y retinal ganglion cells,
complex cells therefore have marked non-linearities in their responses. Some
complex cells respond most strongly to moving bars or edges, often showing
a preference for movement in one direction perpendicular to the optimal
orientation of the stimulus.

Hubel and Wiesel also described a third class of "hypercomplex" cell,
with a receptive field much like that of a complex cell but with greatest
response to a bar or edge not extending beyond the receptive field (Fig.
2.16).

Later studies (e.g. Gilbert, 1977) found simple cells with the same
characteristic, and it is better to think of a property of "end-inhibition"
possessed by some simple and some complex cells than to think in terms of
a third class of cell.

Cells in cat striate cortex show no selectivity for wavelength in their
responses, whereas some of those in monkey cortex do. Dow and Gouras
(1973) found cells with receptive fields in the foveal region which showed
opponent colour responses, sometimes throughout the field and sometimes
superimposed on line-shaped excitatory and inhibitory regions. Michael
(1978) found that some concentric cells in monkey striate cortex have dual-
opponent responses (p.46), always involving red and green.

Functional Architecture in the Visual Cortex

Our description of Hubel and Wiesel's findings has so far ignored the
structure of the visual cortex and the relationship between the arrangement
of cells and their receptive fields. The visual cortex is by no means a
homogeneous mass of tissue in which cells with different kinds of response
are scattered randomly. Instead, it shows an astonishingly precise and regular

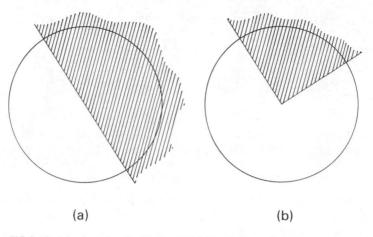

(a)   (b)

FIG.2.16.   A cortical cell with "end-inhibition." The cell does not respond
to a long edge extending beyond its field (a) but does respond to an edge
ending within its field (b).

arrangement of different cell types which Hubel and Wiesel (1962) call
"functional architecture."

Like any region of cerebral cortex, the striate cortex is a folded sheet of
cell bodies and fibres about 3 to 4 mm thick. Cell bodies tend to segregate
into layers of greater and lesser density, and six main layers, some with
subdivisions, can be recognised under the microscope (Fig. 2.17). Below
these layers is the white matter, made up of the axons running between this
region and other cortical regions or lower brain structures. Within the cortex,
fibres run mainly perpendicularly to the surface, and the sideways spread of
fibres across the cortex is limited to quite short distances.

So, the only visible structure in the striate cortex is the layering of cell
bodies. What happens, however, when we probe with an electrode and ask
what responses cells in each part of the cortex show? The first feature we
find is an orderly retinotopic mapping of the visual world onto the surface
of the cortex, just like that in the laminae of the LGN, with the left and
right halves of the visual field mapped onto the right and left cortices
respectively. Cortical cells therefore have the same topographic relation to
each other as their receptive fields have in the visual field. However, the map
is not metrically accurate, as the receptive fields of cells responding to stimuli
in the centre of the visual field are smaller than those of cells with peripheral
fields. Consequently, the cortical area devoted to the central part of the
visual field is proportionally larger than that devoted to the periphery.

Now, let us zoom in and concentrate on one small part of the cortex, in
which all cells have fields from one part of the retina. As an electrode is
moved gradually across the cortex, the fields of cells do not move across the
visual field in a smooth way. Instead, roughly every millimetre, there is a

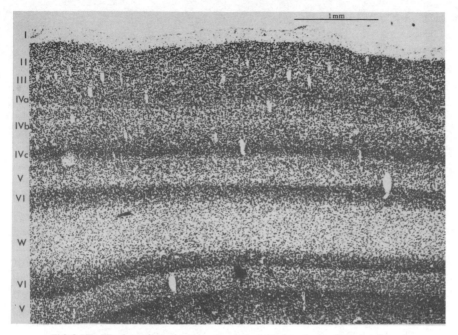

FIG.2.17.   Section of monkey visual cortex stained to show cell bodies. Note the layers into which the cortex is divided. Reproduced from Hubel and Wiesel (1977) with permission of the author and publishers.

jump from fields in one part of the visual field to fields in an adjacent part. Hubel and Wiesel (1977) explained this finding by suggesting that the cortex is divided into roughly square blocks of tissue, about 1 mm by 1 mm, extending from the surface to the white matter, which they call *hypercolumns*. Within a hypercolumn, cells have different receptive fields, which overlap a good deal, but all these fields fall within some single retinal area called the *aggregate field*. In the part of the cortex corresponding to the fovea, the aggregate field is about 0.1° across, while in the periphery it is 3° or more across. Note that the size of a field is measured as the angle subtended at the eye by an object just filling it.

Within a hypercolumn, there is further organisation still. First, it can be divided into two parts according to which eye is most effective in driving the cells. Recall that in the LGN, input from the two eyes was segregated into separate laminae. In layer IVc of the cortex, where fibres from the LGN terminate, this segregation is maintained; cells have concentric fields and respond to their optimal stimulus presented in one eye only. In other layers, however, cells have *binocular fields*; they respond to their optimal stimulus if it is presented to either eye.

Even so, cells always respond more strongly to stimuli in one eye than in the other, and are said to show *ocular dominance*. Within a hypercolumn, cells with different ocular dominance are segregated into two subdivisions. These ocular dominance columns form bands of cells across the cortex with alternating eye preferences, and with appropriate staining techniques they can be made visible, as in Figure 2.18 (LeVay, Hubel, & Wiesel, 1975).

Finally, each hypercolumn is further subdivided. If an electrode penetrates the striate cortex perpendicular to its surface, all the cells, both simple and complex, which it encounters have the same orientation preference. With an oblique penetration, a series of cells are found which have the same preference, then there is a jump to a new preference, and so on. Hubel and Wiesel (1962) explained these findings in terms of columns of cells sharing the same orientation preference. These are about 0.05 mm across and each hypercolumn contains about 20, so that the full 180° range of orientations is represented in each hypercolumn, in steps of about 10°.

Again, it has been possible to confirm this inference from electrode tracks by making orientation preference columns visible. Hubel, Wiesel, & Stryker (1978) exposed monkeys to moving vertical stripes while injecting them with radioactively labelled 2-deoxyglucose, a substance taken up by active nerve cells. The resulting pattern of radioactivity in slices of striate cortex showed the positions of columns of cells with a vertical orientation preference (Fig. 2.19).

Figure 2.20 summarises the functional architecture of the cortex as it has been determined so far. Information from each part of the visual field is fed to a hypercolumn containing tens of thousands of cells, each with slightly

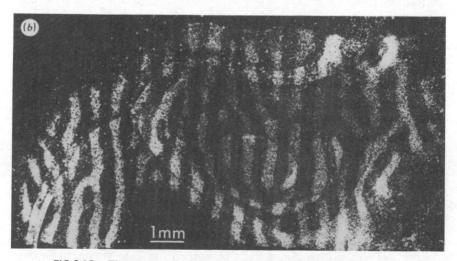

FIG.2.18.   The pattern of ocular dominance columns in the visual cortex revealed as alternating light and dark bands by autoradiographic methods. Reproduced from Hubel and Wiesel (1977) with permission of the author and publishers.

different fields falling within the aggregate field of the hypercolumn. In one half of the hypercolumn, cells are predominantly driven by input from the right eye and in the other half by input from the left. Each half is divided into columns of cells sharing the same orientation preference, and there are enough of these to represent all the possible orientations of straight edge stimuli in steps of about 10°.

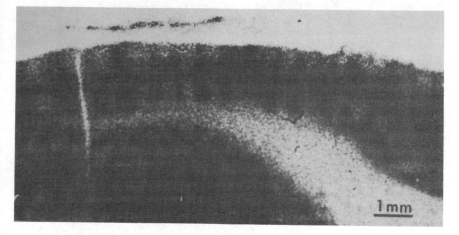

FIG.2.19. Autoradiograph of section through visual cortex revealing columns of cells responding to vertical edges as dark stripes. The uniformly dark band across the centre of the cortex is layer IV, in which cells have no orientation preference. Reproduced with permission from Hubel, Wiesel, & Stryker, (1977). Copyright (c) 1977 Macmillan Journals Limited.

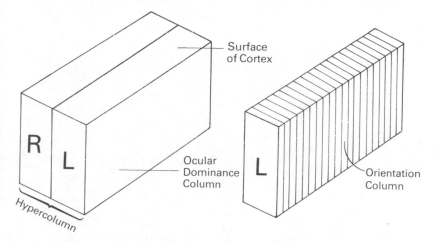

FIG.2.20. Diagram of functional architecture of a hypercolumn, divided into two ocular dominance columns R and L, each divided into orientation columns.

CONCLUSIONS

At the beginning of this chapter, we asked how much could be learned about vision by recording from single cells in the nervous system with a microelectrode. We have now seen, if only in outline, the tremendous amount of knowledge of the properties of single cells in visual systems which has been obtained by this method. In the mammalian visual pathway, we know the receptive fields of cells in the retina, optic nerve, LGN and striate cortex, the topography of these areas and something of how the receptive fields are formed.

A clear implication of these findings is that visual pathways do not copy the retinal pattern of light into a pattern of neural activity and then transmit this faithfully to be displayed in the brain. Instead, single cells respond to particular kinds of *change* of light intensity over both time and space. This means that as a person or other mammal moves about in the environment the continually shifting pattern of activity in the striate cortex will be a complex transformation of the shifting pattern of light entering the eye. In Chapter 3 we ask how this transformation can be described and why it is carried out.

3 Interpreting the Neurophysiology of Vision

So far, our description of the vertebrate visual system has been a catalogue of the different responses of different types of neuron to light. One question which can be asked about these responses is *how* they occur, and we have looked briefly at the synaptic connections in the retina which underly the fields of retinal ganglion cells. Equally as important as this kind of physiological analysis is the question of *why* single cells have the responses which they do. To answer this question, it is not enough to describe the responses of single cells to patterns of light. We must also interpret these responses in terms of a theory of the whole system of which the cell is a part.

As an analogy, imagine trying to understand how a clock works without knowing what it does. By dismantling the clock, it would be possible to describe each of its parts in turn and to explain how the movement of each one influences the next. But it would not be possible to understand the *function* of each part without knowing what the whole mechanism is doing. We would need to know that its purpose is to mark out fixed intervals of time and that an arrangement of pendulum and escapement is a way of doing this. Only then would we understand the functions of these components.

In the case of an animal's visual system, understanding the overall function of the mechanism involves two things. The first is the nature of the *input* to the system; the spatio-temporal patterns of light falling on its retina and the information they carry about the environment. The second is the *output* the visual system must provide; the information about surfaces, objects and events in the environment which an animal needs in order to organise its activities.

61

By combining the answers to these two questions, we should be able to achieve a specification of the job the system has to do. We will know what information the animal needs to detect and how that information is carried in the pattern of light falling on the retina. We can then go on to devise a theory of how the information is actually extracted from the input, and finally ask how this process is carried out by the neurons whose properties we have already studied with a microelectrode.

The distinctions between these questions have been made clearly and forcefully by Marr (1982), and we draw extensively on his ideas in this and later chapters. In his terms, the first problem is to devise a *computational* theory which specifies the job the visual system must do, the second problem is to find *algorithms* which can process information in the way required by the computational theory, and the third problem is to understand how these algorithms are *implemented* by neurons. All these stages are necessary for understanding the neurophysiology of vision. As Marr puts it:

> trying to understand perception by studying only neurons is like trying to understand bird flight by studying only feathers: it just cannot be done. In order to study bird flight we have to understand aerodynamics; only then do the structure of feathers and the different shapes of bird wings make sense. (Marr, 1982, p.27)

How would these principles be applied to the relatively simple visual system of the horseshoe crab? A computational theory of crab vision would specify what information the animal needs from the optic array to organise its activities. As we argued in Chapter 2, these would include such things as the positions relative to itself of the bright disc specifying the water surface and moving shadows specifying potential predators. The second step would be to devise algorithms able to process the pattern of light at the eye so as to make the required information explicit. Finally, we would ask what role the processes of adaptation and lateral inhibition play in implementing these algorithms, and what further physiological processes are involved.

From this point of view, there is still much work to be done on the visual system of *Limulus*. We have seen that the pattern of activity in the optic nerve contains information about steep spatial and temporal gradients in light intensity at the eye. The information required by our computational theory is therefore *available* at this stage, but it has not been made *explicit*; the activity of a cell in the optic nerve does not signal the presence of an edge. In the crab's nervous system further processes must take place to yield a representation of the structure of the environment, which the crab can use to organise limb movements.

When we turn to vertebrates, and especially mammals, the application of Marr's principles raises still more difficult problems. We begin our discussion of theories of the mammalian visual system by considering two well-established ways of understanding the properties of single cells. These treat single cells as detectors of either geometrical features or spatial frequencies. We argue that neither of these treatments provides an adequate computational theory; then we go on to consider Marr's interpretation of retinal ganglion cell and cortical cell properties.

SINGLE CELLS AS "FEATURE DETECTORS"

The theory that single cells in the optic nerve, LGN and striate cortex are detectors of geometric features in the pattern of light falling on the retina begins, as a computational theory should, by considering the input to the visual system. It asks how a two-dimensional pattern such as that in Figure 3.1 can be represented economically, and argues that a full description of it could be achieved by transmitting information only about the positions of dark-bright boundaries, or *edges*. Information specifying the intensities at each point within a region of uniform intensity is redundant; it is not required for a full description of the pattern.

This argument suggests that greater economy of representation could be achieved in a visual system by feeding the output of the mosaic of light receptors to a mosaic of "edge detectors"; units connected to the receptors in such a way that they respond only if an edge falls on them. The output of these edge-detectors would be a complete version of the original pattern, but a much compressed one.

This imaginary system looks very much like a retina containing ganglion cells with concentric fields. If the pattern in Figure 3.1 were projected onto such a retina, ganglion cells with fields in the uniformly light and dark areas would remain silent while those with fields lying along the edges would respond (Fig 3.2a). The input would therefore be fully described by the pattern of activity of retinal ganglion cells, at least to a limit of accuracy imposed by the sizes of the cells' fields. We can say that retinal ganglion cells respond to geometrical *features*, such as edges, in the input pattern.

When we consider cells further along the visual pathway, we find two changes in the geometrical features to which they respond. First, more and more highly specified features are required to elicit a response from a cell. X and Y cells in the optic nerve and LGN respond to an edge of any orientation; cortical simple cells respond to an edge or a bar of a specific orientation, and cells with end-inhibition respond only to an edge or bar of the correct orientation ending within the receptive field. Secondly, the location of a feature on the retina has less effect on a cell's response; complex cells respond to an edge or bar wherever it falls in the receptive field.

FIG.3.1.   Artificial pattern of dark
and light areas.

It therefore appears that the visual pathway is hierarchically organised
and that the responses of cells at successively higher levels represent more
and more abstract properties of the input pattern. Hubel and Wiesel
originally argued that the connections of cortical cells follow a hierarchical
scheme of this kind, in which simple cells are driven by LGN input, complex
cells by simple cells, and hypercomplex by complex. Although this hypothesis
is supported by the fact that simple but not complex cells are found in the
cortical layer where LGN fibres terminate (Gilbert, 1977), it is seriously
weakened by Stone's (1972) evidence that complex cells are driven
monosynaptically from the LGN with shorter latency than simple cells.

Even so, in the feature detection view, these cells form the bottom layers
of a hierarchy of cells (so far undiscovered) which respond to progressively
more and more abstract geometric features. The cells in the next level up
might respond to simple geometrical patterns such as angles, defined by the
activities of particular combinations of complex and hypercomplex cells. At
the top of the hierarchy are cells responding only to stimuli such as particular
items of food or particular social companions. A cell claimed to be near the
top of the hierarchy is one discovered in the inferotemporal cortex of a
monkey by Gross, Rocha-Miranda, and Bender (1972) which responded
most strongly to the silhouette of a monkey's paw. The proposal that there
are cells in the human nervous system responding only to highly abstract
stimulus classes has been dubbed the "grandmother cell" or "yellow
Volkswagen detector" theory.

An eloquent statement of this framework for understanding the properties
of single cells in visual systems can be found in Barlow (1972), and we will
have more to say in Chapter 7 about the theory that vision involves a
hierarchical system of units recognising more and more complexly defined
features. For the moment, though, we will stay with the lower levels of the

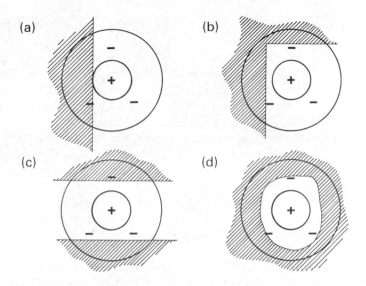

FIG.3.2.   (a) Straight-line boundary between dark and light areas falling in the field of a centre-on ganglion cell. The inhibitory surround component is decreased relative to the excitatory centre component and the cell therefore responds. In (b), (c) and (d), patterns of light fall on the field which illuminate the same surround area as in (a) and therefore evoke the same response from the cell.

presumed hierarchy and ask whether it provides a valid computational theory of what single cells are doing.

Objections to the Feature Detection Theory

The crucial objection to the feature detection view is that single cells are *not* detectors of features such as oriented edges. Consider an on-centre X cell in the optic nerve or LGN. An edge in the outside world may give rise to a light-dark boundary grazing its receptive field centre. If this happens, the cell will respond as the illumination of the surround relative to the centre decreases. But for the cell to be an "edge detector" it must respond *only* to straight light-dark boundaries and *not* to any other pattern. A retinal ganglion or LGN cell does not meet this requirement, as there is an indefinite number of other patterns which would elicit an equally strong response. Figure 3.2 shows how a corner, bar or spot would elicit the same response from such a cell as an edge.

The easiest way to see this point is to imagine you are trying to work out what is going on in the cell's field by monitoring its response. In this case, you would have little success, as the strength of the response would tell you how much centre–surround contrast was present, but not how it was distributed.

The feature detection theory would meet this argument by saying that the presence of an edge is not signalled by the activity of a single retinal ganglion or LGN cell but by the activity of a row of these cells. If simple cortical cells were connected to a row of LGN cells they would therefore act as edge detectors. Exactly the same argument can be made against the claim that cortical cells are detectors of geometrical features, however. The strength of a simple cell's response to an edge does vary with the orientation of the edge in its field, but it *also* varies with its contrast and position. The response of the cell therefore does not provide unambiguous information about the pattern of light in its field. A particular rate of response may mean that there is a low contrast edge of optimal orientation or a high contrast edge of a different orientation (Fig. 3.3a).

Similarly, the response of a cell to a bar or a slit is determined not only by the orientation of the stimulus but also by its contrast, position and width. Figure 3.3b illustrates how a wide slit of optimal orientation can elicit the same response as a narrow slit of a different orientation. Finally, further ambiguity arises because the responses of many cortical cells are influenced not only by light but also by such things as sound (Fishman & Michael, 1973) and the angle of tilt of the animal's body (Horn & Hill, 1969).

If the patterns of light falling on the retina are only of the kind shown in Figure 3.1, then the ambiguity problem will not arise. In such a pattern,

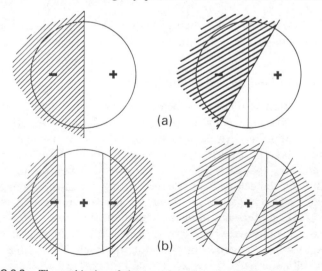

FIG.3.3. The ambiguity of the response of a cortical simple cell. In (a), a low-contrast edge of optimal orientation and a high-contrast edge of a different orientation evoke the same response. In (b), a slit of optimal orientation but wider than the excitatory area evokes the same response as a slit of optimal width but different orientation.

contrast is present only at edges and corners, and all edges and corners have the same contrast. The pattern of activity in an array of retinal ganglion cells stimulated by a pattern of this kind would therefore pick out the edges in it reliably. The light reflected from natural surfaces and objects in the visual world does not come in patterns like that in Figure 3.1, however. With few exceptions, surfaces have *texture*, and the intensity of light they reflect in an observer's direction varies greatly.

Imagine, for example, a black cat lying on a white carpet. If we measure the intensity of light reflected along a line across the scene, we would not find it fall from a constant high value to a constant low value at the edge of the cat, and rise again at the other side. Instead, the texture of tufts of the carpet and hairs on the cat would cause the intensity to fluctuate greatly over both surfaces. Almost everywhere in the pattern of reflected light there would be enough contrast to elicit a response in a cell with a concentric field. If light reflected from this scene were the input to an array of cells with concentric fields, then their outputs would *not* pick out the outline of the cat; instead they would give a complex pattern of activity in which the problem of finding edges would be no easier than that of finding them in the input.

One way to solve this problem would be to blur the input pattern so that the fine pattern reflected from textured surfaces would disappear, leaving only differences in average light intensity over large areas. After such blurring, a response by a cell with a large concentric field would more reliably indicate the presence of the edge of a large object. This is the horseshoe crab's solution; overlap in the fields of view of adjacent ommatidia means that fluctuations of light intensity over the eye are smoothed and information about the fine detail of textured surfaces is lost. The horseshoe crab does not, however, need to recognise cats lying on carpets or, more realistically, patterns of colour markings on a fish. It needs only to spot a dark silhouette moving against a bright background.

In the mammalian eye, the fine structure of light reflected from textured surfaces is available at the retina, and consequently a centre-surround comparison is not adequate for detection of edges, except in an artificial world of uniformly dark objects against a uniformly white background. We can conclude that single cells in the optic nerve, LGN and visual cortex are not detectors of local geometrical features; rather, the activity of any one cell carries ambiguous information about the pattern of light in its field.

SINGLE CELLS AND SPATIAL FREQUENCIES

In the "feature detection" view, single cells detect the presence of geometrical features at particular points in the pattern of light falling on the retina. This is a *local* analysis of the pattern, analysing it into its component features, and detection of its large-scale, *global* organisation must occur at some later point by detection of groups of features. One reply to the argument that single cells are not really feature detectors is to argue that they do not carry information about local properties of the input at all, but instead about global properties; in particular, about *spatial frequencies*.

What are spatial frequencies? When we described Enroth-Cugell and Robson's work, we showed how spatial patterns of light intensity can be described mathematically in the same way as temporal patterns. Just as the temporal pattern of air pressure produced by a tuning fork can be described by a sinusoidal relationship having a particular frequency, wavelength and amplitude, so can the spatial pattern of light intensity produced by a sinusoidal grating.

Most musical instruments do not produce pure sinusoids but a more complex waveform made up of a number of *harmonics* added to the fundamental frequency. Harmonics are multiples of the fundamental frequency, and a musical instrument typically produces a series of harmonics, decreasing in amplitude with increasing frequency. Figure 3.4 illustrates how the addition of two harmonics to a fundamental gives a complex waveform.

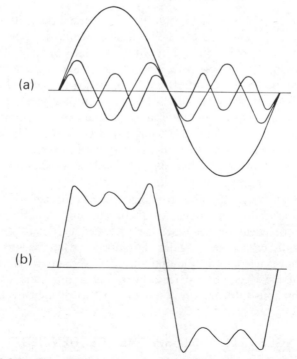

(a)

(b)

FIG.3.4. The synthesis of a complex waveform (b) by the addition of a fundamental frequency, its third harmonic and its fifth harmonic (a). The harmonics have one-third and one-fifth the amplitude of the fundamental.

Just as we can create a complex waveform by adding sinusoids of different frequencies and amplitudes, so we can do the reverse and break down a waveform into its component sinusoids, using a mathematical process known as *Fourier analysis*. Applied to a grating, Fourier analysis would yield the amplitude of each sinusoidal component present, and this spectrum of amplitudes at different frequencies is called the *Fourier transform*. In a grating, light intensity varies along only one axis, but a pattern in which intensity varies along all axes can be transformed in the same way. The low spatial frequency components in a pattern represent its large-scale properties, while the high-frequency components represent the fine details. This is illustrated by Figure 3.5, which shows the effects of filtering out either the high or the low spatial frequencies in a photograph.

The concept of spatial frequency allows us to describe the response of a single cell as a function of the frequency of a sinusoidal grating focused onto its receptive field, rather than as a function of different geometrical stimuli. In particular, we can ask what frequency of sinusoidal grating elicits the maximum response from a cell and how selective it is in its responses to different spatial frequencies.

Responses of Single Cells to Gratings

Retinal ganglion cells with concentric fields will necessarily respond selectively to different spatial frequencies. Above a certain frequency, there is no net change of illumination of either centre or surround at onset and offset of the grating and therefore no response from the cell. The smaller the receptive field of the cell, the higher the maximum spatial frequency to which it will respond. At any given distance from the centre of the cat retina, there is little variation in the field sizes of either X or Y cells (Peichl & Wässle, 1979) and so there will be little variation in spatial frequency tuning.

FIG.3.5. Left: the result of filtering out high spatial frequencies from the photograph in the centre. Right: the result of filtering out low spatial frequencies. The first filtering blurs the picture while the second leaves its outlines. Original photograph copyright (1984) Bill Gillham and Sam Grainger. Filtered versions courtesy of John Frisby, University of Sheffield.

Similarly, LGN cells with fields at the same distance from the centre do not vary in their spatial frequency tuning and are as unselective in their responses to gratings as retinal ganglion cells. Things are different in the visual cortex, however; simple and complex cells are more narrowly tuned to spatial frequency and each hypercolumn contains cells with a wide range of optimum spatial frequencies (Fig. 3.6). The response of a cell to a grating is measured by its *contrast sensitivity*; the reciprocal of the threshold contrast required to obtain a criterion response from the cell.

In the cat striate cortex, the optimum spatial frequencies of cells range from 0.3 to 3 cycles/deg, with all values represented at points out to about 10° eccentricity (Movshon, Thompson, & Tolhurst, 1978). In the monkey, the range is rather higher, from 2 to 8 cycles/deg (De Valois et al., 1982), presumably reflecting the monkey's greater visual acuity. The selectivity of cells can be measured by their *bandwidth;* the ratio of the spatial frequencies at which half the maximum contrast sensitivity is obtained. Bandwidths are measured in octaves by taking the logarithm to base two of the ratio (Fig. 3.7). In both cat and monkey striate cortex, bandwidths range from less than one to about three octaves, with a median value just over one. These bandwidths are considerably less than in the LGN.

The responses of cortical cells to sinusoidal gratings would be expected from what we have already described of their responses to edge, bar and slit stimuli. A cell with a vertical bar as its optimum stimulus, for example, will give its peak response to a vertical grating with wavelength twice the

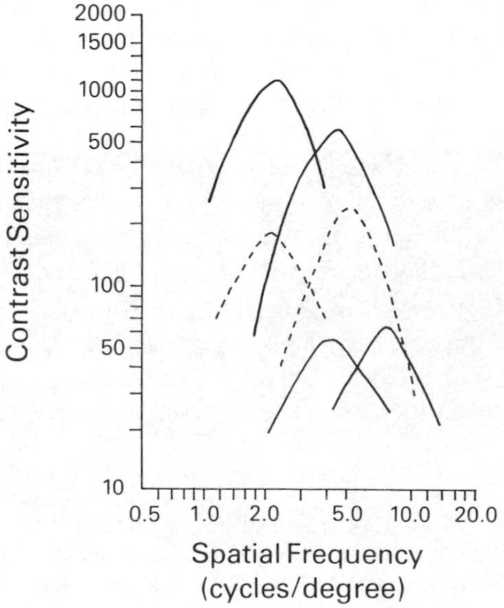

FIG.3.6. Responses of cells within one hypercolumn of visual cortex to sinusoidal gratings of different frequencies. Responses are expressed as contrast sensitivity, which is the reciprocal of the grating contrast required to elicit a criterion response from the cell. Note that peak sensitivities range from 2 to 8 cycles/deg. Reproduced from De Valois et al. (1982) with permission of the publishers.

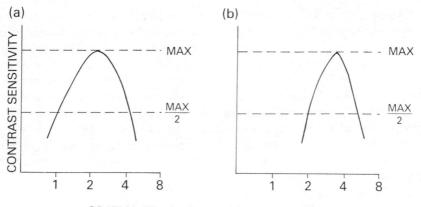

FIG.3.7.   Measurement of the spatial frequency selectivity of a cortical cell.
Cell (a) has peak sensitivity at 2.3 cycles/deg and a bandwidth of 2 octaves.
Cell (b) has peak sensitivity at 3.2 cycles/deg and a bandwidth of 1.3 octaves.

width of the bar, provided the grating is lined up with the boundaries of the
excitatory and inhibitory regions. There is no conflict between the two sets
of findings, and the problems arise when we come to consider their
interpretation.

Why Are Cells Selective for Spatial Frequency?

At first sight, the selectivity of cortical cells for spatial frequency suggests
that a Fourier analysis of the pattern of light at the retina is carried out in
the striate cortex, and that a cortical cell signals not the presence of a local
feature but a global property of the pattern, the amplitude of the spatial
frequency to which it is tuned. It is important to realise, however, that the
fact that cortical cells are selective for spatial frequency does not *prove* that
the visual system decomposes its input into sinusoidal components any more
than the fact that cells are selective for orientation of edges proves that it
analyses input into local geometric features.

   In fact, the theory that the visual cortex performs a global Fourier analysis
is not supported by the physiological evidence. If it were correct, single cells
would be tuned to a narrow band of spatial frequencies and would be
sensitive to their presence throughout the visual field. Instead, cells respond
over a range of spatial frequencies of an octave or more and have fields of
limited size. A further problem is that cells are sensitive to the phase of
sinusoidal components; in other words, where the peaks and troughs fall in
the receptive field. Again we have a problem of ambiguity of single cell
responses.

The conclusion to be drawn from the evidence is that the visual cortex performs a local analysis of the input pattern, but the hypercolumn analysing each piece of the pattern contains multiple channels tuned to different spatial frequencies. This model of the visual system is supported not only by physiological evidence but also by evidence on the visibility of gratings to human observers. Early evidence was obtained by Campbell and Robson (1968) and by Graham and Nachmias (1971), who discovered that thresholds for detection of different components in compound gratings were the same as those for the detection of the components presented individually. These findings indicated that visual input is processed in multiple independent channels, each analysing a band of spatial frequencies.

This model leads us to ask why each hypercolumn in the striate cortex contains cells with different spatial frequency tuning. One answer, proposed by De Valois, Albrecht, and Thorell (1982) among others, is that separate Fourier analyses are carried out of the pattern of light falling in each aggregate field. If an object has a characteristic spatial frequency "signature", then the pattern of activity in cells with different tunings could specify its presence in the aggregate field. The problem with this argument, as Braddick (1981) points out, is that, apart from printed letters, objects which we recognise usually subtend too large a visual angle for their Fourier transform to be represented in a single hypercolumn. Recognition of an object would have to involve further processing of information from many hypercolumns.

Another, more promising possibility is that multiple spatial frequency tuning is an important characteristic of a system designed to detect edges. This may seem a paradoxical suggestion, but it is an important part of the theory of vision developed by Marr (1976) and Marr and Hildreth (1980), to which we now turn.

MARR'S THEORY OF THE VISUAL PATHWAY

At the beginning of the chapter, we presented Marr's (1982) argument that the properties of single cells in the visual pathway cannot be understood without a computational theory of vision. Marr has attempted to provide such a theory, explaining how the pattern of light falling on the retina is transformed into a symbolic representation of the environment, in which the positions, orientations and movement of surfaces are made explicit.

The theory proposes that this is done in a series of stages, which we will be describing in later chapters. For the moment, we are concerned only with the first stage, in which the *raw primal sketch* is built up from the pattern of light on the retina. The raw primal sketch is a representation of the pattern of light in which information about the edges and textures of objects and surfaces is made explicit. If the theory is to specify how this representation is created, it must solve the problem of edge detection in natural images which the "feature detection" theory failed to tackle. Marr (1976) and Marr and Hildreth (1980) have devised an edge-finding algorithm consisting of a series of mathematical operations performed on an image. We will outline the important characteristics of these operations and then consider Marr and Hildreth's argument that they are performed by the mammalian visual system.

The Algorithm

An algorithm for finding edges begins by locating changes, or *gradients*, in light intensity in the image. The simplest algorithm which could be used to do this would be one which computed differences in light intensity in each region of the image. We can picture this as applying a rectangular "mask" divided into two regions of equal size systematically to each region of the image, and computing the difference between the amounts of light falling in each half of the mask. Any value other than zero indicates that a gradient in intensity is present. Note that the field of a simple cell in the visual cortex is just such a mask.

This algorithm would be adequate for detecting gradients in an image such as Figure 3.1, where all edges are equally sharp, or, in other words, all gradients of intensity are equally steep. A characteristic of *natural* images, however, is that gradients of light intensity *vary* in their steepness, from steep (at sharp edges) to shallow (at fuzzy edges). This variation in the steepness of intensity gradients has important consequences for the mask algorithm (Marr, 1976). The size of the mask relative to the scale of the intensity gradient sets a limit on the range of gradients which the algorithm can locate. If the mask is small, then shallow gradients cannot be located, as there will be little difference in light intensity between the two sides. As mask size is increased, shallower gradients can be located, but at the same time information about the location of steep gradients is lost. Applying masks of a uniform size to a natural image is therefore not a satisfactory algorithm for finding edges.

In order to deal with this problem, Marr and Hildreth (1980) propose that location of gradients is carried out by a number of *parallel* operations, each concerned with locating gradients of a particular range of steepness. The first stage of their algorithm is therefore to take the image and transform it into a number of independent representations. In each of these, there is a different upper limit on the steepness of gradient present. Loosely speaking, this is achieved by blurring the image to a greater or lesser extent; the more it is blurred, the shallower the steepest gradient that can be present.

If the input is represented as an array of light intensity values (or *pixels*), then blurring is carried out by replacing each value in the array with the average of it and neighbouring intensity values. A simple way to do this would be to average together all values lying in a circle around each pixel; obviously, the greater the radius of the circle, the more the image will be blurred. Marr and Hildreth's algorithm does not perform the blurring in quite this way; an average is taken of intensity values in a circle around each pixel, but the values are weighted by a Gaussian function. The contribution of values to the average decreases the further they lie from the centre of the circle, according to a Gaussian (normal) distribution. The degree of blurring is determined by the width of the Gaussian distribution, measured by its standard deviation.

Why is a Gaussian function used to blur the image? Another way of expressing the effect of blurring is to say that it limits the band of spatial frequencies present in the output; the more the image is blurred, the lower the upper limit on spatial frequency. The aim of the blurring operation is therefore to limit the range of spatial frequencies present in the output, but this aim is in conflict with the requirement that spatial information present in the image—the *locations* of gradients—is preserved. The more efficient the filtering of spatial frequencies, the more spatial information will be lost. For reasons which the mathematically skilled reader will find discussed in Marr and Hildreth (1980), the optimal trade-off between these requirements is achieved by using a Gaussian function in the blurring operation.

To sum up so far, we have seen that a single "mask" algorithm cannot deal with the range of gradients present in a natural image. Marr and Hildreth (1980) solve this problem by passing the image through a set of two or more *Gaussian filters,* which replace the array of light intensity values (denoted by I) in the image with a set of arrays of values of G*I; the Gaussian-weighted averages of neighbouring values of I. These filters have Gaussian functions of different standard deviations, or widths. The wider a filter is, the lower is the highest spatial frequency it will pass and the shallower is the steepest gradient in its output. Figure 3.8 illustrates the effects of filtering an image with Gaussian filters of two different widths.

Now we come to the second operation performed by Marr and Hildreth's algorithm; the location of intensity changes in the multiple, differently blurred representations of the image. The mathematical operation used to measure change is *differentiation.* If we take a function describing how one quantity y varies with another quantity x and differentiate it, we obtain a function describing how the *rate of change* of y varies with x. For example, consider a car travelling at constant speed. If we take the function relating its distance travelled to time, and differentiate it, we obtain a constant. This is the car's velocity, which does not vary with time.

The result of differentiating a function is called its *first derivative*, and this can itself be differentiated to obtain the *second derivative*, which describes how the rate of rate of change of y varies with x. If the function relating

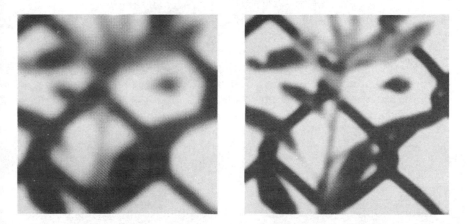

FIG.3.8. An image (above) blurred by Gaussian filters of two different widths (below). The more blurred picture is produced by the wider filter. Reproduced from Marr and Hildreth (1980) with permission of the author and publishers.

the distance travelled by a falling stone to time is differentiated, the first derivative (the stone's velocity) does vary with time; the stone's velocity increases as it falls. If this function is in turn differentiated, the second derivative is a constant, the stone's acceleration under gravity.

Gradients of light intensity in an image could be measured by taking the first derivative of intensity, but, for reasons of economy of computation, Marr and Hildreth's algorithm takes the second derivative. Figure 3.9 illustrates, for a one-dimensional intensity gradient, how the second derivative changes in the region of the gradient. Where it has a positive value, the

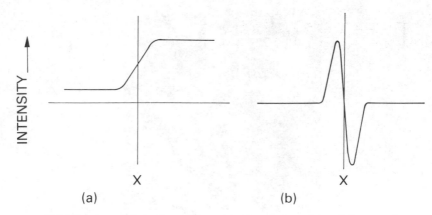

FIG.3.9. A spatial gradient of intensity (a) and the values of the second derivative of intensity (b) around a point X. Note that the second derivative crosses zero at X.

gradient of intensity is increasing, and where it has a negative value the gradient is decreasing. Note particularly that values of the second derivative pass through zero (a *zero-crossing*) at the gradient.

In Marr and Hildreth's algorithm, this operation is carried out on a two-dimensional pattern of light intensity, using an operator called the Laplacian (∇^2). The important feature of the Laplacian is that it is non-directional; its value measures the extent to which the intensity gradient is changing in the region of a point in the image, but does not convey any information about the direction in which this change occurs. Again, the interested reader will find detailed arguments for the use of the Laplacian in Marr and Hildreth (1980).

In the second stage of Marr and Hildreth's algorithm, the Laplacian operator is applied independently to each of the arrays yielded by the Gaussian filters. The result is a set of arrays of values of the Laplacian, denoted by $\nabla^2 G*I$. A wide $\nabla^2 G*I$ filter yields an array capturing only the large-scale changes in intensity in the image, while the output of a narrow $\nabla^2 G*I$ filter also contains information about small-scale changes. In order to locate gradients in the image, we now need to find, in each array, where the values of $\nabla^2 G*I$ pass through zero; that is, where positive and negative values of $\nabla^2 G*I$ are adjacent to one another. Once these zero-crossings are located, rows of zero-crossings sharing the same orientation (*zero-crossing segments*) are located.

We have now reached a stage where Marr and Hildreth's algorithm has yielded a set of representations of the image made up of zero-crossing segments. These make explicit the location and scale of intensity changes present in the original image, and Figure 3.10 illustrates the zero-crossings obtained from an image with $\nabla^2 G*I$ filters of three different widths.

FIG.3.10.   The results of passing an image (upper left) through $\nabla^2 G$ filters of three different widths. Upper right, lower left and lower right: zero-crossings obtained with a narrow, an intermediate and a wide filter. Reproduced from Marr and Hildreth (1980) with permission of the author and publishers.

It is clear from the illustration that this information does not specify the edges of objects and surfaces. Its significance is that it captures the properties of the image needed to locate natural edges in it.

The final step in the construction of the raw primal sketch is to *combine* information about the locations of zero-crossings from the independent $\nabla^2 G$ channels. The raw primal sketch is a rich description of the intensity changes in the input pattern, but in symbolic form. It is made up of tokens called edge segments, bars, terminations and blobs. What rules govern the combination of information from different $\nabla^2 G$ channels in forming this representation?

Marr and Hildreth argue that changes in light intensity which occur at the edges of natural surfaces, and which therefore need to be represented in the raw primal sketch, are localised in space. They will therefore give rise to zero-crossings in a range of widths of $\nabla^2 G$ channel. In particular, a zero-crossing in any one channel should be matched by zero-crossings in all the narrower channels. The only kind of intensity change which would give rise to a zero-crossing in a wide channel not matched by one in a narrower channel would be a diffuse, spread out change such as that caused by a diffraction pattern. It is just this kind of change which Marr and Hildreth argue will not be relevant to finding the edges of surfaces.

The algorithm for forming the raw primal sketch can make use of this constraint on the intensity changes associated with edges of surfaces, and can assume that edges will give rise to zero-crossing segments in adjacent ∇^2G channels. The first rule for constructing the raw primal sketch is therefore that matching zero-crossing segments in adjacent channels give an *edge-segment* in the sketch.

In some situations, a zero-crossing segment in a wide channel may be matched by two parallel ones of opposite contrast in a narrow channel; this situation is represented in the raw primal sketch by a *bar*. The ends of bars are represented by *terminations*, and closed loops of edge segments are represented by *blobs*. Even at this stage, the outlines of objects are not picked out; the raw primal sketch of a cat lying on a carpet would contain edge segments picking out its boundary and the edges of its limbs, but tokens would also be present representing the intensity changes over the surfaces of the cat and carpet. As we will see in Chapter 5, it is the job of later stages to sort these tokens out into higher level groups representing the layout of objects in the scene. An example of the raw primal sketch obtained from an image by Marr and Hildreth's algorithm is shown in Figure 3.11.

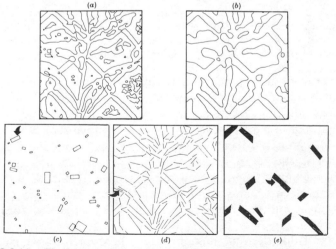

FIG.3.11.   The zero-crossings obtained from the picture in Figure 3.8 using a narrow and a wide ∇^2G filter are shown in (a) and (b). These are combined to give the raw primal sketch; the locations of blobs, edge segments and bars are shown in (c), (d) and (e). Reproduced from Marr and Hildreth (1980) with permission of the author and publishers.

Implementation

Marr and Hildreth's algorithm for computing the raw primal sketch can be implemented by computer, but is it implemented by the mammalian visual pathway? Does it provide a theory of what the various classes of cell are doing? Marr and Hildreth claim that it does and that cells in the visual pathway carry out the computations involved in the first stages of the algorithm.

They argue first that the function of X retinal ganglion cells is to compute $\nabla^2 G * I$. Recall from Chapter 2 that the response of an X cell is a linear function of the difference between the average intensities of light in the centre of the field and in the surround. The contribution of intensity to both components is weighted according to a Gaussian distribution (Enroth-Cugell and Robson, 1966).

Marr and Hildreth demonstrate that, given certain realistic assumptions, this computation of the difference of two Gaussians is equivalent to computing $\nabla^2 G * I$, and they argue that values of this function are signalled by the response rates of X cells. This hypothesis raises a problem; if zero-crossings are to be detected in an array of $\nabla^2 G * I$ values, both positive and negative values must be available, but a nerve cell cannot give a negative response. Marr and Hildreth propose that this is why both on- and off-centre cells exist. The first type carries positive values of $\nabla^2 G * I$ and the second negative values.

In this interpretation, cells with concentric fields do not signal the presence of an edge. Their role is the humbler one of making a measurement on the pattern of light in their fields which can then be used to locate zero-crossings. The simplest rule for locating a zero-crossing in the pattern of X cell activity would be to find adjacent on- and off-centre cells which are both active. Finding a zero-crossing segment would require the further step of detecting a set of adjacent pairs of active cells (Fig. 3.12), and Marr and Hildreth argue that some simple cells in the visual cortex do exactly that. Again, these cells should not be seen as detecting edges but instead as making *measurements*, of the positions, strengths and orientations of zero-crossing segments, from which the locations of edges can later be deduced.

According to Marr, the known properties of the visual pathway therefore take us to only an early stage in visual perception; the computation of zero-crossing segments. How these are combined into the raw primal sketch by the nervous system is not known, though some simple cells may detect bars, and cells with "end-inhibition" may be involved in the detection of terminations and blobs.

An important feature of Marr and Hildreth's algorithm is that it explains why cells with differing spatial frequency sensitivities are found in the visual cortex. These represent $\nabla^2 G$ filters of different widths, probably formed by

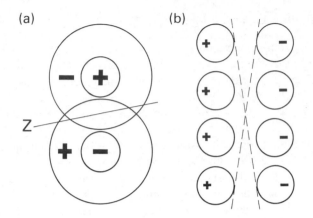

FIG.3.12.   Marr and Hildreth's scheme for the detection of zero-crossing segments by cortical simple cells. In (a), the fields of an on-centre and an off-centre LGN cell overlap. If both are active, then a zero-crossing Z must lie between them and an AND gate connected to them would detect it. In (b), an AND gate connected to parallel rows of on- and off-centre cells (field surrounds not shown) will detect a zero-crossing segment falling between the dashed lines. Adapted from Marr and Hildreth (1980).

pooling the outputs of LGN X cells with overlapping fields. This model is supported by Maffei and Fiorentini's (1977) finding that cells with the highest spatial frequency sensitivity occur in the layer of the striate cortex where LGN fibres terminate. These cells make up the narrowest $\nabla^2 G$ channel, and their outputs are presumably pooled to drive cells in other layers making up wider filters.

As well as finding support from neurophysiology, Marr and Hildreth's argument that the visual pathway performs the $\nabla^2 G*I$ computation is buttressed by evidence from studies of the ability of human observers to detect gratings and other spatial patterns of light. We mentioned earlier that this evidence demonstrates the existence of multiple independent channels tuned to different bands of spatial frequency, and Wilson and Bergen (1979) have proposed a model of these channels. Spatial information is processed in each part of the visual field by four independent channels, and, in each one, a difference of two Gaussians computation is performed on the spatial pattern of light.

The four channels have Gaussian functions of different widths. The two narrower channels have sustained properties, responding to stationary patterns, while the two wider channels have transient properties, responding to fluctuating patterns. The widths of all four channels increase with increasing distance from the fovea. There is a striking correspondence between these channels and the fields of cells in the visual pathway. The smaller sustained channel corresponds to X retinal ganglion cells and the smaller transient channel to Y cells, while the larger channel in each class suggests a pooling of the responses of X and of Y cells to give the wider filters required by Marr and Hildreth's algorithm. Both neurophysiological and psychophysical evidence therefore demonstrate the existence in the visual system of the independent spatial filters required for computation of the raw primal sketch.

Computation of Movement

Marr and Hildreth's (1980) algorithm represents the intensity changes in a stationary pattern of light in a form which can be used to locate edges of objects and surfaces in the world. In the natural environments of animals and people, objects and surfaces often move, and Marr's theory also deals with the perception of movement. Marr and Ullman (1981) propose that the first stage in movement perception is the tagging of edge segments in the raw primal sketch with their direction of movement. This could be computed at one of three stages; from raw intensity values, after zero-crossing segments have been detected, or after the raw primal sketch has been formed.

As we saw in Chapter 2, the movement-sensitive cells in the retinas of many vertebrates compute direction of movement from raw intensity values by measuring the correlation between a change in light intensity at one point and a similar change a short distance away (Barlow & Levick, 1965). A high correlation indicates movement from the first point to the second. Although the W cells in the mammalian retina probably operate in this way, Marr and Ullman argue that it would be more economical to combine the computation of edge information with that of information about movement.

The algorithm they propose for doing this is differentiation of $\nabla^2 G * I$ with respect to time. Figure 3.13a shows the profile of $\nabla^2 G * I$ values around a zero-crossing at X; if the whole pattern of light is moving to the right, the values of $d(\nabla^2 G * I)/dt$ are as in Figure 3.13b, while if it is moving to the left they are as in Figure 3.13c. Movement to the right gives a positive value of the time derivative at point X while movement to the left gives a negative value. The algorithm can therefore compute direction of movement with a resolution of 180°; poor though this is, it is in fact the best that can be done if the input to the movement detector is from a field which is small relative to the extent of the moving edge.

Marr and Ullman argue that the time derivative of $\nabla^2 G * I$ is computed in the retina and signalled by Y retinal ganglion cells, positive and negative values of the derivative being carried by on- and off-centre cells respectively. The non-linearity of Y cell responses does pose some problems for this

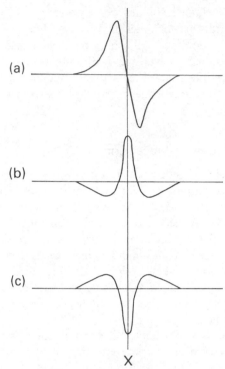

FIG.3.13. A gradient of light intensity at X gives the profile of $\nabla^2 G*I$ values in (a), with a zero-crossing at X. If the gradient is moving to the right, the time derivative of $\nabla^2 G*I$ is as in (b), while if it is moving to the left it is as in (c). The sign of the time derivative at a zero-crossing therefore specifies direction of movement. Adapted from Marr and Ullman (1981).

theory, but Marr and Ullman point out that only the sign of the time derivative needs to be signalled, and not necessarily its exact value.

The simplest system capable of detecting a zero-crossing segment moving in a particular direction would combine the outputs of X and Y cells in the way shown in Figure 3.14. The AND gate is connected to parallel rows of on- and off-centre X cells and also to an overlapping row of Y cells. If these are on-centre, an output from the AND gate will indicate a zero-crossing segment of the correct orientation moving to the right, while if they are off-centre it will indicate one moving to the left. Many simple cells in the visual cortex are sensitive to movement and show direction preferences, and Marr and Ullman propose that such cells are connected according to the pattern in Figure 3.14.

There is less direct evidence for this scheme than for the detection of zero-crossing segments by X cells and simple cells, but it does make sense of two observations. First, it requires that Y cell fields be larger than X cell fields in the same part of the retina. Secondly, it explains why Y retinal ganglion cells should conduct impulses more quickly, as computation of the time derivative of $\nabla^2 G*I$ will take longer and give rise to a delay relative to the X cells' signals.

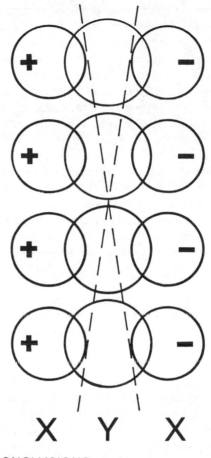

FIG.3.14. Marr and Ullman's scheme for simple cortical cells detecting a zero-crossing moving in a particular direction. Parallel rows of on- and off-centre X LGN cells are connected to an AND gate as in Figure 3.12. The larger overlapping fields between them are of Y cells, also connected to the AND gate. If these are on-centre, the system will respond when a zero-crossing segment moving to the right falls between the dashed lines, while if they are off-centre it will respond to one moving to the left (field surrounds not shown). Adapted from Marr and Ullman (1981).

CONCLUSIONS

What conclusions can we draw about the relative merits of these three approaches to understanding the transformations occurring in the visual pathway? Discussions of this issue often contrast the feature detection and spatial frequency interpretations and try to decide between them, but we follow Marr in regarding both these approaches as inadequate, and feel that their weaknesses lie in points they have in common. Both have their roots in a problem in visual perception, which we will explore in Chapter 7, of how objects are recognised despite the indefinite number of possible patterns of light at the retina which may specify them. One theory argues that this is done by detecting the invariant set of geometric features specifying an object; the other that invariant spatial frequency components are detected. Both, however, hold that invariant properties are detected by cells in the visual cortex.

The feature detection and spatial frequency theories therefore assume a large degree of commitment of the visual cortex to a particular kind of abstraction of information; that required to identify objects. Now the problem with this view is that information is also needed to specify the layout of an animal's or person's environment. An animal needs information not only about the kinds of object or other animals around it, but also about their positions relative to itself and each other and about how they are moving. In both the feature detection and spatial frequency theories, this kind of information is discarded at an early stage in the visual pathway.

Marr's theory contrasts strongly with the other two on this point. Marr sees the visual cortex as doing no more than computing the raw primal sketch; a transformation of the pattern of light into a symbolic form which still retains all the information about position and movement present in the input. The raw primal sketch is a rich representation of the input to the visual system which can be used as input by a wide variety of processes concerned with recognising objects, analysing the three-dimensional structure of the environment, computing patterns of movement and so on.

We have already mentioned one strength of Marr's theory—its analysis of the structure of natural patterns of light and the information they can provide—and we see a second strength in the less committed role it gives to the physiology of the visual cortex. We therefore conclude that this theory offers at present the best framework for interpreting the physiology of the mammalian visual pathway. This is not to say that the hypothesis that the raw primal sketch is computed by the retina, LGN and visual cortex is proven; indeed its strength is that it makes potentially testable predictions about the physiology of the visual pathway.

We will mention just three of the predictions which Marr and Ullman (1981) list. First, there must be pooling of X cell inputs from the LGN to form at least one wider ∇^2G channel, and simple cells detecting zero-crossing segments should take their input from LGN cells in just one channel. Secondly, there should be cells which are driven by a set of cells with the same field and same orientation preference but with different spatial frequency sensitivities, and which therefore detect edge-segments from zero-crossing segments in adjacent ∇^2G channels. Thirdly, direction-selective simple cells should be driven by both on- and off-centre X cells and by either on- or off-centre Y cells, according to the scheme of Figure 3.14.

One direction for further neurophysiological research should be the testing of these and other hypotheses made by Marr's theory. Another direction concerns the problem, sure to be in the back of the reader's mind, of what happens after the striate cortex. Can we trace the visual pathway further into the cortex and find what transformations take place in later stages?

Physiological techniques have been applied to these questions, but the answers they have yielded are bewildering in their complexity. Single-cell recordings from the *prestriate cortex*, the area of occipital and temporal cortex anterior to the striate cortex, have revealed a number of "maps" of the visual field comparable to that in the visual cortex. The location and number of these vary according to the species; the cat is known to have 12 and the owl monkey 8, while the rhesus monkey has at least five; V2, V3, V3A and V4, in area 18, and the middle temporal area (MT) in the superior temporal sulcus.

The details of these findings are summarised in a review by Van Essen (1979), but two general points about the prestriate areas deserve mention. First, the topographies of these maps are often complex; they may be partial representations of the visual field or may involve multiple representations of the same part of the visual field in different parts of the map. Secondly, the visual areas are not arranged in a straightforward pathway from one to the next, as the interconnections between them in the rhesus monkey demonstrate (Fig. 3.15).

Even the primary visual cortex (V1) has more complex connections than we have described so far; it sends outputs to several visual areas but also receives reciprocal inputs from several. It even sends an output back to the

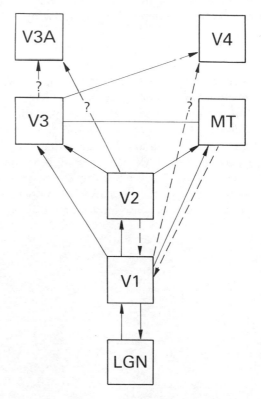

FIG.3.15. Pathways linking visual cortical areas of the rhesus monkey. Question marks denote uncertain projections and broken lines sparse projections. Adapted from Van Essen (1979).

LGN, the significance of which is not known. It is clear we are dealing with a system of multiple reciprocal connections and not with a step-by-step pathway.

What kinds of receptive field do cells in these different visual areas have? Zeki (1978) has studied the receptive field properties of large numbers of cells in each visual map. He found that almost all cells in all the maps are binocularly driven, without the ocular preferences found in the striate cortex. Otherwise, the pattern turns out to be different in different areas. In V2, V3 and V3A, most cells are orientation selective, while in V4 and the STS less than half are. In V4, however, many cells have opponent-colour properties, which are rare or absent in other areas, while in the STS, but in no other areas, nearly all cells are direction selective.

Zeki interprets these results in terms of a "parcelling" model; the simple representation of the visual field in the striate cortex (V1) is parcelled out to be analysed in parallel by a series of specialist processes, one working on colour, one on movement and so on. This explanation is consistent with the pattern of multiple pathways connecting the prestriate areas, and also with the further stages of Marr's theory of vision, in which processing occurs in a "modular" way, with specialist modules working independently on the raw primal sketch in different ways to build up an overall representation of the input.

Tantalising though these findings are, we really have no clear idea what kinds of transformations of patterns of neural activity take place beyond the striate cortex. As things stand, our knowledge of the neurophysiology of mammalian vision goes no further than the processes by which spatiotemporal change in the input pattern is made explicit in the retina, LGN and striate cortex. It is therefore time now to leave the neurophysiological analysis of vision and to discuss its analysis at other levels. From now on we consider what Marr calls "computational" and "algorithmic" theories of perception, and ask what processes might link patterns of light at the retina to the control of animals' and people's activities, without attempting to work out how they are implemented by nerve cells.

II

PROCESSING
RETINAL IMAGES

4

Introduction:
Approaches to the Psychology
of Visual Perception

In Part I of this book we introduced you to some of the developments and theories which have emerged from the study of the neurophysiology of vision. We ended with a discussion of David Marr's work. He has provided perhaps the most comprehensive theory to date of how the retinal image is translated into a set of assertions about the "features" (edges, bars, blobs) contained within it. However, such an understanding of early visual processing leaves us some way off understanding *perception*. When we view the world we see much more than a collection of primitive elements such as those represented in the raw primal sketch. Indeed it may require careful introspection to reveal simple components such as edges or patches of colour at all. Instead, when we view the world we see solid objects at various distances from us. We perceive these objects at rest or in motion as we ourselves move our eyes, heads and bodies to explore the world. And, perhaps most importantly, the world that we view is endowed with meaning. We know the significance of the structures we view—their uses and their names. Though we can only speculate about the perceptual experiences of creatures other than ourselves, it seems likely that their visual worlds are also organised into categories of importance to them.

When we discussed Marr's work in Chapter 3, we described the three different levels of theory which he argues must be distinguished if we are to understand a complex information-processing task such as visual perception. For any process (and vision consists of very many processes), we should first formulate a *computational theory*, which describes what is being computed and why. Next we may consider the *algorithms* for achieving the computation, and the *representations* which form the input to and output from these algorithms. Finally we may describe the *implementation* of the algorithm, whether in neural tissue or in a computer. When we consider processes of vision more complex than the recovery of simple assertions about edges or blobs, our knowledge of neural implementation is very scanty. Our discussion of perception in this section of the book is set at the level of computational theory, representation and algorithm. It is to the psychology, rather than the physiology, of vision that we must now turn.

In this part of our book we consider how perceptual organisation, depth and movement perception, and recognition might be achieved as a result of the processing of retinal images. The retinal image has been seen as the input on which later processes operate in almost all accounts of visual perception. We are thus primarily concerned with those findings and theories that have emerged within this "traditional" approach to visual perception. The focus of much of this research has been on human perception, and this is undoubtedly due at least in part to the historical underpinnings of psychology in the philosophy of mind. Before embarking on the details of the topics in this section, we feel we should outline very briefly how such theories of visual perception have evolved.

It is only relatively recently that a separate science of "psychology" has emerged. During the 17th and 18th centuries, scholars interested in natural philosophy made discoveries about light and eyes, and discussed epistemological issues in ways which were to colour subsequent thinking about visual perception well into this century. On the physical side, an understanding of image-formation by lenses, and the observation by Descartes of a retinal image formed on the back of a bull's eye, led to a long-standing belief that the eye functions much like a camera (or *camera obscura* in the days of da Vinci and Kepler), and that the starting point for vision is an image. However, it was obvious that the images produced by cameras and by eyes are lacking in many of the qualities that we perceive in the world. Images are flat, static and meaningless. Visual perception reveals a solid, mobile and meaningful world. It seemed that perception must therefore involve processes that go beyond the information present in the image. On the philosophical side, the empiricists such as Locke (1690) and Berkeley (1709) argued that perception was somehow constructed from more primitive sensations through a process of learning through association. Though nativist philosophies were also voiced, in which knowledge of the entities of "space," or "time" were considered inborn, or divinely given, it is probably not too much of an overgeneralisation to say that it is the empiricist tradition which has dominated modern thinking in psychology. We do not delve here into the controversy between the "nativists" and the "empiricists," but instead simply agree with Boring (1942) that:

No simple exposition of this great and largely fruitless controversy can, however, be adequate to its complexities. For one thing, almost every protagonist turns out, whatever he was called, to have been both nativist and empiricist. Everyone believed that the organism brought something congenitally to the solution of the problem of space; everyone believed that the organisation of space may be altered or developed in experience. (p.233)

The dominant empiricist position in the 19th century led to the attempted analysis (often using introspective methods) of perceptions into their component sensations by the *structuralists*, and considerable debate about which elements or attributes should be considered as fundamental (see Boring, 1942). By analysing elementary sensations it was hoped that eventually the complexities of human thought could be unravelled, since all complex ideas must ultimately have been derived through sensory experience. The mechanisms whereby perceptions were constructed from sensations, through reference to knowledge previously acquired through learning, were also discussed, most notably by Helmholtz (1866), whose idea of perception involving unconscious inference or conclusions is still echoed by contemporary theorists (e.g. Gregory, 1973). Compare their statements:

. . . such objects are always imagined as being present in the field of vision as would have to be there in order to produce the same impression on the nervous mechanism. . . The psychic activities that lead us to infer that there in front of us at a certain place there is a certain object of a certain character, are generally not conscious activities, but unconscious ones. In their result they are equivalent to a *conclusion* . . . (Helmholtz, 1866, trans 1925, pp.2–4).

. . . we may think of sensory stimulation as providing *data* for *hypotheses* concerning the state of the external world. The selected hypotheses, following this view, are perceptions (Gregory, 1973, pp.61–3).

Thus a view of perception as indirect and inferential persists today, though the methods used to study vision have become more sophisticated, and some rather different ideas about perception have been voiced in the years between Helmholtz and Gregory. We mention some of these landmarks in method and theory here very briefly.

Towards the end of the 19th century, the content of perception was commonly studied using the methods of analytic introspection—though Fechner's psychophysical methods (1860) saw the beginning of a more "objective" way to study the senses. However, introspectionist methods were largely abandoned in the United States, following J. B. Watson's lead in 1912. Watson put forward his case for behaviourism (Watson, 1913, 1924), in which mentalistic notions such as "sensations" and "perceptions" were replaced by objectively observable "discriminative responses." The behaviourists argued that we can never know how animals, or other people, experience the world, and hence should only observe their behaviour, to examine how their responses are related to variations in the stimuli presented. Ironically, while classical behaviourism provided the methodological tools for the comparative study of perception, it did not consider it legitimate to explain any observed differences in the perceptual capabilities of different species in terms of internal processes. The methods of contemporary psychology are still influenced by the behaviourist tradition, although students of perception, on the whole, now regard subjects' verbal reports of their perceptual experience as legitimate "responses" to be recorded and analysed.

At much the same time as Watson was developing behaviourism, the European Gestalt psychologists reacted against the structuralist assumptions that perception could be reduced to sensations. They retained an introspective, though phenomenological approach. They were nativist in philosophy, maintaining that perceptual experience was the result of certain dynamic field forces within the brain. We discuss Gestalt ideas further in Chapter 5.

Gestaltists apart, most other movements in the psychology of perception have been empiricist in flavour, and most have implicitly or explicitly assumed that perception should be regarded as some process of interpretation or construction from the incomplete information provided by the retinal image. Two movements, closely related to each other, which emphasised such complexities of human perception, flourished transiently during the 1940s and 1950s. The first of these, "transactional functionalism" (Kilpatrick, 1952), rested on the demonstrations of Ames (Ittelson, 1952). Ames' displays included a trapezoidal window which looked rectangular, a collection of sticks which could be seen as a chair, and perhaps best known, a curiously constructed room, which (when viewed statically and monocularly) appeared room-shaped but did strange things to the apparent sizes of people standing or walking within it (see Fig. 4.1).

Such demonstrations were used to illustrate the apparently infinite number of objects which could give rise to any single retinal image, and to emphasise the probabilistic and inferential nature of seeing. What one sees will be what one expects to see, given one's lifetime of perceptual experience. While transactional functionalism stressed the individual's history as important in determining his or her perception, the "new look" (e.g. Bruner & Goodman, 1947) stressed the importance of individual differences in motivation, emotion and personality in influencing what they might see. Cantril (in Wittreich, 1959) for example claimed that one observer, whose husband walked across the Ames room, persisted in seeing him remain constant in size, while the stranger accompanying him shrank or grew. Wittreich confirmed this observation with some of the married couples he tested.

During the 1960s, associationist explanations of perceptual learning and discriminative responding gave way to a new "cognitive psychology" of

FIG.4.1. The Ames room The room is perceived as being of conventional shape, with right-angled corners and rectangular windows. The people standing inside the room appear to be of very odd sizes. In fact it is the room which is oddly shaped—the people are both of normal height. Photograph copyright © Eastern Counties Newspapers Ltd. Used by permission.

perception, attention and memory. Attempts were made to describe the stages which intervened between stimulus and response. The revolution in information technology provided a new metaphor for psychology, in which information from the senses was seen to be processed in ways not unlike the processing of information in a computer. Processes of sensory coding, storage and retrieval of information were all discussed, and the development of computer models of some of these processes was seen to be a legitimate goal of psychological theorising. If a machine could be designed which could "see," its computer program could constitute the implementation of a theory of how seeing is achieved by humans. (See Boden, 1977, for an introduction to the field of artificial intelligence [A.I.].) Marr's (1982) theory represents perhaps the most sophisticated attempt yet to explain the information processing operations involved in vision within a framework which cuts across the boundaries between physiology, psychology and artificial intelligence.

In this very cursory discussion of the history of visual perception there has been one notable omission. We have here mentioned theories which have taken an "impoverished" retinal image as the starting point for perceptual processing. In Part III of this book we describe a quite different—controversial—theory, which was first proposed by J.J. Gibson (1950a, 1966, 1979). This theory suggests that the "input" to a perceptual system is structure in the entire optic array, and transformations in the array over time. Gibson denies that perception involves construction, interpretation or representation, and his theory thus stands apart from those that we have mentioned here. (Though, paradoxically, one can draw some parallels between some of Gibson's ideas and those of both the Gestaltists and the behaviourists—two diametrically opposed schools. We shall have more to say about this in Chapter 8.) In this part of the book, however, we are concerned to explore how far we can explain the perceptual accomplishments of people and animals when those perceptual activities *are* seen as the end-products of the processing of retinal images. This is the mainstream of visual perception theories, and we defer any challenge to it for the moment.

A unifying principle in the psychology of visual perception has been that unless the perceiver makes assumptions about the physical world which gave rise to a particular retinal image, perception just isn't possible. The only dispute has been over how specific such assumptions need to be. For some contemporary theorists, these assumptions are thought to be quite specific and may be learned through an individual's lifetime experience—for example the assumption that windows or rooms are rectangular. For others, the assumptions may be more general and hard-wired (that is, built into the central nervous system and not dependent on learning), such as the assumption that similarly oriented texture elements should be grouped together (see Chapter 5). Many theorists have argued that perceptual parsimony is achieved (at the cost of occasional error or illusion), by making use of specific world knowledge to infer, from sensory data, what it is that gave rise to that data. Thus tentative "object hypotheses," obtained by accessing stored information in memory, may constrain and guide the interpretation of incoming sensory data. Such perceptual theories may be described as involving a strong "top-down" or "conceptually-driven" component. Many A.I. models of perception fall into this category and some of these will be discussed in Chapters 5, 6 and 7. Other models (e.g. Marr, 1976) have been developed largely along "bottom-up" or "data-driven" lines. In such theories very general constraints are incorporated within each stage of information processing, but specific world knowledge is only recruited into the act of seeing when relatively low-level stages of information-processing produce ambiguous results. One of Marr's many achievements is his demonstration that a great deal of the processing of images can be achieved without recourse to specific world knowledge.

OVERVIEW OF MARR'S THEORY OF VISION

In each of the chapters which follows in this section, we describe some of the ideas which have been important historically, and then end with a description of Marr's theory of the topic under discussion. Of those theories which have emerged within the "information-processing" tradition, Marr's is the most compatible with our aim to account for animal, as well as human, perception. Although his aim has been to provide a theory which may be applicable to human perception, and hence he relies at least in part on human psychophysical evidence to support his statements, he stresses that the same kind of analysis could be applied to visual perception in other species. Most importantly, his level of "computational theory" demands that we always consider what is being computed from light, and why. Ecological, as well as physiological considerations would allow us to tailor a theory in the spirit of Marr to the beast in question.

> Vision, in short, is used in such a bewildering variety of ways that the visual systems of different animals must differ significantly from one another. Can the type of formulation that I have been advocating, in terms of representations and processes, possibly prove adequate for them all? I think so. The general point here is that because vision is used by different animals for such a wide variety of purposes, it is inconceivable that all seeing animals use the same representations; each can confidently be expected to use one or more representations that are nicely tailored to the owner's purpose. (Marr, 1982, p.32)

Because Marr's theory is of some importance to this section of the book, but appears dotted around the different chapters contained here (which also discuss the work of people other than Marr), we take this opportunity to provide a brief summary of the important points that he makes.

An image, the input for visual processing, represents intensity over a huge array of different locations. This array of intensity values is created by the way in which light is reflected by the physical structures which the observer is viewing, and focused by the observer's eye. The goal of early visual processing is to create from the image a description of those structures— the shapes of surfaces and objects, their orientations and distances from the viewer. This is achieved by constructing a number of distinct representations from the intensity values in the image. The first representation is the *primal sketch*. The primal sketch describes the intensity changes present in the image and makes more global structures explicit. We have already described, in Chapter 3, how the *raw primal sketch* is formed. The raw primal sketch consists of a set of statements about the edges and blobs present, their locations, orientations and so on. From this complex and rather messy representation, larger structures—boundaries and regions, can be found through the application of grouping procedures. This more refined description is known as the *full primal sketch*, and in Chapter 5 we describe how it can be derived.

The full primal sketch captures many of the contours and textures within an image, but a description of an image is only one aspect of early visual processing, where the goal is to describe surfaces and shapes relative to the viewer. Marr sees the culmination of early visual processing as a *viewer-centred* representation, which he calls the *2½D sketch*. This is obtained by an analysis of depth and motion and shading, as well as the structures assembled in the primal sketch. We describe some of the processes which contribute to the formation of the 2½D sketch in Chapter 6.

The 2½D sketch describes the layout of structures in the world from a particular vantage point. We need such a representation to guide any action we may need to take, whether simple eye movement or complicated locomotion. However, a further, and equally essential aspect of vision is the *recognition* of objects. In order to recognise what object a particular shape corresponds to, a third representational level is needed—one centred on the object, rather than on the viewer. This third level consists of *3D model representations*, and these we describe in Chapter 7. It is at the stage of formation of the 3D model representations that a stored set of object descriptions is contacted. As far as possible, previous stages of visual processing proceed in a bottom-up fashion, making use of general constraints rather than any specific object "hypotheses."

Thus Marr's theory involves a number of distinct levels of representation, each of which is a symbolic description of some aspect of the information carried within the retinal image. A variety of different processes transform one representation to another, and we describe some of these processes in the chapters which follow.

5 Perceptual Organisation

In Chapter 3 we saw how processes which identify simple local features in an image, such as edges and blobs, may be implemented by nerve cells. In this chapter we turn to consider how such low-level descriptions may be organised into larger perceptual "chunks." When we view the world we do not see a collection of edges and blobs—unless we adopt a very analytical perceptual attitude—but see instead an organised world of surfaces and objects. How is such perceptual segregation achieved? How do we know which parts of the visual information reaching our sensory apparatus belong together? These are the questions addressed in this chapter. The first part of the chapter concentrates on human perception, since it was through the study of this that many of the principles of perceptual organisation became established. We return to the broader perspective of animal vision when we consider how such perceptual principles may be exploited in natural camouflage and advertisement. In the final part of the chapter we turn to artificial intelligence approaches to perceptual organisation.

As we discussed in the last chapter, the psychology of human visual perception during the late 19th and early 20th century was dominated by associationism. It was assumed that perception could be analysed in terms of its component sensations, and that complex ideas were the result of associating together simpler ones. However, as the Gestalt psychologists pointed out, an analysis of perception into discrete sensations overlooks some important aspects of form and structure. Each of the arrangements shown in Figure 5.1 possesses the quality of "squareness" despite being composed of quite different elements. A tune is recognisable despite being played in a different key or at a different speed. The spatial and temporal

FIG.5.1.   Each of these three forms is seen as being square, despite being composed of quite different elements.

relationships between elements are as important as the absolute size, location or nature of the elements themselves, and a sensation-based account of perception fails to capture this.

Even Wundt (1896) recognised that a simple structuralist analysis failed to capture certain perceptual phenomena: "A compound clang is more in its ideational and affective attributes than merely a sum of single tones (Wundt, 1896, trans. 1907, p.368)." But it was the Gestalt psychologists, notably Wertheimer (1923), Köhler (1947) and Koffka (1935), with whom the catch-phrase "the whole is greater than the sum of its parts" became identified. We will first describe the Gestalt ideas about perceptual organisation, and then go on to consider more recent accounts.

AMBIGUOUS PICTURES

The world that we view appears to be composed of discrete objects of various sizes which are seen against a background comprised of textured surfaces. We usually have no difficulty in seeing the boundaries of objects, unless these are successfully camouflaged (see later), and there is generally no doubt about which areas are "figures" and which comprise the "ground." However, it is possible to construct pictures in which there is ambiguity about which region is "figure" and which "ground." Edgar Rubin, one of the Gestalt psychologists, used the face/vase picture (Fig. 5.2) to illustrate this. The picture can be seen either as a pair of black faces in profile, or as a white vase, but it is impossible to maintain simultaneously the perception of both the faces and the vase. The contour dividing the black and white regions of the picture appears to have a one-sided function. It "belongs" to whichever region is perceived as figure. People viewing this picture usually find that their perception of it shifts from one interpretation to the other, sometimes quite spontaneously. The artist M. C. Escher exploited this principle of perceptual reversibility when he produced etchings in which there is figure/ground ambiguity (see Fig. 5.3).

FIG.5.2. This picture, devised by E. Rubin in 1915, can be seen *either* as a pair of black faces in silhouette, *or* as a white vase.

FIG.5.3. M.C. Escher's "Circle Limit IV." Courtesy Gemeentemuseum, The Hague. Copyright © SPADEM 1984. Used by permission.

It is also possible to construct pictures so that the internal organisation of a particular figure is ambiguous. Jastrow's duck–rabbit picture (Fig. 5.4) may be seen as a duck (beak at the right), or a rabbit (ears at the right), but not both simultaneously. Some abstract and "op"-art may be perplexing to view because no stable organisation is apparent (see Fig. 5.5).

The perception of such ambiguous displays is interesting in its own right, and psychologists have investigated the factors influencing which organisation of an ambiguous display will be preferred, and also the factors determining perceptual reversals (for example see Attneave, 1971; Hochberg, 1950; Pheiffer, Eure, & Hamilton, 1956). In all these examples, the perceptual "data" remain the same, while the interpretation of them varies. It seems as though there must be a strong "top-down" component in such perceptions. Higher levels of perceptual interpretation appear to be continually constraining and guiding the lower levels of image analysis.

FIG.5.4. Duck or rabbit? This ambiguous picture was introduced to psychologists by J. Jastrow in 1900.

FIG.5.5. V. Vasareley's "Supernovae." Courtesy Tate Gallery, London. Copyright © SPADEM 1984. Used by permission.

However, these ambiguous pictures have been cleverly constructed, and our perception of them is not necessarily typical of normal processing. Ambiguity generally does not arise in the real world, or in most pictures. Rather than having constantly shifting interpretations, we usually see a stable and organised world. For example, viewing Figure 5.6a in isolation, most people would report seeing a hexagon, while those viewing Figure 5.6b report seeing a picture of a three-dimensional cube, even though Figure 5.6a is an equally legitimate view of a cube, viewed corner on. Figure 5.7 is seen as a set of overlapping circles, rather than as one circle touching two adjoining shapes which have "bites" taken out of them. Why, given these possible alternative perceptions, do we see these pictures in these ways?

GESTALT LAWS OF ORGANISATION

The Gestalt psychologists formulated a number of principles of perceptual organisation to describe how certain perceptions are more likely to occur than others. Some of their principles were primarily to do with the grouping of sub-regions of figures, and others were more concerned with the segregation

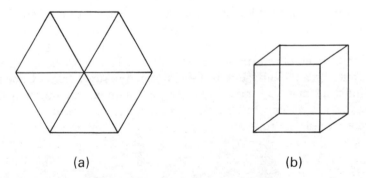

(a)   (b)

FIG.5.6.   The form at (a) looks like a hexagon, while that at (b) looks like a cube. Of course (a) is also a legitimate view of a cube.

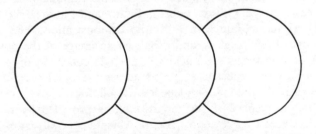

FIG.5.7.   Most people would see this as a set of overlapping circles, although two of the shapes might have "bites" taken out of them.

of figure from ground. However, since sub-regions of a figure need to be grouped in order for a larger region to be seen as "belonging together" as a figure, we will discuss all these principles together.

Proximity

One of the most important factors determining the perceptual organisation of a scene is proximity of the elements within it. Things which are close together are grouped together. In Figure 5.8a the perception is of columns, because the horizontal spacing of the dots is greater than their vertical spacing. In Figure 5.8b we see rows, because the horizontal spacing of the dots is the smaller, and Figure 5.8c is ambiguous; the dots are equally spaced in both directions. Proximity in depth is a powerful organising factor. The central square in a Julesz random-dot stereogram (see Chapter 6, p.134) is not visible until the two halves of the stereo pair are viewed in a stereoscope. Dots with the same disparity values are then grouped together and the square is seen as a distinct figure floating above its background.

Similarity

Things which look "similar" are grouped together. The examples shown at the top of Figure 5.16 (p.109) appear to consist of two distinct regions, with a boundary between them. The elements on one side of this boundary have a different orientation to those on the other. In Figure 5.9 the perception is of columns, even though the proximity information suggests rows, illustrating that similarity may over-ride proximity information. The question of *how* similar items must be in order to be grouped together is an empirical one to which we will return.

Common Fate

Things which appear to move together are grouped together. A camouflaged animal will only remain well-hidden if it remains stationary. As soon as it moves it is easier to see. Gibson, Gibson, Smith, and Flock (1959) illustrated grouping by common fate with a simple demonstration. They sprinkled powder on two sheets of glass, and projected an image of the powder onto a screen. While the sheets were held still a single collection of powder was seen. As soon as one sheet was moved across the other, viewers saw the powder segregated into two independent collections, by virtue of the movement in the display. A further example is provided by random-dot kinematograms (see Chapter 6, p. 155), in which a central region of texture is revealed through the apparent motions of the elements it contains. Johansson (1973) has produced an even more dramatic demonstration of

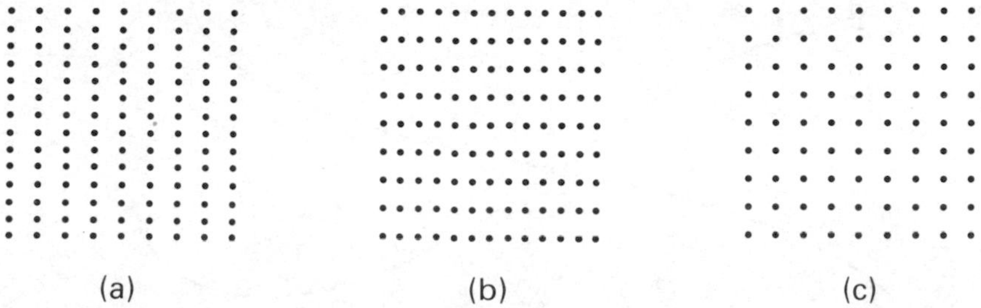

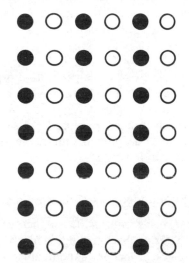

FIG.5.8. The dots in (a) form columns because they are nearer vertically than horizontally. At (b) we see rows, the dots here are nearer horizontally; (c) is ambiguous, the dots are equally spaced in both directions.

FIG.5.9. This picture is seen as columns. Similarity in brightness of the dots over-rides proximity.

the power of movement to confer organisation. He attached lights to the joints of a darkly-clothed actor and filmed him as he moved in a dark room, so that only the lights were visible. When the actor was at rest, observers reported perceiving a disorganised collection of points. As soon as the actor walked, their perception was of a moving human figure. We shall return to discuss the perceptual organisation of such complex displays in Chapter 13.

Good Continuation

In a figure such as Figure 5.10, one tends to perceive two smooth curves which cross at point X, rather than perceiving two irregular V-shaped forms touching at X. The Gestaltists argued that perceptual organisation will tend to preserve smooth continuity rather than yielding abrupt changes. Quite dissimilar objects may be perceived as "belonging together" by virtue of a

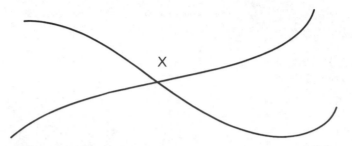

FIG.5.10. This is seen as two smooth lines which cross at X, rather than as two V-shapes touching at X.

combination of proximity and good continuity (see Fig. 5.11). Good continuation may be thought the spatial analogy of common fate.

Closure

Of several geometrically possible perceptual organisations, that one will be seen which produces a "closed" rather than an "open" figure. Thus the patterns on the left and right of Figure 5.1 are seen as squares rather than crosses, because the former are closed. The Gestaltists suggested that the stellar constellation "the plough" might be seen as a plough because of closure and good continuation.

Relative Size, Surroundedness, Orientation and Symmetry

All other things being equal, the smaller of two areas will be seen as figure against a larger background. Thus Figure 5.12a will tend to be perceived as a black propellor shape against a white background since the black area is the smaller. This effect is enhanced if the white area actually surrounds the black as in Figure 5.12b, since surrounded areas tend to be

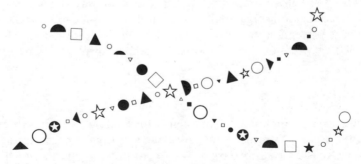

FIG.5.11. Quite dissimilar shapes may be grouped together through a combination of proximity and good continuation.

seen as figures. However, if we orient the figure so that the white area is arranged around the horizontal and vertical axes then it is easier to see this larger area as a figure (Fig. 5.12c). There seems to be a preference for horizontally or vertically oriented regions to be seen as figures. Also we may note that both these sets of patterns are symmetrical. Symmetry is a powerful perceptual property, and may be more salient perceptually than non-reflected repetition (Bruce & Morgan, 1975). Examples of symmetry and repetition are shown in Figure 5.13. Symmetrical areas tend to be perceived as figures against asymmetrical backgrounds. Figure 5.14 shows how relative size, orientation, symmetry and surroundedness may all operate together so that it is difficult, if not impossible, to see anything other than the black areas as the figures in this picture. The reader will note the perceptual stability of

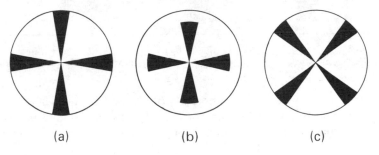

(a)   (b)   (c)

FIG.5.12. The preferred perception of (a) is a black propeller on a white background. This preference is enhanced if the white area surrounds the black as at (b). If the orientation of the forms is altered, so that the white area is oriented around the horizontal and vertical axes, as at (c), then it is easier to see the larger, white area as figure.

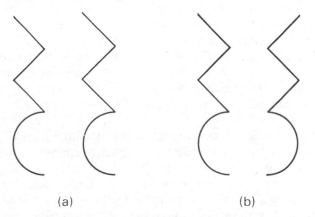

(a)   (b)

FIG.5.13. At (a) one form is repeated without reflection around a vertical axis. This arrangement is not as perceptually salient as the arrangement shown at (b), where repetition with reflection around the vertical axis produces bilateral symmetry.

FIG.5.14. This picture clearly shows black shapes on a white background. The black shapes are vertically oriented, symmetrical, small (relative to the background) and surrounded by the background.

this picture, compared with the ambiguity of Figure 5.2, in which the relative sizes, surroundedness and symmetries in the display favour neither the "faces" nor the "vase" particularly strongly.

The Law of Prägnanz

For the Gestalt psychologists, many of these laws were held to be manifestations of the Law of Prägnanz, introduced by Wertheimer. Koffka (1935) describes the law: "Of several geometrically possible organisations that one will actually occur which possesses the best, simplest and most stable shape (p. 138)."

Thus an organisation of four dots arranged as though they were at the corners of a square (Fig. 5.1, right) might well be seen as a "square" since this is a "better" arrangement than, say, a cross or a triangle plus an extra dot. The square is a closed, symmetrical form which the Gestaltists maintained was the most stable.

While the Gestaltists accepted that familiarity with objects in the world, and "objective set," might influence perceptual organisation, they rejected an explanation solely in these terms. A major determinant of perceptual organisation for them was couched in terms of certain "field forces" which they thought operated within the brain. The Gestaltists maintained a *Doctrine of Isomorphism*, according to which there is, underlying every sensory experience, a brain event which is structurally similar to that experience. Thus when one perceives a circle, a "circular trace" is established, and so on. Field forces were held to operate to make the outcome as stable as possible, just as the forces operating on a soap bubble are such that its most stable state is a sphere. Unfortunately, there has been no evidence provided for such field forces, and the physiological theory of the Gestaltists has fallen by the wayside, leaving us with a set of descriptive principles, but without a model of perceptual processing. Indeed some of their "laws" of perceptual organisation today sound vague and inadequate. What is meant by a "good" or a "simple" shape, for example? Recent workers have attempted to formalise at least some of the Gestalt perceptual principles.

RECENT APPROACHES TO PERCEPTUAL ORGANISATION

Hochberg and Brooks (1960) tried to provide an objective criterion for the notion of "goodness" of shape by presenting subjects with line drawings (Fig. 5.15) and asking them to rate the apparent tridimensionality in these figures. They argued that as the complexity of the figures as two-dimensional line drawings increased, so there should be a tendency for the figures to be perceived as two-dimensional representations of three-dimensional objects. They made a number of measurements on the figures and looked for those which correlated well with perceived tridimensionality. The best measure was the number of angles in the figure. This measure seems to represent "complexity." The more angles the figure contains, the more complex it is in two dimensions, and the more likely it is to be perceived as a representation of a "simpler," three dimensional object. A second measure which correlated well was the number of differently sized angles. This reflects the asymmetry in the 2D figure, since a figure in which many of the angles are of the same size is more likely to be symmetrical than one in which many differently sized angles are present. A final measure was the number of continuous lines. This reflects the discontinuity present, since the more continuous lines there are, the more discontinuities must be present between each. Thus the more complex, asymmetrical and discontinuous the 2D pattern, the more likely it was to be perceived as representing a projection of a 3D figure. Hochberg and Brooks then applied their measures to a set of new figures and found they correlated well with the perceived tridimensionality in these.

Thus it is possible to express Gestalt ideas such as "good shape" more precisely. In similar vein we now consider recent attempts to tackle the problem of grouping by similarity. How similar must items be before they are grouped together? It is unlikely that they must be *identical*, since no camouflage can ever perfectly match its surroundings, yet we know that camouflage can be remarkably successful. But if identity is not required, what are the important variables that determine grouping by similarity? This has been investigated by seeing how easily two different regions of a pattern,

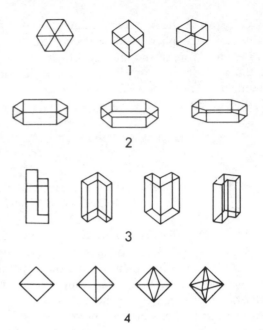

FIG.5.15. Examples of the forms used by Hochberg and Brooks (1960). In each of rows 1–4, the figure at the left is most likely to be seen as two-dimensional, and that at the right is most likely to be seen as a two-dimensional projection of a three-dimensional object. From Hochberg (1978). Reprinted by permission of Prentice-Hall, Inc, Englewood Cliffs, New Jersey.

or more naturally textured image, segregate perceptually from each other. The logic of this is that the more the elements in two different regions cohere with one another, by virtue of the perceptual similarity which exists between them, the less visible will be the boundary between these two regions.

Olson and Attneave (1970) required observers to indicate where the "odd" quadrant lay within a circular display of simple pattern elements (see Fig. 5.16). They found that the quadrant was most easily spotted if the elements within it differed in slope from those of the rest of the display (e.g. < ∨) and was most difficult to find if the elements differed in configuration, but not in the slopes of their component parts (e.g. < >). Similar conclusions were reached by Beck (1972) who asked his subjects to count elements of one type (e.g. <) which were distributed randomly within a display containing elements of a different type (e.g. >). Again he reasoned that the more the odd elements stood out from the background elements, and grouped with each other rather than with the background, the easier they would be to isolate and count. Like Olson and Attneave, Beck found that slope differences led to faster counting than configurational differences.

Such findings are interesting as they demonstrate that the variables that influence grouping by similarity are not necessarily the same as those which would influence the judged *conceptual* similarity of the same elements viewed individually by humans. Thus L and ⟨ might be considered more similar (both letter L, with one example tilted) when viewed as a single pair, than would L and ⌐. However, when large numbers of these elements are

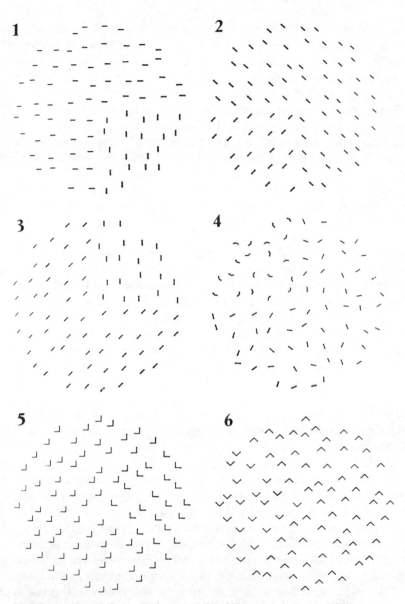

FIG.5.16. Some of the displays used by Olson and Attneave (1970) to investigate grouping by similarity. In the displays marked 1, 2 and 3, the lines in one region are of a different orientation to the rest, and the odd region is easy to spot. In display 4, odd elements are curved, and the odd region is reasonably evident. In displays 5 and 6, the configurations, but not the slopes, of the elements differ from one region to the next. Here it is much harder to spot the odd quadrant. Reprinted by permission from American Journal of Psychology, copyright © 1970 by the University of Illinois Press.

combined, it is the difference in the common orientations of two populations which is perceptually more salient than the difference between the conceptual identity of the individual members. Julesz (1965) stresses that in similarity grouping we are looking at spontaneous, preattentive visual processing, which precedes the identification of patterns and objects, and which is quite different from deliberate scrutiny. In some textures it is possible to discern that an odd region is present by carefully examining and comparing individual pattern elements, just as one can "find" a camouflaged animal by careful inspection. Such processes of scrutiny however are at a much higher level than the grouping mechanisms we are discussing here.

Julesz (1965, 1975) extended the study of grouping by similarity to include more naturally-textured images in which brightness and colour were varied as well as slope and configuration of elements. First, and most simply, he noted that two regions would be segregated if there was a clear brightness or colour difference between them, and that brightness and colour grouping appeared to operate by "averaging" rather than by taking detailed account of statistical differences in the brightness distributions. If two halves of a pattern are constructed so that one half contains mostly black and dark grey squares (with a few light grey and white ones), and the other contains mostly light grey and white squares (with a few dark grey and black ones), then a clear boundary is seen between the two regions. If however one region contains mostly black and light grey squares, and the other contains mostly dark grey and white ones, then no clear boundary is perceived even though the composition of the two pictures with respect to the relative frequencies of the different types of square is still quite different. Here it is the *average* brightnesses in the two halves of the pattern which matters, not the details of the composition of these average brightnesses.

Similarly, if a region is composed mostly of red and yellow squares (with a few blue and green ones) and the adjacent area is mostly green and blue (with a few red and yellow squares) then good segregation is achieved. If one region is mostly red and green, and the other mostly yellow and blue, then the segregation is not as clear. Julesz (1965) proposed that the perceptual system imposes a "slicer" mechanism. A region of similar brightness or similar wavelength could be grouped together as distinct from another region where the "average" brightness or wavelength differed from the first.

The spatial distribution or "granularity" of different regions is also important however. If two regions have the same overall average brightness, but with the pattern elements distributed differently, so that they are spaced apart in one region and clumped together in the other (see Fig. 5.17), a perceptual boundary will be evident. Finally, in other work on region discrimination, Julesz confirmed the findings of Olson and Attneave, and Beck, in demonstrating the importance of differences in slope in perceptual segregation.

Julesz tried to tie together a number of observations on perceptual grouping in terms of the formal statistical properties of the patterns being viewed. He made the strong claim that two regions can not be discriminated if their first and second order statistics are identical—where these statistical properties are derived mathematically using either Markov processes (for generation in one dimension), or techniques from random geometry for two-dimensional generation (Frisch & Julesz, 1966; Julesz, Frisch, Gilbert, & Shepp, 1973). Differences in the first order statistics of patterns capture differences in their overall brightness. Differences in second order statistics capture differences in granularity and slope. While such attempts to capture the variables determining similarity grouping in formal mathematical terms have been thwarted by counterexamples, the general principles seem to hold. Pattern elements need not be identical in order to be treated together by grouping processes. Such grouping processes seem to operate between elements of similar brightness, wavelength, slope and granularity. These properties correspond to those which we know are extracted early on in visual processing (see Chapters 2 and 3), and correspond to the properties captured by the descriptions in Marr's "raw primal sketch." We return to consider Marr's work towards the end of this chapter.

Thus we have seen how recent work in the area of perceptual grouping has quantified the Gestalt principles of "good shape" and "similarity." However, all of the above work has made use of artificial patterns and textures. Can these laws of perceptual organisation be demonstrated in more natural settings?

CONCEALMENT AND ADVERTISEMENT

In this section we return to the broader perspective of animal vision, to demonstrate how the Gestalt principles can give some insights into the ways in which the colouration and shapes of animals can help to conceal or to

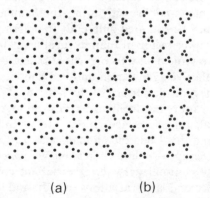

FIG.5.17. The average brightness in region (a) is the same as that in (b), but the dots in (b) are clumped together more than those in (a). A clear boundary is seen between the two regions.

(a)   (b)

reveal them. The study of camouflage in nature in addition provides us with a way of exploring the ways in which perceptual grouping processes in other species may be similar to, or differ from, our own.

Animals which remain concealed from predators have a greater chance of surviving and reproducing, and a predator also stands a better chance of getting food if it is not easily visible to its own prey. In order to remain concealed an animal should not stand out as a figure against its background, but needs instead to blend with it. On the other hand, for the purposes of breeding or defending territory, animals may need to be conspicuous to potential mates or competitors. Under such circumstances the animal may need to stand out as a distinctive figure against its surroundings. Whether an animal will be camouflaged or conspicuous depends on its behavioural needs and the habitat in which it lives. Some animals may need to remain hidden for much of the time but have the potential of occasionally giving a highly distinctive display or warning sign. This can be achieved by temporarily revealing distinctive surface features which are normally hidden beneath wings or tails, or by changing skin colour, coat or plumage to meet changing circumstances. To understand why a creature is coloured in a particular way we need to consider ecological factors as well as perceptual ones.

Merging and Contrasting

An animal that needs to be hidden should avoid standing out as a figure against its background. An animal that needs to be seen should stand out as a figure distinctly from its background. The way in which this is achieved will depend upon the nature of the background habitat.

An animal can blend with a uniform background by being of similar average colour and brightness. Many species are coloured fairly simply to match the habitat on which they live—for example tropical tree-snakes are green and polar bears are white. Some animals show seasonal variation in their colouration to match their changing habitats. The Arctic fox is white in the winter and brown during the summer. In other species, different animals may be coloured differently in differing environments. The peppered moth is darker in urban than in rural areas for example.

A more radical way to prevent standing out as a figure, and one which is more effective against non-uniform habitats, is to break up the perceptual cohesiveness of the surface of the body by *disruptive colouration*. Dissimilar surface areas are less likely to be grouped together as a single figure. If some of the patches of surface colour are in turn similar to elements in the background this leads the animal's surface to be grouped together with its habitat. Disruptive colouration along with *background picturing* is an efficient method of camouflage where the habitat contains different coloured and shaped elements and variations in light and shade. The tree frog shown in

Figure 5.18 is a good example of a creature whose surface markings incorporate these features. An artificial example is given by the green, brown and black mottled pattern painted on tanks and combat jackets to achieve camouflage for human military purposes.

In these examples of camouflage we see exploitation of the principle that grouping by similarity (with the background habitat) may over-ride grouping by proximity (of adjacent parts of the animal's surface). Effective disruptive colouration must match the background in terms of average brightness, colour and density of markings. Where the background texture elements have some intrinsic orientation, as in Figure 5.18, surface markings must be similarly oriented.

Conversely, in order to be conspicuous, an animal needs to have high brightness or colour contrast with its background. The all-black crow is a distinctive form against grassland or stubble field. In addition, the outline of an animal's body or of significant signs or structures can be enhanced by *outlining*. Many butterflies have contrasting borders around the edges of their wings, and some fish may have black edges to emphasise their distinctive fin shapes. Since flat structures are less conspicuous as figures than solid ones (see p.114), and solid bodies have no single contour line (the particular contour which will correspond to the animal's outline in an image of it will depend on vantage point), it makes sense that only "flat" structures such as

FIG.5.18. This African frog is well camouflaged when seen against the bark of the tree on which it habitually rests. Its asymmetrical markings show disruptive colouration along with background picturing. However, the shadow cast by the frog's head on the bark could reveal it. Photograph by P. Ward. Copyright © Bruce Coleman Ltd. Used by permission.

butterfly wings or fish fins should be outlined in this way (Hailman, 1977). More frequently, we find local outlining to emphasise the shape of a patch which serves as a courtship or warning signal. Such patches are often outlined in white or black in fish and birds.

Symmetry and Regularity

Symmetrical forms stand out more readily as figures against their backgrounds than do asymmetrical ones. Since animals are bilaterally symmetric, those that need to be hidden must reduce their apparent symmetry. Camouflaged snakes may rest in irregular coils so that the symmetry of surface markings is not evident. The frog in Figure 5.18 has asymmetrical markings which make it less visible as a separate figure. Conversely, symmetry and repetition may be employed to enhance an animal's outline or internal features. Butterflies which have dramatic markings on their wings become highly salient symmetrical figures when their wings are spread. Signal patches can also be made conspicuous by virtue of their shape. Regular geometric forms such as circles, squares and triangles are perceptually salient figures, and they are also rare in the habitats of animals, so that surface markings which are geometrically regular will be additionally distinctive due to their dissimilarity to background elements. Hailman (1977) suggests that the common use of circular signal patches may be because they are regular, and hence unusual, rather than functioning as eye mimics. Triangular patterns can be seen on the breeding plumage of some male birds such as peacocks, and rectangular patches are found on the wings of some ducks. In many birds and fish we find another kind of regularity in the form of repeated markings—the series of tail spots on cuckoos and head stripes on sparrows for example.

Countershading and Reverse Countershading

A creature might be well camouflaged in terms of matching the colours and contrasts in its background, but could still be apparent as a distinct figure by virtue of its solidity. There will be a distinct depth difference between the upper part of a cylindrical body and the surface upon which it rests, which may be revealed to an observer by stereopsis or motion parallax (see Chapter 6). This will lead to grouping by proximity in depth and by common fate, just as central regions of texture can be revealed in random-dot stereograms and random-dot kinematograms (see Chapter 6). Many birds use sideways movements of their heads to reveal prey by motion parallax. A solution to this problem is to be as flat as possible, either behaviourally, by crouching, or structurally, by becoming flat during the course of evolution. Moths and flatfish, by virtue of their flat shapes, are at minimal depth differences from the surfaces on which they rest. Crouching also reduces the likelihood that an animal will be revealed by the shadow it casts. The head of the frog in Figure 5.18 casts such a shadow on the bark.

Creatures that inhabit environments where there is a strong light source have the additional problem of unequal illumination of their surfaces, leading to self-shading, which again will tend to reveal. This can be compensated for by *countershading*. A countershaded animal has its darkest surface areas where the most light strikes its body, and is lighter where less light is incident (Thayer, 1918). The zebra's stripes may in part serve a counter-shading function. The black stripes are at their broadest (and hence the coat on average is at its darkest) where the body receives most light.

The clearest examples of countershading are found among the fish, who often have dark dorsal and light ventral regions. This means that they are relatively concealed from air-borne predators where their darker backs will be seen against the murk of the water, and also concealed when viewed by a predator swimming beneath them, as their light undersides are now seen against the brighter sky above. The countershading evident in an animal can usually be explained in terms of the direction of the habitual light source and the shape of its body. Caterpillars that live on the undersides of leaves have "reverse" countershading, with their undersides which receive the most light, darker than their backs.

If appropriate countershading can serve to conceal an animal then *reverse* countershading could act to reveal it. There are some animals, who lead their lives in upright posture, who are lighter dorsally and darker ventrally. In the male bobolink (a kind of blackbird) reverse countershaded plumage, in which the head and back are white, is adopted for the breeding season, where the bird needs to be distinctive, but is discarded during winter, when the bird's plumage is darker dorsally (Hailman, 1977).

Immobility and Camouflage

However well concealed a stationary animal may be, grouping by "common fate" would tend to reveal it if it moved. It therefore benefits a camouflaged animal if it can remain still for a large proportion of the time. In many species, while the adults may be brightly coloured for courtship or aggressive purposes, the young may have quite different plumage or coats which merge with their backgrounds. Whether the young of a species are camouflaged or not will depend on the habitat in which the nest or den is sited, and on the behaviour of both young and parents. For example, if the nest is on open ground, and both parents leave it to forage, then camouflage of the young is more important.

However, as Cott (1940) pointed out, while immobility is advantageous to concealment, it is not essential. A green tennis ball is harder to follow than a white one on a grass court. Thus even if an animal is active, it will be harder to spot or track it if merges with its background. Some creatures have markings which appear to make it harder to track their movement. Many snakes which flee in defence (Jackson, Ingram, & Campbell, 1976), and some fish, have longitudinal stripes which may deceive observers since they appear to remain still as the animal moves forward. Of course movement is one of the easiest ways for an animal to reveal itself when it needs to be conspicuous. Some make use of temporal redundancy by making repetitive or stereotyped movements of their bodies in their displays, and others repeatedly flash signal patches beneath their tails or wings.

PERCEPTUAL ORGANISATION IN OTHER SPECIES

These examples of animal colouration thus illustrate how the Gestalt laws may be useful to help understand camouflage and concealment principles, at least when assessed by human vision. However, a successful camouflage for a particular species is not necessarily that which prevents its detection by a human visual system. It is the properties of the predator's, the prey's and the conspecific's visual systems which are important. Some species may not appear well-hidden to us, because their colours are different from those of their habitats. However, provided they need to be hidden from colour-blind species, only the brightness levels are important. Conversely, crab spiders which match the flowers on which they live may be well concealed to our eyes and to the eyes of many of their predators, but they may be detectable to any insect prey which have good sensitivity to ultra-violet radiation (Eisner, Silberglied, Aneshansley, Carrel, & Howland, 1969). How can we find out whether an animal's colouration is having its apparent (to our eyes) effect of hiding an animal or making it conspicuous?

It is possible to examine how accurate are our own perceptual intuitions about the relative degrees of concealment attained by camouflaged animals by observing the "success" that different surface markings confer to an animal in terms of its survival. This can be done through observation of natural situations or through experiment. For example, a radical change in the predominant colouration of the peppered moth has been observed in areas where industrial pollution is present. At one time, darker members of the peppered moth species were rare. Over the last 200 years or so, in areas where buildings and trees are polluted with soot and grime, the predominant colouration in the moths has changed. Darker members are much more frequent than lighter ones, while in rural areas the lighter moths are still common. This suggests that the avian predators which feed on such moths find light moths distinctive on dark backgrounds in the same way that we do. In industrial areas the gene for darker colouration has conferred an advantage on those possessing it, enhancing their chances of surviving and reproducing (Kettlewell, 1973).

As well as such "natural" experiments, it is possible to conduct controlled experiments in which members of a prey species are placed against different backgrounds and then exposed to predators. The success of a particular camouflage can be assessed in terms of the number of prey that survive! Sumner (1934), for example, reared mosquito fish in differently coloured tanks. These are fish that, in common with many others, adjust their colours to tone in with their surroundings. After seven to eight weeks those fish reared in a black tank were very dark, while those raised in a white tank were a much paler buff or grey. Equal numbers of the "black" and "white" fish were transferred into experimental tanks which were painted black or pale grey, and exposed to the Galapagos penguin as predator. Of the fish which were appropriately colour-adapted 32% were eaten, as compared with 68% of those which were inappropriately colour-adapted. Thus the Galapagos penguin seems to find fish of high contrast to their background more easily than those of low contrast, again in agreement with our own perceptions. More dramatic experiments involve artificially colouring the prey species before exposing them to predation (e.g. Croze, 1970).

Experiments such as these are not always ethically acceptable (most people would be unhappy if the prey used in such studies were mammals or birds rather than fish or insects). A further experimental way of assessing degree of concealment without the sacrifice of too many animals is illustrated by Pietrewicz and Kamil (1977). They conducted operant conditioning experiments in which blue jays were trained to detect moths in colour slides. Interestingly they showed that the birds were sensitive to the orientation of the moths (whether their heads were pointing up, down, or horizontally), as well as to the degree of visual similarity existing between the moth's markings and those of the bark against which it was photographed. Only the latter aspect is noticeable to us.

Observing the "success" of various surface markings is, of course, not the only way to study perceptual organisation in other species. Hertz (1928, 1929) for example describes some delightful experiments with jays and bees in which she investigated aspects of their figural perception directly as they searched for food from arrangements of objects. She concluded that for the jay birds (though not for the bees), perceptual organisation was very similar to our own. To appreciate fully the adaptive significance of animal colouration requires continued research along these lines.

WHY DO THE GESTALT LAWS WORK?

We have shown that many of the Gestalt laws are useful descriptive tools for a discussion of perceptual organisation in the real world, but we are still some way from having an adequate theory of *why* the principles work and *how* perceptual organisation is achieved. We mentioned earlier how the Gestalt psychologists themselves attempted to answer both these points with their model of brain field forces. What alternative answers would contemporary theorists provide?

Marr's (1976, 1982) approach to vision emphasises that we should always consider what general assumptions about the world can be brought to bear on visual processing, to constrain the range of possible interpretations for any particular image. The Gestalt principles of organisation may work because they reflect a set of sensible assumptions that can be made about the world of physical and biological objects. Because the same kind of surface reflects and absorbs light in the same kind of way, the different subregions of a single object are likely to look similar. Because matter is cohesive, adjacent regions are likely to belong together, and will retain their adjacency relations despite movement of the object. The shapes of natural objects tend to vary smoothly rather than having abrupt discontinuities, and many natural objects (at least those which grow) are symmetrical. A solid object stands upon (and hence is at a different depth from) the surface on which it rests, and objects tend to be small compared with the ground. A perceptual system which made use of such assumptions to interpret natural images would generally achieve correct solutions to perceptual organisation, unless deceived by a camouflage exploiting these very same assumptions. It is perhaps not surprising that in our perception of unnatural displays (such as the patterns used by experimental psychologists or the authors of textbooks), we employ the same set of assumptions that serve us well in interpreting natural images.

However, having a set of descriptive principles, even if we know why they work, is still only a starting point for a full information processing theory of grouping processes. We need to know *how* such principles can be applied to primitive elements recovered from images—edges, blobs and so on—in order to recover the potentially significant structures present. It is research in artificial intelligence (A.I.), which has attempted to provide such a *process* theory of perceptual organisation, which is much more powerful than a purely *descriptive* theory, such as that of the Gestaltists or more recent workers like Julesz. Marr's (1976) early visual processing program implements such a process theory and makes extensive use of Gestalt principles to achieve perceptual organisation. Before describing Marr's work, we will digress briefly to introduce you to other research in A.I. which has attempted to formalise organisational processes, by making use of a rather different set of constraints.

ARTIFICIAL INTELLIGENCE APPROACHES
TO GROUPING

Scene Analysis Programs

Many researchers in A.I. during the 1960s and 1970s attempted to solve what became known as the "segmentation problem." This is the problem of dividing up a visual scene into a number of distinct objects. Most researchers avoided the complexities of natural images, and restricted their programs to a world of matt, white prismatic solids which were evenly illuminated. Figure 5.19 shows a line drawing of the outlines of such a collection of objects. Viewed analytically, Figure 5.19 is just a collection of straight lines in a variety of orientations. However, our spontaneous perception of such a scene is more likely to be of a collection of distinct *objects*. Thus this scene is readily described by our visual apparatus as being made up of two blocks and a wedge, with one block partially occluding the other two structures. Here again we have an example of perceptual organisation. Somehow we know that the regions labelled a, b and c belong together as one structure, distinct from d, e and f which belong to another. The Gestalt psychologists might argue that the perception of regions a, b and c as belonging together provides a closed, simple and symmetrical interpretation, but this does not

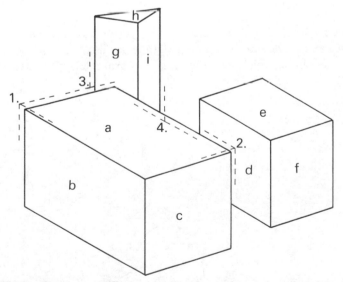

FIG.5.19. We have no difficulty in seeing that regions a, b and c belong together (likewise d, e and f; g, h and i). Guzman's program SEE interpreted pictures like this by examining the junctions present. Examples of arrow junctions are shown at 1 and 2, and T junctions are shown at 3 and 4. What other kinds of junction are there in this picture?

really address the question of *how* such a solution is achieved by visual processing.

This was the kind of problem tackled by Guzman (1968), Clowes (1971) and Waltz (1975) amongst others, who set out to try to write computer programs which could "see" objects from collections of lines such as these. The common principle in all their work was a consideration of the *junctions* present in these figures. A junction is a point where two or more lines meet. Different junction types have different implications for the possible arrangement of surfaces within the picture. Thus Guzman suggested that the presence of an *arrow* junction would generally imply that the edges which formed the fins of the arrow belonged to a single body, while a *T* junction generally implied that the shaft and the cross-bar of the T belonged to different bodies. Figure 5.19 shows how these principles apply in our example.

Guzman's program SEE considered only junctions, and incorporated his own informal intuitions about the interpretations of different junction types. Clowes tackled the problem of junction specification more systematically, and employed a more sophisticated notion of how different junction types in the image relate to the organisation of *objects* in the "scene" depicted. This was achieved by considering the nature of the *edges* depicted by the junction lines (Clowes, 1971, Huffman, 1971), as well as the nature of the intersection of these lines. Edges may be *convex, concave* or *occluding* (see Fig. 5.20). Only certain combinations of edge types are compatible with a particular configuration of lines at a junction. By ensuring that edges were consistently labelled along their entire length, Clowes' program OBSCENE was able to interpret pictures successfully provided that no more than three lines met at a single junction. The program was also able to "reject" certain pictures as "impossible" (see Fig. 5.21 for example), whereas SEE would simply accept such examples as objects.

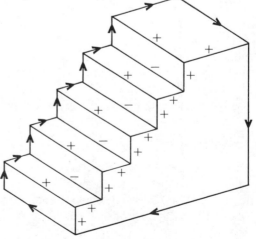

FIG.5.20.   Three different kinds of edge are shown; concave (+), convex (−), and occluding (>).

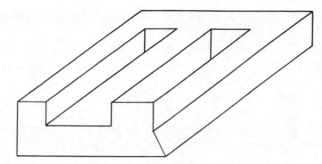

FIG.5.21. An impossible object. From Clowes (1971). Reproduced by permission of the North-Holland Publishing Company, Amsterdam.

The most elegant example of work of this type was that of Waltz (1975), who introduced a fourth edge type, the crack, and whose program accepted pictures of scenes containing shadows. Once shadows are introduced, the possible labellings for a particular type of junction increase dramatically, since a number of different types of edge could now be present. Nevertheless, Waltz's program was able successfully to parse scenes containing shadows. His work illustrates how adding more information in the form of light and shading may actually aid the interpretation of a scene by providing additional local constraints.

While such A.I. programs are intrinsically interesting, and point out the complicated processing which may underly our everyday ability to perceive patterns such as these, they are of limited importance. The programs work by incorporating the constraints of their visual worlds, but the particular constraints employed are specific to the world of white prismatic solids—an artificially manufactured world which our visual systems did not evolve to perceive. The principles embodied within these segmentation programs would fail to recover the significant structures in natural images. Natural objects may have internal markings, texture and shading. Straight lines and angular junctions are rare (cf. Chapter 3, p.67). Indeed A.I. segmentation programs of the above type either start with a line drawing as input, or make use of initial programs to find the edges in images of prismatic solids by using the assumption that edges are straight, along with higher level knowledge about "likely" places to find lines (e.g. Shirai, 1973).

Marr's Program

Of more interest to our discussion is a processing model which can recover structures from natural images of everyday objects and surfaces, despite their noise, texture and shadow. Such a program has been produced by Marr (1976, 1982), whose early visual processing program finds occluding and internal contours from images such as those shown in Figure 5.22. We

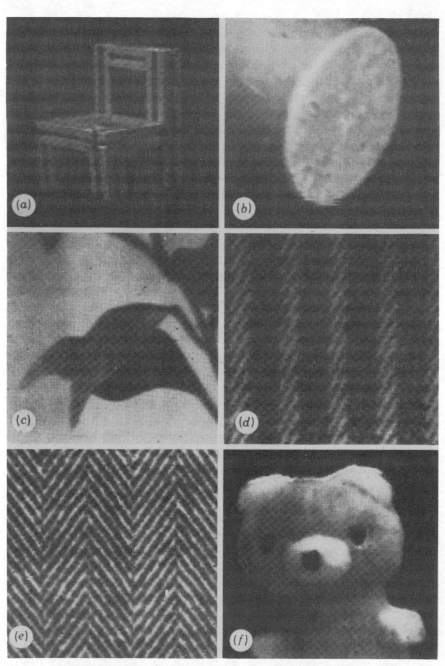

FIG.5.22. Examples of the images analysed by Marr's (1976) early vision program: (a) a chair; (b) a rod; (c) a plant; (d) and (e) textures and (f) a teddy bear. Reproduced with permission from Marr (1976).

have already considered some of Marr's ideas in Chapters 3 and 4. He proposes that cells in the retina and visual cortex of mammals function to locate *zero-crossings* (see p. 76) in the retinal image, which serve as the first step towards recovering information about edges in the world. A comparison of the zero-crossings found by sets of cells with different receptive field sizes leads to a set of assertions about the "features" present at each location in the image. This set of assertions is the *raw primal sketch*.

The primitives in the raw primal sketch are edges, bars, blobs and terminations which have the associated attributes of orientation, contrast, length, width and position. The representation of a straight line would consist of a termination, then several segments having the same orientation, then a final termination. The raw primal sketch is very complex and messy (see the examples in Figs. 3.10, 5.29 and 5.30), and from it we need to recover global structures as well as internal structures and surface texture.

This is achieved in the next stage of early visual processing by the recursive assignment of *place tokens* to small structures, or collections of structures, in the raw primal sketch. These place tokens are in turn aggregated together to form larger units, in a cyclical manner. Place tokens can be defined by the *position* of a blob, or of a short line or edge; by the *termination* of a longer edge, line or elongated blob, or by a small *aggregation* of tokens. Grouping of these place tokens can proceed by *clustering* nearby place tokens on the basis of changes in spatial density (see Fig. 5.23), by *curvilinear* aggregation, which produces contours by joining aligned items which are near to one another (see Fig. 5.24) and finally by *theta aggregation*. Theta aggregation involves the grouping of similarly oriented items in a direction that relies upon, but differs from, their intrinsic orientation. Theta organisation can for example be used to recover the vertical stripes in a herringbone pattern where all the individual texture elements are oriented obliquely (see Fig. 5.25).

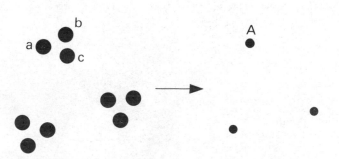

FIG.5.23. Place tokens corresponding to small dots can be grouped together by proximity to yield higher-order place tokens. Here, place tokens at a, b and c are grouped to yield a place token at A, and likewise for the other dots in this figure.

The grouping together of place tokens thus relies upon local proximity (adjacent elements are combined) and similarity (similarly oriented elements are combined), but more global considerations can also influence the structures detected. For example, in curvilinear aggregation, a "closure" principle could allow two edge segments to be joined even though the contrast across the edge segments differed due to illumination effects (see the image in Fig. 5.26). Marr's program therefore embodies many of the Gestalt principles that we earlier discussed at length.

FIG.5.24. Curvilinear aggregation will group place tokens at a, b, c, d and so on to yield a single structure A.

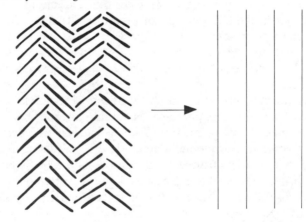

FIG.5.25. Theta aggregation can recover the vertical orientation of the stripes of a herringbone pattern.

FIG.5.26. Curvilinear aggregation along with the application of a closure principle could reveal the contour a–b–c–d, despite the different contrasts of the edge segments along this contour. This pattern of shading might arise if a tube was illuminated in the direction shown.

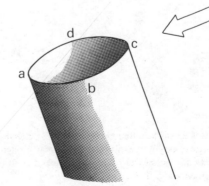

The grouping procedures use the construction of tokens at different scales to locate physically meaningful boundaries in the image. It is essential that different scales are used in order to recover different kinds of surface properties. "Thus if the image was a close-up view of a cat, the raw primal sketch might yield descriptions mostly at the scale of the cat's hairs. At the next level the markings on its coat may appear . . . and at a yet higher level there is the parallel stripe structure of these markings (Marr, 1982, p. 91)." For a herringbone pattern we know both that the "bones" are short parallel segments oriented at 45°, and that these form vertical stripes.

Boundaries due to changes in surface reflectance (where two different objects overlap, for example), or to discontinuities in surface orientation or depth, can be revealed in two ways. First, boundaries may simply be marked by place tokens. The elliptical boundary perceived in Figure 5.27 may be produced by the curvilinear aggregation of the place tokens assigned to the termination of each radial line. Second, boundaries may be revealed by discontinuities in parameters that describe the spatial organisation of an image. Changes in the local density of place tokens, their spacing or their overall orientation structure could all be used to reveal such boundaries. Thus the boundary in Figure 5.28 cannot be defined by place tokens, but is revealed by the discontinuity in the common orientations of all the small elements in the image.

This last example also illustrates how Marr's theory can be applied to the problem of texture and region discrimination tackled by Julesz (see p. 110). While Julesz tried to arrive at a universal mathematical formula to explain why some texture boundaries were perceptually evident, although others were invisible without scrutiny, Marr provided a process theory which provides a more powerful explanation. Julesz's explanation was purely descriptive; Marr showed *how* a set of descriptive principles can be used to recover texture and larger structures from images. Indeed Marr's grouping principles fare better than Julesz's mathematics at accounting for the perceptibility of texture discontinuities (Marr, 1976).

FIG.5.27. The elliptical boundary could be revealed by curvilinear aggregation of the place tokens assigned to the ends of the lines.

FIG.5.28. The boundary seen here could be revealed by discontinuities in the orientations of all the small elements in the two regions.

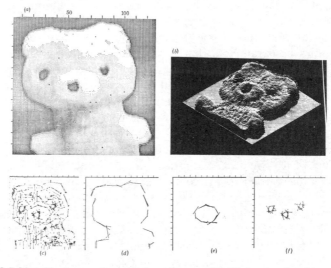

FIG.5.29. The image of a teddy bear (Figure 5.22 (f)) is printed at (a), and shown as an intensity map at (b). At (c) is shown the location of all the small edge segments in the raw primal sketch. The structures which emerge after grouping operations are shown at (d), (e) and (f). Reproduced, with permission, from Marr (1976).

The successfulness of Marr's early visual processing program can be judged by its ability to recover the occluding contours from the image of a teddy bear (see Fig. 5.22f), and to reveal the internal contours of the bear which correspond to eyes, nose and muzzle outlines (see Fig. 5.29). Such structures are recovered without recourse to high level knowledge. The program knows nothing of the usual shape of a teddy bear's head, and does not find the contours which correspond to its eyes because it "expects" to find them. Marr's theory of early visual processing thus contrasts strongly with some computer models, or more general theories of visual perception

FIG.5.30. The image of a plant (Figure 5.22 (c)) is printed at (a). At (b) is shown the location of all the small edge segments in the raw primal sketch; (c) and (d) show some structures which are formed by curvilinear aggregation. The grouping procedures cannot separate the two leaves, and the single structure at (e) appears. If the program is told that segments 1 and 2 in the original image do not match, then the separate structures (f) and (g) are found. Reproduced, with permission, from Marr (1976).

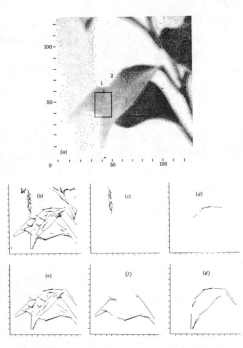

where expectations and "object-hypotheses" guide every stage of perceptual analysis (e.g. Roberts, 1965; Gregory, 1980). The processing of natural images by Marr's program works because the program embodies grouping principles which reflect *general* properties of the world. Things which are oriented similarly, or lie next to each other, are more likely to "belong together" than things which are oriented dissimilarly and spaced far apart.

Marr's program resorts to higher-level knowledge only in cases of ambiguity. For example, in the image of a plant (see Figs. 5.22 and 5.30), the segmentation procedures fail to separate the contours of the two overlapping leaves. In this case the program needs to be "told" that the different contour segments do not belong together as a single structure. While this ambiguity is indeed present when starting from a static "monocular" image, the additional information gained from stereopsis or motion parallax from the leaves of a real plant could allow the correct grouping to be achieved without such downward-flowing information.

CONCLUSIONS

The Gestalt psychologists, through the study of our perception of simple patterns, gave us insights into the organisational principles which may apply to the perception of the world. The study of natural camouflage and concealment shows that these principles fare well in describing the utility of various surface markings of animals. Marr has shown how such principles can be incorporated within a processing model which reveals the structures hidden in the messy data obtained from natural images. To the extent that other animals have similar figural perception to ourselves, we might similarly explain their early visual processing in terms of the elaboration of structures present in the primal sketch.

It should be noted here however that Marr (1982) does not regard his early visual processing program as solving the "figure-ground" or "segmentation" problem as traditionally conceived. The goal of early visual processing is not to recover the "objects" present within a scene—for the division of a scene into component objects is an arbitrary and ambiguous affair. Which should we regard as the "objects" to be recovered—a crowd of people, each individual person, or the eyes, ears and nose of each? Such consideration depends on the use to which the information is to be put. Marr instead sees the goal of early visual processing as to describe the surfaces present in the image. The recovery of the full primal sketch, in which some potentially significant structures such as occluding edges may be found, is only one aspect of early visual processing. Other valuable information about the kinds of surface discontinuities present can be gained from considering information about depth and motions present in the image. In this chapter we have largely ignored the problem of how depth and motion are analysed. We have merely mentioned their importance. It is to the analysis of depth and motion that we turn in Chapter 6.

6

Perceiving Depth
and Movement

At the end of the last chapter we described how Marr's early visual processing program recovers aspects of the structure of images from an initial array of intensities. As we pointed out, Marr sees the goal of early visual processing as furnishing a description of the surfaces being viewed by an observer. The recovery of occluding and internal contours is one aspect of this, but the full primal sketch is still essentially a description of the *image*, rather than of the *world*. The visual world which we view consists of surfaces extending away into the distance, and solid objects resting on them at different distances and with their surfaces inclined differently towards us. In addition, the pattern of light reaching the retina is never static. The eyes, heads and bodies of observers move, and objects and animals in the scene being viewed move likewise.

In this chapter we consider the optical information available to animals which allows them to perceive the layout of surfaces in the world, the relative distances of objects from themselves and the motions of these objects and of themselves.

PERCEIVING THE THIRD DIMENSION

The psychology of perception has been dominated by the apparent paradox of three dimensional vision. As we discussed in Chapter 1, for some purposes the eye can be thought of as a camera, with the lens and internal fluids acting to focus light onto a mosaic of retinal receptors. At any instant of time therefore one can conceive of the pattern of excitation of retinal receptors as a "picture," curved around the back of an eyeball. Though curved, the image is essentially two dimensional, and yet our perception is of a three dimensional world. How might depth be recovered?

The problem of how we recover the third dimension was tackled resolutely by the British empiricist philosophers, notably by Berkeley (1709). Berkeley's views have come to dominate our thinking on many aspects of perception. The British empiricists rejected any notion that ideas were implanted in the mind at birth, saying instead that all complex ideas had to be built up by the association of simpler ones. Since all information is received via the organs of sense, ultimately all knowledge must be achieved by the associating together of simple sensations. It was assumed that the third dimension must be perceived by associating together visual "cues"with the position of objects felt by touch.

Convergence and Accommodation

The primary cues which Berkeley suggested could become associated with the felt positions of objects were the different angles of inclination of the eyes (see Fig. 6.1), different degrees of blurring of the image and different degrees of strain in the muscles around the lens.

Today we would refer to the different angles of inclination of the eyes as the degree of *convergence* and we would include both blurring and strain under the heading of the *accommodation* of the lens (see Chapter 1, p.21 and Fig. 6.2). Convergence and accommodation are often listed in introductory texts as "physiological" cues to depth. They are "cues" because these signals must be learned through association with non-visual aspects of experience. There is, however, a potentially much more important physiological source of information about relative distance for creatures with binocularly overlapping fields of vision.

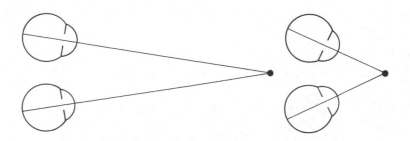

FIG.6.1.   The eyes swing inwards to focus on a near object.

Stereopsis

At close range, animals with overlapping visual fields have stereoscopic information available to them from the disparate images obtained at the two eyes. Each eye sees a slightly different view of the world due to the horizontal separation of the two eyes. You can confirm this by alternately opening and closing each eye. The world will appear to shift laterally.

Figure 6.3 shows the geometrical properties of the two retinal images which give rise to disparity. If the two eyes are focused on object A, the images in each eye cast by A are said to lie on *corresponding points* on the two retinas. The images cast by a nearer or more distant object, such as B, will fall on *disparate* points on the two retinas and the amount of disparity will depend upon the distance between B and A. Thus it can be seen that if the brain can compute disparity this will give precise information about the relative distances of objects in the world.

Neurophysiologists have discovered cells in the cortex of cats, monkeys and other species which fire maximally when both eyes are exposed to stimuli which fall on disparate areas of the two retinas, (Blakemore, 1970; Hubel & Wiesel, 1970; Clarke & Whitteridge, 1973). Hubel and Wiesel (1970) for example contrasted the properties of such "binocular depth cells" in area 18 of the visual cortex of the macaque monkey with "ordinary" binocularly driven cells they had earlier found in area 17. Whereas ordinary cells responded to stimulation in either eye alone, as well as when both eyes were presented with stimuli falling on corresponding points, the binocular depth cells of area 18 responded hardly at all with monocular input, and responded most to disparity in a particular direction. In the cat, binocular depth cells are found in area 17. We could think of such cells as measuring the disparities present in a visual scene.

It is possible to create strong depth impressions from pictures by sending to each eye separately the projective drawing that the eye would see if an actual object in depth were presented. Wheatstone (1838) is usually attributed with the invention of the first *stereoscope*, shown in Figure 6.4. He drew the view of a block as it appeared to each eye, and then with an arrangement of mirrors sent the left eye view to the left eye of an observer and the right eye view to the right eye. The result was that the observer saw a "solid" object in depth. It is possible to arrange such stereo demonstrations in a

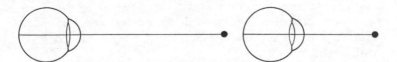

FIG.6.2.   The lens accommodates, by becoming thicker, when the eye focuses on a near object.

number of ways, all of which depend on separating out the left and right eye views, and then sending these separately to each eye. A common technique is to use *anaglyphs*. Here one view is drawn in red and one in green, and the two superimposed. The viewer looks through glasses containing a red filter to one eye and a green filter to the other, so that only one of the images is passed to each. The resulting perceptions of solid objects in depth are of course illusory. No actual solid object exists, but the disparities which

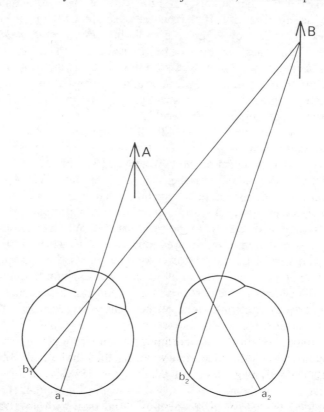

FIG.6.3.   The eyes are focused on an object at A, and the image of A falls on corresponding points on the two retinas (a_1 and a_2). The images of a more distant object B, fall on disparate points on the two retinas (b_1 and b_2).

would exist if an object were present have been captured in the anaglyphs. The brain thus receives the information that it would receive if an actual 3D object were presented, and the phenomenal impression reflects this. Frisby (1979) provides numerous examples of anaglyphs and his book is well worth consulting.

While it seems relatively easy to appreciate how disparity might be computed, and the neurophysiological evidence indicates that cells in the cortex may indeed measure the disparities present in the images to the two

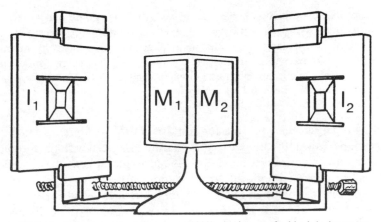

FIG.6.4.   Wheatstone's stereoscope (1838). A picture of a block is drawn as it would appear to the left eye (I_1) and to the right eye (I_2). If these two images are sent to each eye separately, via mirrors M_1 and M_2, an observer sees a single cube in depth. Adapted from Boring (1942).

eyes, it is less easy to appreciate why our phenomenal impressions of objects in the real world, or of illusory forms in a stereoscope, are of *single* objects. If you focus on a pen held near your eyes, you will experience double images of more distant objects, but it is nonetheless true that within a certain range of distance a single percept is obtained. If the eyes fixate a given point, the region of space within which single vision is possible is known as Panum's fusional area. How is this fusion achieved? How do we know which parts of one eye's image *correspond* to particular parts in the other? This problem of establishing correspondences between one view and another slightly different one recurs in various forms throughout this chapter.

It used to be thought that the forms presented to each eye were recognised independently and then the images were matched and fused. For example, Sherrington (1906) suggested:

During binocular regard of an objective image each uniocular mechanism develops independently a sensual image of considerable completeness. The singleness of binocular perception results from the union of these elaborated uniocular sensations. The singleness is therefore the product of a synthesis that works with already elaborated sensations contemporaneously proceeding. (p.380)

However, not all agreed with this—particularly given the strange results which could be obtained using stereoscopes. For example, Darwin received a communication from A.L. Austin in New Zealand:

Although a perfect stranger to you, and living on the reverse side of the globe, I have taken the liberty of writing to you on a small discovery I have made in binocular vision in the stereoscope. I find by taking two ordinary carte-de-visite photos of two different persons' faces, the portraits being about the same sizes, and looking about the same direction, and placing them in a stereoscope, the faces blend into one in a most remarkable manner, producing in the case of some ladies' portraits, in every instance, a *decided improvement* in beauty. (Galton, 1907, p.226)

Darwin passed this information on to Galton, who confirmed these observations. Ross (1976) suggests that Galton disagreed with the monocular combination explanation because the binocular perception of two different faces was so unlike an "optical" combination of the faces.

A more serious challenge to the recognition and fusion theory came with the important work of Bela Julesz in the 1960s, summarised in his 1971 book. Julesz developed *random dot stereograms* as a tool to explore the processes of stereopsis.

A random dot stereogram is shown in Figure 6.5. Both members of the stereo pair consist of a uniform, randomly generated texture of black and white dots. There is no recognisable form present in either member of the pair. However, if the stereogram shown in Figure 6.5 were to be viewed in a stereoscope the viewer would see a central square of texture floating above the background. This is because the stereogram in fact contains disparate "forms" camouflaged by the background texture. Each half of the stereogram contains identical background elements. The central regions, corresponding to the perceived square, also match, but are displaced inwards from the background as shown in Figure 6.6. The gaps which remain after this lateral shifting are then filled in with more texture. Thus when viewed in a stereoscope the eyes are presented with the disparities which would be present if an inner square of texture were actually held above the background texture of random dots.

This simple demonstration makes it difficult to maintain any theory of stereopsis which depends on the recognition and fusion of monocular contours. It could be argued that *local* patterns of black and white dots are detected and matched, but Julesz (1971) provides evidence against this. For example, fusion can be achieved from stereograms in which one member of the pair is blurred, reduced in size, or has "noise" added to it such that any local patterns are disrupted.

Julesz proposes that stereopsis proceeds by a point-by-point comparison of dots of the same brightness value. He argues that brightnesses must be the same since fusion cannot be achieved if one member of a random-dot stereogram has reversed contrast to the other, i.e. if black dots in one image correspond to white dots in the other. If individual dots are matched, why is the percept obtained from a random-dot stereogram so stable? The number of possible matches between individual dots in such stereograms is huge;

FIG.6.5. A random-dot stereogram of the kind devised by Julesz.
If this pair was viewed in a
stereogram, a square would be seen
floating above the background.
Photograph courtesy John Frisby,
University of Sheffield.

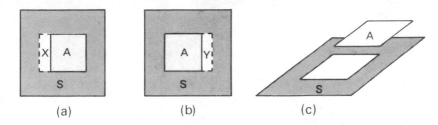

(a)   (b)   (c)

FIG.6.6.   (a) and (b) are the two halves of a random-dot stereogram shown
in simplified form. Both have the same surrounding texture (S). A central
region (A) has been shifted to the right in (a) and to the left in (b). The gaps
left have been filled in with more texture (X and Y). If such a stereogram was
constructed, and viewed in a stereoscope, the central square would be seen
floating above the background, as shown at (c). Adapted from Julesz (1965).

Figure 6.7 illustrates the problem of false targets in stereoscopic fusion. This
figure shows how a viewer might in principle end up seeing any number of
lace-like depth planes, yet in practice observers all reach the same, simple
solutions to such stereoscopic puzzles.

Julesz suggests that the *global stereopsis* mechanism selects a match based
on a uniform set of disparity measurements.

> Thus, to obtain local stereopsis of a few edges or dots, one can visualize how
> the binocular disparity units will maximally fire for similar receptive fields in
> the two retinae of the same shapes, orientations and retinal ordinates. On the
> other hand, for complex textured surfaces, another level of neural processing
> has to be evoked that evaluates the possible local solutions and selects the
> densest firing units of the same disparity. This processing I will call global
> stereopsis, and it is on another level of complexity from the commonly quoted
> local stereopsis of the textbooks. (Julesz, 1971, p.150)

Julesz's own model of the process of global stereopsis is not couched in
neurophysiological terms, but in the form of an elaborate mechanical
metaphor—*the spring-coupled magnetic dipole model*. The model is designed
to encompass amongst other things the phenomenon of *hysteresis* (Fender &

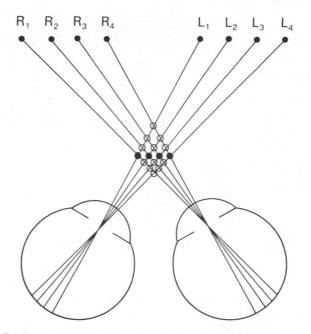

FIG.6.7.   Both eyes look at four dots, but the correspondence between the two retinal projections is ambiguous. Each of the dots L_1 to L_4 could match any of the four projections of dots R_1 to R_4. "False" matches are shown as open circles in the projection field. Correct matches are shown as filled circles. Adapted from Marr and Poggio (1976).

Julesz, 1967). Normally, stereograms can only be fused if the disparities presented to the two eyes are not too great, specifically not greater than Panum's fusional limit. Once a random dot stereogram has been fused by an observer, however, the disparity can be increased to 20 times Panum's fusional limit, without loss of stereoscopic sensation. The phenomenon is rather like the attractiveness that is held between opposite poles of magnets once they have contacted—it becomes remarkably difficult to pull them apart.

The phenomenon of hysteresis has influenced several models of stereopsis which include *cooperativity* between local measures to achieve global stereopsis. However, as Marr (1982) points out, hysteresis may reflect the operation of a memory buffer rather than reflecting the mechanism of stereo fusion itself. Marr and Poggio (1976, 1979) have produced two different stereo algorithms, the first showing cooperativity and the second relying on a short-term memory system. These algorithms were both developed after a consideration of the constraints to be embodied in any theory of stereopsis. As we have already seen, in Marr's view, a computational theory in which such constraints are made explicit, must be formulated prior to any algorithms for achieving this computation (see also Chapters 3, 4 and 5). Marr and Poggio point out that stereo matching should take place between elements which are reliably related to surface markings and discontinuities. Intensity arrays—which would be used to match "points of the same brightness level" (Julesz)—are thus poor candidates for the matching process. Raw primal sketch descriptions like edges and blobs might be candidates for stereo matching, though in fact Marr and Poggio (1979) make use of zero-crossings for the matching process.

The computational theory of stereopsis formulated by Marr and Poggio takes into account the following constraints of the physical world:

> 1) A given point on a physical surface has a unique position in space at any one time and 2) matter is cohesive, it is separated into objects, and the surfaces of objects are generally smooth in the sense that the surface variation due to roughness, cracks, or other sharp differences that can be attributed to changes in distance from the viewer, are small compared with the overall distance from the viewer. (Marr, 1982, p.112)

These physical considerations give rise to three constraints in the matching of stereo images. First, the logic of the physical world dictates that a pair of candidate image elements to be matched must be physically similar if they are to have originated from the same point on an object's surface (the compatibility constraint). Secondly, any item in one image should only match one item in the other image (the uniqueness constraint). Finally, the disparity should vary smoothly almost everywhere in an image (the continuity constraint).

These matching constraints can be successfully embodied within an algorithm which can "solve" random-dot stereograms (Marr & Poggio, 1976). The solution gradually drops out of a network of excitatory and inhibitory connections which take account of these three constraints simultaneously. See Frisby (1979) for a simple account of this.

Marr and Poggio's second algorithm (1979) is more complex. It is more closely tied to psychophysical observations of stereo fusion, in which there is evidence that stereo matching may proceed within independent spatial-frequency tuned channels. For example, Julesz and Miller (1975) showed that high spatial frequency "noise" added to stereograms did not disrupt the binocular fusion obtained between lower spatial frequency components in the image, provided that there was no overlap in the spatial frequencies of the noise and the image. Marr and Poggio (1979) therefore suggest that the image is analysed by a set of channels of successively finer resolution. The low spatial frequency channels control vergence movements of the eyes which cause finer channels to come into correspondence. Interim results are held in a temporary memory, the 2½D sketch. Marr and Poggio suggest that the inputs to this stereo matching process should be the zero-crossings obtained using V^2G filters of different widths (see Chapter 3).

While Marr and Poggio's two algorithms for stereopsis are both elegant, and succeed in "solving" the stereo pairs they are tested on, they do not easily accommodate all the psychophysical evidence on stereopsis. For example, if an outline is provided for the camouflaged square in a random-dot stereogram then stereo fusion is improved (Saye & Frisby, 1975). This facilitation occurs even if the stereogram is flashed very briefly (Mayhew & Frisby, 1981), and is thus unlikely to be given simply by the improved control of vergence movements. Mayhew and Frisby (1981; also Frisby & Mayhew, 1980) have developed a rather different computational model, in which the process of stereo matching is seen as intimately linked with the elaboration of descriptions in the raw primal sketch. This contrasts with Marr, who views stereopsis as a more-or-less separate module of visual information processing. The constraints that Mayhew and Frisby make use of are rather different from Marr's. Perhaps the clearest difference lies in their inclusion of a *figural continuity* constraint. For each zero-crossing in one eye's image, candidate matches are established from the other eye's image. Such candidates must be within a certain disparity, and they must be zero-crossings of the same sign and similar orientation to the target. If there are several candidate matches, most can be eliminated by checking whether other zero-crossings in the near vicinity of the candidate bear the same figural relationship to it as those in the near vicinity of the target. Such a procedure successfully eliminates false matches from natural and random-dot stereo pairs.

There are numerous contemporary models which attempt to account for stereoscopic fusion (Marr, 1982, criticises most of them). Some are formulated in physical or mathematical terms (Julesz, 1971; Sperling, 1970) and some in computational terms (Marr & Poggio, 1976; Frisby & Mayhew, 1980). Many accounts assume that stereopsis is achieved prior to, or in parallel with the elaboration of the forms present in the image, i.e. that it is a relatively low-level process, operating as a separable module in Marr's theory, uninfluenced by higher-level processes.

However, it may be that factors involved in the process of stereopsis are more cognitive than many such models imply. First, we should note that while fusion is impossible between reversed contrast random-dot stereograms, it *is* possible between reversed contrast *line* stereograms, where black lines in one member of the stereogram correspond to white lines in the other. This suggests that there may be some interaction between local stereopsis mechanisms operating on low-level measurements of the image, and other mechanisms which operate on disparities between more global *contours*. Mayhew and Frisby's approach, in which stereopsis and grouping processes are interlinked, may provide a way to explain such phenomena. Second,

Harris and Gregory (1973) produced stereograms in which each eye was stimulated with disparate *illusory* contours (illustrated in Fig. 6.22). They found that for forward-going contours, three-dimensional illusory contours were observed across the gaps between the sectors. This observation suggests that in some situations stereopsis may be based on the *apparent* configurations presented to each eye rather than relying solely on the actual figural information present.

That higher level cognitive factors may over-ride local depth information is perhaps most strikingly demonstrated by Gregory's "hollow face" illusion (e.g. Gregory, 1973; see Fig. 6.8). If a hollow mask of a face is viewed from a distance of a few feet, the impression is of a normal face, with the nose nearer to the observer than the forehead. Only at very close range indeed does the stereoscopic information dominate over the cognitive interpretative processes. It appears that "top-down" processes may need to be invoked to account fully for the processes of global stereopsis.

This account of stereopsis has necessarily been superficial. Whole books have been devoted to the subject and the interested reader is advised to consult Julesz (1971), Gulick and Lawson (1976), and the relevant sections of Kaufman (1974) and Marr (1982) for further details.

One-eyed humans can be accurate at gauging distance (as you will see if you close one eye and try reaching for objects), and creatures with panoramic vision and little binocular overlap include birds which can take flight, navigate and land. Convergence, accommodation and stereopsis can work only over relatively short distances. There must therefore be sources of information other than these to tell animals about the distances of objects in their world. Given the "flat" retinal image, what can these sources be?

Pictorial Cues to Depth

As well as the physiological cues, there are the "pictorial" cues to depth, so-called because artists since the Renaissance have employed them to convey an impression of depth in their work. If certain features can give depth information on a canvas then perhaps those same features may be used by the brain in its interpretation of the "flat" retinal picture.

Many of these pictorial cues are simple consequences of the geometry of the retinal image. Consider for convenience the properties of images cast by objects on a plane perpendicular to the line of sight, the "frontal plane" (see Fig. 6.9). We can think of such an image as capturing the geometrical properties of retinal images, ignoring the curvature of the latter.

The size of an image cast by an object is small if the object is far away, as at C in Figure 6.9, and becomes larger as the object approaches the frontal plane, as at A in Figure 6.9. Thus the *relative size* of an image depends upon its distance. If we consider naturally occurring surfaces,

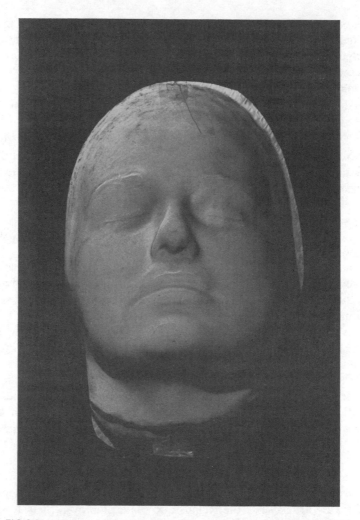

FIG.6.8. This is a picture of a hollow mask, illuminated from behind. In real life, as in this photograph, we see a normal face, with the tip of the nose nearer to us than the eyelids. Photograph by Sam Grainger.

receding away from the frontal plane and consisting of large numbers of stochastically regular texture elements, the image cast by such a receding plane will contain a *gradient* of image size. As we will see in the third part of this book, the notion of a gradient is central to some approaches to space perception, but for the moment we are treating it as a "cue" for the perception of distance.

Perspective is perhaps the best known pictorial cue to depth. The horizontal separation of images cast by the two sides of a pair of railway tracks is larger for the nearer portions of the tracks and smaller for the more distant portions. The image cast by parallel lines at the frontal plane converges as the lines recede horizontally from the observer.

Because our eyes are elevated above the ground which supports us and other objects, there are also differences in the *height* in the visual field of images cast by objects at different distances. The further away an object is from the observer the higher in the visual field its image will be cast. The "cues" of relative size, perspective and relative height all result from the geometry of the retinal image, and all three operate together whenever objects are viewed by the eye (see Fig.6.10).

Shadow is an important aspect of pictures (or images) which conveys an impression of solidity, and in Chapter 5 we described how animals may be

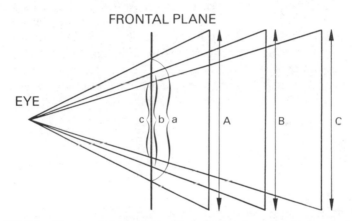

FIG.6.9. The size of the image cast by an object decreases with increase in distance.

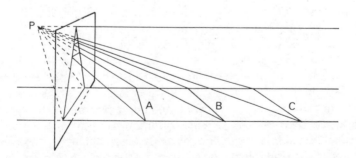

FIG.6.10. In this diagram, an observer at P looks at a set of square units on the ground (paving slabs perhaps). The image formed at the frontal plane illustrates how the "cues" of relative size, perspective, and relative height are all simple consequences of the geometry of image formation. Adapted from J. J. Gibson (1950a). Copyright © by Houghton Mifflin, Boston. Used by permission of the publishers.

countershaded to counteract this. In Fig. 6.11, the "humps" in one image become "dents" in the other, due to the different pattern of light and shadow created by inverting one frame to form the second. We seem to assume that light comes from above (from the sun or room lighting) when interpreting such shadow information.

Just as the images cast by objects are smaller when they are at a distance so they are also less clear, less bright and have slightly different spectral properties. This is because light is scattered and absorbed by particles in the atmosphere—and different wavelengths are scattered to different degrees (see Chapter 1). Figure 6.12 gives a powerful impression of depth because of the way in which the light reflected by the distant hills has been scattered—though there are also other cues, such as relative size, operating here.

Another cue which operates when viewing most natural scenes is that of *interposition* or overlay. Figure 6.13 is seen as circles, with one on top of another. This is not the only possible interpretation, we might see the drawing as representing adjacent shapes, one circular and the others with "bites" taken out of them. Usually however we interpret the irregular image as representing a "good" shape (cf. Gestalt principles discussed in Chapter 5) which is partially covered by another good shape.

Dynamic Cues

So far we have considered a static observer viewing an unchanging scene—an untypical situation. In addition to physiological cues to depth, and pictorial cues, modern cue theory also considers how movement of an observer, or of objects, can signal relative distance by *motion parallax*.

Consider Figure 6.14. Here we see an eye viewing two similar objects at different distances. As the eye moves, the image cast by object B travels further across the retina than that cast by object A. Conversely, if the eye were still, and objects A and B moved across the line of sight at constant and equal speed, the image cast by the nearer object would travel further across the retina than the image cast by the more distant one. Relative speed of motion of different portions of the retinal image could therefore signal relative depth. In Part III of this book we consider in great detail how information of this kind may inform an animal or person about the layout of the world and their own movements within it.

Thus while the retinal image contains many inherent ambiguities, various signs, cues or clues available in the total retinal picture are correlated with distances in the world and allow the "lost" third dimension to be recovered by the observer. At this point it should be noted that at least some aspects of depth perception appear to be innate rather than learned, even in humans, who are not independently mobile at birth. We will be considering some of this evidence in Chapter 10. For the moment we should simply point out

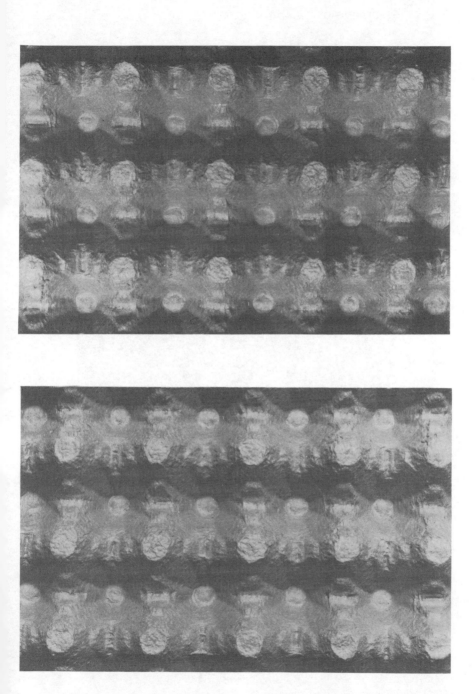

FIG.6.11.   The picture below was formed by inverting the one above. Humps in the top picture become dents in the bottom picture. Photograph by Sam Grainger.

143

FIG.6.12. The image of the near hills is brighter and clearer than the image of the distant ones, from which the light has been scattered by the atmosphere. Photograph by Mike Burton.

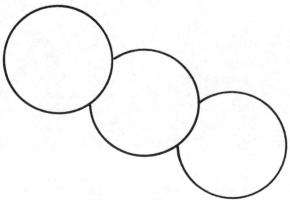

FIG.6.13. Interposition

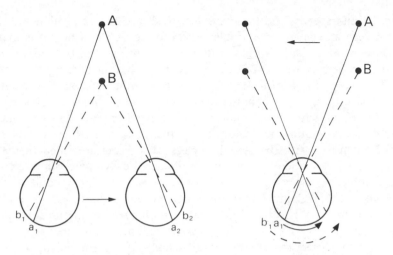

FIG.6.14.   Motion parallax. The observer looks at two objects (A and B) at different distances. If the observer moves (as in the left diagram), or the objects move at equal speed (as in the right diagram), the image of the nearer object B moves further across the retina ($b_1 - b_2$) than does the image of A ($a_1 - a_2$).

that it does not seem as though all the "cues" to depth need to be learned through associating visual information with the felt positions of objects.

In the context of our discussion of depth perception we have already mentioned one aspect of motion. We now move on to discuss further aspects of the perception of motion, again from the starting point of the retinal image.

OBSERVER MOVEMENT AND OBJECT MOTION

For the majority of this chapter we have treated the human observer as if he or she were stationary and viewing an unchanging world. The problem of understanding the visual processing of retinal images becomes vastly more complicated once one begins to contemplate how movement in the world or by the observer is encoded. Most animals—including ourselves—actively explore and sample their visual worlds with eye, head and body movements, and the motions of items in the world may signal events of interest or danger.

Eye Movements

The eyes themselves are never at rest. We can distinguish a number of different types of human eye movement, characterised by different sizes, latencies and speeds, and these are described in Chapter 1. While all these various eye movements are problematical for accounts of how it is that we perceive a stable visual world (since there is movement of the retinal image every time the eyes are moved), there is evidence that they are in fact essential for the perception of form. It is possible to examine perception without eye movements using the technique of *stabilised retinal images*. This can be achieved by attaching to the cornea of the eye a contact lens on which is mounted a miniature projector. Since the contact lens, and hence the projector, moves with the eye, the images of objects presented to the eye remain focused on identical retinal coordinates. Loss of perception of colour and contour occurs within seconds of stabilisation (Heckenmuller, 1965). Pritchard (1961) claimed that form perception is disrupted in a rather interesting manner. He presented observers with patterns, pictures and words and his subjects reported that they disappeared, and sometimes reappeared, in fragments, such that "meaningful" chunks were preserved. Thus the stimulus word BEER might be reported as PEER, BEE and BE at different times. While this again suggests a role for "top-down" processes, the effects may have been produced by occasional slippage of the lens system (Cornsweet, 1970), or may have resulted from reporting bias on the part of the observers. Nevertheless, the general conclusion from the stabilised image experiments is that movement of the image across the retina is *vital* for perception.

However, a consideration of eye movements alone immediately raises the problem of how it is that we know whether it is ourselves (eyes, head, body) or objects in the world moving, since movement of the image on the retina could be produced either by object movement or by movement of the observer.

Distinguishing Movement of the Eyes from Movement in the World

Consider a stationary eye viewing an isolated object as in Figure 6.15. As the object moves across the line of sight, the image it casts will move across the retina—it will be cast on different receptors as it travels. In this situation we correctly perceive ourselves as still and the object as moving. Now suppose we move the eye, but the object remains stationary. Again the image will move across the retina—but this time we will perceive the object at rest and ourselves as moving. Finally, consider what happens when the eye tracks a moving object. The image is cast on the same part of the retina, just as when neither the eye nor the object moves, but now movement *is* perceived.

It appears again that the information contained within the retinal image is ambiguous. In order to perceive correctly what is moving and what is at rest, the visual system as a whole must also take into account information

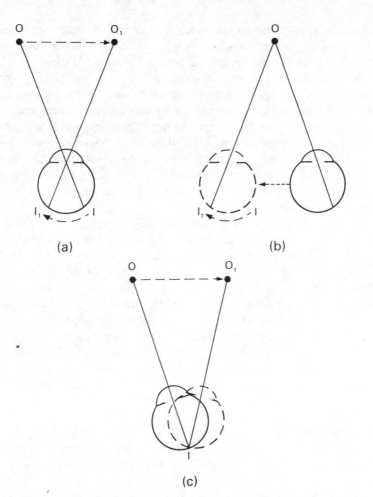

FIG.6.15. At (a), a stationary eye views a moving object O. As O moves to O_1, its image I moves across the retina to I_1. At (b) the same image movement $(I–I_1)$ is produced when the eye moves but the object remains stationary. At (c) the eye moves to track the movement of the object. O moves to O_1, but its image remains at the same place, I.

about the way the eyes and body are moving. Gregory (1972) has suggested that two systems must be involved in movement perception—the image-retina system and the eye–head system. Information from the eye–head system is used to disambiguate that from the image–retina system.

Account could be taken of the movement of eyes and body in one of two ways. One possibility is (Sherrington, 1906) an *inflow* theory in which afferent signals from the eye muscles are taken into account when movement in the retinal image is interpreted. Helmholtz (1866) proposed instead an *outflow* theory where it is efferent commands sent to the muscles (described by Helmholtz as an "effort of will") which are used in interpreting image movement. Early evidence seemed to favour Helmholtz's theory. If the eye is moved passively, by pressing on the side of the eyeball, the visual world appears to move. If signals from the muscles were being processed, such passive movement should be compensated for as easily as movement actively initiated by the observer. If the eye is immobilised by paralysing drugs or some mechanical wedge (Mach, 1914; Brindley & Merton, 1960), subjects report that the visual world appears to move when they attempt, unsuccessfully, to initiate eye movements. Here it appears that the commands to the muscles are being taken into account despite the fact that no actual change in the muscles results.

However, both these lines of evidence may be criticised. First, passive movement of the eye does not necessarily mimic normal changes in the muscles. Second, Stevens, Emerson, Gerstein, Kallos, Neufield, Nichols and Rosenquist (1976) report a more careful investigation of the effects of muscle paralysis. Following an attempted *saccade,* their subject reported a kind of displacement, or relocation of the visual world *without* movement. Stevens et al. suggest that a *spatial system* compares information from the retina with commands sent to the muscles, in the way suggested by Helmholtz, but that this system is responsible for maintaining a perceptually stable spatial world without being involved in motion perception. Two further systems were suggested by Stevens et al. to account for their effects; an *eye position system*, which uses afferent information from the eye muscles, and a *pattern system*, which analyses motion in the retinal mosaic.

Normally there will be a great deal of information from the background against which any object appears which can disambiguate the interpretation of image movement. Stevens et al. suggest that movement in part of the retinal mosaic is interpreted as movement of an object in the world, while movement of the whole mosaic is interpreted as an eye movement, without any need to involve efferent information at all. Small-scale motion of the entire array is interpreted as tremor, and leads to pattern processing. Large-scale motion is interpreted as saccadic, and leads to suppression of pattern processing. This illustrates how some apparent ambiguity in the retinal image may disappear when one considers the information available in the entire mosaic, rather than a restricted portion of it, a point to which we will return later in the book.

Integrating Information from Successive Fixations

Human observers and some animals typically sample their visual worlds with a series of discrete fixations, separated by saccades. No visible blur is apparent when our eyes dart from location to location. Indeed there is evidence that processing during a saccade is suppressed (Volkmann, 1976), and Stevens et al. (1976) suggest that suppression is triggered by large-scale movement of the entire retinal mosaic. Somehow we must be able to integrate these successive "snapshots" to produce our perception of a stable visual world.

The problem of integrating successive slightly different retinal images may be thought analogous to the problem of fusing the two retinally disparate images when stereopsis is achieved. In both cases the brain must discover which aspects of the retinal image *correspond* to the same objects and match them accordingly. We hope that the discussion of stereopsis above will have indicated that the correspondence problem is not trivial. It is no easier to solve when one considers integrating successive fixations.

If a view from one discrete sample of the visual world is to be matched with a second slightly different view obtained at a later point in time it is necessary to postulate some sort of *memory* to preserve the first view for comparison with the second. Information-processing psychologists have identified one such short-lived visual memory system which at first might seem a likely candidate to mediate the integration of successive glimpses. This short-lived visual memory system is known as *iconic memory* (named by Neisser, 1967). Its properties were first fully investigated by Sperling (1960).

Sperling conducted a series of experiments to investigate limits in the span of apprehension. If a human observer is presented very briefly with an array of, say, three rows each containing four letters, typically they can report only three or four of the total array of 12 letters. Observers state that they can "see" more letters than they can report. Sperling asked observers to report only a single row of such a display, by giving them a cue (high, medium or low-pitched tones for the top, middle and bottom rows respectively) *after* the offset of the display. If the cue followed the display immediately, then observers could report about three items from each four item row, suggesting that 75% of the letters were available for report immediately after presentation. As the delay between display offset and the presentation of the tone was increased so the number of items reported from any row declined, until at about 500 msec delay, with light pre- and post-exposure fields, there was no advantage to be gained by asking for partial report over full report.

Iconic memory therefore seems to preserve visual information from a briefly glimpsed scene for a period of 500 msec or more (depending on the pre- and post-field illumination levels). During this time iconic memory appears to decay passively. Information in iconic memory appears to be in an uninterpreted form, since only physical cues can be used to give a partial report advantage (Von Wright, 1968, 1970; Sperling, 1960).

Could this be the memory system which serves to integrate successive views as observers fixate different portions of a scene? Hochberg (1968) and Turvey (1977b) argue strongly that it could not, since iconic memory is tied to anatomical, specifically retinal, coordinates. Thus it can serve no useful integrative function, since we have just replaced the problem of comparing different retinal snapshots with that of comparing different iconic snapshots. It seems that a memory system at a more abstract level than the iconic would be needed to serve this integrative function.

There is good evidence from a number of studies that information from iconic memory may be coded into a rather longer-lasting short term visual memory. For example, Posner and Keele (1967) asked subjects to make same-different judgements of pairs of letters. The "same" pairs could be either physically identical (A A) or the same in name alone (A a). When both letters were presented simultaneously, physical matches (A A) were achieved more quickly than name matches (A a). The advantage of physical over name matches declined as the interval between the presentation of the two letters increased, until at an inter-stimulus interval of about 1.5 seconds the two types of judgement were made equally slowly. Posner and Keele suggested that the physical match advantage was obtained because the letters matched at the level of a physical code as well as a name code. This physical code faded over the 1.5 sec interval. Using non-verbal materials Phillips and Baddeley (1971) demonstrated that the physical code might be much longer lived than this, and Phillips (1974) describes some elegant experiments in which he directly compared the properties of iconic memory with those of the short-term visual store (STVS). Iconic memory may be masked by the presentation of a bright light or pattern immediately after the test stimulus, is tied to anatomical coordinates and is not affected by pattern complexity. STVS is not disrupted by masking, not tied to anatomical coordinates but is affected by pattern complexity. In STVS, less is retained from complex than from simple patterns. These observations suggest that STVS is a limited capacity short term store at a more "schematic" level than iconic memory.

Hochberg (1968) implicated such a memory system in the integration of successive views of objects, labelling it a *schematic map*. Hochberg conducted a number of studies in which he mimicked successive local sampling of the entire visual field by revealing partial glimpses of objects to observers, in a technique called *successive aperture viewing*. A line drawing of an object might be displayed section by section through a hole as shown in Figure 6.16. Observers were able to recover object structure from these glimpses, see spontaneous reversals in depth and correctly notice the "impossibility" of certain configurations. Hochberg argued that the partial views were integrated at the level of the schematic map just as they would be if the observer were exploring a complete object with a succession of fixations.

However, Hochberg's schematic map does not serve to combine successive glimpses in a passive, "data-driven" way. Instead, he suggests that one may need previously acquired knowledge about the properties of objects to integrate successive views of them: "It seems most plausible to me that they

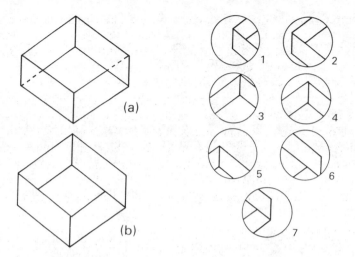

FIG.6.16.   (a) shows a figure which is ambiguous in depth and (b) shows an impossible figure. Observers notice ambiguity and impossibility if a figure is viewed piece by piece through an aperture, as illustrated in frames 1–7. Adapted from Hochberg (1968).

(schematic maps) are built up not only from the successive views of a given object or scene but from *previous experiences* as well (Hochberg, 1968, p. 325)." And elsewhere: "A schematic map is a matrix of space-time expectancies (or assumptions) (Hochberg, 1968, p. 324)."

Thus described, Hochberg's idea bears some similarity to Minsky's (1977) notion of "frame systems" (Turvey, 1977b). Minsky (1977) does not explicitly discuss the problem of integrating successive fixations made by the eyes alone, but addresses instead the broader problem of integrating successive views of an object or scene as the whole observer moves around or within it. He suggests that prior knowledge of an object such as a cube leads to the establishment of a coherent interlinked system of frames. Each frame corresponds to a symbolic description of one view of the cube. As the observer moves around a cube, different faces of it become visible and others are concealed from view. Minsky suggests that rather than recomputing the description of each viewpoint anew, the correct frames in the system would become available when information about an impending movement became available.

This kind of theory is strongly empiricist. Just as cue theory implies that people must learn to use indirect clues in order to perceive distances, Hochberg's or Minsky's theory implies that we must know about object properties in order to integrate successive views of them. As yet, however, no detailed theory of how such correspondences are achieved has been proposed.

Perceiving Object Motion

So far, we have considered some of the processes which might be involved when an observer perceives stable objects given a sequence of discrete glimpses of them. Let us now consider how movement can be perceived and object structure recovered when an object is in motion. We now assume that the observer is stationary.

Although the situation of a continuously moving object viewed by a static observer appears very different to that of an observer sampling a stationary world with a series of discrete fixations, some analyses of movement perception have essentially regarded one of the central problems as being the same, namely that of establishing correspondences between a sequence of distinct images. Thus Ullman (1979) states:

> The correspondence problem is that of identifying a portion of the changing visual array as representing a single object in motion or in change. The notion of a "correspondence" comes about when the problem is considered (as it is in much of this work) in the context of a sequence of images, such as the frames of a motion picture. The problem then becomes one of establishing a match between parts of one frame and their counterparts in a subsequent frame that represents the same object at a later time. (p.4)

Thus for at least some workers in the field of artificial intelligence an understanding of motion perception starts with working out how correspondences are established between "snapshots" of the changing retinal pattern captured at different moments.

The justification for analysing the perception of motion in this way is given partly because it is possible to perceive movement in the absence of continuous translation of the retinal image. This phenomenon of *apparent motion* was extensively investigated by the Gestalt psychologists, notably by Wertheimer (1912). If an observer is presented with a display in which two lines in different locations are alternately exposed, at certain interstimulus intervals (which depend on the spatial separation, luminance and duration of the lines) the observer reports seeing the first line move across to the position of the second, i.e. the observer sees not two lines alternately appearing in different locations, but one line which moves smoothly from place to place. Thus it appears that change in retinal position can be a sufficient condition for the perception of movement (though we have already noted that it is not a necessary condition, as when the eye tracks a moving target). Since apparent movement and real movement are phenomenally so similar, a strong case can be made for regarding the perception of real movement as the integration of a succession of discrete views.

Ullman's analysis of motion perception therefore starts with the correspondence problem in apparently moving displays. He argues that correspondences are established on the basis of matches between primitive *elements* of figures such as edges, lines and blobs, rather than between whole figures. That is, matches are built up between the kinds of descriptive units found in the raw primal sketch. (Note the similarity between this and the theories of Julesz (1971) and Marr and Poggio (1976, 1979), who establish matches between elements, rather than entire patterns, to achieve stereoscopic fusion.) Ullman presents a number of demonstrations to support his case. In one of these, observers were presented with a "broken wheel" display (see Fig. 6.17) in which every other spoke is incomplete. If the "wheel" is rotated by x degrees between successive frames, where x is greater than half the angle between the spokes of the wheel, the observer sees the wheel breaking into three distinct rings. The innermost and outermost rings rotate anti-clockwise while the middle ring appears to rotate clockwise. This would be expected if matches were established between line segments, but would not be expected if the entire figure were being matched from frame to frame. If figural matching were occurring one would expect to perceive clockwise rotation of the whole wheel.

Ullman provides an elegant computational account of how correspondence can be achieved by making use of a principle of "minimal mapping." Suppose that one frame of a film consists of elements A and B, and a second frame consists of elements A' and B', displaced relative to A and B. The correspondence problem is to establish whether A or B is to be matched with A'. Ullman achieves this by establishing an *affinity measure* for each possible pairing. The closer together in space, and the more similar in description are the two elements in a pair, the greater will be their affinity (based on the simple assumption that near, similar matches are more likely to belong together than more distant, dissimilar matches). To solve the

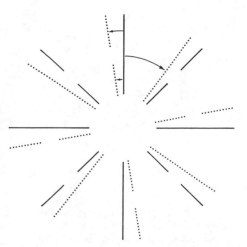

FIG.6.17. The solid lines show the first frame of Ullman's "broken wheel" configuration, and the dotted lines show the second frame when it is viewed in apparent motion. Under certain conditions the wheel is seen to split into three rings, with the outer and inner ones moving anticlockwise and the central one moving clockwise, as shown by the arrows. Adapted from Ullman (1979).

correspondence process for an entire display of several elements a solution is found which minimises matches with poor affinities and maximises those with strong affinities. A global solution is thus obtained through a set of local measures.

Once the correspondence problem has been solved (though Ullman's solution is not necessarily that used by the human visual system, see Marr, 1982), it is possible to recover the three dimensional structure which gives rise to a particular set of motions. The kinetic depth effect (Wallach & O'Connell, 1953) provides perhaps the best known example of the recovery of structure from motion. If a shadow is cast by a rotating wire shape onto a screen (see Fig. 6.18), a viewer can readily perceive the shape of the structure behind the screen from the dynamic shadow pattern. Ullman's own demonstration of the recovery of structure from motion involves the images of a pair of co-axial counter-rotating cylinders (see Fig. 6.19). When static, the display looks like a random collection of dots. Once it moves however the observer has a clear impression of one cylinder inside another, with the two rotating in opposite directions. Ullman has shown that it is possible to recover structure from motion if one assumes that the motion arises from *rigid* bodies. Given this rigidity assumption, his structure-from-motion theorem proves that structure can be recovered from three frames which each show four non-coplanar points in motion.

The interested reader is referred to Ullman's book (Ullman, 1979) for a fuller discussion of the processes of establishing correspondences and recovering structure from motion. Throughout his book Ullman, like Marr, attempts to provide a computational account which makes use of general constraints (e.g. assume motion is of a rigid object) rather than knowledge

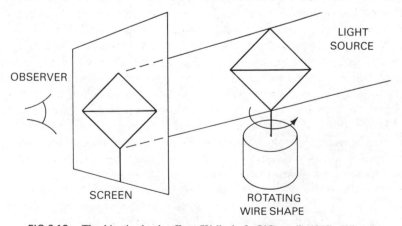

FIG.6.18. The kinetic depth effect (Wallach & O'Connell, 1953). When a wire shape is rotated behind a screen on which its shadow falls, observers see the dynamic shadow pattern as a solid shape in motion.

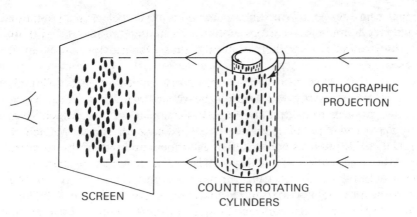

FIG.6.19.   Illustration of the principles behind Ullman's (1979) counter-rotating cylinders display. The screen shows the pattern of dots which would arise if the images of two, co-axial, glass cylinders covered with blobs were projected orthographically onto a screen. As the cylinders are rotated in opposite directions, the pattern of dots on the screen changes. Observers who view a film of the screen can recover the structure of the counter-rotating cylinders from the pattern of apparent motions present.

of specific objects. Thus Ullman's account has less of a "conceptually driven" flavour than, say, Hochberg's schematic maps or Minsky's frame system theory.

Motion Detectors Revisited

In Chapter 2 we described how directionally selective cells in the visual system of rabbits, cats and monkeys have been discovered which respond to motion within their receptive fields, indicating that motion might be considered a primitive property of the visual system to which detectors are directly attuned. In the preceding paragraphs however we have been considering a much less direct account of some aspects of motion perception.

These approaches may not be in opposition however, since it is likely that several systems may be involved in the perception of motion. Braddick (1980) for example has distinguished between two types of apparent motion— one which may depend on the stimulation of low-level "motion detectors," the other which seems to depend on higher-level, more cognitive factors.

Braddick has examined the factors which affect the perception of apparent motion in *random-dot kinematograms* (Julesz, 1971). A random-dot kinematogram (r.d.k.) is composed of successive frames of random texture, in each of which there is no perceptible form. However, the dots in a central portion of each pattern are displaced by a constant amount from one frame to the next, while the background texture remains the same. The dots comprising the central region are seen to move as a whole revealing a boundary between the moving figure and the stationary surround. (Random-dot kinematograms are therefore rather like random-dot stereograms—in the latter, the central region is segregated by virtue of a common spatial disparity that the central elements possess, while in the former, the region is segregated by a common translation over time.)

The parameters of apparent motion in r.d.k.s are not the same as those of apparent motion in line and figure stimuli as investigated by the Gestalt psychologists. In r.d.k.s the spatial displacement and inter-stimulus intervals must be much smaller than those which will produce apparent motion between two lines. For example, the inter-stimulus interval must be less than 100 msec for a 100 msec exposure of each r.d.k. frame (Braddick, 1973), but may be up to 300 msec for line stimuli (Neuhaus, 1930). Apparent motion is not seen in an r.d.k. if successive stimuli are presented to different eyes, though this is possible with line displays. Apparent motion in r.d.k.s is abolished if the inter-stimulus interval is bright, whereas in line displays it can be seen with dark or bright inter-stimulus intervals.

In classic line or configurational displays a number of interesting phenomena can be obtained which seem to demand a higher-level, more cognitive interpretation. For example, apparent motion can be seen between two different shapes, say a circle and a square, with the shape apparently changing as the form "moves" from one location to the other. Kolers (1963) showed that if the path of an apparently moving line was impeded by a third figure, the line would appear to move in depth to avoid the "obstacle." Finally, in the Ternus display (Ternus, 1926) illustrated in Figure 6.20, the entire configuration of elements is seen to move from place to place, even though the central element actually remains in the same location from frame to frame. This group movement occurs only if the inter-stimulus interval is greater than 40 msec (Pantle & Picciano, 1976). (While this last example might seem to counter Ullman's claim that correspondences are established

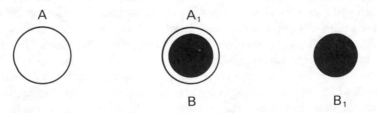

FIG.6.20.   A Ternus display. A and A_1 are the positions of two dots in the first frame of an apparent motion display. B and B_1 are the positions of dots in the second frame. Under certain conditions, observers see the entire configuration A–A_1 shift sideways to B–B_1. (N.B. The form of the dots from one frame to the next is identical. Open and filled circles have been used here to distinguish one frame from the next.)

between primitive elements rather than entire forms, his analysis is in fact able to account for "coherent" perception of the Ternus display [Ullman, 1979] .)

Therefore Braddick (1980) concludes that apparent motion in r.d.k.s is:

> a low-level "short-range" process (that) may tentatively be identified with the response of directionally sensitive neurons in the visual pathway to discontinuous stimulation. The more interpretative phenomena of apparent motion may then be associated with the higher-level process that determines the criterion of smooth perceived motion. (Braddick, 1980, p. 140)

Braddick here suggests that it is only the short-range processes of apparent motion that may be a consequence of the firing of directionally selective neurons (see Chapter 2). Such neurons may underlie our ability to detect discontinuities in the direction of motions present in a dynamic display. Discontinuities in motion directions may themselves reflect discontinuities in the surfaces being viewed, and hence could give important information to aid the segmentation of a scene. (See Marr (1982), who describes an algorithm by Batali which recovers discontinuities in the directions of motion present between successive frames of randomly textured and natural images.) Short-range processes of this kind may be quite distinct from the more sophisticated, "higher-level" analysis of correspondences and structure from motion, which we have been considering in this chapter.

It is in fact quite sensible that many different systems should seem to be involved in the perception of real and apparent motion. Different kinds of analysis are required for different types of moving stimulus. In the periphery of the visual field motion serves an orienting function. A flashing or moving light will cause human observers to turn their eyes and/or heads automatically to fixate the object. Such orienting functions may be mediated in part by the superior colliculus (see Chapter 2, p.52). Once fixated, a moving object may need to be recognised and tracked, which will involve a number of different, presumably cortical, systems. To a large extent different contemporary theorists are attempting to explain different aspects of the perception of moving stimuli. One further aspect of motion perception which has not as yet been discussed is the perception of relative motion in complex displays. This will be covered later in Chapter 13.

To summarise this chapter so far, we have seen how binocular disparity, along with other information (or "cues") in retinal images may allow us to recover the "lost" third dimension. We have discussed how humans sample their worlds with a variety of eye movements, and considered how an observer might disambiguate retinal image information about whether they, or objects in the world, are moving. Because observers actively sample their visual worlds, there is a need to integrate successive fixations, and information-processing psychologists have proposed some sort of memory system to accomplish this. Turning to the perception of object motions, we discussed how the correspondence problem has been seen as a central issue in some treatments of the perception of real and apparent motion (Ullman, 1979). However it appears that many systems may be involved in different aspects of the perception of motion.

MARR'S THEORY OF THE 2½D SKETCH

Many of the issues that we have introduced in our discussion of the perception of depth and movement have been incorporated within a single theoretical treatment by Marr (1982). Marr sees the goal of early visual processing as the production of a description of the visible surfaces of the environment, so that their dispositions and layouts are described with respect to the viewer. This description he terms the 2½D sketch, and it is built up from several different sources. The contour, texture and shading information available from the full primal sketch, stereopsis, and the analysis of motions present, all contribute to the 2½D sketch, which acts as a buffer store in which partial solutions can be stored as processing proceeds. The label "2½D" derives from the assumption that the sketch captures a great deal about the relative depths and surface orientations, and local changes and discontinuities in these, but that some aspects are represented more accurately than others.

> Very locally we can easily say from motion or stereopsis information whether one point is in front of another. But if we try to compare the distances to two surfaces that lie in different parts of the visual field, we do very poorly and can do this much less accurately than we can compare their surface orientations. (Marr, 1982, p. 282)

For these and other reasons Marr concludes that the 2½D sketch represents surface orientation much more accurately than depth (see Fig. 6.21). Only local changes in depth may be represented to any degree of accuracy.

Discontinuities in depth are signalled primarily by stereopsis mechanisms and by the presence of occlusion. Occlusion may be specified by the presence of occluding contours in the primal sketch and by discontinuities in the pattern of motions present. Information about surface orientation is given by stereopsis, by surface and textural contours, and by an analysis of structure from motion.

Once these properties are obtained, Marr sees the representation in the 2½D sketch as comprised of a set of vector-like primitives, which may be depicted as a set of "needles" (see Fig. 6.21). The length of each needle

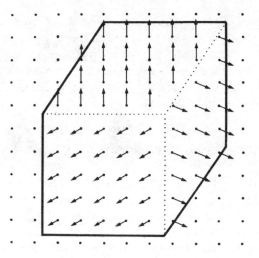

FIG.6.21. The 2½D sketch of a cube. The surfaces of the cube are represented by a set of vector primitives, like needles. The length of each needle represents the degree of tilt of the surface, and the orientation of the needle represents the direction in which the surface slants. From D. Marr (1982). Copyright © 1982 by W.H. Freeman & Company. Used by permission.

describes the degree of tilt of that part of the surface, and the orientation of each needle describes the direction in which the surface slants. In addition, the distance from the viewer to each point on the surface could be represented very roughly by a third, scalar quantity (which is not shown in Fig. 6.21).

Where there is insufficient information present from the early visual processing modules to produce a full description in the 2½D sketch, various *interpolation procedures* may be invoked. For example a uniform area when viewed by the two eyes contains no disparities. The depth of that part of the viewed surface must be obtained by interpolation from regions where contrasts are present. Marr suggests that "illusory" or "cognitive" contours (see Fig. 6.22) may be the results of some kinds of interpolation processes.

Earlier in this chapter we mentioned how Turvey (1977b) and Hochberg (1968) discussed the kind of short-term visual memory system that would be necessary for the integration of successive glimpses of the world gained through eye movements. Could the 2½D sketch serve this function? Probably not, since Marr argues that this must be based on a *retinocentric* frame.

> ... if one used a frame that had already allowed for eye movements, it would have to have foveal resolution everywhere. Such luxurious memory capacity would be wasteful, unnecessary, and in violation of our own experience as perceivers, because if things were really like this, we should be able to build up a perceptual impression of the world that was everywhere as detailed as it is in the centre of gaze. (Marr 1982, p. 284).

FIG.6.22. "Cognitive" or "illusory" contours. An apparent boundary is seen where the edge of the large white triangle would lie, if such a triangle were actually present.

If anything, the 2½D sketch shares more in common with iconic than with schematic memory, but any simple equation of Marr's 2½D sketch with the temporary buffer stores proposed by other information-processing theorists is probably unwise at present.

A Note on Modularity

The 2½D sketch serves the dual function of providing information about the layout of surfaces and, in so doing, implicitly solving the "segmentation" problem by making explicit the discontinuities between different surfaces and objects. Thus while most treatments of visual perception would regard it as quite legitimate to have separate chapters on "grouping," "depth" and "movement", for Marr, such divisions would be misleading. Although Marr views the organisation of the visual system as inherently *modular*, so that stereopsis, structure from motion, shape from shading and so on, may all be studied in relative isolation, his modules do not map comfortably onto those offered in traditional or other A.I. accounts of visual perception. perception.

Marr sees the 2½D sketch as the end-product of *early* visual processing. While the 2½D sketch remains to be implemented in a working computer program, the suggestion is that it can be established largely without recourse to downward-flowing information. Recall the image of a plant (Chapter 5) which could not be fully "solved" at the level of the primal sketch without knowledge that two separate structures were present. This knowledge would be available at the level of the 2½D sketch because of the discontinuities in depth at these "hidden" boundaries revealed by stereopsis and motion parallax. Thus when we start from the real input to human vision—which is binocular and dynamic—there are few ambiguities that cannot be resolved through a full consideration of the products of a number of early visual processing "modules." In Marr's theory, unlike many other contemporary ones, we do not need to know or hypothesise what we are looking at in order to describe at least some aspects of its shape fully. However, to describe the scene being viewed appropriately within a viewer-centred frame is still only an early stage in perception. There must be other processes which allow us to categorise the image of a plant as being that of a "plant," and a "rubber-plant" at that. It is to such processes of recognition that we turn next.

7

Object Recognition

An essential part of the behaviour of animals and people is their ability to *recognise* objects, animals and people which are important to their survival. People are able to recognise large numbers of other people, the letters of the alphabet, familiar buildings, and so on. Animals may need to recognise landmarks, suitable prey, potential mates or predators and to behave in the way appropriate to each category.

If we assume that the information available to a person or animal is a static two-dimensional image on the retina, a problem immediately arises in explaining visual recognition. Take the example of a person recognising letters of the alphabet; the problem is that an infinite number of possible retinal images can correspond to a particular letter, depending upon how the letter is written, how large it is, the angle at which it is seen and so on (Fig. 7.1). Yet somehow we recognise all these patterns of light as corresponding to the same letter.

Or consider the problem of recognising a friend's face; the image of their face on the retina will depend upon the lighting conditions and their distance, angle and facial expression. Again, all these images are classified together, even though some (such as a full-face and a profile view) are quite dissimilar and more like the same views of different faces than they are like each other (Fig. 7.2). Some animals will face the same problem; a young chick or duckling, for example, must remain close to its mother in order to obtain warmth and protection from predators. If it is separated from its mother it runs towards her, and to do this it must be able to recognise her from any angle and in any posture. Again, an indefinite number of different retinal images result in the same behaviour.

FIG.7.1.   All these different shapes are classified as the letter A.

These are all illustrations of the problem of *stimulus equivalence*; if the stimulus controlling behaviour is a pattern of light, or image, on the retina, then an infinite number of images are equivalent in their effects, and different from other sets of images. Obviously, all the images corresponding to a particular thing, whether letter of the alphabet, face or bird, must have something in common, but the problem is to find just what this is and how this thing in common is detected. It is this problem which we will be considering in this chapter.

SIMPLE MECHANISMS OF RECOGNITION

Many animals, particularly simpler ones such as insects and fish, solve the stimulus equivalence problem by detecting something relatively simple which all images corresponding to a particular object have in common. A good example is the three-spined stickleback. Males of this species build nests and defend them against other males by performing threat displays. A stickleback must therefore be able to recognise rival males and discriminate them from other fish and from objects drifting by. The retinal images of rival males will obviously vary greatly, depending upon the other fish's distance, angle and posture, and it seems that classifying these images separately from those of other fish will need elaborate criteria.

In fact, as Tinbergen (1951) discovered, the stickleback manages successfully with quite simple mechanisms of recognition. Tinbergen observed the strength of sticklebacks' aggressive responses to a range of models and found that they would readily attack a crude model of another fish, *provided* it had the red belly colour characteristic of male sticklebacks. Indeed, a crude model with a red belly elicited more attack than an accurate one without (Fig. 7.3).

A feature of an object or animal—such as the red belly of a stickleback— which elicits a response from an animal, is called a *key* or *sign stimulus*, and it greatly simplifies the problem of recognition. As long as red objects and

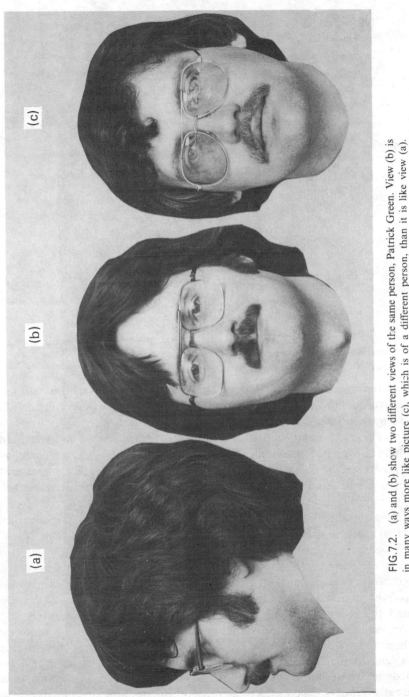

FIG.7.2. (a) and (b) show two different views of the same person, Patrick Green. View (b) is in many ways more like picture (c), which is of a different person, than it is like view (a). Photographs by Sam Grainger.

165

INEFFECTIVE
MODEL

EFFECTIVE
MODEL

RED

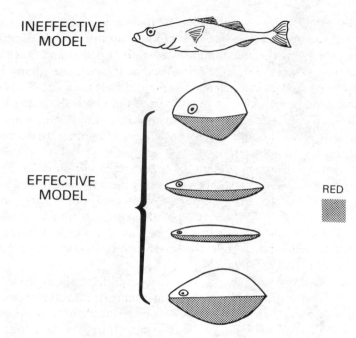

FIG.7.3. An accurate model of a stickleback without a red belly (top), is
less effective as a stimulus to elicit aggression from a male stickleback than
any of the cruder models below. Adapted from Tinbergen (1951).

fish with red markings are rare in the stickleback's environment, it can use
the key stimulus to recognise rivals and does not need to use information
about another fish's detailed structure and colouration.

The stickleback's recognition of a rival male does depend on more than
just the presence of a patch of red of a certain size in the retinal image, as
Tinbergen also found that a model with a red patch on its back was attacked
less than one with an identical red patch on its belly, and that a model in
the "head-down" posture of an aggressive fish was attacked more than one
in a horizontal posture. Even so, the presence of this distinctive feature
allows a much simpler means of recognition to be effective than would
otherwise be the case.

Many other examples are known of key stimuli being important in the
recognition by animals of other members of their species, and we will
mention two other examples from Tinbergen's work. One is the recognition
of female grayling butterflies by males. Tinbergen found that males would
fly towards crude paper models moving overhead and that their response
was not affected by the colour or shape of the model. The key stimulus
turned out to be the pattern of movement of the model; males would fly
towards it if it imitated the flickering and up-and-down movements of a
butterfly, but not if it moved in a smooth way. Although butterflies do waste

time chasing other males, or butterflies of the wrong species, this simple mechanism of recognition does prevent responses to other kinds of insect.

Another example is the recognition by nestling thrushes and blackbirds of their parents. When the parents bring food to the nest, the young birds turn towards them and gape, opening their mouths wide to be fed. Tinbergen found that gaping is elicited by a moving dark silhouette above the birds' eye level, of any shape and size. Presumably this simple mechanism of recognition is adequate because the chances of anything other than a parent resembling the key stimulus are low.

Key stimuli may also be important in the recognition of prey. Toads feed by snapping at insects flying past them, capturing them with their long sticky tongues. Ewert (1974) found that they recognise insects by fairly simple criteria, as they will snap at small cardboard squares, as long as these are moving. Although toads are selective for the size and speed of movement of cardboard squares, they are clearly not able to recognise insects on the basis of details of their appearance.

The toad's category of "prey" is not perfect, particularly as it excludes motionless insects. In the toad's normal environment, however, this is not a problem, as the flies and other insects on which it feeds must move about if they are to find food and mates. The toad can exploit this fact and use a simple rule for recognition, as long as there are relatively few inedible objects around which resemble insects in their size and pattern of movement.

In all these cases, relatively simple recognition mechanisms work effectively. For other animals, they often cannot, and one such situation is where animals must recognise other members of their species individually, for example where there is a dominance hierarchy in a group. Any simple colour markings or other structures which could act as key stimuli will be common to all individuals and so recognition must be on the basis of more subtle details.

Birds such as chickens are particularly interesting because they show a transition from the use of simple rules to recognise other individuals early in life to the use of more complex ones. The ability of a chick to recognise its mother from any angle and in any posture takes some days to develop, through a process of learning called *imprinting* (Bateson, 1966). When they first hatch, chicks have a strong following response to almost any conspicuous moving object. They do show some selectivity, for example following a blue or red object more readily than a green or a yellow one (Kovach, 1971), but the range of things they will follow is still wide; for example, young chicks will run for long periods in a running wheel towards a bright rotating light (Bateson & Jaeckel, 1974). As imprinting occurs, the chick's following response becomes more selective, and narrows down to familiar objects. In the chick's natural environment, it would come to approach only its mother and to avoid all other moving objects, but chicks will also imprint upon any other object, such as a plastic bucket or wellington boot, to which they happen to be exposed.

Adult chickens are able to discriminate visually between individual other chickens, as Ryan (1982) has shown using an operant conditioning procedure. He found that chickens could discriminate slides of one bird in a variety of poses from slides of other birds and could transfer this discrimination to novel sets of slides. Similarly, Rosenfeld and Van Hoesen (1979) have shown that monkeys can easily learn to discriminate slides of one monkey's face seen from many angles from slides of other monkeys' faces.

Thus for some animals the problem of recognising significant objects may be reduced to the problem of detecting localised key stimuli or features which in the natural world are unambiguous cues to appropriate action. Such local features may be quite simple—it is easy to see how a "redness" detector might function in the stickleback, and not too difficult to conjecture how this might be coupled with a rather crude configurational analysis to explain observed preferences for the location of the red patch and the posture of the model. However such mechanisms are also relatively inflexible. The toad surrounded by dead flies would starve, the chick who follows the first mobile object it sees may become imprinted on an ethologist, and the male stickleback may waste its time threatening a bus passing the laboratory window.

Other animals, especially primates, have more flexibility in their perception and action and are able to recognise and discriminate on the basis of more complex and subtle criteria. In these cases, as in human perception, the problem of how stimulus equivalence is achieved is a difficult one, as we will see in the remainder of this chapter.

MORE COMPLEX RECOGNITION PROCESSES

We may speculate that at least some behaviour in humans may be under the control of "key" stimuli. For example, some workers (e.g. Fantz, 1961) have claimed, controversially (see Ellis, 1975, for a critique), that human infants show innate preferences for face-like patterns. On the whole however it is through a process of learning that we come to classify certain configurations as equivalent and distinct from others. The human infant learns to recognise the faces of its parents irrespective of angle, expression or lighting. A mother will still be "mummy" to her child after she has curled her hair, and a father will still be "daddy" if he hasn't shaved for a few days. Later, the child will learn to distinguish teachers and friends from strangers, family pets from strays, and the long process of formal education enables most to decipher the intricacies of written language. What kinds of internal representations allow for the recognition of complex configurations, and what kinds of processes operate on the retinal image to allow access to these internal representations? These have been the questions posed in the study of human pattern and object recognition.

Much early work on human pattern recognition focused on the problem of recognising alphanumeric patterns. There is good reason for such work, since researchers in computer science have had the applied aim of making computers able to recognise such patterns so that they might, for example, achieve automatic sorting of letters with hand-written postal codes. The emphasis on alphanumerics was unfortunate in other ways, since the problem of stimulus equivalence is rather different for alphanumerics than for objects. Letters must be recognised despite changes in their form, but they are only two-dimensional patterns, so that other problems in object recognition are minimised. Nevertheless the area of alphanumeric recognition is worth discussing briefly since it serves to introduce, and to dismiss, certain theoretical approaches to the broader area of object recognition.

Template Matching

The simplest account that we could offer of how we recognise alphanumeric characters would be that of *template matching*. For each letter or numeral known by the perceiver there would be a template stored in long-term memory. Incoming patterns would be matched against the set of templates, and if there were sufficient overlap between a novel pattern and a template then the pattern would be categorised as belonging to the class captured by that template. Within such a framework, slight changes in the size or angle of patterns could be taken care of by an initial process of standardisation and normalisation. For example all patterns could be rotated so that their major axes (as discovered by other processing operations) were aligned vertically, with the height of the major axis scaled to unity (see Fig. 7.4). In addition, some pre-processing or "cleaning up" of the image would be necessary. Both humans and other animals (Sutherland, 1973) cope very well with broken or wobbly lines in the patterns they recognise.

Such a template-matching scheme could work provided that such normalising procedures were sufficient to render the resulting patterns

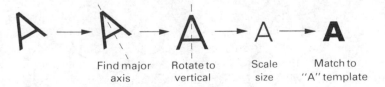

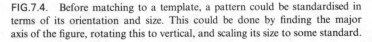

FIG.7.4. Before matching to a template, a pattern could be standardised in terms of its orientation and size. This could be done by finding the major axis of the figure, rotating this to vertical, and scaling its size to some standard.

unambiguous. Unfortunately this is almost impossible to achieve, even in the simple world of alphanumerics. An "R" could match an "A" template better than its own, and vice versa (see Fig. 7.5). The bar which distinguishes a "Q" from an "O" may be located in a variety of places (see Fig. 7.6). At the very least we would need more than one template for each letter and numeral, and it becomes difficult to see how children could learn letters and numbers in such a scheme.

Template-matching schemes also fail to account for the facts of animal discrimination. Sutherland and Williams (1969) showed that rats trained to discriminate an irregular from a regular chequerboard pattern readily transferred this learning to new examples of random and regular patterns (see Fig. 7.7). As Sutherland (1973) points out, the configuration in Figure 7.7d should match better with a "template" for pattern 7.7a than for b, but it is treated by the rats as though it were more like b than a. It is also difficult to see how a template-matching model could possibly be applied to the more general area of object recognition, where the problem of stimulus equivalence is magnified. However, a template-matching process can operate successfully if the form of the characters it must recognise can be constrained. Thus the computer which recognises account numbers on the bottom of cheques matches these to stored templates. The character set has been

FIG.7.5. The bold figures show possible templates for an A (left) and an R (right). The dashed figures show how an R (left) and an A (right) could match another letter's template better than their own.

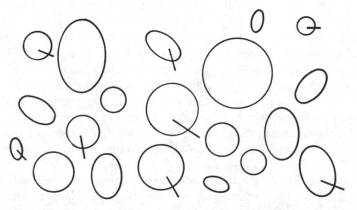

FIG.7.6. What distinguishes the Q's from the O's? Not the precise form of the circle, nor the precise location or orientation of the bar.

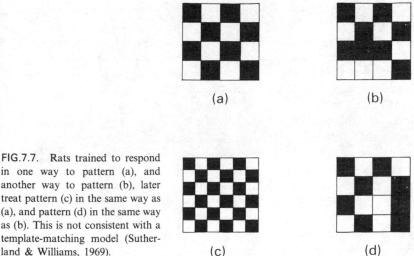

(a)   (b)

FIG.7.7. Rats trained to respond in one way to pattern (a), and another way to pattern (b), later treat pattern (c) in the same way as (a), and pattern (d) in the same way as (b). This is not consistent with a template-matching model (Sutherland & Williams, 1969).

(c)   (d)

constrained however, so that the numerals have constant form, and in addition are made as dissimilar to one another as possible to avoid any chance of confusion. The characters which humans recognise are not constrained in this way.

Feature Analysis

When we consider how it is that we know the difference between an A and an R, or a Q and an O, it seems that there are certain critical *features* which distinguish one from another. The bar which cuts the circular body of a Q is essential to distinguish it from an O, whereas the precise form of the circle is less crucial. Perhaps a model in which combinations of features were detected would be more successful than one based on templates.

Feature analysis models of recognition were popular with psychologists and computer scientists during the 1960s while physiologists such as Hubel and Wiesel were discovering "feature detectors" in the visual cortex of cats and monkeys (see Chapter 3). Perhaps the most influential model for psychology was Selfridge's (1959) Pandemonium system, originally devised as a computer program to recognise Morse Code signals, but popularised as a model of alphanumeric recognition by Neisser (1967), and Lindsay and Norman (1972). An illustration of a Pandemonium system is shown in Figure 7.8.

The system consists of a number of different classes of "demon." The most important of these for our purposes are the *feature demons* and the *cognitive demons*. Feature demons respond selectively when particular local configurations (right angles, vertical lines etc.) are presented. The cognitive

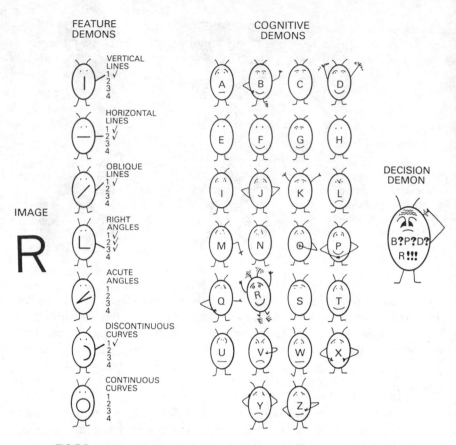

FIG.7.8. A Pandemonium system for classifying letters. Each of the feature demons responds selectively to a different feature in the image, and signals the number of features present to the cognitive demons. Each of the cognitive demons represents a different letter, and "shrieks" louder the more of its features are present. (Extra features inhibit the responses of cognitive demons.) The decision demon selects the letter which is being shouted the loudest. Liberally adapted from Selfridge (1959) and Lindsay & Norman (1972).

demons, which represent particular letters, look for particular combinations of features from the feature demons. Thus the cognitive demon representing the letter H might look for two vertical and one horizontal line, plus four right angles. The more of their features are present, the louder will the cognitive demons "shout" to the highest level, the decision demon, who selects the letter corresponding to that represented by the cognitive demon who is shouting the loudest. Thus in this system individual characters are represented as sets of critical features, and the processing of any image proceeds in a hierarchical fashion through levels of increasing abstraction. It is this kind of model which Barlow (1972) and others used to interpret the properties of simple cells in the visual cortex (see Chapter 3). Simple cells were thought to be acting as the feature demons in the Pandemonium system, passing information on to cells which responded to increasingly abstract properties. The notion of a "Grandmother cell" or "yellow Volkswagen detector" arose in this context.

A Pandemonium system can learn to give different weights to different features according to how well these features discriminate between different patterns, and can in principle accommodate certain kinds of contextual effect. These are a ubiquitous feature of human pattern recognition and Figure 7.9 shows one example of how context affects the recognition of letters. The same shape can be seen as H or as A depending on the surrounding letters. Within a Pandemonium system we might allow higher level demons to "arouse" those at lower levels which correspond to particularly likely patterns, so that they would need less sensory evidence to make them shout sufficiently loudly to win over the decision demon (cf. the integration of contextual and physical feature information in a variety of models of word recognition, e.g. Morton, 1969).

However, as a general model for human pattern and object recognition the Pandemonium system is unsatisfactory. Ultimately it rests on a description of patterns in terms of a set of features, which are themselves like mini-templates. One of the reasons that Pandemonium was so popular was that it seemed consistent with the neurophysiology of the visual cortex; but we have already seen that the simple cells cannot be thought of as "feature detectors" (see Chapter 3). While this may not matter for a purely psychological or computational theory of recognition, there are other problems. Feature-list descriptions fail to capture overall structural relations which are captured, albeit too rigidly, by more global templates. Thus the Pandemonium system depicted in Figure 7.8 would confuse an F with⊤and a T with⊥, confusions that humans typically do not make. In addition, the Pandemonium system, in classifying patterns, discards all information which distinguishes different instances of the same pattern. The output of the decision demon would be the same irrespective of the particular version of the letter A shown. We need a way of talking about recognition which allows us to describe the differences between patterns as well as being able to classify together those which are instances of the same type. We need to preserve such differences so that other kinds of classifications can be made. We recognise someone's hand-writing, for example, by the particular shapes of the letters they produce. Thus we need a representational format which captures aspects of structure which are essential for the classification of an

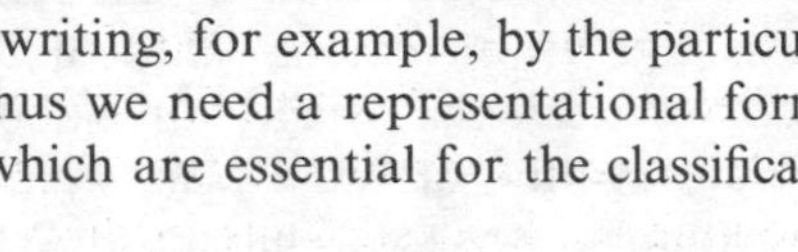

FIG.7.9. The same shape may be seen as an H in one context and an A in another (from a demonstration by Selfridge).

TAE CAT

item but preserves at some other level structural differences between different instances of the same class.

Structural Descriptions

A general and flexible representational format for human pattern and object recognition is provided by the language of structural descriptions. Structural descriptions do not constitute a theory of how recognition is achieved, they simply provide the right type of representation with which to construct such a theory. A structural description consists of a set of propositions (which are symbolic, but not linguistic, though we describe them in words), about a particular configuration. Such propositions describe the nature of the components of a configuration and make explicit the structural arrangements of these parts. Thus a structural description of a letter T might look like Figure 7.10a.

Using the language of structural descriptions it is possible to construct "models" for particular concepts and categories against which any incoming instance can be matched. Such models capture obligatory features of the structure but may be less particular about other details. Thus the "model" for a letter T might look like Figure 7.10b. It is essential that a horizontal line is supported by a vertical line, and that this support occurs about half way along the horizontal line. But the lengths of the two lines are less important. Figure 7.10c shows examples that would be classified as letter Ts by this model, and Figure 7.10d shows examples that would fail.

Structural descriptions are also easier to apply to object recognition than "templates" or "feature" representations. A picture of an object (or a "retinal image" of an object) can be described by a series of structural descriptions at increasing levels of abstraction from the original intensity distribution. There are thus a number of possible "domains" of description (Sutherland, 1973).

Take for example the two drawings shown in Fig. 7.11. These drawings can be described within a number of distinct domains, which can broadly be grouped together as being either "two-dimensional" or "three-dimensional." The 2D descriptions describe the picture or image present, and this image can be described in increasingly abstract or global terms. It may be described as a collection of points of different brightnesses, as a collection of lines, or as a group of regions. These different levels of description are reminiscent of the different stages of elaboration of the primal sketch, through the aggregation of small edge segments up to larger contours or aggregated texture regions (see Chapter 5). Whatever the level of description in the 2D domain, whether points, lines or regions, the representations established for these two pictures would look very different. It is within the domain of 3D description that the equivalence of these two pictures can be

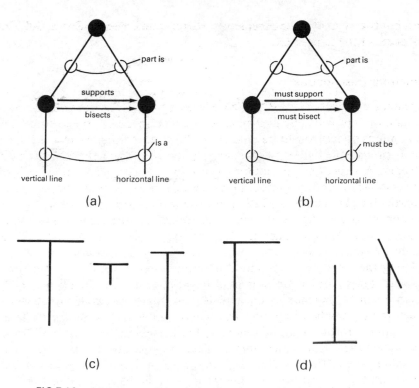

(a)   (b)

(c)   (d)

FIG,7,10   (a) A structural description for a letter T. The description indicates
that there are two parts to the letter. One part is a vertical line, the other a
horizontal line. The vertical line supports and bisects the horizontal line. (b)
A model for a letter T. This is like the description at (a), but the essential
aspects of the description are specified. For something to be a T, a vertical
line must support, and must bisect, a horizontal line, but the relative lengths
are not important. (c) Shapes which would be classified as Ts by the model.
(d) Shapes which would fail to be classified as Ts.

established. Three-dimensional descriptions are couched in terms of surfaces,
bodies and objects. The two pictures shown in Figure 7.11 are equivalent
only at the level of an object description which is independent of the vantage
point.

The description above again illustrates the thrust of Marr's term "2½D"
sketch for the representation of *surfaces,* from the point of view of the
observer. Marr's 2½D sketch falls somewhere in between the 2D and 3D
groups of descriptions in Sutherland's scheme.

Thus two different projections of the same object will have different
structural descriptions in the picture domain, but will be equivalent in the
object domain (see Fig. 7.11). Provided that structural descriptions are
established at all these possible levels, we can capture both the equivalences
between different views of the same object and their differences. Our problem

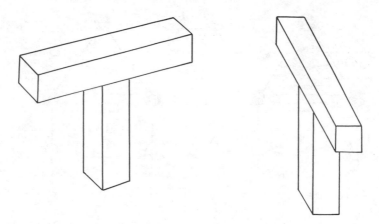

FIG.7.11. These two forms are quite different in terms of their two-dimensional description. They are equivalent only in the three-dimensional domain.

now is to consider how structural descriptions at the 3D level can be constructed, stored and matched, and to examine the extent to which the construction of 3D representations can proceed in a "bottom-up" fashion.

Winston (1973) has illustrated the use of structural descriptions in object recognition to show how object concepts might be learned by giving examples. His program learns to recognise simple toy block structures such as those illustrated in Figure 7.12 which contains examples of an "arch," a "pedestal" and a "house."

The computer program is presented with examples of each, as well as "near-misses," in order to build up models for each concept. The procedure for a pedestal might go as follows. First, the program would be presented with an example of a pedestal (Fig. 7.13a) to which it would assign the structural description shown in Figure 7.14a. Thus a pedestal is described as having two parts, with one part being a "brick" and the other part being a "board," with the former supporting the latter. Then the program would be presented with the sequence of "near misses" shown in Figure 7.13b–d. For Figure 7.13b, the description would again show two parts, with one a brick and the other a board, but the relationship between these is now different. The board is beside the brick, and the program is told that this is *not* a pedestal. By comparing this description of the near miss with that of the structure labelled "pedestal" the program can construct a model for a pedestal in which the support relation is made obligatory. For something to be a pedestal one part *must be* supported by the other. The other examples in the training sequence (Fig. 7.13) further constrain the eventual model for a pedestal (Fig. 7.14b). The eventual model shows that for something to be a pedestal, an upright brick must support a lying board.

House   Pedestal   Arch

FIG.7.12. Three of the toy block structures learned by Winston's program. Adapted from Winston (1973) with his permission.

(a) Pedestal   (b) Near miss

(c) Near miss   (d) Near miss

FIG.7.13. A pedestal training sequence. Adapted from Winston (1973) with his permission.

(e) Near miss

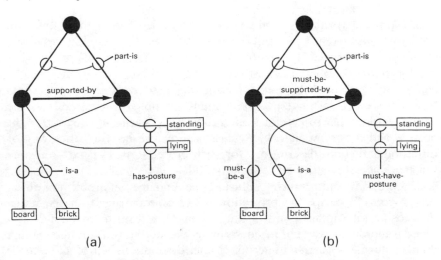

(a)   (b)

FIG.7.14. (a) A description of the pedestal in 7.13a. (b) A model for a pedestal built up after training on a sequence of pedestals and near-misses. Adapted from Winston (1973) with his permission.

177

Our choice of a pedestal to illustrate this process of learning a structural model from examples was deliberate. The pedestal is like a three-dimensional letter T (see Fig. 7.10), and the structural description for a pedestal is very similar to that described for a T, except that the "parts" of the pedestal are themselves three-dimensional objects like a brick and a board, instead of the horizontal and vertical lines in the letter T. Thus this kind of representation can be used for two-dimensional written characters, or three-dimensional objects.

To return to Winston's program, a process similar to that used for the pedestal can be used to derive a model for a house (Fig. 7.12). Here the eventual model would specify that a brick *must* support a wedge (the roof). As for the pedestal, both the support relations and the nature of the objects is quite tightly specified. However in the case of an arch (Fig. 7.12) there is more flexibility. While the "upright" structures in the arch model *must* be bricks and *must not* touch each other, the structure which they support can be a brick, or a wedge, or maybe even any object at all. An arch is still an arch whatever the shape at the top.

Winston's program is here operating in the object domain. It can accept any projection of a brick or wedge and label these accordingly. However the structural descriptions for brick and wedge must themselves be specified at a different level of the program. At an even lower level, the line drawing which serves as input must be parsed into separate objects using the procedures described in Chapter 5. The initial stages of the program make use of programs like Guzman's (see p.120, Chapter 5) to group regions of the picture together.

The problems with Winston's system are buried within these low-level programs which furnish the descriptions on which the "learning program" operates. As we noted in Chapter 5, scene analysis programs of the kind developed by Guzman, Clowes and Waltz work by making use of the constraints inherent in the kinds of scene they describe. But the constraints of the mini-world of matt prismatic solids are not the constraints of the natural world. While something similar to Winston's learning program might provide a theory of visual object classification, we need a better way of furnishing structural descriptions for such procedures to operate on—one which is not restricted to an artificial world.

To do this, we must return to consider the fundamental problem of object recognition. To recap, the projection of an object's shape on the retina depends on the vantage point of the viewer. Thus if we relied on a *viewer-centred* coordinate system for describing the object (one in the picture domain, to use Sutherland's terminology), descriptions would have to be stored for a great number of different vantage points. Minsky (1977) has in fact suggested that the linking together of a number of different views in the form of a *frame system* (see Chapter 6, p.151) could provide the basis for recognition. However, if we can describe the object with reference to an *object-centred* coordinate system, (i.e. build a structural description in the "object" domain) then it would be possible to reduce the number of object models stored, ideally to only a single one per distinguishable object. This was what Winston attempted to do with an artificial world.

The problem is then to find a way of describing the object within its own coordinate system *without* confining the discussion to an artificial world, and/or using knowledge of an object-specific kind. If one has to rely on object-specific knowledge then we would have to know what an object was before we could recognise it—an obvious paradox. However it seems likely that knowledge of *some* constraints is essential to parse objects—the question is, how specific are these?

MARR AND NISHIHARA'S THEORY OF OBJECT RECOGNITION

David Marr, along with Nishihara (Marr & Nishihara, 1978), outlined the foundations for one possible solution to this problem. An object must be described within a frame of reference which is based on the shape itself. To do this, we must be able to set up a canonical coordinate frame (a coordinate frame which is determined by the shape itself) for the shape *before* the shape has been described.

The appropriate set of descriptive elements (primitives) for describing a shape will depend in part on the level of detail that the shape description is to capture. The fingers of a human hand are not expressed in a system which uses primitives the size of arms and legs. To get around this problem, Marr and Nishihara suggest that we need a *modular* organisation of shape descriptions with different sized primitives used at different levels. This allows a description at a "high" level to be stable over changes in fine detail, but sensitivity to these changes to be available at other levels.

First we need to define an *axis* for the representation of a shape. Shapes which are elongated or have a natural axis of symmetry are easier to describe, and Marr and Nishihara restrict their discussion to the class of elongated objects which can be described as a set of one or more *generalised cones*. A generalised cone is the surface created by moving a cross-section of constant shape but variable size along an axis (see Fig. 7.15). The cross-section can get fatter or thinner as long as its shape is preserved. The class of generalised cones includes geometric forms like a pyramid or sphere, as well as natural forms like arms and legs (roughly). Objects whose shape is achieved by growth are often describable by one or more generalised cones, and so we can talk about object recognition in the natural world, rather than an artificial one. In the discussion which follows we will generally be talking

AXIS

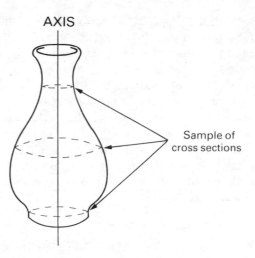

Sample of
cross sections

FIG.7.15. One example of a generalised cone. The shape is created by moving a cross-section of constant shape but variable size along an axis.

talking about the recognition of shapes comprised of more than one generalised cone, so that there will be more than one axis in the representation. For example, a human figure can be described as a set of generalised cones corresponding to the trunk, head, arms and legs. Each of these component generalised cones has its own axis, and together these form the component axes for a representation of a human.

A description which uses axis-based primitives is like a stick figure. Stick figures capture the relative lengths and dispositions of the axes which form the components of the entire structure. The relative thicknesses of these components (e.g. the human trunk is thicker than a leg) could also be included in the representation, though for simplicity we will omit this detail here. Information captured by such a description might be very useful for recognition since stick figures are inherently modular. We can use a single stick to represent a whole leg, or three smaller sticks to represent the upper and lower limb segments and the foot. At a still finer level, we can capture the details of toes with a set of much smaller sticks. At each level of description we can construct a 3D model where each 3D model specifies:

1. A single model axis. This provides coarse information about the size and orientation of the overall shape described.
2. The arrangements and lengths of the major component axes.
3. Pointers to the 3D models for the shape components associated with these component axes.

This leads to a hierarchy of 3D models (illustrated in Fig. 7.16) each with its own coordinate system.

The first "box" in Figure 7.16 shows the single model axis for a human body with the relative dispositions of the component axes (corresponding

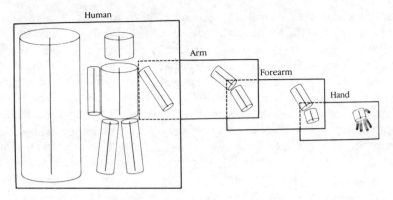

FIG.7.16. A hierarchy of 3D models. Each box shows the major axis for the figure of interest on the left, and its component axes to the right. From Marr and Nishihara (1978). Reproduced with permission of author and publishers.

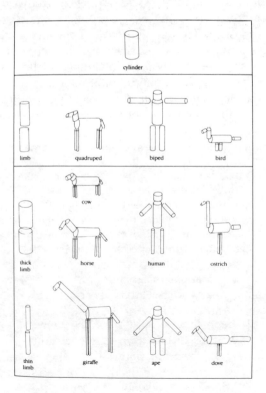

FIG.7.17. A catalogue of 3D model descriptions at different levels of specificity. Reproduced from Marr and Nishihara (1978) with permission of author and publishers.

to head, body, legs and arms). The axis which corresponds to the arm forms the major axis for the "arm model" (next box in the figure), in which the component axes of upper arm and forearm are shown, and so on through to the details of the fingers of a human hand. Such a hierarchy of 3D models is called a 3D model description. Recognition is thought to be achieved when a match is established between a 3D model description derived from an image, and one of the stored catalogue of 3D model descriptions corresponding to known objects. These may in turn be organised hierarchically, in terms of the specificity of their descriptions (see Fig. 7.17). Thus a "human" figure can be matched to the general model for a biped, or the more specific model for a human. Ape and human are distinguished by the relative length of the component axes in the model description for a biped.

Now we need to address the question of how such 3D model descriptions can be derived *prior* to accessing the catalogue. We need to derive the axes from an image without knowing what object it is that the image represents. In fact it can be shown (Marr, 1977) that we can make use of the occluding contours of an image to find the axis of a generalised cone, provided the axis is not too foreshortened. The only assumption needed is that these contours come from a shape which is comprised of generalised cones.

We have already seen, in Chapter 5, how Marr's early visual processing program derives contour information from an image without "knowing" what shape it is looking for. Occluding contours in an image are those which show the "silhouette" of the object (see the outline of the head of the bear in Fig. 5.29, or the donkey in Fig. 7.20). As Marr points out, silhouettes are infinitely ambiguous, and yet we interpret them in a particular way:

> Somewhere, buried in the perceptual machinery that can interpret silhouettes as three-dimensional shapes, there must lie some source of additional information that constrains us to see silhouettes as we do. Probably, but perhaps slightly less certainly than in the analyses of motion and stereopsis, these constraints are general rather than particular and do not require *a priori* knowledge of the viewed shapes. (Marr, 1982, p.219)

Let us examine the assumptions which Marr suggests allow us to interpret silhouettes so consistently.

1. Each line of sight from the viewer to the object should graze the object's surface at exactly one point. Thus each point on a silhouette arises from one point on the surface being viewed. We can define the *contour generator* as the set of points on a surface that projects to the boundary of a silhouette (see Fig. 7.18).
2. Nearby points on the contour in an image arise from nearby points on the contour generator on the viewed object (see Fig. 7.18).
3. All the points on the contour generator lie in a single plane.

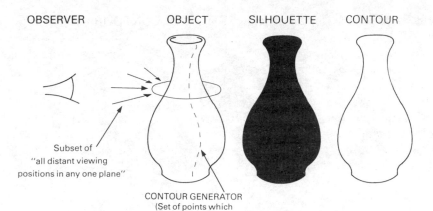

FIG.7.18.   An object, its silhouette and its contour. The set of points which projects to the contour (the contour generator) is shown. For this figure, all three assumptions (see text) hold for all distant viewing positions in any one plane. Adapted from Marr (1977) and Marr (1982).

This third is the strongest assumption, but is necessary in order to distinguish convex and concave segments in the interpretation process. If this assumption is violated, then the wrong conclusion might be reached. For example, the occluding contour in the image of a cube, viewed corner on, is hexagonal (see Fig. 7.19). Because we assume the contour generator is planar, we could interpret such a silhouette wrongly. In the absence of any other information from internal lines or motion, we might interpret the contour as belonging to a spindle shape like one of those drawn, or simply as a flat hexagon. In fact the points on the cube which gave rise to this contour do not lie in a single plane. It is this assumption of a planar contour generator which may lead us (wrongly!) to interpret the moving silhouette of someone's hands as the head of a duck, or an alligator, while playing shadow games.

Marr has shown that if a surface is smooth, and if these assumptions hold for all distant viewing positions in any one plane (see Fig. 7.18), then the viewed surface is a generalised cone. Thus shape can be derived from occluding contours *provided* the shape is a generalised cone, or a set of such cones. Vatan (cited by Marr & Nishihara, 1978 and Marr 1982) has written a program to derive the axes from such a contour. Figure 7.20 shows how his program derives the component axes from an image of a toy donkey. The initial outline was formed by aggregating descriptions from the raw primal sketch, in the same way as for the teddy bear's head (Chapter 5). From this initial outline, convex and concave segments are labelled and used to divide the "donkey" into smaller sections. The axis is derived for each of these sections separately, and then these component axes are related together to form a "stick" representation for the entire figure.

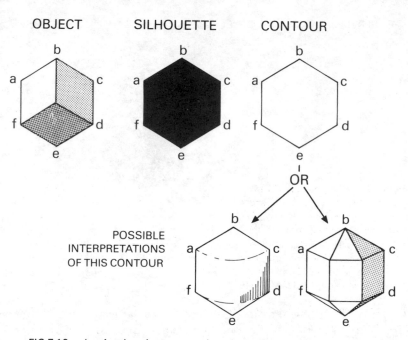

FIG.7.19.   A cube viewed corner on gives rise to the silhouette and contour shown. The contour generator (a–b–c–d–e–f) is not planar. This silhouette might be seen simply as a hexagon, or interpreted as one of the spindle shapes shown.

Now these axes derived from occluding contours are viewer-centred. They depend on the image which in turn depends on the vantage point. We must transform them to object-centred axes, and to do this we must make use of the *image-space processor*. The image-space processor operates on the viewer-centred axes and translates them to object-centred coordinates, so that the relationships between the different axes in the figure are specified in three, instead of two dimensions. Use may be made of information from stereopsis, texture and shading to achieve this, but it may also be necessary to use preliminary matches with stored 3D model descriptions to improve the analysis of the image. Thus, for recognition, Marr does envisage that there is a continuous interplay between the derivation of an object's description and the process of recognition itself: "We view recognition as a gradual process that proceeds from the general to the specific and that overlaps with, guides, and constrains the derivation of a description from the image (Marr, 1982, p. 321)."

In summary then, Marr and Nishihara have outlined a scheme in which an object-centred representation, consisting of an axis-based structural description, can be established from an image and used to access a stored catalogue of 3D model descriptions in order for recognition to be achieved.

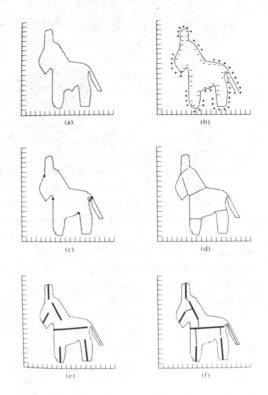

FIG.7.20. (a) An outline of a toy donkey. (b) Convex (+) and concave (−) sections are labelled. (c) Strong segmentation points are found. (d) The outline is divided into a set of smaller segments making use of the points found at (c) and rules for connecting these to other points on the contour. (e) The component axis is found for each segment. (f) The axes are related to one another (thin lines). Reproduced from Marr and Nishihara (1978) with permission of author and publishers.

Once an initial match has been established, use may then be made of downward-flowing information to refine the analysis of the image. These ideas are speculative; only a few isolated details of these derivation and recognition processes have been specified sufficiently clearly to implement them, and the system itself rests on a number of assumptions and observations about the perception of stick figures and silhouettes which have a rather ad hoc flavour. Nevertheless, in comparison with other schemes in artificial intelligence, Marr and Nishihara's theory is notable. It is much more applicable to the world of everyday objects than is, say, Winston's; and much more precisely specified than other all-embracing theories such as Minsky's.

CONCLUSION

In this chapter we have outlined some of the problems posed by the recognition of objects from retinal images, and have seen how contemporary work in artificial intelligence has attempted to overcome these problems. We are still a long way from developing a computer program which can recognise everyday objects with the ease that we do, and some way off understanding how we ourselves perform everyday tasks such as recognising human faces (discussed further in Chapter 13). Whether theories such as Marr and Nishihara's can be developed to deal with specific problems such as face recognition remains to be seen.

CONCLUSION TO PART II

In this section of the book we provided a rapid survey of the kinds of theories which are needed to explain how we organise and interpret the information contained within retinal images. A retinal image is messy, flat and static—and thus it must be interpreted, either by making explicit use of object hypotheses, or implicit use of general constraints in the physical world. Within the "retinal image" framework, an approach such as Marr's, which emphasises the implicit use of natural constraints, holds the greatest potential for talking about animal as well as human vision. At various points in this section we attempted to provide an introduction to the very important theoretical progress which has been achieved by Marr and his collaborators.

   However, a major disadvantage of this general approach to visual perception is that it treats perception very much in isolation from action. Although real and exciting progress has been made in understanding how we construct representations of the world which might allow us to act upon that world appropriately, very little has been said about how these representations are in fact used. In the next part of the book, we try to redress this balance. To do this, we introduce a rather different framework for visual perception from the traditional "retinal image" approach.

III DETECTING INFORMATION IN THE TRANSFORMING OPTIC ARRAY

8

Introduction to the Ecological Approach to Visual Perception

In the second part of this book we sketched an explanation of how an account of form, space and movement perception could be given in terms of the conventional starting point of the retinal image. The impression gained is that visual perception must involve large amounts of computation from instant to instant—building elaborate symbolic descriptions from primitive assertions, inferring distances from a variety of cues, taking account of signals to move eyes, and so on. The slightly different images reaching the two eyes must be combined to form a single three-dimensional percept, and views of the world glimpsed at different moments must also be integrated to result in the perception of a stable world containing objects in motion.

In this part of the book we consider a rather different framework for visual perception. This alternative, "ecological," approach emphasises the information which may be available in extended spatial and temporal pattern in the optic array, to guide the actions of animals and people, and to specify events of importance or interest. For the moment, we may regard the two approaches as complementary, with the "ecological" framework operating at a more global level of analysis than the computational accounts we have been considering until now. However, many of those working within the ecological framework regard their theoretical orientation as antithetical to that of information-processing theorists such as Marr. Inevitably we must confront some of these differences, though we leave the details of the arguments until Chapter 14.

The ecological approach to visual space perception was developed over a 35-year period by J.J. Gibson, (Gibson, 1950a, 1966, 1979; see also Reed & Jones, 1982). Gibson's theory of perception takes as its starting point not a "retinal image," which is passively sensed, but the ambient optic array, which an observer actively samples. In Chapter 1 we introduced the notion of an optic array and described how eyes have evolved to detect the spatial and temporal pattern contained within it. Gibson maintains that it is flow and disturbances in the structure of the total optic array, rather than bars, blobs or forms in an "image," which provide the information for perception, which unambiguously informs the observer both about the world and about him or herself simultaneously. In this ecological approach, perception and action are seen as tightly interlocked and mutually constraining. More controversially, Gibson's is a "direct" theory of perception, in which he maintains that information is "picked up" rather than "processed." Before we embark upon an introduction to Gibson's ideas, we should state that we disagree with his notion of "direct perception" in its strong form. Nevertheless, we feel that his theory has been important in inspiring some fascinating research, in which optical variables of higher order than local intensity values have been taken as the input to vision, and shown to provide important sources of information for the control of action (Chapters 9-12), and the apprehension of events (Chapter 13). We think it appropriate to devote this chapter to a description of why and how Gibson developed his theory, before going on to make use of some of his ideas in the remaining chapters of this section.

J. J. GIBSON'S THEORY OF PERCEPTION

During World War II Gibson addressed himself to the problem of how to train pilots quickly, or how to discriminate potentially successful from unsuccessful pilots prior to training. The most difficult, and hence dangerous, aspects of flying are landing and take-off. To land a plane successfully you must know where you are located relative to the air strip, your angle of approach, and know how to modify your approach so that you are aiming for the right position at the right speed. Gibson felt therefore that good depth perception was likely to be a prerequisite of good flying. He discovered however that tests based on the pictorial cues to depth, and training measures devised to make people capitalise on depth information, had little success when applied to the problem of training pilots. Here was a clear practical example of the perception of relative distance, and yet attempts to improve "depth perception" were fruitless.

Such observations led Gibson to reformulate his views of visual perception radically. In his 1950 book he began by suggesting that the classical approach to "depth" or "space" perception be replaced by an approach which emphasised the perception of *surfaces* in the *environment*. This emphasis remained throughout his subsequent books. Gibson's theory emphasises the *ground* on which an animal lives and moves around, or above which an insect, bird or pilot flies. The ground consists of surfaces at different distances and slants. The surfaces are composed of texture elements. Pebbles, grains of sand, or blades of grass are all elements of texture which, while not identical, possess statistical regularity—the average size and spacing of elements of the same kind of texture will remain roughly constant for different samples. Some surfaces surround objects, and these objects may be attached to the ground (rocks, trees), or detached and independently mobile (animals). Object surfaces, like ground surfaces, have texture. The environment thus consists of textured surfaces which are themselves immersed in a medium (air). Gibson argues that we need an appropriate geometry to describe the environment, which will not necessarily be one based on abstractions such as "points" and "planes," as conventional geometries are. An ecological geometry must take surfaces and texture elements as its starting point. "A surface is substantial; a plane is not. A surface is textured; a plane is not. A surface is never perfectly transparent; a plane is. A surface can be seen; a plane can only be visualized (Gibson, 1979, p.35)."

The structure which exists in the surfaces of the environment in turn structures the light which reaches an observer; we saw simple examples of this in Chapter 1. Gibson argues that it is the structure in the light, rather than stimulation by light, which furnishes information for visual perception. Stimulation per se does not lead to perception, as evidenced by perceptual experience in a Ganzfeld (Metzger, 1930; Gibson & Dibble, 1952; Gibson & Waddell, 1952). Diffuse unstructured light, as might be obtained by placing halves of table-tennis balls over the eyes and sitting in a bright room, produces perception of nothingness. To perceive things, rather than nothing, the light must be structured. In order to describe the structure in light we need an "ecological" optics (Gibson, 1961), rather than a description at the level of the physics of photons, waves and so on. The physics of photons coupled with the biochemistry of photoreceptor action can be used to explain how light is emitted and propagated and how receptors are stimulated by it, but not how the world is perceived. An ecological optics must cut across the boundaries between physical and physiological optics and the psycology of perception.

Gibson rejected the claim that the retinal image is the starting point for visual processing. He argued that it was the total array of light beams reaching an observer, after structuring by surfaces and objects in the world, which provided direct information about the layout of those surfaces and objects, and about movement within the world and by the observer. Gibson pointed out that the total optic array contains information over space and time which unambiguously specifies layout and events. In Chapter 1 we described how light is structured in the optic array, and here we remind you briefly of the important points.

The ambient optic array at any point above the ground consists of an innumerable collection of light rays of different wavelengths and intensities. Some have been reflected by air particles, others by the surfaces in the world. These rays form a hierarchical and overlapping set of solid angles. The solid angles corresponding to the tiniest texture elements are nested within those which correspond to the boundaries of larger regions or objects. Changes in the pattern or properties of the light from one solid angle to another signal boundaries in the world, where for example one object partially conceals or occludes another object, or the ground.

Gibson maintained that the optic array contained *invariant* information about the world, in the form of higher-order variables, where traditional psychologists saw ambiguity and insufficiency in the retinal image. An example of an invariant is given by Sedgwick's (1973) "horizon ratio relation." The horizon "intersects" an object at a particular height, and Sedgwick showed that all objects of the same height, whatever their distance, are cut by the horizon in the same ratio. An observer's task is to detect such invariant information by actively sampling the dynamic optic array. For example, the gradient of image size provided by the light reflected from textured surfaces receding away from an observer provides a continuous metric of the visual world. The rate of change of texture density, Gibson claims, can be detected directly, and unambiguously specifies the layout of surfaces in the world. In Chapter 6 we considered gradients of texture as one "cue" for depth perception. For Gibson, they are of more fundamental importance. Figure 8.1 shows examples of how texture gradients (of artificially regular proportions) can give impressions of surfaces receding into the distance. Figure 8.2 shows how the local shape of a surface may be given by the change in texture density gradient.

FIG.8.1.   Examples   of   texture density gradients.

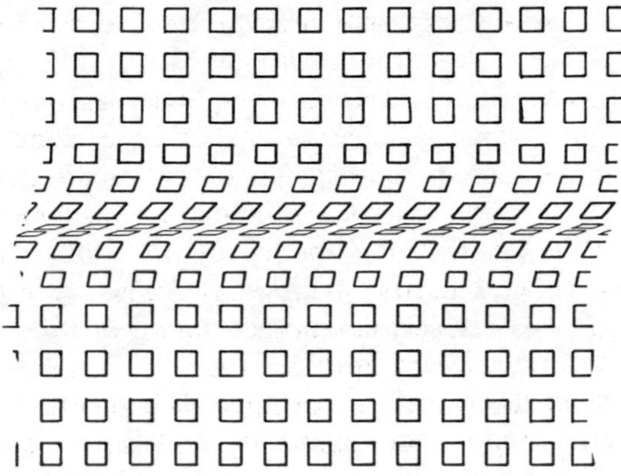

FIG.8.2. Surface shape and slant can be revealed by texture.

Gibson and co-workers (Gibson 1950b; Gibson & Cornsweet, 1952; Beck & Gibson, 1955) have shown that changes in phenomenal slant are produced by changes in texture density gradients in viewed images, though the relationship between the two is not straightforward. Phenomenal slant is proportional to, but less than, actual slant. Gibson (e.g. 1975) later criticised these experiments on the grounds that they studied optical slant, i.e. the perceived slant about a plane perpendicular to the line of sight, rather than geographical slant—that relative to the ground surface. Hence the observer's task was not ecologically valid.

Gibson originally termed his theory a "ground" theory of perception (Gibson, 1950a) in contrast with traditional "air" theories. In Gibson's view, the perception of objects should never be considered in isolation from the background texture on which they lie. Take the example of an observer viewing an object at a certain distance. Traditional "simplification" of this situation would lead to the schematisation in Figure 8.3—where we can see that the same image could potentially be cast by an infinite number of objects of different sizes, inclinations and distances from the observer. Gibson (1950a) called this kind of theory an "air" theory of visual perception because images are discussed as though cast by artificially smooth objects devoid of any background.

Gibsonian optics would depict the situation rather differently. Rather than considering an image cast by, for example, a tree suspended in a perceptual vacuum, Gibson would consider the total array of light reaching the observer. Assuming for the moment a stationary eye and world, the optic array would contain information about a continuous ground receding from the observer in the form of a texture density gradient. The size of this particular tree would be given by the amount of texture it conceals. Since a tree itself has texture, the fact that the tree is vertical, rather than inclined away from or towards the observer would also be specified by the lack of

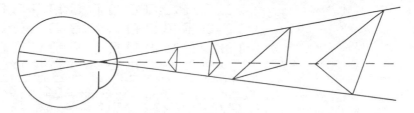

FIG.8.3.   The kind of drawing typically used by students of visual perception
to illustrate the ambiguity of the retinal image.

change in the texture density in the relevant portion of the optic array, that
corresponding to the tree's trunk. Thus this particular pattern of light
unambiguously specifies a tree of a particular size at a particular distance.

> Distance therefore is *not* a line endwise to the eye as Bishop Berkeley thought.
> To think so is to confuse abstract geometrical space with the living space of
> the environment. It is to confuse the Z-axis of a Cartesian coordinate system
> with the number of paces along the ground to a fixed object. (Gibson, 1979,
> p.117)

Gibson sees the important information about the layout of surfaces (he
rejects the term "space" perception) as coming from a variety of gradients
of information in the optic array, and gradients of texture, colour, brightness
and disparity are all mentioned. However, it is misleading to consider the
information available to such a "static" observer, since Gibson believes that
movement is *essential* for seeing. "What is clear to me now that was not
clear before is that structure as such, frozen structure, is a myth, or at least
a limiting case. Invariants of structure do not exist except in relation to
variants (Gibson 1979, p.87)."

Variants in information are produced by movement of the observer and
the motion of objects in the world. The fact that observers *actively* explore
their world allows powerful information from *motion perspective* to tell them
both about their position relative to structures in the world and about their
own movements. When an observer moves (as in Fig. 8.4) the entire optic
array is transformed. Such transformations nonetheless contain information
about both the layout and shapes of objects and surfaces in the world, and
about the observer's movement relative to the world. "Perception of the
world and of the self go together and only occur over time" (Gibson, 1975,
p.49).

Figure 8.5 shows an example of motion perspective. As an observer walks
past a collection of objects at different distances the relative motions present
in the changing optic array will be specifically correlated with the layout of
such objects. Indeed as an observer moves in any way in the world this

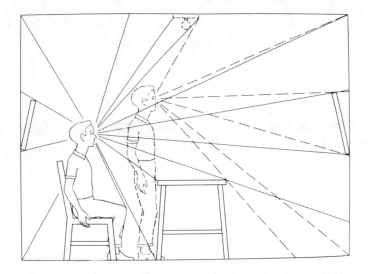

FIG.8.4. When an observer moves the entire optic array is transformed. From Gibson (1966). Copyright © 1966 by Houghton Mifflin Company, Boston. Used by permission.

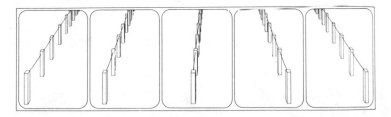

FIG.8.5. Successive views of a row of fence posts as an observer moves past them. The observer travels from right to left between each of the frames from left to right. From Gibson (1950a). Copyright © 1950 by Houghton Mifflin Company, Boston. Used by permission.

locomotion will always be accompanied by *flow* in the optic array. The nature of optic flow patterns is specific to certain types of movement, (see Figs. 8.6–8.8). If a pilot is trying to land an aeroplane (Fig. 8.6) there will be streaming in the optic array radiating out from the point at which he is aiming. This point is known as the *pole* of the optic flow field. The array of optical texture elements (produced by light reflected from the texture elements in the world) expands centrifugally, with elements successively passing out of the bounded visual field of the observer and new elements emerging at the pole. If one was sitting on the roof of a train facing backwards there would be a continuous inward streaming of optical texture elements towards the point from which one was travelling (Fig. 8.7). If you chose the softer

FIG.8.6.   The optic flow field for a pilot landing an aeroplane. From Gibson
(1950). Copyright © 1950 by Houghton Mifflin Company, Boston. Used by
permission.

FIG.8.7.   The optic flow field for a person sitting on the roof of a train,
facing backwards.

option of remaining seated at a train window the flow pattern would be as
in Figure 8.8.

   Gibson (1979) described the relationship between optic flow and locomotion more formally in the following way:

   1. Flow of the ambient array specifies locomotion and non-flow specifies
      statis.

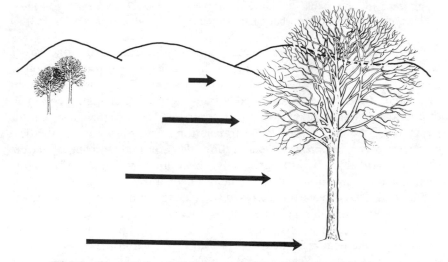

FIG.8.8.   The optic flow field for a person sitting on a train and looking out of the window as they travel from right to left through this terrain.

2. Outflow specifies approach and inflow specifies retreat from.
3. The focus or centre of outflow specifies the direction of locomotion in the environment.
4. A shift of the centre of outflow from one visual solid angle to another specifies a change in the direction of locomotion, a turn, and a remaining of the centre within the same solid angle specifies no change in direction (abridged from Gibson, 1979, pp.227–9).

That flow in the optic array may be sufficient to specify observer movement is dramatically demonstrated by the fairground amusement called the haunted swing. Here a person is seated in a stationary swing while the room rotates around them. The optical information is identical to that which would be produced if the observer, rather than the room, were being spun, and the subjective impression for the observer is the same—only by closing their eyes can they escape the nauseating sensation of being turned head over heels. In the next two chapters we will discuss in more detail how optical flow patterns may be used to inform animals and people of their actions in the world.

The fundamental importance of observer movement in Gibson's perceptual theory is reinforced by his notion of *perceptual systems* to contrast with the traditional "senses." Gibson (1966, 1979) claimed that it was an entire perceptual system whose job it is to "see."

Receptors are *stimulated* whereas an organ is *activated* . . . the eye is part of a dual organ, one of a pair of eyes, and they are set in a head that can turn,

attached to a body that can move from place to place. These organs make a
hierarchy and constitute what I have called a *perceptual system*. (1979, p.53)

Movement by the observer, whether of body, head or eyes, is one way in
which variant information is obtained. The other way is through motion or
change in objects in the world—i.e. through *events*. Events include objects
or animals translating, rotating, colliding or growing, changing colour or
disappearing. All such events are accompanied by disturbances in the
structure of the optic array. Rigid translation of an object across the field
of view involves the progressive accretion, deletion and shearing of texture
elements. An object will progressively cover up (or "wipe out") texture
elements in the direction of its movement, uncover (or "unwipe") them from
behind and shear the elements crossed by the edges parallel to its movement
(see Fig. 8.9). If the object changes its distance from the observer this change
will be accompanied by magnification (if approaching) or minification (if
receding) of the texture elements of its own surface, and the covering up or
uncovering of texture elements of the background. Texture elements which
are covered up by object motion in one direction are uncovered by motion
in the reverse direction. The same is true of observer movement. Texture
elements which pass out of the observer's view when movement is in one
direction will reappear if the movement is reversed. Gibson claims that this
principle of *reversible occlusion* underlies the observer's impression of a
constant and stable visual world where even those surfaces momentarily
hidden are still "perceived".

Once one considers the total array of light there is no ambiguity about
whether it is oneself or objects in the world which are moving. Eye movements
do not change the structure of the ambient optic array, they simply allow a
different portion of the array to be sampled. Movement of the head and

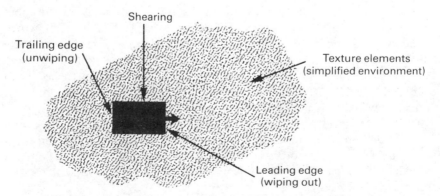

FIG.8.9. As an object moves, elements of background texture are progressively wiped out (covered up) by its leading edge, unwiped (revealed) by
its trailing edge, and sheared by edges parallel to its direction of movement.

body is always accompanied by a systematic flow pattern in the *total* array. Movement of an object within the world produces *local* disturbances in the structure of the array. Thus the major distinction between movement within the world or on behalf of the observer can be specified unambiguously by different flow patterns in the optic array. Note that Stevens et al. (1976; see Chapter 6, p.148) also discussed how different patterns of motion in the entire retinal mosaic could be used to disambiguate motion perception, though the details of their argument are quite different from Gibson's.

Gibson's approach to the psychology of perception became progressively more radical. While in his 1950 book his major aim seemed to be to consider the nature of the visual information in the optic array within a psychophysical framework, in his later work (Gibson, 1966, 1979) he became more interested in defining a totally new approach to perception. In the ecological approach to perception the animal and environment are viewed as intimately inter-linked. The end product of perception is not seen as an internal representation of the visual world—a "percept." Rather the animal is seen as detecting *affordances*. The affordance of some surface or object in the environment is what it offers the animal—whether it can be grasped or eaten, trodden on or sat upon. The notion of an affordance can be traced back to the Gestalt psychologists, and particularly Koffka's idea of the "demand character" of an object. "To primitive man each thing says what it is and what he ought to do with it . . . a fruit says 'Eat me'; water says 'Drink me'; thunder says 'Fear me' (Koffka, 1935, p.7)."

A sawn-off tree trunk of the right flatness and size affords "sitting-on" by a human, or "hopping-on" for a frog. Gibson makes the strong claim that there is information in the light to specify the affordances of the environment. "This is a radical hypothesis, for it implies that the 'values' and 'meanings' of things in the environment can be directly perceived (Gibson, 1979, p.127)."

Thus when the light specifies that a surface is flat, extended and substantial its property of affording support to terrestrial animals is implicitly given. While it is relatively easy to appreciate that affordances like "supporting" or "graspable" might be specified in the optic array, it is much less easy to appreciate how qualities such as "eatable" or "writable-with" could be contained within the light. At the point where Gibson claims that a letter-box affords the posting of letters by humans of western culture, his theory is the most controversial. Nevertheless, the concept of affordances provides a powerful way to bridge the gap that exists in more cognitive theories between "perception" and "action." Within the theory of affordances, perception is an invitation to act, and action is an essential component of perception. However, Gibson's claim that all of perception can be understood without appeal to linguistic or cultural mediation is problematic, and we will return to this issue later.

Gibson thus asserts that optical information specifies surfaces of support, falling-off places, impending collision and so on. And, he claims, affordances are perceived directly, without the need for mediation by cognitive processes. The major task for the ecological psychologist is to discover the invariant information that animals have evolved to detect, and to discover the mechanisms by which they become attuned to this information. Gibson denies the need for "memory" in explaining perception. Incoming percepts are not matched against previously laid down traces, rather the perceptual system has evolved to "resonate" to certain invariant information. The concept of "resonance" is left rather vague by Gibson. For our purposes it is sufficient to stress that the theory suggests that there should be receptors or receptor networks which should be sensitive to variables of higher order than "features" such as lines and edges.

Gibson decries the traditional laboratory experiment in perception in which observers are presented with "stimuli," devoid of context. In such situations the optical information is indeed impoverished but this will only tell us how a human observer copes with artificially impoverished inputs, and may tell us nothing of perception in the optically-rich real environment. He denies that ambiguous figures and illusions should be the starting point for a psychology of perception. While these may be interesting, and may be analysed in terms of the invariant information that they contain, they are not characteristic of normal perception. In the real world such perceptual distortions are rare. Additionally, Gibson regards the perception of *pictures* (the focus of much research in perception) as involving two components— the direct perception of the picture as a picture, i.e. as a flat surface, and the indirect perception of what it is that the picture represents. The picture of an apple, for example, as a flat surface, affords little apart from inspection. The affordances of the object depicted, the fact that it is an apple, can be grasped, thrown and eaten, are perceived indirectly and without ever fooling an adult observer into actually trying to reach for and eat the picture. Everyday perception is of the "direct," not the "indirect" kind.

Perhaps the best way to illustrate the difference between the approach of Gibson and his students and that of other perceptual theorists is to contrast their explanations of a number of specific topics. We have already seen how the problem of whether oneself or objects in the world are moving is dealt with by Gibson, but what about other "problems" in perception?

Size Constancy

Perceptual constancies have often been used to demonstrate the indirect and inferential nature of seeing. An object at distance $2x$ metres from an observer casts an image on the retina which is half the size of the image cast by that same object at distance x metres from the observer, and we have already seen (in Chapter 6) how relative size of retinal images may be thought of as a "cue" for the perception of depth. However, if you watch a friend walk down the street he or she does not appear to shrink to half size each time the person's distance from you doubles. Our perception of the sizes of objects is remarkably constant, provided the distances are not too great.

The traditional view of this phenomenon is that the brain must take account of the perceived distance of objects (as given by various cues) and scale perceptual size up accordingly. The consequence of this is paradoxical. While relative image size may act as a cue to distance, the distance thus assessed is then used to judge the apparent size of the viewed object. Gibson views the problem differently. Because, he argues, texture gradients provide a continuous and constant scale for the perception of the world, there is no problem of size constancy scaling. The size of any object is given by the scale of the background at the point where the object is attached (Gibson, 1950a).

Size constancy breaks down over large distances. In the laboratory perceived size tends towards image size, but Gibson (1947) showed that in an open, ploughed (and hence textured) field, estimates of the height of a distant stake merely became more variable at great distance rather than the error being in one direction. Size constancy also fails if we view objects from a height, rather than at a horizontal distance. Thus, from the top of a high building, people on the pavement below us appear insect-like in their proportions. Traditional theory would explain this in terms of absence of cues to distance. Gibson would say that when viewing from a height, the absence of the ground removes the continuous scale of texture necessary for accurate size perception.

Stereopsis

In Chapter 6 the reader was introduced to the problems associated with matching two disparate images into single three-dimensional percepts. It was suggested that global stereopsis was achieved on the basis of large numbers of computations and comparisons at a local level. Students of Gibson (e.g. Michaels, 1978) deny that visual perception involves the matching of two distinct images. No-one has ever suggested that tactile perception involves such a synthetic step—yet when one feels an object under a cloth, each hand must obtain a quite different tactile impression. It has always been implicitly assumed that we know objects directly by touch, and yet logically the problem of the resulting "singleness" of tactile perception is the same. Therefore if tactile images need not be compared and integrated, why consider binocular vision to involve the comparison and fusion of two retinal "pictures"? Michaels and Carello (1981) feel that perceptual theory has been misled by the camera metaphor.

> Just as Gibson took issue with the idea of discrete retinal snapshots, we will take issue with the supposition that the information has two parts, one to each eye, and that these two parts require fusion. And, just as he found it more convenient to consider the information for monocular motion perception to be transformations over a third dimension (time), we might reconsider binocular information in terms of transformations over a third dimension of space. . . . Transformations over time describe the successive order of an optic array and so constitute monocular kinetic information. Similarly, transformations over space describe the adjacent order of two arrays and constitute binocular static information—what will be called the binocular array. (Michaels and Carello, 1981, p.119)

In these terms the task of the ecological perceptual theorist is to understand the invariant information obtained by binocularity, i.e. in the transformations which obtain from one eye's view to the other. It is claimed that invariants can be shown to specify the distances of objects, to remove the ambiguity of monocular shape information and can specify the shapes and sizes of particular objects (Michaels, 1978).

Perceiving Forms in Motion

In Chapter 6 we described the conditions in which "apparent" motion may be perceived when an item is displaced between successive frames of a film. The phenomenal similarity between real and apparent motion has justified the analysis of motion by perceptual theorists in terms of the comparison of successive retinal snapshots. In contrast, Gibson (1968) regarded the stimuli of apparent motion displays as preserving the transformational information which is present in a real moving display. In both cases, he would claim, the stimulus information contains transformations over time which specify the path of the motion. Gibson would argue that the perception of motion depends on the *direct* registration of this information. Clocksin (1980) has demonstrated that the types of edges present, and the orientations of surfaces in the world can be recovered "directly" from the optical flow information available to a locomoting observer. Thus a Gibsonian analysis of movement of objects or of observers would commence with an analysis of the information available in a continuously changing optic array. Clocksin starts with optical flow, and recovers edges.

We could contrast this with the approach of Ullman, considered in Chapter 6, who starts his analysis of motion perception with a sequence of static images, from which he recovers edges and then establishes correspondences between successive images over time. Both Clocksin and Ullman are researchers in artificial intelligence, concerned to provide explicit computational theories of perception. Both regard a consideration of the information available in the light reaching an observer to be fundamental to the development of adequate theories of perception, and both are attempting to avoid the use of object-specific, "downward-flowing" information in their accounts. Their difference lies in the nature of the information which forms the starting point for their analyses. For Ullman it is an image, for Clocksin it is flow.

Gibson's Theory in Perspective

Gibson's theory is radical indeed. It stands apart from the mainstream of perceptual theory. Some have likened Gibson's ideas to those of the Gestaltists, who took a similar phenomenological approach to seeing. However the Gestaltists were nativist in philosophy, while Gibson sees learning as important; and the Gestaltists sought to explain perceptual phenomena in terms of the physiology of the brain, unlike Gibson. It would be as legitimate to compare Gibson with the behaviourists, who looked at stimuli and responses but did not care to speculate on intervening stages of processing—but the behaviourists saw animals as prodded into action by discrete stimuli or sensations, while for Gibson, perception and action are intimately interlinked. Thus Gibson's approach is unique and has until recently been ignored by the vast majority of perceptual psychologists. This is largely because the difference between Gibsonian and traditional accounts of perception is more profound than might be appreciated from the preceding pages. The differences between the two approaches are not just psychological but verge on the philosophical. Traditional perceptual theory holds that perception is indirect and mediated by higher cognitive processes. We do not "just see" the world but actively construct it from fragmentary perceptual data. Gibson is a "direct realist." He holds that perception is direct and unmediated by inference and problem solving. However, at least some of the distinction between a "direct" and an "indirect" theory may be muddied by conceptual and logical confusion (Shaw & Bransford, 1977).

Much of the remainder of this book has a distinctly Gibsonian flavour, particularly in Chapters 9 and 10, as we talk about the detection of information from optic flow patterns, and how this might be used to guide the actions of animals and humans in their worlds. However, unlike much of the work in ecological optics, we are concerned to describe physiological and computational models of how this information might be detected. We do not consider it adequate to claim that the observer just "resonates" to "invariants" picked up "directly", but would concede that for some purposes one can demonstrate how patterns of light may be used to guide action, without detailed enquiry about how the information contained within light is processed. Different levels of analysis suit different purposes, and we return to these issues in Chapter 14. In addition, we see a distinction between the kinds of visual processing which might be used to guide locomotion through, and manipulation of objects in, the world, and the kinds of visual processing which might be involved in *understanding* the visual world in conceptual terms. For Gibson (1979), the two kinds of perception apparently do not differ. Thus just as a tree stump affords "sitting on," so a mail-box affords "posting letters," to a human being in a Western culture. In both cases perception is not mediated, in the inferential sense of the word, though humans may have to learn how to use the invariant information in the optic array. However, a fundamental aspect of human cognition is the ability to manipulate symbols and images in order to plan, reflect and reminisce. It seems likely that such "cognitive" activities are intimately involved in at least some aspects of human perception, and hence in this way too our approach is much less radical than Gibson's. In other animals we may wish to consider how "mental maps" of their environments are established and used. Such considerations appeal to notions of internal representations, "memories" of a kind, that Gibson would not consider appropriate to the subject matter of perception.

Our own aim is to present a pragmatic, rather than a theoretically "pure," account of a variety of perceptual accomplishments, and for many such accomplishments a "weak" version of the Gibsonian approach provides a more comfortable level of analysis than does the "retinal image" approach. In the remaining chapters of this section we will consider aspects of "dynamic" visual perception by animals and humans, but we will not adhere too strictly to a Gibsonian style of analysing these activities. However it should be said that the majority of the research we will describe in this section has been conducted by people influenced by, and sympathetic to, Gibson's position. The subject matter and the approach of this section will feel very different to that of Part II. In Chapter 14 we will tackle these differences explicitly and explore the possibilities for reconciliation and synthesis.

9 Visual Guidance of Animal Locomotion

A crucial part of Gibson's critique of traditional theories of visual perception is his argument that they neglect the relationship between perceiver and environment. It is because of his emphasis on this relationship that Gibson came to describe his own approach as *ecological*. An ecological outlook on vision leads us to ask two kinds of question. First, what information is available in the spatiotemporal pattern of light to specify the structure of the environment and events in it? Secondly, what information does an animal or person *need* from the pattern of light in order to organise their actions?

We saw in Chapter 8 some of the ways in which Gibson tackled the first question, and in Chapters 9–13 we discuss further ways in which the optic array provides information for vision. We attempt to put this problem in the context of the second question, and stress the need to understand the role of visual perception in animals' and people's actions. We begin, in this chapter, by considering how animals use information in light to guide their movement around the physical environment of solid objects and surfaces.

HOW ANIMALS MOVE ABOUT

The information which an animal needs to guide its movement through the environment—to perch on a branch, to detour around an obstacle, to jump over a ditch, and so on—will depend on the way in which it moves about; whether it burrows, runs, swims or flies. Means of locomotion are in turn constrained by the environment an animal lives in. The fundamental division of biological environments is into water and land. A watery environment— sea, lake or river—can in turn be divided into two kinds of potential habitat—the substrate and the open water. Many animals living in the substrate do not move about at all but are attached to the bottom and filter their food from water currents. Coral, sponges and bivalve molluscs such as oysters are examples of such sessile animals.

Many other species either move about on the surface of the substrate— examples include starfish and snails—or burrow in it, as do many annelid worms and some bivalve molluscs. For such animals, information about the chemical composition of the water, the chemistry and texture of the substrate and the direction of the force of gravity is often sufficient to control their movement around the environment and to enable them to locate sources of food and potential mates. The role of vision in guiding movement in such animals is often restricted to the detection of sudden changes in light level which specify possible predators.

One reason why many aquatic animals living on the substrate make only limited use of vision to guide locomotion is that they move slowly. Because of the viscosity of water, an animal like a lizard or rabbit, even if magically equipped with gills, would not be able to run about at its usual speed on the sea floor; animals such as lobsters and crabs are the fastest walkers over the bottom of watery environments. An animal moving slowly over the sea floor has less need to plan a course to avoid obstacles, because it is less likely to have enough kinetic energy to do itself any damage if it collides with one. A starfish or limpet encountering an obstacle simply creeps around it. The particular value of light is that it gives information about the positions of objects and surfaces beyond immediate tactile contact, and such information is not useful to a starfish or limpet.

Speed of movement is only one of a number of factors influencing the evolution of animals' visual capacities, however. Some bottom-living aquatic animals may make good use of vision. Crabs and octopuses live on the sea-floor, and locate nooks and crannies among rocks where they are relatively safe from predators, discriminate between different kinds of prey and engage in complex social behaviour. Vision plays some part in guiding these forms of behaviour, which rely on the ability to detect complex information in light.

In open water, animals can move at greater speeds, although whether a species can exploit this possibility depends upon its body size. The viscosity of water prevents small animals from generating sufficient power to move at any speed, and small planktonic animals such as shrimp simply swim to maintain their vertical position, often using the direction of maximum light intensity to orient themselves.

All larger animals which swim continuously in open water show similarly streamlined body shapes and modes of swimming, determined by the mechanics of moving through water; fish, sharks and marine mammals (whales and dolphins) swim by undulating movement of the body, whilst squid use a unique jet propulsion mechanism. These animals need to detect obstacles and other animals at a distance, and most of them use information available in light to do so. Dolphins and other cetaceans also use an echolocation system based on ultrasonic cries, while some fish species living in murky water detect objects in their surroundings by distortion of their own electric fields (Heiligenberg, 1973).

When we turn to consider the terrestrial environment, we again find species which move slowly over the surface of the earth, or burrow under it, but we also find a greater variety of ways of moving around the environment rapidly. Insects, spiders, reptiles, birds and mammals move by walking, running and jumping, while birds, bats and many insects can also fly.

As in water, light provides information specifying the layout of an animal's surroundings and, as light penetrates further through air than through water, information about surfaces is available up to greater distances than in water. We have seen in Chapter 1 the two kinds of eye which enable land animals to exploit this source of information; the vertebrate eye and the compound eye of arthropods. Only one group of land animals can move about at speed without vision; these are the bats, which, like dolphins, detect reflections of their own ultrasonic cries (Griffin, 1958).

This general survey of the animal kingdom shows us some ways in which the physical properties of an animal's habitat and the way it moves around it may influence the extent to which it will make use of information in light. This will depend upon many factors, including the amount of ambient light in its habitat, the extent to which it is absorbed by the medium, and the animal's mode of locomotion.

Environment and locomotion can constrain perception in more subtle ways than just determining which sensory modality is most appropriate. For example, animals which move about at speed in open water or air will have as a potential source of information variables in the optic flow field which are not available to animals which move only intermittently. In the rest of this chapter, we will discuss examples of animals which move about at speed through air, and will ask whether they do in fact detect variables of the optic flow field and use them to guide walking, running or flying. We will consider three problems which are posed for perception in such animals; maintaining a stable path through air currents, detecting surfaces in the surrounding environment and detecting the distances of surfaces.

HOW INSECTS STEER A STRAIGHT COURSE

An insect flies by beating its wings rapidly, twisting them as it does so, so that on each downstroke air is driven backwards and downwards. This generates a force on the insect with two components—an upwards force, or lift, and a forward force, or thrust. The aerodynamic principles by which these forces are produced are well understood, at least for larger insects (Pringle, 1974).

Simply beating the wings will not ensure *stable* flight, however. The direction and magnitude of the force produced by the wingbeat must be controlled to prevent the insect rolling, yawing or pitching (see Fig. 9.1). A degree of stability is provided by insects' anatomy. The abdomen, particularly if it is long, as in the locust, acts as a rudder to counteract pitch and yaw, and in all insects the centre of lift is above the centre of gravity, giving pendulum stability against roll. In these ways, deviation from a stable flight attitude generates a correcting force.

This inherent stability is augmented in all actively flying insects by "active reflexes"—negative feedback loops operating through the insect's nervous system and muscles. Receptors detect information specifying rotation around one of the axes, and the wings, limbs or abdomen move so as to correct the rotation. One source of information specifying rotation is the pattern of airflow over the insect. In the locust, for example, the rate of air flow over either side of the head during flight is detected by sensory hairs, and a difference in the two rates, which specifies yaw, generates steering movements of the legs and abdomen (Camhi, 1970).

In completely still air, or in air moving as a homogeneous mass at a uniform speed, this kind of change of pattern of air flow unambiguously specifies a rotation caused by the insect's own movement. Corrective movements of the wings, legs and abdomen will keep the insect on a straight and stable course.

Often, however, the air an insect flies through moves in irregular currents, gusts and eddies too small for us to detect but large enough to deflect a flying insect. For an insect flying through fluctuating air currents, air flow

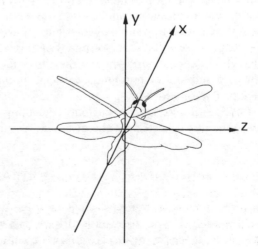

FIG.9.1. The three orthogonal axes through a flying insect. Rotation around axis x is rolling; around axis y is yawing and around axis z is pitching.

over the body provides ambiguous information about the insect's path relative to the environment. An insect which simply regulated its path relative to the air around it would fly in an irregular, "drunkard's walk" path as it was blown about by fluctuating air currents. Such a flight path would be maladaptive for many insects, as they would be unable to fly any distance through the environment in order to reach new food sources.

We would therefore expect insects to be able to detect turns relative to the fixed environment around them as well as relative to the air in which they fly. What information in the optic flow field could specify such turns? Locusts maintain stability in the rolling plane by detecting both the direction from which diffuse light intensity is the greatest and the angle of the horizon relative to the body axis (Goodman, 1965). In a locust's natural environment, these two sources of information unambiguously specify the direction of the force of gravity, whatever the air around the insect is doing.

These two means of ensuring stable flight have their limitations. First, the orientation of the horizon is useful only to insects flying over open country, as locusts do when migrating, but not to insects flying through a cluttered environment of vegetation. Secondly, neither mechanism can correct yawing turns and prevent an insect flying round and round in circles. A further means by which insects can maintain stable flight, which overcomes both these problems, is through the *optomotor response*.

The first demonstration of the optomotor response (Kalmus, 1949) studied the control of walking rather than flying, and a typical experiment is shown in Figure 9.2. A fly walks on a platform surrounded by a cylinder with vertical stripes on its inside surface. As the cylinder is turned, the fly turns in the same direction, so that the velocity of flow of texture in the optic flow field is minimised.

Rotation of the cylinder causes a flow of optic texture in a uniform sideways direction throughout the optic flow field, but what would this pattern of flow specify about a fly's natural environment? It would not specify movement of the environment as, outside an optomotor experiment, the whole environment would never move in a uniform way (Gibson, 1966). Instead, it would unambiguously specify rotation of the fly due to movement of the surface it is resting on.

An illustration of this point is provided by situations where stationary human observers are presented with uniformly moving texture in a large part of the visual field. Such situations are rare, or must be contrived experimentally (note that forward locomotion does not produce *uniform* flow of texture), but they often cause a powerful impression of self-movement. The reader may have experienced such an effect by standing in shallow water at the seashore and looking straight down. As the water rushes out after each wave, an observer has a strong illusion of moving in the opposite direction. A similar effect can occur at a railway station, when uniform flow

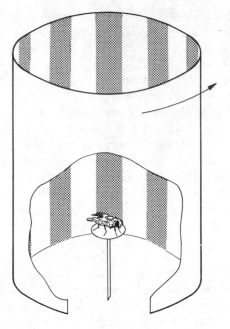

FIG.9.2. Experiment to demonstrate the optomotor response of a
walking fly.

created by movement of a train on a nearby platform can be interpreted as
movement of the observer's own, stationary train. We shall have more to
say about control of human posture and balance by vision in Chapter 10.

In an optomotor experiment, a fly detects a pattern of optic flow which
specifies its rotation relative to the environment, and makes the appropriate
turning movements of its legs to reduce sideways optic flow to a minimum.
Can this ability to detect uniform flow throughout the optic flow field also
be used to correct yawing turns during flight? Many insects, if suspended in
the air by a rod glued to the back, will beat their wings as if flying, and
their turning responses to artificial optic flow fields can be measured.

The fruitfly *Drosophila melanogaster* is one example of an insect which
shows the same optomotor response during tethered flight as a walking fly
does to a rotating striped drum. A fruitfly responds to a striped pattern
moving sideways across its visual field with a yawing turn, made up of three
components; an increase in the difference between the amplitudes of beat of
the two wings, sideways deflection of the abdomen and hind legs, and
inhibition of the "hitches," or transient reductions in wingbeat amplitude,
which occur spontaneously and independently on the two sides of the body
during normal flight (Götz, Hengstenberg, & Biesinger, 1979).

There is no reason why uniform flow of optic texture should not also be
used to detect pitching and rolling turns as well as yawing ones, and the

fruitfly's optomotor response does indeed operate in these two planes also (Blondeau & Heisenberg, 1982; see Fig. 9.3). This means of detecting pitching and rolling will be effective in a cluttered environment where the horizon is not visible. It is important to stress that these rotating striped patterns simulate the optic flow caused by rotation of the insect, whether the rotation arises from its own movement or from an air current or from both. Since all these situations require the same corrective manoeuvres, there is no need for an insect to discriminate between them. We see here an example of the ecological principle that animals detect only that information in light which they need to control their actions.

It is obvious how these optomotor responses act to maintain stable flight by a fruitfly or other insect, but can they also keep an insect on a straight path through fluctuating air currents? In principle, they can play a part in doing this. Each time the insect is rotated by an air current, flow of texture will generate an opposing *torque*, or turning force. The insect will therefore keep the direction of its thrust constant relative to the environment. Its actual path will be determined by the resultant of its thrust and the air current, and the insect will therefore follow a zig-zag path. Nevertheless this

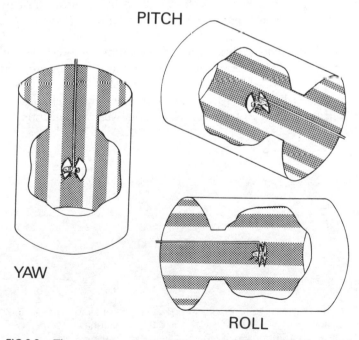

PITCH

YAW

ROLL

FIG.9.3. The optomotor response of a tethered fly to rotation of a drum in all three planes. In each case, the fly turns to minimise velocity of flow of optic texture. Adapted from Blondeau & Heisenberg (1982).

path will have a component in a constant direction, and the insect will not fly around in circles.

This argument makes an unrealistic assumption, however, which is that there will be no optic flow unless the insect turns. This would be nearly true if the insect were at a considerable height above the ground and at a great distance from landmarks, so that motion parallax was only slight. If an insect flies near the ground, however, passing close to vegetation or other objects, there will be movement everywhere in the optic flow field, except at its *poles*, which specify the direction of movement (see Fig. 8.6). The rate of of movement in any part of the optic flow field will depend on its angular separation from the poles, on the distance of corresponding landmarks from the insect and on the insect's velocity. These relationships are illustrated in Figure 9.4.

Unless an insect is flying at high altitude, the optic flow field will therefore be an elaborate pattern of regions of different rates of movement, generated by the insect's *translatory* movement, and the effects of *rotatory* movement will be superimposed on this pattern. If the optomotor responses we have been considering are to play a role in keeping an insect on a straight course by counteracting turns, then optic flow caused by rotation must in some way be filtered out from that caused by translation. How might this be achieved?

Reichardt (1969) has analysed the yawing optomotor response and has proposed a model of its control. In his model, receptor cells are connected to movement detectors, which respond to movement in a preferred direction in the same way as directionally selective retinal cells in vertebrates (Chapter 2, p.50). Reichardt analyses the mechanism of movement detection in detail,

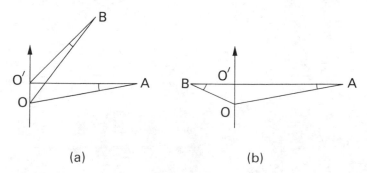

(a)   (b)

FIG.9.4. The relation between distance, angular position in the optic flow field and velocity of flow. (a) Objects A and B are equidistant to the observer but B is nearer to the pole of the optic flow field. As the observer moves in unit time from O to O′, texture reflected from A moves through a greater angle. (b) Objects A and B are equidistant from the pole of the optic flow field, but B is nearer the observer than A. As the observer moves from O to O′, texture reflected from B moves through a greater angle.

but our concern is with the next stage of the model, in which the outputs of all movement detectors sharing the same preferred direction are summed together. This summation of the responses of movement detectors is illustrated in Figure 9.5, and our question is whether this model can resolve the components of optic flow caused by rotation and by translation.

In Figure 9.5, the outputs of direction selective movement detectors around the eye are summed by a "rotation detector." Each movement detector gives a positive output to clockwise movement and a negative output to counter-clockwise movement. Consider undisturbed forward flight first; Figure 9.5a shows the directions and rates of flow over each part of the eye, and (as long as landmarks on the two sides are at approximately the same distance) it is apparent that the outputs of the detectors on the two sides will cancel out.

Consider next a counter-clockwise rotation of the insect, causing a uniform clockwise flow superimposed on the pattern in Figure 9.5a. The result of

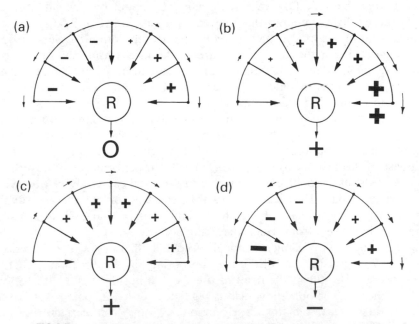

FIG.9.5. A model of the control of the optomotor response. Movement detectors connected to receptors signal the direction and rate of flow in each part of the optic flow field and a rotation detector R sums their outputs. Clockwise and counter-clockwise flow give positive and negative outputs respectively. (a) Optic flow during forward flight. (b) Effect of rotation superimposed on forward flight. (c) Optic flow caused by sideways movement. (d) Optic flow caused by a nearby surface on the left. Arrows indicate magnitude and direction of optic flow. Sizes of "+" and "−" symbols indicate magnitude of movement detector output.

adding the two patterns is shown in Figure 9.5b, and the rotation detector now yields a positive output, which can be coupled to motor mechanisms to give a clockwise corrective turn. Similarly, a clockwise rotation will cause a negative output from the rotation detector and a counter-clockwise correction.

Disturbances to flight will not necessarily be purely rotatory, however, but will usually also involve a translatory component. Figure 9.5c shows the effects of a purely translatory disturbance, in which the insect is blown sideways, to the left. The optic flow will cause a positive response from the rotation detector and therefore a clockwise turn which will tend to return the insect towards its original path. The "rotation detector" does not therefore *resolve* the rotatory and translatory components of a disturbance to flight but generates a corrective turn appropriate to deal with either or both and so keep the insect on an average straight course.

A consequence of a model of this kind, which Götz (1975) has pointed out, is that the optic flow caused by a nearby object on one side during undisturbed flight simulates that caused by a rotation (Fig. 9.5d). Further elaboration of the model may therefore be needed, although Götz (1975) has suggested that the apparent failure of the mechanism may in fact be adaptive for fruitflies, generating straight flight in an empty environment and frequent turns in patches of vegetation, with the result that the fly spends more time in food-rich areas.

One feature of the model shown in Figure 9.5 is that it assumes information from all parts of the visual field is summed equally. Collett (1980) has argued against this assumption, and has provided evidence that it is not correct in the case of the hoverfly *Syritta pipiens*. The flight performance of hoverflies is one of the most sophisticated among insects, and can easily be observed on a summer day. They can fly forwards, sideways or obliquely, through grass, flowers and foliage, hover in a stable position, and fly accurately towards the flowers from which they take nectar.

One component of Collett's model of hoverfly flight control is detection of optic flow over the part of the eye appropriate for the direction of flight. In forward flight, this is the front of the eye, but in sideways flight it is the side of the eye. The optic flow field is regulated so that its pole is kept over one of these areas, and this clearly involves a more complex and flexible model than that of Figure 9.5. Perhaps similar complexities occur in other insect species, although the ability of the hoverfly to fly with great accuracy in any direction may well mean that its perceptual capacities are unusually elaborate. We should be alert to the possibility of different mechanisms in different species of insect, related to different ecological demands.

The problem of maintaining a stable path or position in a moving medium is faced by other animals besides insects. Being larger and more powerful, birds will not be affected by small air currents, but stronger currents may be important in two sorts of situation. Hummingbirds, which hover in a stable position to feed from flowers, may need to detect and correct disturbances of their position by wind in the same way as hoverflies, and birds navigating over long distances must correct effects of crosswinds on their flight path.

Fish living in moving water face similar problems to those of airborne insects. Trout, for example, maintain their position in fast-flowing streams, and it seems likely that they do so by detecting information in the optic flow field specifying movement relative to their surroundings. The study of optomotor processes in fish and birds would present greater difficulty than in insects, but it would be interesting to know whether similar mechanisms are involved.

DETECTING SURFACES

Our next problem is one which is shared by a wider range of actively moving animals, including large terrestrial animals which are not troubled by air currents. It is the problem of detecting the surfaces of solid objects surrounding a moving animal. This is necessary to avoid collision with obstacles, or to orient a flying animal towards a surface on which it can alight. The three dimensional layout of the world can be retrieved from a stationary retinal image or a pair of images, in the ways discussed in Chapter 6, but we shall look at evidence that at least one insect species uses information in the optic flow field to do this.

The housefly, *Musca domestica*, as well as showing a standard optomotor response to a revolving striped drum, will also turn so as to follow the movement of a single vertical stripe on a drum (Reichardt & Poggio, 1976). As the stripe rotates, the fly follows its movement in such a way as to keep the stripe in the centre of its visual field.

What information in the pattern of light reaching its eyes might a fly be using to track a vertical stripe? Reichardt and Poggio (1976) found that the yawing torque of a fly presented with a single vertical stripe was determined by three factors. One is the angle between the stripe and the long axis of the fly's body. The second is the angular *velocity* of the stripe. For a given position of the stripe, the fly will turn more quickly if the stripe is moving away from the centre of the visual field more quickly. In this way, the fly has a simple ability to extrapolate from the stripe's rate of movement and predict its future position. Finally, the fly's torque shows small random changes causing it to turn irregularly, which can be observed either when the fly is placed in a homogeneously lit environment, or when it is fixating a stationary stripe.

Why should this fixation of a moving or stationary vertical stripe be of any significance to a housefly in normal life? Flies feed on a variety of kinds of organic matter, making short flights between potentially nutritious surfaces where chemoreceptors in their feet allow them to assess their luck in finding food (Dethier, 1955). Could fixation of a vertical stripe be the outcome of a system normally guiding the airborne fly towards a surface?

Imagine a fly in an artificial world of vertical dark cylinders against a diffuse white background. If the fly keeps aligned towards the edge of a cylinder in the same way as it does towards a stripe on a rotating drum, it will fly towards the surface of a cylinder, where it may land. If the cylinders move, or the fly is buffeted by air currents, control of torque by angular position and velocity will still guide it to the target. Now, let us make this artificial environment more realistic, in two stages. First, keeping all objects uniformly dark against a diffusely lit background, can the system deal with variation in shape and orientation of surfaces?

Wehrhahn and Reichardt (1973) have shown that similar principles control the lift/thrust responses of houseflies, so that a single horizontal stripe moving vertically can be fixated. The system therefore works around two axes and can guide the fly to a surface tilted at any angle. Further, Reichardt and Poggio (1976) show that patterns other than vertical stripes vary in their "attractiveness"; that is the proportion of its time a fly spends fixating them. Perhaps the attractiveness of different geometrical patterns reflects in some way the likelihood that different sorts of natural surface will be nutritious.

Reichardt and Poggio (1976) argue that the random component in the fly's torque is important in preventing fixation of a sub-optimal pattern, or, in the natural environment, preventing flight towards an unpromising surface. We can imagine the airborne fly as surrounded by surfaces competing for fixation; as it switches its direction of flight about between them, through random fluctuations in torque, it will spend most time fixated on the optimal one and so fly towards it.

There is a second way, however, in which we must make this environment more realistic. The real world does not contain uniformly dark objects against a diffuse background, but objects with textured surfaces. Consider an insect flying about among the branches of a tree. At any instant, the optic array will contain a mass of solid angles of light reflected from texture elements such as veins or patches of colour on leaves. The *stationary* optic array does not now specify where the boundaries of objects lie, nor their relative distances. As soon as the insect moves, however, such information is available in the optic flow field. The boundaries of leaves are specified by discontinuities in the rate of flow of optic texture. That reflected from a distant leaf will move at a different, lower rate from that reflected from a nearer leaf. In Gibson's (1966) terms, wiping and shearing of texture are available to specify three-dimensional layout.

In further experiments, Reichardt and Poggio (1979) demonstrated that flies have some ability to detect wiping of texture. They presented tethered flies with a vertical stripe of a random-dot texture against a background of the same texture (see Fig. 9.6).

As we would expect, if both stripe and background either remained stationary or moved together, the flies did not fixate the stripe. Certain patterns of *relative* movement between stripe and background did, however, cause flies to fixate the stripe; the most effective patterns were oscillation of stripe and background at different frequencies or with the same frequency but with a phase difference of 90° or 270°. In a fly's natural environment, there would be relative movement in the optic flow field as it flew near a textured surface in front of a more distant, similarly textured background. Fixation of a small region of moving texture would therefore guide the fly towards a nearby landing surface.

Fixation of moving texture keeps a housefly on a course towards a potential landing surface, but the problem now arises of how the fly's landing manoeuvres are guided. Flies do not simply crash into surfaces (unless they are made of glass—why should be clear in a moment!) but land using a stereotyped series of manoeuvres, beginning with forward extension of the front legs.

A looming surface straight ahead is specified by centrifugal flow in a wide area of the optic flow field; a pattern which can be simulated by presenting a fly with a rotating disc on which a spiral is painted. Depending on the direction in which the disc is rotated, either inward or outward movement of edges is generated. If a housefly is suspended in front of a disc rotated

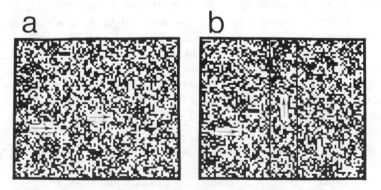

FIG.9.6. Random-dot patterns used by Reichardt & Poggio (1979) to study figure-ground discrimination by flies. In (a), a vertical stripe moves with the background, while in (b) it moves in a different direction to the background. The relative movement in (b) allows both flies and people to detect the stripe. Reproduced from Reichardt & Poggio (1979), with permission of the author and publishers.

so as to give an expanding pattern, it will immediately give the landing response, whereas a disc rotating in the opposite direction elicits no response (Braitenberg & Ferretti, 1966).

The information available in the optic flow field to specify the boundaries of surfaces is therefore used by the housefly to orient to surfaces and to initiate landing manoeuvres when it approaches one closely. No doubt the rules relating flight to optic flow which we have described are only a part of the fly's flight control system; it is possible, for example, that a fly switches between cruising flight, in which obstacles are avoided, and exploratory flight, in which they are approached. A combination of both experimental and observational analysis will be needed to explore further the ways flies and other insects steer between and towards obstacles.

It seems likely that other animals moving about through a cluttered environment—a fish swimming through coral, a deer running through a wood or a squirrel running between branches—use the same sources of information in the optic flow field to detect the layout of objects surrounding them. Many manoeuvres of this kind, however, will require information about the *distances* of surfaces from an animal, as well as their positions relative to one another; can the optic flow field provide distance information?

DETECTING DISTANCE

Distance Information in the Retinal Image

The ways discussed in Chapter 6 of extracting depth information from a static retinal image—accommodation, binocular disparity, image size and so on—are potentially available to animals, though to varying extents. The compound eye of insects does not accommodate, and this source of information is available only to animals with single-chambered eyes. The range of distances over which binocular disparity is useful depends upon the distance between the two eyes, and will be greater for vertebrates than for insects. Even so, at least one insect species does detect distance in this way; the extent of a preying mantis' strike at a small insect is determined by the disparity in positions of the image of the target in the two eyes (Rossel, 1983).

Two vertebrates which rely only on the "traditional" cues to depth in obtaining distance information are the chameleon and the toad. Both these animals capture prey such as insects by orienting towards the target and striking at it with the tongue. The extent of the strike is accurately related to prey distance, and the chameleon obtains this information from the degree of accommodation of its lens when the prey is optimally focused (Harkness, 1977), while the toad uses both accommodation and binocular disparity (Collett, 1977).

The use of information available in a static retinal image is particularly suitable to the technique of prey capture these animals employ, in which the direction and distance of a rapid strike is preset while the animal is stationary. This kind of control of movement is called *open-loop*, meaning that while the movement is executed no further information from the environment can modify it. In *closed-loop* control of movement, on the other hand, movement is continually modified by information from the surroundings; an insect's optomotor response is under closed-loop control, for example.

For the toad, obtaining depth information from a pair of static retinal images may reflect a more fundamental feature of its behavioural organization, as Lock and Collett (1979) have obtained evidence suggesting that toads do not move through their surroundings under smooth, closed-loop control in the way that flies do, but in a series of "chunks" of movement controlled in an open-loop fashion by information detected at the start of the "chunk".

Lock and Collett found that toads approach a prey item which is beyond the 10 cm range of their strike in a series of walks and/or hops. Each of these "walks" lasts about 2 sec and takes the toad about 40 cm, but once it begins, moving the target does not alter the toad's bearing until the walk is completed. The bearing of the next walk is in the direction of the new position of the target. Likewise, a walk continues to completion even if the target disappears during it. Figure 9.7 illustrates how a toad tracks a moving

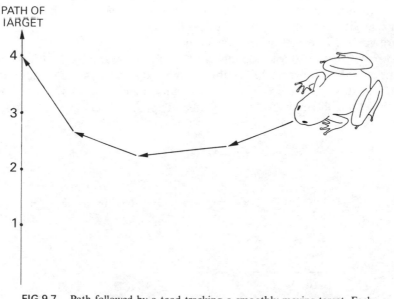

FIG.9.7.   Path followed by a toad tracking a smoothly moving target. Each arrow represents a "walk" lasting about 2 sec.

target in a series of walks, each in the direction of the target's position at the outset.

A toad's approach to distant prey is therefore organised in a "chunked" way; information in the light reaching its eyes before a walk begins is used to set the bearing of that walk, which then is executed under open-loop control without further feedback control. This information could be obtained from the static optic array, or from the optic flow field during the previous walk, or both. The latter seems unlikely to be an important source of information, as a toad sets out on the correct bearing to an object as soon as it appears.

Lock and Collett found in further experiments that toads are able to detect the distance as well as the bearing of a target from the static optic array; there is a straightforward linear relation between target distance (if the target is outside snapping distance but inside the range of one walk) and walking distance. Again, moving the target or making it disappear during the walk did not affect the length of the walk.

These findings do not exhaust the toad's visual abilities, however; it can also detect the size and position of a barrier between itself and a target. Lock and Collett (1980) used two kinds of barrier, a chasm and a paling fence (Fig. 9.8). A toad confronted by a chasm will leap across it if it is not too wide, or step into it if it is not too deep. If it is both too wide and too deep, it turns away. In the case of the paling fence, a toad either sets out directly towards the prey or directly towards one end of the fence, depending upon the widths of the gaps in the fence. Again, the bearing of the first walk is in one direction or the other, indicating that optic flow is not necessary to provide the information the toad needs.

Clearly, toads do not hop about at random snapping at prey items whenever they happen to fall within striking distance. Instead, they make their way through the obstacles surrounding them by means which are at the same time both remarkably efficient and apparently clumsy. It is a puzzle

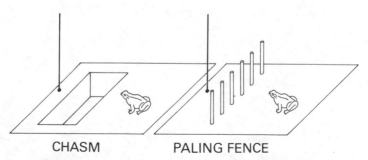

CHASM   PALING FENCE

FIG.9.8. Obstacles used by Lock and Collett (1979) to study a toad's approach to its prey.

why organisation of the toad's movement should be "chunked" in this way; one possibility, suggested by Lock and Collett, is that it reflects some basic design principle of the amphibian nervous system. Whatever the reason, however, this kind of behavioural organisation is one which must rely on retrieving depth information from the static optic arrays at the two eyes.

An example of an insect relying on the stationary optic array for distance information is the honeybee, when locating a familiar source of food. By training honeybees to feed from a dish at a certain distance from a landmark, and then varying the size and distance of the landmark, Cartwright and Collett (1979) showed that some bees would search at the distance at which the angular size of the landmark at the eye was the same as during training.

Gauging distance from angular size requires knowledge of the actual size of an object, and so does not seem a generally useful tactic for an insect to adopt. In this situation, however, it is perfectly adequate. A bee does not need information about the distances of objects surrounding a food source; it needs to be able to return to it, and does so by matching its retinal image to that remembered from its previous visit, making the ecologically reasonable assumption that the layout and position of large objects in the environment will not change over a period of hours or days.

In general, we have seen two sorts of situations where animals can rely exclusively on depth information in the stationary retinal image. One is where the extent and direction of a chunk of movement is preset and then continues under open-loop control, and the other where a place in the environment can be recognised by matching its image to a stored one. As we saw in the last chapter, though, the optic flow field surrounding a moving animal provides further sources of distance information, and we might expect these to be used by animals moving about under closed-loop control. We would expect such sources of information to be particularly important to insects, as the cues of accommodation and binocular disparity are of such limited use to them. In vertebrates, we might expect to find information from optic flow used alongside other cues.

Distance Information from the Optic Flow Field

The simplest kind of information in the optic flow field specifying distance is motion parallax; the further an object is from the eye the more slowly optic texture reflected from it moves. Thus a flow field containing patches of texture moving at different rates provides information about the *relative* distances of surfaces around the animal. It cannot specify *absolute* distance, as the rate of optic flow is also a function of the animal's velocity.

In some situations, an animal's speed relative to its surroundings may be constant, so that rate of flow is a measure of object distance, but in many situations this assumption may not hold. Movement of the air or water, for a flying or a swimming animal, or the slope of the ground for a running animal, make the relationship between commands to muscles and actual velocity unpredictable. Since distance information is needed if the animal's velocity is to be obtained from flow, it seems that rate of texture flow is not a promising means of detecting distance.

Simple rate of flow is not the only parameter of what is happening in the optic flow field, however. Lee (1980b) has demonstrated that a more complex parameter *can* provide distance information independently of an animal's velocity. Strictly speaking, it does not specify distance but *time to contact*; that is, the time that will elapse before the animal collides with a surface, assuming that it is moving with constant velocity. Time to contact is likely to be a useful piece of information to animals; for example, to a bird or insect approaching a surface and needing to time its landing manoeuvres correctly, or to a horse needing to time its jump over a fence.

What is this parameter of the optic flow field, and how does it specify time-to-contact? Lee's argument goes as follows. Figure 9.9 shows a schematic representation of an animal approaching a surface with constant closing velocity. A surface on the right is approaching an eye on the left with velocity V. At time t it is a distance $Z(t)$ away, in units of the diameter of the eye, for convenience. A texture element P on the surface has an image P' projected on the retina. At time t, P' is a distance $r(t)$ from the centre of the expanding optic flow field and moving outwards with velocity $v(t)$.

From similar triangles, $\dfrac{1}{r(t)} = \dfrac{Z(t)}{R}$

Differentiating with respect to time, and inverting, $\dfrac{r(t)^2}{v(t)} = \dfrac{R}{V}$

Since $R = Z(t)\, r(t)$, $\quad \dfrac{r(t)}{v(t)} = \dfrac{Z(t)}{V}$

This ratio $r(t)/v(t)$ is the ratio at time t of the distance of any point from the centre of an expanding optical pattern to its centrifugal velocity. Since it is equal to $Z(t)/V$, it specifies time to contact if V is constant. In other words, the time elapsing until contact with a surface is specified by a simple ratio derivable from its dynamic projection on the retina. Two studies of animal distance perception have demonstrated that this parameter, which Lee calls τ, is used to organise movement during approach towards an object, and we will look at each of these in turn.

The first concerns the gannet (*Sula bassana*), a seabird which hunts by flying over the sea at heights of up to 30m. When it detects a fish below the surface, it dives almost vertically into the water to seize the fish in its beak. At the start of the dive, the gannet assumes a swept-back wing posture (Fig. 9.10) which allows it to steer, presumably keeping the fish at a fixed point

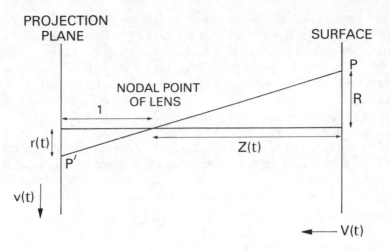

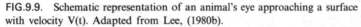

FIG.9.9. Schematic representation of an animal's eye approaching a surface with velocity V(t). Adapted from Lee, (1980b).

FIG.9.10. Successive wing positions of a diving gannet. The wings are streamlined as the bird strikes the water. Drawing by John Busby, reproduced from Nelson, B. (1978), with the permission of the publishers.

point in its visual field. Gannets enter the water at speeds of up to 24m/sec (54 m.p.h.) and would be injured if they kept their wings extended at this speed. When less than a second away from the water surface their wings are therefore stretched back into a streamlined posture. If the wings are streamlined too soon, steering accuracy will be lost, whereas if they are streamlined too late, the bird will be injured. There is therefore an optimum time to contact at which to streamline, and Lee and Reddish (1981) argue that this can be obtained from the parameter τ.

If closing velocity is constant, τ directly specifies time to contact. The situation is more complex for the diving gannet, however, because the bird's velocity increases throughout its dive as it accelerates under gravity. Lee and Reddish show that, for an accelerating dive, the actual time to contact t_c is given by:

$$t_c = \tau(t) + t_d - \sqrt{t_d{}^2 + \tau(t)^2} \qquad (1)$$

Equation (1) shows that time to contact is given by both $\tau(t)$ and t_d, the duration of the dive, and so it appears that τ alone cannot specify when the gannet should streamline. However, Lee and Reddish argue that a strategy based on τ could still work, if the bird waited until τ reached a margin value τ_m and streamlined at a time t_i after this point. In this case, the time to contact t_c at which the bird would streamline would be given by:

$$t_c = \tau_m + t_d - \sqrt{\tau_m{}^2 + t_d{}^2} - t_i \qquad (2)$$

Lee and Reddish filmed gannets' dives and, by single frame analysis, obtained values of t_c and t_d for each of a large number of dives. Figure 9.11 shows the data they obtained and the curve generated by equation (2) which best fits the points. Lee and Reddish argue that strategies of timing streamlining which involve computation of the actual time to contact (from height, velocity and acceleration), or streamlining at a particular velocity or at a particular height, would all give relationships between t_c and t_d which match the data less well than does the τ strategy.

The gannet therefore appears to use the parameter τ to detect the optimum time to streamline its wings as it approaches a single, uniform surface. Another situation in which we might expect τ to be useful is where a flying animal is landing on a surface. A series of manoeuvres will be necessary in order to land safely, and these will need to be executed at the appropriate times before landing.

Earlier, we described the housefly's landing response to an optic flow field specifying a looming object. This flow field is similar to that of the diving gannet, and could provide information about time to contact in the same

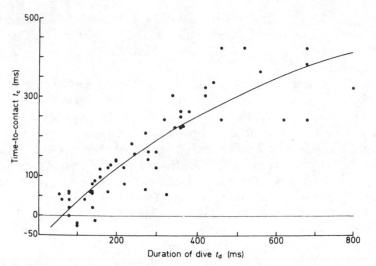

FIG.9.11. Relationship between the duration of a gannet's dive and the time to contact at which it streamlines. The curve is the best fit generated by equation (2) to the data. Reproduced with permission from Lee & Reddish (1981). Copyright © 1981 Macmillan Journals Ltd.

way. Is the fly's landing timed using this information? Wagner (1982) has shown, from single frame analysis of films of houseflies landing on small black spheres, that landing begins with a deceleration approximately 0.2 sec before contact, and that the optic flow field provides information specifying the distance from the object at which to start decelerating.

The parameter showing the least variance at the point of deceleration was what Wagner termed "relative retinal expansion velocity" (RREV), defined as the ratio of the rate of expansion of the image of the target to its size:

$$\text{RREV} = \frac{da}{dt} \cdot \frac{1}{a}$$

where a is the solid angle subtended by the target at the eye.

Wagner's RREV is essentially the same parameter as Lee's τ, as it measures the centrifugal velocity of the image of the edge of the target relative to its distance from the centre of the image. Where we are considering an animal approaching an object rather than a continuous textured surface (as in the gannet example), it is useful to express the parameter as relative rate of expansion of the image of the object.

In natural situations, a fly will be surrounded by objects of different sizes and shapes, and the optic flow field will contain many patches of texture moving at different rates, each with a different τ value specifying the time to contact if the fly were to turn towards it and approach it directly.

Wagner suggests that flies do not detect distances of objects around them independently of their own speed and direction of flight, but rather detect potential times to contact, which are directly useful in timing landing manoeuvres.

These two examples suggest that it may sometimes be misleading to think of depth perception as having the role of providing an animal with a metrically accurate picture of its surroundings. In many circumstances, animals will not need information about absolute distances of objects. We have seen that it is difficult to get such information from an optic flow field, because of the problem of independently gauging the animal's speed, but that the flow field does provide a parameter which can be used in heuristic, ecologically adequate strategies of timing approach to an object or a surface.

A problem for further research is how widely other species use the optic parameter τ. Does an insect or bird use it in steering a course around obstacles as well as in approaching them? Is it used by running animals in assessing the distance of a barrier, or the width of a chasm which must be jumped over? How useful is it for animals such as squirrels or monkeys which jump between branches of trees?

These questions will be easier to answer with insects, though it seems likely that principles which emerge there will be relevant to vertebrates also. Vertebrates which need to monitor distances as they move about, and which have little binocular overlap, are as reliant on information in the optic flow field as are insects. Things may become a good deal more complex, however, with animals such as cats and primates, where there is the possibility that depth perception may involve detection of interactions between patterns of optic flow and binocular disparity. Even so, we will see in the next chapter evidence that a striking variety of human activities are timed by detecting the parameter of optic flow τ.

CONCLUSIONS

The experiments we have described in this chapter provide evidence that Gibson's analysis of the information available in the optic flow field is useful for understanding how animals obtain information needed to guide movement through the environment. We have seen, for example, that flies detect uniform lateral flow, centrifugal flow and relative rate of expansion in order to control flight and landing manoeuvres.

As well as showing that Gibsonian principles are useful in understanding animal vision, these examples make two further points. The first is that the perception of the layout of the environment need not be considered as a problem of constructing a metrically accurate three-dimensional representation of it. We should always begin by asking why the animal needs to detect surfaces or their distances and what constraints applying in its normal environment could make simple solutions adequate. A gannet may not need to detect its height above sea-level instant by instant, but only to detect the optimum point at which to streamline its wings as it dives, and the parameter τ can provide this information.

The second point concerns a criticism often made of Gibson's theory, which is that it ignores the physiology of perception and is vague about how information available in light actually is detected. As we argue in Chapter 14, we agree that Gibson did not address the physiology of vision adequately, but this is no reason for believing that a Gibsonian style of analysis of the information available in light is incompatible with neurophysiological analysis; indeed, we believe, work on insect vision shows that the two approaches can work well together.

Consider the optomotor response of an insect to a rotating drum. This shows that the insect detects the direction of optic flow over a wide area of the visual field, and Gibson's theory tells us what such a pattern of stimulation would mean in a normal environment. It is then possible to proceed with physiological analysis of how the insect's nervous system is organised to detect this pattern of optic flow and to control patterns of muscle contraction accordingly.

Optic flow results in a flowing pattern of stimulation of ommatidia, and in Reichardt's (1969) model, multiplicative interaction between adjacent ommatidia signals the direction of optic flow over each part of the eye. Recent neurophysiological work (e.g. Hausen, 1976) has begun to show how the outputs of such movement detectors are combined further back in the fly's nervous system into the directionally selective responses to wide-field flow required by a model such as that in Figure 9.5.

This example of work on insect vision demonstrates that there need be nothing vague or mysterious about picking up information in the optic flow field, and that an ecological level of analysis of perception is a vital part of formulating the problem which perceptual mechanisms solve; a formulation which is necessary before physiology can get under way. Perhaps a way into making the same kind of link in vertebrate vision will be analysis of the physiological basis of the detection of a parameter such as τ.

10 Visual Guidance of Human Action

In Chapter 9 we discussed how the flight paths of insects, the locomotion of toads and the diving of gannets may be guided by information obtained from patterns of optic flow. In this chapter we discuss aspects of locomotor behaviour in higher animals, particularly man. We describe how research conducted within an ecological framework has helped us to understand aspects of human action which were largely ignored by traditional approaches to human perception.

While the mental life of insects is presumably relatively uncomplicated, that of humans is complex and creative. We do not simply "respond" to the information which reaches our senses, but encode and reflect upon it, and can describe our world to others. Nevertheless, just like lower animals, we must maintain posture and safe footing, and negotiate obstacles while moving around the world. We duck to avoid missiles, or move our arms and hands appropriately to catch them. We stop at the edge of a cliff, jump over puddles, or brake the car when an animal darts across the road.

Following Lee (1977) we can classify the types of information necessary for controlling such locomotor activities into three kinds—*exteroceptive, proprioceptive* and *exproprioceptive*. Exteroceptive information about the layout of surfaces in the environment, and the position of objects or course of events within the environment is needed to guide action in the world. The most important source of exteroceptive information for humans and many other animals is vision. Proprioceptive information about the movement of body parts relative to one another is necessary for coordinated bodily actions, and is gained through mechanical receptors in joints and within the vestibular system, but also through vision (try bringing the tips of both your

229

index fingers together with your eyes open and then with them closed). Exproprioceptive information about the position of the body or parts of it *relative to* the environment is also necessary for maintaining balance and guiding action through the world, and again vision provides powerful information of this kind.

Lee's classification departs from the traditional division of sensory systems into exteroceptors and proprioceptors, but his three-fold system is more suitable for discussions of locomotor behaviour. In the examples of locomotor behaviour we discuss below we will show how vision provides important information of all three kinds, this information being given by the dynamic properties of optic flow patterns.

In this chapter we first discuss how vision guides gross postural adjustments which allow us to duck to avoid missiles, or to maintain our balance while standing. We then consider finer aspects of locomotion and describe how it is that we negotiate a smooth path through a variable terrain. These are activities that humans share with other land-living animals, but we will go on to consider the visual guidance of behaviour peculiar to humans, such as driving cars or catching and hitting balls in sport. The way in which vision is used to guide this wide variety of activities appears to involve very general principles, some of which we have already met in Chapter 9.

POSTURAL ADJUSTMENTS

Avoiding Objects on Collision Course

An object approaching an observer on a collision path needs to be avoided. A strong empiricist tradition might suggest that infants would need considerable experience of the tactile consequences of an approaching object before reacting to the visual information specifying collision. However, it appears that infants may have an innate appreciation of particular patterns of optic flow. Bower, Broughton and Moore (1970) demonstrated that babies as young as eight days old would show defensive distress reactions when a foam rubber cube was pushed towards them. It appears that babies who are too young to have experienced the effects of colliding objects can respond appropriately to those apparently on collision course. Of course their reactions might be based on the change in air pressure created by the real approaching object rather than on the optical information specifying collision. However, Bower et al. (1970) and Ball and Tronick (1971) also tested young babies' reactions to dynamic optical displays in which no air pressure changes were present.

The displays were created by casting the shadow of a real object onto a screen in front of a supported infant. As the object was moved towards the light source, the shadow cast by it expanded in size, creating a "looming" image. Babies showed characteristic reactions to such displays. Their heads went back and their arms and hands were raised to cover their faces. Distress was also evident. While Bower et al. reported that the reactions exhibited were somewhat less strong to an apparent than to a real object, Ball and Tronick reported no difference in the strength of the reactions in the two cases. The reactions given to these looming patterns were in marked contrast to the indifference shown when the pattern cast specified an object which was approaching on a non-collision path, or when it specified an object receding from the child (a shrinking as opposed to a looming pattern). Schiff, Caviness and Gibson (1962) reported similar responses in infant rhesus monkeys presented with looming patterns.

It may be that behaviour in this situation is based on detecting τ (see Chapter 9), the optic variable which specifies time to contact. Schiff and Detwiler (1979) have shown that adult humans are able to estimate when an object which had been approaching on a filmed collision course would have hit them, and that their judgements were influenced little by whether the object was filmed against a textured or a blank background. This suggests that adults can use the rate of looming of the image of an obstacle in the absence of information about the rate of background texture deletion to estimate τ. Adults do systematically underestimate τ in this situation, (see also McCleod and Ross, 1983), but this would seem an ecologically sound strategy. It is better to duck too soon than too late! It would be interesting to examine more microscopically the timing of reactions by infant humans and monkeys to patterns looming at different speeds to see whether there is evidence that their behaviour is controlled by the detection of τ.

Maintaining Balance

As adults (at least when sober) we take for granted our ability to remain upright on two feet. As every parent knows, however, the ability to stand and eventually to walk unsupported is an achievement which is gradually mastered by the infant with months of unsteadiness and falls on the way. The gymnast on the narrow beam, the ballet dancer on points or the circus artiste standing on a cantering horse must all learn to maintain balance in new and changing circumstances.

There are a number of different sources of information which may be used to control balance. These include information from receptors in the feet and ankle joints, information from the vestibular system—the organ of balance—and information received through the eyes. A simple demonstration suggests that visual information may be extremely important in maintaining posture. Try standing on one leg with eyes open and then with them closed. With eyes closed you will probably sway and perhaps even fall over, despite the information still being received from your feet, ankles and vestibular system.

The importance of vision in maintaining balance has been more formally demonstrated by Lee and his colleagues (Lishman & Lee, 1973; Lee & Aronson, 1974; Lee & Lishman, 1975) in an experimental arrangement known as the "swinging room." The room essentially consists of a bottomless box suspended from the ceiling. The subject stands on a floor and the walls of the room can be moved backwards or forwards around them, without their knowledge. The walls of the room are covered with wallpaper to provide a visual texture. When the room is moved towards the subject, this produces the same expanding optic flow pattern which would be produced if the observer were in fact swaying towards the wall. If the room is moved away from the observer this produces a contracting optical flow pattern as though the observer were swaying away from the wall. This is illustrated in Figure 10.1.

Using this apparatus Lee and his colleagues conducted a number of experiments in which they showed that vision could provide exproprioceptive information which could be used to control balance. In one experiment Lee and Aronson (1974) placed toddlers (aged 13–16 months) within the swinging room. After a period of acclimatisation in which the infant's normal stability while standing could be assessed, they tested the infant's reactions to slight movement of the wall of the room while the child was standing facing it. When the room was moved towards the subject he or she was observed to sway, stagger or fall in a direction away from the wall. This was not merely a defensive reaction to the "looming" pattern (cf. p.230) because the child staggered or fell towards the wall when it was moved away from them (see Fig. 10.1). Indeed some of the children became distressed during the

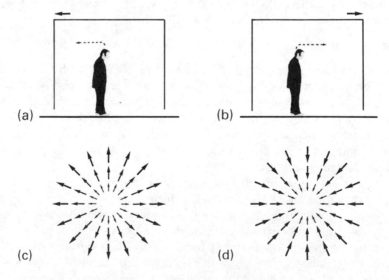

FIG.10.1.   An adult or child stands in the swinging room. (a) The room is moved towards the subject and s/he sways or falls backwards. (b) The room is moved away, and s/he sways or falls forwards. (c) The expanding optic flow pattern which would result from movement of the room towards the subject. (d) The contracting optical flow pattern which would result from the movement of the room away from the subject.

procedure and for them the experiment had to be prematurely terminated.

The responses shown by these children were entirely consistent with those that would be expected if the child interpreted the optic flow produced by movements of the room as resulting from its own postural sway. An outward flow, obtained when the room is moved towards the child, is consistent with sway towards the wall. The child then compensates for its apparent sway by moving backwards, and vice versa. It appears that in children acquiring the skill of balancing on two feet, visual information can over-ride the veridical information about the actual posture obtained from the feet, ankles and vestibular system. Lee and Aronson suggest that it is vision which "tunes up" the sensitivity of these mechanical systems, and point out that visual information is a better source for the child to rely on while the feet and ankles are maturing and growing. Such observations may explain why congenitally blind children are slower than sighted ones in learning to stand and to walk, and blind adults show more body sway than sighted adults (Edwards, 1946).

Even for sighted adults, however, it appears that visual information may over-ride that obtained from mechanical or vestibular receptor systems. A familiar example of this is when one experiences one's own stationary train as moving while another departs from the next platform, an example of induced movement (see Chapter 13). Lee and Lishman (1975) were able to affect body sway and stability in adults in normal and novel stances by movements of the swinging room. In one experiment they tested adults standing normally, on a sloping ramp, on a pile of foam pads (a "compliant" surface), or on their toes. Their degree of body sway was measured accurately with a sway meter when they stood with eyes open or eyes closed, or within the swinging room. Their body sway with eyes open could be "driven" by movements of the swinging room. Thus if the room was moved backwards and forwards in a regular, sinusoidal manner, the body was also seen to sway sinusoidally, linked to the movement of the walls. While this visual driving was observed in all four stances, it was greatest for adults standing on the compliant surface, where the information from the foot and ankle receptors was the most impoverished.

In a further experiment, Lee and Lishman had subjects adopt novel balancing postures such as the "Chaplin" stance (feet aligned at 180°) or the "pinstripe" stance (one foot angled behind the calf of the other leg while holding a weight in the hand opposite to the supporting leg). In such circumstances the adults, like the children in Lee and Aronson's study, could be made to stagger and fall by movements of the swinging room. They described the subject as like "a visual puppet; his balance can be manipulated by simply moving his surroundings without his being aware of it (Lee & Lishman, 1975, p.94)."

We have seen above that vision appears to play an important role in affecting gross postural adjustments. Babies respond to the exteroceptive information in looming patterns and try to avoid the "objects" which are about to collide with them. Toddlers and adults make use of exproprioceptive information from vision when maintaining balance. We now turn to consider how we use vision when we are actively negotiating terrain during locomotion.

WALKING, RUNNING AND JUMPING

It is obviously difficult to walk or run safely without adequate vision, but it is not necessarily obvious at how many different levels visual information is used to guide locomotion.

At the coarsest level, vision can inform moving animals of their direction of movement through the world. Any movement is accompanied by flow in the optic array, and the form of the flow pattern is precisely related to the direction of the movement. We have already considered in Chapter 8 how patterns of flow specify the direction in which a human or animal is moving.

Visual information is also needed in order to avoid colliding with objects in the path of the movement or to steer a path through openings, and to specify the kind of terrain which lies ahead. At a coarse level, this includes discovering surfaces of support and avoiding "falling-off" places.

Detecting Falling-Off Places

From the moment they are independently mobile, young animals must avoid falling off dangerous edges. Adult humans generally avoid accidentally stepping over the edge of a cliff, but would an unattended infant avoid crawling off? This was the question posed by E.J. Gibson which led to the development of the "visual cliff" (Gibson & Walk, 1960). The apparatus is shown in Figure 10.2. It consists of a raised platform which divides two checkerboard surfaces (giving optical "texture"). One of these is at a similar level to the platform (the shallow side), the other is considerably lower (the deep side). Both sides provide surfaces of support, however, since the deep side is covered with a sheet of glass which is at the same level as that covering the shallow side. Thus both the shallow and deep sides have a surface which could safely support an animal or child, but the optical information given by the deep side specifies a sharp drop. Gibson and Walk showed that the young of all species which guide themselves mainly by vision, when placed on the central platform, would avoid venturing onto the glass covering the deep side. Human infants aged 6–14 months would not cross the glass even when encouraged by their mothers who were standing on the other side of it. Young animals placed on the glass showed defensive reactions.

By manipulating the size of the texture elements on the surfaces, and the distances of these from the central platform, Gibson and Walk were able to

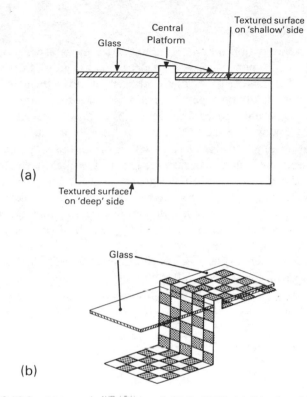

FIG.10.2. The visual cliff (Gibson & Walk, 1960). (a) Side view, (b) shows textured surfaces beneath the glass.

explore which variables were important in guiding the behaviour of the animals tested. If the squares on the deep side were made larger, so that the perceived density of the squares as seen from each side of the platform was equivalent, the animals still avoided the deep side, suggesting that motion perspective, rather than texture density, was the important variable. However, if the actual depth of each surface was made the same (i.e. both shallow), but one was patterned with smaller sized squares than the other, there was still a slight tendency to prefer the optically shallow side, suggesting some role for texture density. These observations suggest that by the time they are mobile (immediately for chicks and lambs, after 6 months or so for humans), young creatures can make use of motion perspective and also perhaps texture density changes in guiding themselves so that they remain on safe surfaces of support. The experiments on infant responses to looming patterns, along with those on the visual cliff, suggest that some appreciation of depth, or relative depth, may be inborn rather than learned in the way the Empiricist philosophers suggested (see Chapter 6). Bower (e.g. 1966, 1971) describes other observations of infants which are relevant to this issue.

Regulating Gait

We have seen how vision may be used to detect gross aspects of layout—obstacles and cliffs, but vision is also necessary to guide finer aspects of locomotion. The movements of our limbs as we move through the world need to be tailored to the type of terrain we encounter, and the type of terrain needs to be anticipated and the limbs adjusted accordingly. To see why, we must briefly describe the nature of locomotor activity.

An animal or human walks or runs with a smooth and cyclically regular sequence of limb movements (Bernstein, 1967). It propels itself forwards by applying force backwards against the ground as each foot strikes it. When walking, one or more feet (depending on how many the walker possesses) remain in contact with the ground all the time; when running, the animal or human progesses by a series of leaps. The length of each leap ("flight") is determined by the speed at which the animal is travelling and the vertical thrust applied at each stride. Figure 10.3 illustrates this further for those familiar with vectors. For both walking and running it is important that the thrust being applied to the foot on contact is coordinated with the swing-through time of the foot which will next contact the ground, so that this

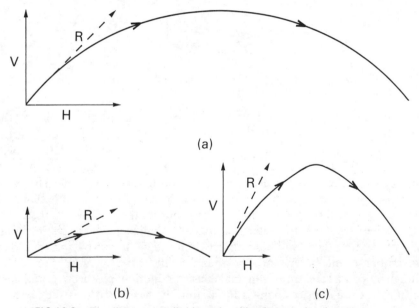

(a)

(b)   (c)

FIG.10.3.   The distance travelled in each stride when running depends upon the vertical thrust (V) and a force reflected in horizontal velocity (H). At (a), both V and H are large, and the flight is long. At (b) the vertical thrust is reduced, and at (c) the horizontal velocity is reduced. In both cases, flight length is reduced. The flight path is not the resultant (R) of vectors V and H, because other forces are operating.

meets the ground in the right way for maximum thrust. For example, if the foot is travelling forward relative to the ground when it contacts it, this will have a braking effect. Thus trained human runners try to lift their knees high so that they can thrust down hard and backwards relative to the ground as each foot strikes it just in front of the hips. The thrust applied at each stride must then give the runner sufficient vertical lift to ensure a long enough flight time so that the next foot can be swung through to its optimum strike position, and so on (Lee, Lishman & Thomson, 1982).

The striking of the ground needs not only to be timed, but the force exerted needs to be modified according to the type of surface encountered. If the ground surface is slippery then a large force will produce skidding rather than the desired propulsion forwards. If the surface is compliant rather than firm then much of the force will be absorbed by the surface rather than moving the animal (try running fast on soft sand), and so more force must be applied in order to maintain speed. If the surface is uneven then the animal may fail to find adequate points of contact between its feet and the ground. Despite these difficulties humans and other animals can normally maintain fairly smooth progress through an environment of variable surfaces provided they can see properly. At night it can be an uncomfortably jarring experience to run across hilly or uneven ground, demonstrating how vision is needed to make fine adjustments to planned foot positions, postures and forces (Lee, 1980a).

It is thus essential that gait is regulated to meet the demands of a particular terrain. Theories of action which stress the "blind" running off of programs of locomotor activity have little to say about this.

There will, in general, be unpredictable influences, both from within and without, which will deviate the activity from its intended course. The activity has, therefore, to be monitored in terms of the program and any deviation corrected by adjusting the ongoing program. It is in this continual process of formulating locomotor programs, monitoring their execution and adjusting them that sensory information plays its vital role. (Lee & Lishman, 1977, p.226)

Lee et al. (1982) have illustrated this adjusting of locomotor programs by sensory information in their studies of the sport of long-jumping. A long-jumper needs to maximise his or her horizontal velocity and vertical thrust at the point of take-off (refer back to Fig. 10.3). Since the jump is measured to the take-off board, and is disqualified if the athlete steps over this, the athlete must try to reach maximum speed as the launching foot strikes the board, with the body postured appropriately to give maximum lift. Athletic coaches encourage their students to develop a standard run-up, which they mark out in paces back from the board, and they may intersperse practice jumps with "run-throughs," where the athlete strikes the board but runs on through the sand without jumping. Such training procedures seem to be based on the assumption that some kind of run-up program can be set up, learned and executed without further modification during the course of the action. Lee et al. (1982) set out to examine whether athletes did indeed maintain a standard run-up in accordance with training procedures.

They filmed the training sessions of three female athletes who ranged from club to olympic standard. A striped marker strip was placed on either side of the track so that the athletes' foot placements could be accurately measured from single frames of the film. Their analysis revealed that the run-up consisted of two distinct phases. Until the athletes were a few strides from the board, their stride patterns were remarkably constant, which presumably reflected their training with standard run-ups. This consistency broke down over the last few strides however. It appeared that the cumulative effect of the small inconsistencies during the first phase meant that the athlete had to adjust her final few strides in order to strike the board accurately. There was a dramatic increase in the variability of stride lengths for the last three strides, while the standard error (a measure of variability) of the footfall positions decreased dramatically over these same few strides, to reach 8cm at the board for the olympic athlete. It appeared that athletes were homing in on the board by adjusting the flight time of each of the last few strides. You will remember that flight length, and hence flight time will be affected by changes in the vertical thrust applied if velocity remains constant (see Fig. 10.3). Lee et al. argue that these few strides are visually guided by the optic flow parameter τ which specifies time to contact with the board. In Chapter 9 (p.222) we showed how τ was derived by considering the relative velocities of optical texture elements. For the examples we will discuss in this chapter:

$$\tau(t) = 1/\text{rate of dilation of retinal image of an obstacle.}$$

In the case of the long-jumper, τ would be given by the inverse of the rate of dilation of the image of the board. The average adjustment which is needed to the vertical thrusts of the last few strides (in order to modulate the flight times) is t'_f/t_f, where t'_f is the required mean flight time of the remaining strides and t_f is the current flight time. t'_f is specified by time-to-contact.

The long-jumper is perhaps an extreme example of precisely timed locomotion, but those of us of meagre athletic ability are still able to run to catch a bus, jumping over puddles and negotiating kerbs and other minor hurdles on the way. These activities are probably visually controlled in the same way as the more precise skill of long-jumping. For many of us however, speedy transport is achieved by driving, rather than running. In the next section we consider how the control of some aspects of driving might also be given by the use of τ.

DRIVING CARS

Braking

Humans, unlike other animals, can propel themselves speedily and effortlessly through the world with the aid of machines. The motor-cyclist or car driver must learn to steer his or her vehicle around corners and obstacles, and must be able to slow down or stop as conditions dictate. A good driver will use the brake in good time, and with the correct force so that the car's speed can be reduced appropriately and smoothly. However if brakes are applied too late (see unsafe driver 3 in Fig. 10.4), or too gently (unsafe driver 2 in Fig. 10.4), the driver will enter the "crash zone" shown in Figure 10.4, which may be fatal.

There are thus two components to braking—knowing when to start and knowing how hard to brake. When following fairly closely behind another vehicle a driver is usually given a clear visual signal to start applying brakes when the brake-lights of the car in front light up. He or she still has to decide how hard to apply the brakes however since normal brake lights give no indication about how much the car in front is slowing. The driver must therefore respond to the optic information which specifies how quickly he or she is closing on the car in front. It is better to brake strongly at first, since this minimises the stopping distance, but the driver must also avoid braking too severely for the car behind to respond in turn. Good drivers

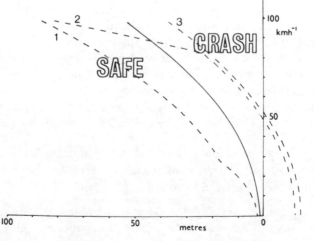

FIG.10.4. To stop safely, a driver must reduce speed (Km per hour) to zero before the distance to an obstacle (metres) reaches zero. The safe driver (1) in this figure achieves this by braking strongly at first, and then more gently. Driver 3 does not start to brake soon enough, and driver 2 brakes too gently. Reproduced from Lee & Lishman (1977) with permission of author and publishers.

drive safe braking distances apart, and this also requires adjustment according to speed and road conditions.

When brakes must be applied to negotiate an "obstacle" (e.g. traffic lights) the driver must decide when to start braking as well as how much pressure to apply. A potentially dangerous situation is encountered by the driver when leaving a fast highway where he or she may have adapted to travelling at a high constant velocity, and may fail to brake sufficiently to negotiate a steeply curved exit road or a roundabout (traffic circle). The driver's ability to reduce his speed accordingly can be enhanced by giving explicit advice on road signs about recommended exit or cornering speeds, or by augmenting the visual information which the driver responds to by constructing fences or painting lines across the road. One of the major through-routes in England, the A1, is particularly dangerous because it is almost of motorway (freeway) standard, hence people drive fast, but it is constantly interrupted by roundabouts (traffic circles) which must be taken slowly. Yellow lines have been painted across the road on the approach to some of these roundabouts, and the lines get closer together nearer the roundabout. The lines themselves give one a vivid impression of speed after the relatively featureless miles preceding them, and the gradual change in the spacing of the lines gives drivers visual information that suggests they are decelerating less quickly than they actually are. This causes drivers to brake harder than they might otherwise.

It would appear that good drivers must be constantly monitoring their distance from other cars and obstacles, and must know about their own and other cars' speeds, acceleration and deceleration in order to brake effectively. However, Lee (1976) has argued that the control of braking can be more economically achieved if the driver responds directly to information about time-to-contact which is available in the optic flow field.

Lee suggests that a driver could register the value of $\tau(t)$ simply from the inverse of the proportionate rate of separation of the retinal images of any two points on the obstacle, e.g. the tail lights of a vehicle. That is:

$$\tau(t) = 1/(\text{rate of dilation of retinal image of obstacle})$$

$$\tau(t) = \frac{(\text{angular separation of the tail lights})}{(\text{rate of separation of the tail lights})}$$

In daylight the driver might make use of the image of the entire car in front, but only tail lights could be used at a distance at night. Lee suggests that a driver could make use of the optic variable τ and its derivative with respect to time, $\dot{\tau}$, to determine whether he is gaining on or receding from the car in front, and so to judge when to start braking for an obstacle or a moving vehicle, and to determine safe following distances and speeds. For example, Figure 10.5 shows a model which Lee (1976; also Lee & Lishman

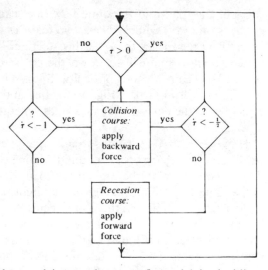

FIG.10.5. Lee's (1976) model illustrates how a driver can maintain a safe distance by maintaining τ and $\dot{\tau}$ at safe values. See Lee (1976) for derivation of these values. Reproduced from Lee & Lishman (1977) with permission of author and publishers.

1977) suggests might describe how a driver makes use of τ and $\dot{\tau}$ in deciding whether he needs to brake (to avoid collision) or to accelerate (to keep up with traffic flow). This figure shows that a driver's deceleration is adequate if $\dot{\tau} > -\frac{1}{2}$ (a figure derived in detail in Lee (1976)). A driver could therefore function safely provided he maintained $\dot{\tau}$ at some marginal value greater than $-\frac{1}{2}$. Lee shows that such an assumption gives quite a good fit to data obtained in experiments where drivers were asked to stop at a specified point which they approached with varying speeds (Spurr, 1969).

Lee also suggests that road safety could be improved by amplifying or adding to the visual information gained from the rear ends of vehicles, particularly at night. By adding a reflectant strip so that the driver sees a progressively wider band of light the closer he approaches a vehicle at night, the information about rate of closure would be amplified, just as the yellow stripes painted across roads (see p.240) amplify information about speed. Information could be added by having an "imperative" brake signal, in addition to the normal brake lights, which would only operate when strong pressure was applied to the brake pedal by the driver in front.

Steering

We have already discussed in Chapter 8 how the optic flow pattern produced by movement along a straight path can inform an observer about the direction in which he or she is travelling. Lee & Lishman (1977) describe how optic flow can be used to guide steering. First, the optic flow line which disappears from view directly underneath the driver—the locomotor flow line—indicates the potential path that would be followed if no correction to the steering was applied. Second, the relationship between the images of the edges of the road and the optic flow lines can inform a driver whether he or she is on or off course. These two features of optical flow patterns could be used by the driver to adjust his steering. When steering on course, the locomotor flow line will lie down the centre of the road and the edges of the road will coincide with optic flow lines. When off-course, neither of these conditions will hold (see Fig. 10.6). Lee and Lishman extend these same principles to the curved optic flow lines generated by a driver steering round a bend.

However, a driver also has to anticipate bends, and begin to slow down before reaching sharp ones. Lee and Lishman suggest that information about time-to-contact (with the edge of the road, for example) could be used here in the same way as in braking on a straight path.

A single variable, τ, therefore seems to be involved in a variety of locomotor activities, which include the defensive reactions of babies, the regulation of gait by long-jumpers, and braking by drivers, as well as the control of diving in gannets described in the last chapter. We now turn from locomotion to consider a rather different set of activities, those involved in catching and hitting balls in sport and play. Here we again find that "time to contact" is an important variable.

BALL GAMES: CATCHING AND HITTING

The problem faced by a human trying to catch a ball in his or her hands is like that of a predator such as the toad catching an insect with its tongue. The path of the "target" must be correctly perceived so that the limbs can be moved to the right positions.

Human infants are able to reach accurately for a moving object at the age when they first reach for stationary ones, by about 18 weeks (Von Hofsten and Lindhagen, 1979). Von Hofsten and Lindhagen studied babies ranging from 12–36 weeks of age and recorded their reactions to a brightly coloured target which was moved at different speeds across their field of vision. Reaching occurred more frequently to slowly moving targets and more often in the older children. Across all age groups those reaches which were made were almost always accurate, suggesting that the babies only initiated a reach when they were likely to be successful. The youngest babies, at 12 weeks, hardly ever attempted to reach, and as they developed they reached first for the "easier," slowly moving targets.

A detailed film analysis of the reaches made by the babies (Von Hofsten, 1980) revealed that they moved their arms in a series of ballistic (open-loop) movements to the point where contact would be made with the moving target. Babies at all ages were remarkably accurate at predicting the path of the target, but the older infants reached for it more "economically," using

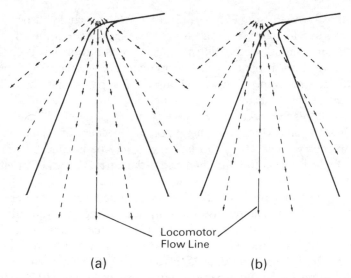

Locomotor
Flow Line

(a)   (b)

FIG.10.6. At (a) the driver is on course. The locomotor flow line lies down the centre of the lane on which the car travels, and optic flow lines coincide with the edges of the road. At (b) neither of these conditions holds, and the driver is off course. Adapted from Lee & Lishman (1977) with permission of author and publishers.

fewer ballistic steps. "While the infants seem to know where to go in order to catch the object most efficiently when they begin to reach, they do not seem to know quite how to get there (von Hofsten, 1980, p.381)."

Even the youngest infants were able to "home in" on the target using discrete moves without looking back at their hands, suggesting that at this age they are able to define the position of their hands in perceived space using information from their joints and muscles.

Thus the prerequisites of catching or hitting appear to be at least partially pre-wired in the human. What seems to develop is the motor skill of getting to the target economically and grasping it, or hitting it, once there. In order to catch a moving ball for example the hand or hands must be oriented correctly and appropriate grasping movements initiated *before* the ball makes physical contact with the hand, while it is still in flight. Alderson, Sully and Sully (1974) studied one-handed catching of tennis balls and found that the fine orienting movements of the hand began 150–200 msec before the ball struck the palm and the grasping movement started 32–50 msec before contact.

While some vision is essential in order to assess the flight path and speed of a moving target in order to initiate these movements it does not seem to be necessary to view the entire trajectory. Whiting and Sharp (1974) studied one-handed catching of tennis balls which were only illuminated for 80 msec of their trajectory. The duration of the dark period which followed this brief illumination was varied from 125 to 445 msec (which included a period of 125 msec assumed to reflect nervous system latency). They found that the function relating accuracy of catching and occlusion duration was U-shaped. Performance was poor if the occluded period was greater than 365 msec or shorter than 205 msec, peaking at 285 msec. It appears that there is an optimal point in the trajectory during which to view the ball in order to predict its path, this being when the time to contact is about 250–300 msec. If the ball is seen too early it gets "lost," possibly because of limitations on immediate memory. If it is seen too late there may be insufficient time to process the flight information and then begin the correct series of orienting movements.

Lee (1980a) has suggested that the 300 msec time-to-contact interval is critical because catchers standardise the duration of their movements and therefore need only to initiate these movements at a specific time to contact. Standard movement durations have been observed in a study by Schmidt (1969) where subjects had to move a slider to hit an approaching target, and also in ball-hitting by baseball batters. Hubbard and Seng (1954) filmed baseball batters and observed that they always began to step forward when the ball was released by the pitcher, but geared the duration of the step to the speed of the ball. The duration of the bat swing was kept constant but its initiation was dependent on ball speed, occurring about 40 msec after the forward foot was planted. Hubbard and Seng also tried to record the head and eye movements made by their sample of batters as they tracked the path of the ball. Though their methods were insensitive, their film analysis did suggest that batters did not track or fixate the ball during the final stage of its flight, nor when it actually made contact with the bat (contrary to the advice given in training manuals). Again it appears that it is information about time to contact picked up earlier in the flight path which is of more importance than the information gained in the final moments before contact occurs.

Recently, Lee, Young, Reddish, Lough, and Clayton (1983) have explored the visual control of hitting in a situation where subjects had to leap up and punch balls which were dropped from varying heights above them, as in volleyball. A ball dropping towards the ground accelerates at a constant rate under the influence of gravity. Its velocity thus increases continuously. Lee et al. suggested that subjects might still make use of τ—the *instantaneous* time to contact at any point in the drop (cf. our discussion of gannets in Chapter 9). τ will always be greater than the *actual* time to contact (t_c) at that point, as illustrated in Figure 10.7. τ depends on the instantaneous velocity, and assumes that this remains constant for the remainder of the drop. But because the ball is accelerating, its average velocity for the remaining drop time will be greater than the velocity used to compute τ, and hence the actual time to contact, t_c, will be less than τ. The overestimation of t_c given by τ depends on the total drop time as illustrated in Figure 10.7.

If subjects were using τ to time their actions, one would predict that each stage of the punching action would occur earlier, the longer the drop time of the ball. For example, if the value of τ used to control a particular stage of the action were 1 sec, Figure 10.7 shows that this corresponds to a t_c of about 0.6 sec for a long drop and about 0.5 sec for a short drop. However the action patterns for the different drop times should converge close to contact, since as Figure 10.7 shows, τ and t_c converge when actual time to contact is less than 250 msec. (It may be for this reason that 250–300 msec is an important time to contact during which to view a ball in flight, since it is at this point that τ can be used to give an accurate measure of the actual time to contact, while still allowing enough time for orienting movements to occur.) By measuring the changes occurring in the angles of the knee and elbow as these were flexed and extended in the punching act, Lee et al. were able to confirm these predictions, and produce evidence that the actions were indeed timed by making use of τ.

We have discussed at some length in this chapter and the previous one how a variety of animal and human activities may be regulated through the detection of fairly simple parameters derived from optic flow. To show that a particular variable, like τ, could be used to control action is much easier to do than to show *how* it is involved at the level of regulating muscle actions. We have ignored this latter problem in our discussion up till now. In the next chapter we deal explicitly with some of the issues raised by the control of action, and consider ways in which vision might be involved in this control.

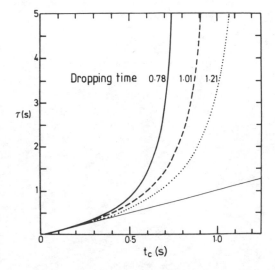

FIG.10.7. The relationship between τ (instantaneous time to contact) and t_c (actual time to contact) for balls dropped from three different heights to yield three different drop times (0.78, 1.01 and 1.21 secs). From Lee et al. (1983). Copyright © The Experimental Psychology Society. Reproduced by permission of the author and the E.P.S.

11 Theories of the Control of Action

In Chapters 9 and 10, we saw that both animal and human perception do involve the detection of some of the parameters of the optic array and optic flow field which Gibson believed to be important. Chicks and babies avoid precipices by detecting motion parallax and texture gradients; flies find landing sites by detecting wiping of texture in the optic flow field and both gannets and people time movement by monitoring the relative rate of expansion of parts of the flow field. The description of the information available in light developed by Gibson is therefore useful in explaining some perceptual processes.

This reflects another feature of the "ecological" approach to perception, which is its emphasis on the role of perception in an animal's or person's action. The traditional approach treats perception and action as quite distinct processes, regarding perception as the processing of the information in the retinal image to yield a symbolic representation of the world, and action as the generation of commands to the muscles. This generation of responses must obviously draw on information about the environment, but the traditional view would be that the two processes could be analysed independently of one another.

In the ecological view, however, perception and action are tightly interlocked processes. Animals and people do not passively perceive the world but move about in it actively, picking up the information needed to guide their movement. There is a continuous cycle between organism and world. The consequence of this viewpoint is that the role of perception is to furnish the information needed to organise action, which in turn implies that an understanding of perception requires an understanding of the systems controlling action. In this chapter, we therefore intend to explore the relationship between perception and action in two contexts; first, the optomotor response of insects and, secondly, the control of human action. We will not be able to provide a clear answer to the question of how vision controls action, but we hope to introduce you to the kind of framework which might be useful for answering this question in the future.

THE OPTOMOTOR RESPONSE

In Chapter 9, we described the turning response of a tethered insect in a rotating drum (p. 209) and argued that the role of this response is to keep an insect on as straight a path as possible through the environment. We mentioned that some progress has been made in uncovering the neurophysiological basis of this response, with the discovery of neurons that respond to uniform movement of a pattern of light over the eye. If the insect's nervous system transforms the spatiotemporal pattern of light intensity at the eye into a pattern of neural activity representing the distribution of movement over the eye, then what is the next stage? How are commands to muscles modulated in order to generate the appropriate turn?

Von Holst (1954) explained the optomotor response in terms of the model shown in Figure 11.1; a command to carry out a movement originates in a "higher centre" of the nervous system and an "efference copy" of the commands to the muscles is retained in a "lower centre." As the movement is executed, there will be a flow of optic texture over the eye and this movement-induced input is called "reafference." The reafferent input can be compared with the input expected from the commands stored as an efference copy in the lower centre. Note the similarity between this model and the one we discussed in Chapter 6, which attempted to explain how the human nervous system compensates for effects of the movement of the eye on the retinal image.

How does Von Holst's "efference copy" model explain the optomotor response? If the insect is stationary, no optic flow over the eye is expected and so a discrepancy is registered if the drum rotates. The discrepancy indicates that the source of the movement is outside the insect and so it turns in order to reduce the discrepancy caused by relative movement. If, on the other hand, the insect initiates a movement in a stationary environment, the resulting reafference corresponds to that predicted from the efference copy and so there is no discrepancy. The theory can therefore account for the insect's ability to initiate movement without being locked into position by the optomotor response.

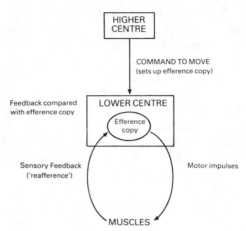

FIG.11.1. Von Holst's efference copy model.

We have already discussed one problem with this theory in Chapter 9, arguing that the sensory information provided by a rotating drum would, in the insect's normal environment, unambiguously specify rotation of the insect. The more important problem for now, however, is that Von Holst's efference copy theory assumes that reafference *can* be predicted from motor commands. In the case of the human eye, this may well be so; given the mechanics of the muscles, inertia of the eyeball and so on, a particular pattern of muscle contraction will yield a predictable rate, direction and extent of movement over the retina. But this will not necessarily be so for a flying or walking animal. The same set of commands to the flight or leg muscles can generate quite different results depending upon patterns of air flow around the animal or the terrain it is walking on. This is a problem of "context conditioned variability," which we will return to later in this chapter.

We would therefore argue that a better model of the optomotor response does not involve reafference but rather a direct comparison between the extent of lateral flow over the eyes and a set point of zero, after which any discrepancy generates appropriate commands to the muscles to turn the insect. This model differs from the efference copy model in not including any means of resolving whether the source of optic flow is the animal's own movement or an external disturbance. As we have argued, however, there is no reason, in many circumstances, for an insect to resolve this ambiguity; all it needs is information specifying what corrective change in its flight is needed.

Discarding a role for an efference copy leaves us with another problem. In Von Holst's model, the insect can make self-initiated movements through commands from a higher centre lying outside the feedback loop controlling movement, but the model we suggest leaves it locked into a fixed position or path of movement as long as there is no movement in its surroundings.

Rather than solve this problem by introducing a higher level in a hierarchical system of behavioural organisation, we suggest that the system of regulation of optic flow which generates the optomotor response is one of a number of regulatory systems. Each one monitors some parameter of optic flow and modulates movement so as to maintain it at some preferred value or within a range of values. A stationary insect does not therefore begin to move because of a command from a "higher centre" but because a different regulatory system has switched into control, and movement is now maintaining a different pattern of optic flow.

Three processes are likely to be important in determining switches between these regulatory systems. First, information detected in the environment will be important; for example, information specifying a food source may bring about a switch from a regulatory system generating cruising flight to one guiding the insect to the food. In other cases, such information may simply trigger a stereotyped response rather than switch in a new regulatory system, as when a shadow moving downwards over a locust's eye causes it to jump.

Secondly, changes in an animal's internal state, such as motivational changes or cyclical changes in arousal will bias switches between regulatory systems, or may cause them to occur in the absence of external changes. Finally, it is likely that semi-random fluctuations between regulatory systems are important; Reichardt and Poggio's (1976) finding of stochastic fluctuation in a fly's fixation of a pattern reflects a process of this kind.

This model of the optomotor response, and especially its extension to other aspects of insect behaviour, is a tentative one which needs to be tested against behavioural evidence. Even so, we have put it forward as an example of one way of integrating perception and action, through regulatory systems maintaining stable patterns of flow of sensory information and movement, each constraining the other. There is no longer any need to postulate a "central executive" watching an internal picture of the world and selecting pieces of behaviour to execute. Instead, stable patterns of regulation of sensory flow switch in and out of control as conditions change.

One advantage of thinking about the organisation of insects' and other animals' behaviour in this way is that it gets us around the puzzle of "how the world looks to an animal." We tend to think of ourselves as in some way located behind our eyes, looking at a picture displayed to us, and we are tempted to wonder what that picture might look like for a fly, fish or horse.

Put more formally, the question is what kind of representation of the environment is present in the animal's nervous system, and we believe that this question is a misleading one if it treats perception in isolation from action. The economical way to organise a nervous system is for perceptual mechanisms to detect whatever information is needed to guide the animal's activities, and no more. Our suggestion is that for many insects the information that is needed is the value of a number of parameters of optic flow which are regulated by competing homeostatic systems.

THE CONTROL OF HUMAN ACTION

In Chapter 10 we described the information available from patterns of optic flow which could be used to guide various human activities, both natural and skilled. We now turn to consider *how* this guidance may be achieved. In order to do this, it is necessary to outline briefly some of the problems in the control of human action, which are, not surprisingly, more difficult than those involved in the control of insect action.

Most theorists are agreed that actions must ultimately be controlled at a high level in the nervous system where something like an "action plan" must be formulated and executed. When we consider the nature of action plans it is clear that at some level the representation must be sufficiently flexible and abstract to allow equivalent ends to be achieved in a variety of ways. Turvey (1977a) gives as an example the observation that we can draw a letter A with a pen on paper, with a finger on someone's back or with a toe in the sand. At least some of these activities may be novel, but are not difficult for us. In the same way we can recognise a letter A drawn in different ways by different people (see Chapter 7). Some abstract representation of the letter perhaps allows for the way in which we can generalise both when perceiving and when acting. Here we see one contrast with the organisation of insect behaviour, where such flexibility of motor control is largely absent.

Suppose then we wished to draw an A in the sand with a toe. Somehow the abstract representation which we wish to particularise must be translated into a specific pattern of motor (i.e. muscle) activity. It might be possible, in principle, to conceive of each muscle involved in this action being independently instructed by commands issued from a high level in the nervous system. Thus our abstract conception of the letter A might be translated into a series of independent commands to a variety of muscles in the leg, foot and toes. This kind of "push-button" metaphor for the control of action has been criticised by Bernstein (1967) whose arguments have been summarised and extended by Turvey and his colleagues (Turvey, 1977a; Turvey, Shaw, & Mace, 1978; Turvey, Fitch, & Tuller, 1982; Tuller, Turvey, & Fitch, 1982; Fitch, Tuller, & Turvey, 1982).

There are two different, but closely associated problems with the push-button metaphor. The first is known as the *degrees of freedom* problem. An "executive" issuing independent efferent commands to all those muscles involved in even the simplest of movements would have a very great deal of moment to moment computation to perform. This first problem is possibly confounded by the second—that of *context-conditioned variability* (Turvey et al., 1982). We have already met this problem in discussing the insect optomotor response, where we pointed out that the consequences of a particular pattern of commands to leg or wing muscles would not be predictable, but would depend upon the external forces acting on the limbs. In the human case, the problem is even greater, as the context in which any particular muscle contraction occurs affects the actual limb movement achieved. The movement produced by a given contraction depends on the current configuration of the parts of the limb, the current motions of the adjoining limb segments, and the external forces against which each muscle must work. An executive pressing the buttons, in such a model, would have to have moment to moment information available about the external forces and the dynamic and static aspects of the current configurations of the limb segments.

Turvey et al. (1978) liken the problem of the push-button executive to that which an air pilot would face if he or she had to control individually each of the mechanical segments used to guide the flight of an aeroplane. At a minimum, an aeroplane has two ailerons at the back of the wings which can be moved up or down to control roll; two elevators on the tail which if moved up or down control pitch, and a rudder at the back which can be moved left or right to control yaw (cf. insect flight in Chapter 9). There is thus one degree of freedom for each of these five hinged parts. If each of these parts had to be altered individually the pilot would be faced with an impossible informational load. Even if the mechanical parts could only be moved to one of eight positions the control system would still have to keep track of 8^5 (32,768) independent states.

Of course no air pilot actually has to cope with this task because the mechanical components of the guidance system are in fact linked. The ailerons are yoked so that when one moves up the other moves down. The rudder is linked to the ailerons so that it moves left when the right aileron goes down: and the elevators on the tail section move together—both up or both down. This linkage reduces the degrees of freedom to two, and the guidance of the aircraft can be achieved with a joystick which also has two degrees of freedom (it can be moved forward or backward for ascent or descent and from side to side to bank or turn.)

Turvey et al. (1978) and Turvey (1977a) suggest that combinations of muscles in animals are similarly linked and constrained to act together as *coordinative structures* which can function relatively autonomously. Spinal reflexes are seen as simple examples of coordinative structures, though even these can involve quite complicated actions. For example, an animal with the upper part of the spinal cord completely sectioned will still repeatedly scratch an itch on its body with whichever foot can most easily reach it.

The concept of coordinative structures goes beyond simple reflex acts however, to include patterns of inter-limb coordination in voluntary acts.

THE CONTROL OF HUMAN ACTION 253

An everyday example is given by the difficulty we experience if we try to beat out two quite different rhythms simultaneously with different hands. The hands seem constrained to act together in this situation. Kelso, Putnam, and Goodman (1983) have demonstrated this more formally. If two hands are required to make movements of different difficulties and directions, the movement of each hand is influenced by that of the other. Such patterns of mutual constraint and interaction would not be expected if an "executive" independently commanded each muscle. Turvey therefore suggests that the executive commands a group of muscles which function cooperatively together.

Coordinative structures thus reduce the degrees of freedom problem, and they may also solve some of the problems of context-conditioned variability. Coordinative structures can take care of the local context in which an action takes place if they behave like mass-spring systems, in which the equilibrium point of a spring to which a mass is attached is not affected however the mass is pushed or pulled. The spring always returns to rest at the same length, without any executive monitoring its movements over time. There is some evidence that human limb movements exhibit similar properties. More radically, coordinative structures may be viewed as *limit-cycle oscillators* (a different kind of oscillator from the familiar mass-spring system). Limit-cycle oscillators are mutually synchronising—they influence one another's behaviour. We have just described how movement in one hand may influence the movement in the other, and such observations suggest that this model of coordinative structures may be a fruitful one to pursue (see Tuller et al., 1982 for a good introduction to these ideas).

Thus coordinative structures may drastically reduce the number of instructions and monitoring that the executive must perform. However, coordinative structures must still be set into action, and their parameters altered to cope with changing environmental circumstances, so our executive still has a role to play. From the above discussion it follows that the instructions issued from the executive must be at a more abstract level than instructions to individual muscles. The executive is seen as controlling the modes of interaction of lower centres. Turvey argues that this form of control should not be viewed as hierarchically organised, with the executive issuing commands which pass unidirectionally and without modification to lower levels. Rather he suggests that the system must be organised as a *heterarchy*, or, more radically, as a *coalition* (see Turvey et al., 1978). In a heterarchical organisation no one part of the system should be seen as dominating the others. All levels in a heterarchy contribute equally to hypothesis-testing and decision-making.

An important structure which contributes to the organisation and control of action is the segmental apparatus of the mammalian spinal cord. The spinal cord can be seen as a set of "segments" (marked out by the vertebrae), within each of which there are neuronal loops which control simple reflexes (like the knee jerk), without involving any "communication" with the brain. Complex voluntary activities may involve the recruitment, modification and elaboration of these simple reflexes, which form the bases for coordinative structures. This may be achieved in part by *tuning* of the segmental apparatus prior to a movement occurring. Turvey (1977a) cites evidence from Gurfinkel, Kots, Krinsky, Pal'tsev, Feldman, Tsetlin, and Shik (1971) in support of the notion of tuning. If a subject is asked to flex one leg, it typically takes about 170 msec between the command and the flexion occurring. If, during this latency period, the knee-jerk reflex is elicited, its amplitude is enhanced relative to a control condition where no command is present. It therefore appears that an instruction issued from the brain to the leg involves the preparation or tuning of the segmental apparatus prior to the actual movement of the leg occurring.

If we continue to consider leg movements, in the more complex activity of walking or running, there is evidence that the organisation of the segmental apparatus of the spinal cord allows the initiation and maintenance of stepping movements of the limbs without sensory input. However the form of the stepping pattern must be tailored to the external forces. This can be achieved by using afferent information obtained from reflex structures and also by tuning the segmental apparatus on the detection of relevant information obtained primarily through vision. In this way a basic pattern of activity can be attuned to the current contextual demands.

Thus the control of action involves both the activation of the relevant coordinative structures and their tuning to meet environmental conditions. Both of these functions can be seen as dependent on the pickup of information from the optic array. The detection of *invariants* may underlie the perception of significant structures towards which the animal or person must manoeuvre, or upon which it must act. The detection of *variation,* i.e. the pattern of change in the optic flow, will determine the precise form that the action must take.

> . . . evolution has thoroughly exploited the principle of separating action-plan specification from tuning. The instinctive rituals are released by stimulation of a simple kind—the red belly of the stickleback, the spot under the herring-gull's beak—but the unfolding stereotypic behaviour is flexible; it relates to the lie of the land, to the contingencies of the local environment. We should suppose that these species-specific action plans are adjusted by the pickup of information about the environment, that is to say, that tuning is environment-related. (Turvey, 1977a, p.246)

Once again however, the details of tuning need not be specified absolutely at a cortical level. Much of it can be achieved by the segmental apparatus.

Indeed given the nature of the interactions at lower levels, many aspects of locomotor adjustment may take care of themselves. This can be achieved in part by some types of *tuning reflex*. An example of this is the tonic neck reflex, which biases the motor apparatus for a movement in the direction of gaze. In humans, directing the eyes and head towards an item of interest may effect reorganisation of the segmental apparatus appropriate to changing the direction of locomotion. Detailed information about the layout of the environment, which modifies the form of the locomotion in the new direction may likewise be taken account of at a segmental level. The executive (something of a misnomer in a heterarchically organised system) cannot, given the degrees of freedom problem, be responsible for the detailed metrical prescription for an act. This must be realised at lower levels, but there is good evidence that the spinal and muscular systems are functionally organised to achieve this.

Thus visual information of different kinds (invariants and variants) must be injected into unfolding activities at appropriate points, after which the coordinative structures which have been activated and tuned can take care of themselves to a large extent. However, Turvey and his colleagues go even further, and devolve the responsibility for these "injections" of visual information to the coordinative structures:

> We do not want a model in which the brain interprets the perceptual information, decides what portion of the information to supply a given coordinative structure, and when to supply it. Instead, the organisation of the coordinative structure should be such as to accept only certain information at certain times. (Fitch et al., 1982, p.272)

Coordinative structures do seem to be organised so that a minimal change in one of their parameters has a maximum effect on behaviour. An animal's speed of running is altered only by the thrust it applies to the ground, other aspects of the step cycle remaining constant. To return to baseball batters (see p. 244), as we mentioned, Hubbard and Seng (1954) showed that batters keep the timing of their swings constant, and deal with balls of varying speed by altering only the speed with which they step forward. Time to contact assessed during the ball's flight thus affects only a single aspect of a complex activity.

The baseball batter serves as an example to summarise the ideas of Turvey and his colleagues which we have presented here. The invariants of the ball-pitching situation (those that specify a ball, a pitcher, etc.) inform the batter that a striking action would be appropriate. The action plan for "striking" will be abstract, and rather than consisting of detailed instructions to individual muscles, will serve to recruit the appropriate coordinative structures. The variants in the situation (e.g., the speed of the ball) will determine how the batter should strike it, but are used to modify only certain components of the action, leaving others constant.

Turvey's arguments remain controversial, and we have given no more than their flavour in this chapter. The details of the anatomical, physiological and experimental evidence for his position have been omitted. However it is hoped that this brief account will serve to illustrate how perception and action might be related within an ecological theory. Indeed in such an approach they cannot be separated. Within this framework an "action plan" is seen as one and the same as a projection of the environment, the product of "perception."

CONCLUSIONS

A fundamental part of the ecological view of perception is that perception and action are interlocked processes. If we are to understand perception, we must know what it is for, and that means we must understand how action is organised. In simple animals such as insects, the principle that perception is for the control of movement may well be sufficient to give us a full understanding of perception. In more complex animals, and especially in people, this viewpoint is relevant only to certain aspects of perception; those involved in the moment-by-moment control of movement—taking strides, hitting a ball, applying brakes and so on. It is not directly relevant to understanding how perception yields information not used in the immediate control of activity but instead stored in some way to influence activity later. The principle of perception being constrained by action is not obviously relevant to a person watching a television programme, for example.

The next two chapters follow up the ecological approach in two different directions. First, we look at some ways in which perception is involved in the moment-by-moment control of animals' actions in their *animate* environment; the prey, predators and conspecifics around them. Then, in Chapter 13, we will ask what the ecological approach has to offer the study of human perception outside the context of moment-by-moment control of movement.

12 Perception of the Animate World

In Chapters 9 and 10, we saw ways in which animals and people detect information in light that specifies the three-dimensional layout of the world, which they need in order to control actions such as diving or long-jumping. Most of our examples concerned the inanimate environment, however, and on the whole we have not considered situations where the position and movement of other animals or other people need to be detected. In this chapter we extend our discussion to such situations and, using the ecological approach of the last three chapters, ask how animals perceive their *animate* environment.

An animal is normally surrounded by many other animals, of many different species, but it only needs information about the activities of those which in some way affect its chances of survival and reproduction. These fall into three categories. The first is *prey*, which carnivorous animals must detect, pursue and capture. Secondly, most species are themselves prey for other species, and they must be able to detect and evade *predators*.

Thirdly, most animals must be able to obtain information about the activities of their *conspecifics*—other members of their own species—with which they must engage in social behaviour. Social behaviour includes mating and the courtship behaviour which may precede it, parental care, play and various forms of competition such as aggression and territoriality. In some species, particularly the social insects and some mammals, it includes elaborate forms of cooperative behaviour in which many individuals engage together in hunting, nest building and other activities.

In all these situations, an animal must be able to perceive what other animals are doing and adjust its own behaviour accordingly. This will involve

257

detection of where another animal is, in what direction it is moving, what posture it is in, and so on. We look at a series of examples of animal social behaviour that require the ability to detect increasingly elaborate information of this kind.

DETECTING ANOTHER ANIMAL'S BEARING

The simplest information about another animal which light can provide is its *bearing* relative to the observer. This is given by the position in the optic array of light reflected from the other animal relative to the axis of the observer's body (Fig. 12.1). For an animal with a single-chambered eye this is equivalent to the retinal coordinates of the image of the other animal or, if the eye is mobile, to the displacement of the eye required to fixate the target. For an insect, it is equivalent to the coordinates of the ommatidia stimulated by light reflected from the other animal. If the other animal is a predator, information specifying its relative position is necessary to move away from it or to take up a defensive posture with the correct orientation. If it is a potential mate or prey, on the other hand, the information is needed to pursue it.

One way of pursuing another animal is to release a stereotyped pattern of movement on detection of an appropriate target, with the direction of the movement preset. We saw one example of this tactic in Chapter 9; a toad turns to face a prey-like target and then its tongue darts out to capture it under open-loop control.

Preying mantises capture the small insects on which they feed in the same way, and the control mechanisms involved have been analysed by Mittelstaedt (1962). Mantises first stalk their prey and then capture it by striking out with their powerful, clawed forelegs. The strike lasts between 30 and 60 milliseconds, which is too rapid for a closed-loop mechanism to guide the claws towards their target. Instead, the strike is controlled in two stages. First, a closed-loop mechanism turns the mantis' head to face the target, so

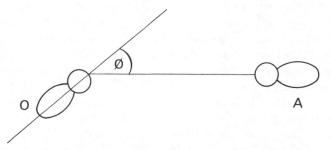

FIG.12.1.   The bearing of animal A from animal O is given by the angle φ.

that light reflected from it falls on ommatidia at the front of both eyes. Then, the position of the head sets the direction in which the forelegs strike under open-loop control (but note that Rossel's (1983) finding, that a mantis will occasionally strike accurately at a target which it is not facing, suggests that this model needs revision).

The way in which toads and mantises capture prey is eminently suited to situations in which a predator can execute a prey-catching movement so quickly that the prey cannot move any appreciable distance during it. Many other carnivorous animals use such "stalk and pounce" tactics, and the cat is a familiar example. Although the mechanisms orienting a cat's lunge onto its prey are less amenable to experimental analysis than those of the mantis, it is possible that similar principles are involved.

If the target animal can move an appreciable distance in the time taken by the pursuer to reach it, then an open-loop mechanism will not work. A closed-loop mechanism, which continually modifies the pursuer's path in response to changes in the target's path, will be necessary. We will look at two examples of how insects track potential mates in this way, considering the details of each case and then making some comparisons.

If two airborne houseflies come close to each other, they may buzz around in a brief flurry and then separate. Land and Collett (1974) filmed such encounters between houseflies of the species *Fannia canicularis* and found that they take the form of a chase, lasting between 0.1 and 2 sec, in which the leading fly is closely followed by the pursuer. The record of one chase (Fig. 12.2) shows how each time the leading fly turns, the pursuer manoeuvres so as to follow it.

Land and Collett were able to reconstruct a pursuing fly's path accurately, given the leading fly's path, by applying two rules governing the pursuer's behaviour. First, as the leader's angular deviation from the pursuer's axis increases, the pursuer turns to reduce the angle. Secondly, when the leader is within 30° on either side of the pursuer's axis, the pursuer detects the leader's angular *velocity* and turns to reduce it also. As a result, the pursuer can begin its turn before the leader crosses its midline. The fly's pursuit behaviour can therefore be explained in terms of its ability to detect two parameters of optic flow; the angular position and the angular velocity of the target. Note that these are the same parameters as those detected by a tethered fly presented with a moving vertical stripe (Chapter 9, p.215).

As well as chasing other flies, male houseflies will chase any small moving object, such as peas fired from a pea shooter. Land and Collett argue that this general pursuit of small moving targets allows males to locate and contact females. How, though, does such a simple form of visual guidance allow males to distinguish females from males, or to discriminate between females of different species? Part of the answer lies in the context of the fly's behaviour; Land and Collett suggest that a male fly can fly and turn more

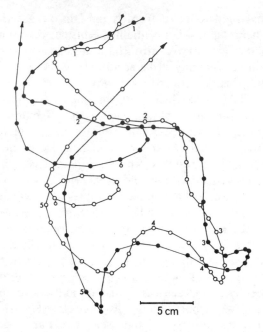

FIG.12.2. Record of a fly chase. Circles show positions of flies at 20 msec intervals (open circles— leader; closed circles—pursuer). Corresponding positions are numbered at 200 msec intervals. Reproduced from Land & Collett (1974) with permission of author and publishers.

5 cm

quickly than a female, so that a male pursuer can catch up with a female but not with a male. Likewise, a pursuer will be unlikely to catch up with a fly of another species because its aerodynamic properties will differ from those of a female of its own species. If the leader is smaller than a conspecific female and therefore able to turn more quickly, or if it is larger and therefore able to fly faster, the pursuer will fall behind.

The chasing behaviour of flies is therefore controlled by two mechanisms working in parallel to regulate the position of a small dark region in the optic flow field. Whether the pursuer catches up depends upon the size and aerodynamic properties of the two flies. If the leader is a female of the same species, these properties will be matched and the pursuer will catch up and mate. It seems unlikely, however, that this mechanism is foolproof, as flies of other species may well be present that are of the same size as females of the pursuer's species. Unless they have some further means of discriminating targets at a distance, houseflies will therefore waste some time in pursuit of the wrong target.

Pursuit of a female by a male hoverfly (*Syritta pipiens*), is a more elaborate business (Collett & Land, 1975). Rather than launching an all-out pursuit, the male hoverfly first "shadows" the female, keeping his body axis pointed straight at her. This fixation of the female is achieved both through small sideways movements (hoverflies are able to fly at any angle to the axis of the body) and by turns. If the bearing of the female is more than about 8° from the male's midline, fixation is achieved by an abrupt turn under open-loop control, which Collett and Land term a saccade, because of its similarity to saccadic movements of the primate eye (Chapter 1, p.28). Errors of less than 8° are corrected by smooth turns under closed-loop control, and examples of smooth and saccadic shadowing are shown in Figures 12.3 and 12.4.

During shadowing, the male also regulates his distance from the female, keeping between 5 and 15 cm from her by flying forwards or backwards. Once the female lands on a flower, the male stops shadowing and darts towards the female in a stereotyped fashion, accelerating rapidly and then making a sudden turn just at the point of landing to bring himself into the correct orientation for copulation.

The control systems governing pursuit of potential mates by male hoverflies are clearly more complex than those of the housefly, and Collett and Land suggest that the hoverfly switches between a number of different control systems, each regulating different aspects of optic flow. One reason for this complexity is the more intricate control of flight in hoverflies, which results in more smooth and accurate tracking than in housefly chases. Another reason is the two-stage pursuit of the female and the need to regulate distance during shadowing so that the stereotyped dart towards the female will be timed correctly.

Surprisingly, however, this sophisticated flight control does not ensure accurate discrimination between female hoverflies and other targets, as males

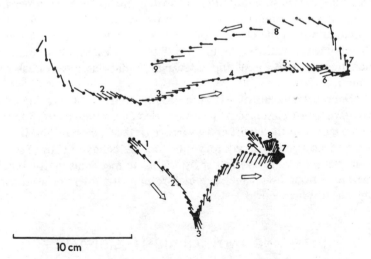

10 cm

FIG.12.3. Record of smooth shadowing by a hoverfly. The shadowing fly (below) adjusts its position smoothly to maintain fixation of the target fly (above). Positions are shown every 40 msec and corresponding positions numbered every 400 msec. Reproduced from Collett & Land (1975) with permission of author and publishers.

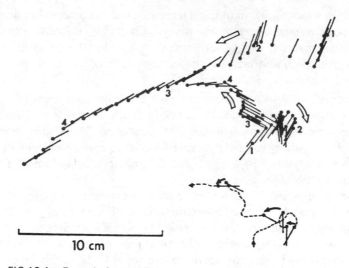

FIG.12.4.   Record of saccadic shadowing by a hoverfly. Positions are shown
every 20 msec and corresponding positions are numbered every 200 msec.
The shadowing fly (below) shows three abrupt shifts in orientation (saccades)
as it fixates the target fly (above), at 11, 16 and 30 x 20 msec. These saccades
are made clearer in the lower diagram. Reproduced from Collett & Land
(1975) with permission of author and publishers.

will sometimes attempt copulation with other males, or with insects of the
wrong species. Discrimination must come at the point when mating is
attempted, although the chances of tracking a male are reduced somewhat
by a phenomenon called "wobbling"; if two males begin to shadow one
another, they go into increasing sideways oscillations in antiphase, which
soon separate them.

   No doubt mechanisms of this kind are involved in both mating and prey
capture in other species, and they will be effective as long as the pursuer can
match the moves of the target and overtake it. It will certainly be interesting
to discover how much predatory and social behaviour in insects and
other simple animals is controlled by the same mechanisms for regulating
parameters of optic flow which are also responsible for steering the animal
through the physical world.

DETECTING ANOTHER ANIMAL'S DISTANCE

For the housefly, detection of the bearing of a potential mate is enough to
guide its social behaviour. As long as it keeps this parameter near zero, it
will fly towards its target, and whether it catches up with it or not is in the
hands of fate and aerodynamics. What problems arise, however, when an

animal does not need simply to get as close to or as far away from another animal as possible, but needs to maintain an optimum distance from it? We have already seen that the male hoverfly maintains a roughly constant distance from the female while shadowing her, and we will look at two other examples of similar behaviour before considering what optical information could specify another animal's distance.

A school of fish may consist of hundreds or thousands of individuals, maintaining fairly constant distances from their neighbours, all swimming in parallel at the same pace and executing turns with a striking synchrony. What information specifies the position and direction of a neighbouring fish? It is known that information both in light and in the pattern of waves of water pressure generated by other fish is used, as blinded saithe (*Pollachius virens*) swim normally in schools but maintain a greater distance from their neighbours than do sighted fish (Partridge & Pitcher, 1980). In order to abolish schooling completely it is necessary not only to blind the fish but also to cut the nerves from the lateral lines.

Another example of the detection of distance is provided by the behaviour of a young chick or duckling towards its mother. We described in Chapter 7 how the young bird begins life with a following response to any conspicuous moving object, and how in the first few days after hatching this response becomes restricted to familiar objects. In the first days of its life, the following response helps a young bird remain within a short distance of its mother or some other imprinted object. Klopfer (1967) found that those 1–2 day-old ducklings which did follow a moving model of a duck spent most of a test period following less than 20 cm behind it. As the model moved, the ducklings moved with it, or, if they fell a short distance behind, ran to catch it up.

Casual observation of older ducklings in the wild shows a different pattern of behaviour; as ducklings search for food, they spend less time close to their mother and sometimes become separated from her by distances of several feet or yards. If this happens, they run or swim towards her at great speed. This suggests that a young bird approaches its mother whenever she is more than a certain "safe" distance away; a distance which increases as the bird becomes older. Keeping as close as possible to the mother at all times would not require detection of distance, but would prevent the young bird from feeding efficiently; a simple ability to detect distance could solve this problem.

The hoverfly, schooling fish and imprinted bird all need to detect the distance of other members of their own species in order to increase their chances of survival and reproduction. The question raised by all three examples is how the distance of the other animal is detected, and, unfortunately, in none of the cases has the question been answered. Even so, we will consider three possible parameters of the optic array which could specify distance and which could be tested experimentally. The first is the angular size of the segment of the optic array filled by light reflected from the other animal. For an animal with a single-chambered eye, this is equivalent to the area of the retinal image of the other animal. This can only give a crude specification of distance, as it will also depend not only on the other animal's size but also on its posture and its orientation relative to the observer.

Even so, angular size would be sufficient under certain constraints. First, the size of the other animal would have to be sufficiently predictable to give the accuracy of regulation of distance needed. Secondly, the variation in angular size as the other animal changed its posture and orientation must not be too great. It is possible that these constraints are met for the hoverfly, as female hoverflies will be of fairly constant size, and the poor accuracy of regulation of distance (between 5 and 15 cm) may be attributable to variation in the distance of the female from the male's horizontal plane (Fig. 12.5). It would be interesting to know whether a male moves closer to a female in its horizontal plane than to one outside it.

Angular size is also a possibility for schooling fish and for birds, and to assess its usefulness we would need to know how much fish and mother birds vary in size and how accurately distance is regulated. For fish, only crude specification by optical parameters may be necessary, as information detected through the lateral line is also used. Mother birds will vary somewhat in angular size, depending upon the direction from which they are seen and on whether they are standing, pecking or sitting. Again, however, crude specification of distance may suffice, as a chick or duckling only needs to detect whether its mother is beyond a safe distance.

A second parameter worth considering in cases such as these is the size of elements of optic texture reflected from the other animal. Beyond a certain distance, the angular size of patterns such as scales, hair or colour markings on the other animal will be too small to resolve. A means of keeping within a certain distance of another animal would therefore be to keep the texture of some part of its body detectable. This tactic will work as long as the average size of texture elements is predictable, which will certainly be the case for hair, feathers and scales.

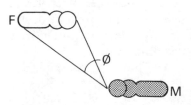

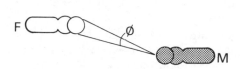

FIG.12.5. The vertical angle φ subtended by a female hoverfly at a constant distance from a male increases the further she is above or below the male's horizontal axis.

This may be a promising explanation for the detection of distance by fish, which often have myopic eyes (Chapter 1, p.21). It is possible that a schooling fish swims sufficiently close to a neighbour to keep texture elements such as scales or colour markings in focus. In effect, it would be accommodating by movement of the whole body rather than by adjustment of the lens. Partridge and Pitcher (1980) argue that distance between fish is governed by a balance between visually-mediated attraction and lateral line-mediated repulsion, and the basis of the attraction component could be a process of keeping scales or other markings in focus.

Thirdly, does motion parallax hold any promise as a means of detecting the distance of another animal? Recall from Chapter 9 that the velocity of flow of optical texture in each region of the flow field depends on its angular distance from the poles, the distance of the surface it is reflected from and on the animal's velocity. It cannot therefore specify absolute distance unless the animal's velocity is constrained. It could, however, be useful to schooling fish in regulating swimming speed; a looming or receding flow field would specify for a fish that it was swimming more or less quickly than the rest of the school.

Chicks or ducklings could use motion parallax to detect distance from their mother, under certain constraints. As a bird such as a pigeon or chick walks, its head moves forwards in a series of jerky steps. What could optic flow during such a step specify? As long as each step took the bird a fixed distance and its mother was in a fixed position in the optic flow field relative to its poles, then the extent of flow during a step would specify the mother's distance (Fig. 12.6). These constraints would be met as long as the bird

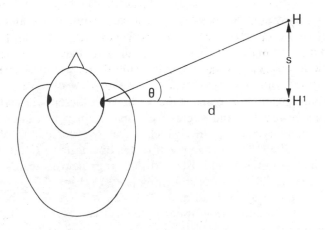

FIG.12.6.   A chick fixating a hen at H, so that the hen lies near to 90° from the pole of the optic flow field. If the chick takes a step of distance s, the image of the hen will move through an angle θ which specifies the distance of the hen d as long as s is constant.

walked at a constant pace over fairly level ground and kept its mother fixated monocularly. Motion parallax would also be affected by the mother's movement, and so, all in all, it would specify distance rather inaccurately. Nevertheless, the degree of accuracy could be sufficient for the bird to detect whether it was dangerously far from its mother.
dangerously far from its mother.

These three parameters could provide the information that many animals need to regulate their distance from conspecifics, and their use could be tested experimentally. It is important to note that they only provide distance information if other factors are constrained. These factors include such things as the size of the other animal, the size of texture elements on its surface and the animal's walking speed. Often, some of these will be sufficiently constrained in the animal's natural environment for simple parameters of the optic array to give distance information accurately enough for the animal's purposes. Great accuracy may often not be needed, particularly where back-up sources of information are available, such as vibration in water for fish or the mother's alarm calls for young birds.

DETECTING ANOTHER ANIMAL'S POSTURE

So far, in discussing how one animal might be able to detect the bearing and distance of another, we have treated the posture and orientation of the other animal as complicating factors which would compromise the specification of distance by a simple parameter such as angular size. In all but the simplest animals, however, social behaviour will depend upon the detection of more information about another animal than simply its bearing and distance. Animals have bodies made up of trunk, head and articulated limbs able to take up a wide range of positions relative to one another, and these relative positions determine the animal's *posture*.

The ability of animals to detect the posture of other animals is demonstrated in many courtship and aggressive displays, in which animals take up particular stereotyped postures which affect the behaviour of the other animal involved. Gulls, for example, threaten by adopting an upright posture with the bill pointing downwards and the wings held forwards, and signal submission with the opposite, crouching posture (Fig. 12.7). The angle of a dog's ears relative to its head and of its tail relative to its body provide information for another dog about its aggressiveness. The "tension" in a baboon's posture, and how far forwards its weight is shifted, signals to another baboon how likely it is to attack. As we will see in the next chapter, facial expressions are particularly important postures in human communication.

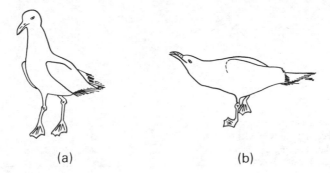

(a)   (b)

FIG.12.7. Threat (a) and appeasement (b) postures of the lesser black-backed gull. Drawn from photographs by N. Tinbergen in Manning, A. (1978).

The problem of detection of posture can be approached within a traditional pattern recognition framework, like that of Chapter 7. One simple possibility is that a particular posture makes colour markings or other key stimuli more visible. Another is that certain configurations of limbs and body are recognised as whole forms. To explain more subtle and flexible perception of posture from the "retinal image" starting point, we could draw on Marr and Nishihara's (1978) arguments, discussed in Chapter 7, on object recognition. Recall that they tackled the problem of how objects could be recognised in any orientation without prior knowledge of what the object is. The solution they suggested was based on the assumption, which would be valid for an animal, that the object is made up of "generalised cones." The axes of the cones can be recovered from a projection of the object, and their lengths and positions in an object-centred frame of reference derived. Although Marr and Nishihara's aim was to explain the *recognition* of complex objects, we could imagine other processes operating on the object-centred representation to recover angles between the axes of limbs and build up a description of the animal's posture.

Such approaches assume that the posture to be perceived is a static configuration projected onto the retina in "snapshot" fashion. They would therefore need to be complemented by a more Gibsonian analysis in cases where animals are able to detect *transformations* of posture. A possible example of this is provided by Turner (1964). Young chicks learn to feed by pecking at small objects on the ground and they have a strong tendency to peck close to the spot where the mother is pecking. Turner made a model hen (Fig. 12.8) which could be made to "peck" at the ground and found that chicks would approach it and peck around its bill as readily as they would approach a real hen. This only happened when the model made "pecking" movements, and the chicks were much slower to approach a stationary model in either an upright or head-down posture. It looks as if

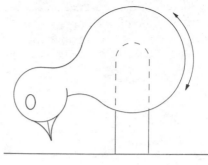

FIG.12.8. Flat cardboard model
of a hen. "Pecking" movements of
the model elicit pecking by chicks.
Adapted from Turner (1964).

chicks may detect a simple change in optic structure — a downwards wiping
of texture — which specifies a pecking action.

It is likely that mammals are able to detect more complex patterns of
transformation of other animals' posture. One important category is the gait
of another animal; the pattern of movement of its limbs relative to one
another as it walks or runs. There is some anecdotal evidence that predators
such as wolves prefer to attack prey moving with an unusual gait (and
therefore probably injured), and this would be an interesting possibility to
follow up more rigorously. We will consider ways in which people detect
information in other people's gait in the next chapter.

DETECTING ANOTHER ANIMAL'S ORIENTATION

As well as the orientations of another animal's limbs relative to each other,
an animal may also need to be able to detect their orientations relative to
itself. This category of information includes first the orientation of another
animal's whole body relative to the observer, and secondly the orientation
of parts of its body such as its head or a limb (Fig. 12.9). We have already
seen one example of one animal detecting the orientation of another's body
relative to itself; a male hoverfly landing on a female turns through the
correct angle needed to achieve the right orientation for copulation. Another
example comes from the social behaviour of the Siamese fighting fish *Betta
splendens*. These fish engage in contests at the boundaries of their territories,
in which they may bite one another, but more often the contests involve
stereotyped displays.

In a threat display, a fish spreads its dorsal, tail and anal fins (Fig. 12.10).
It may turn broadside to its opponent and lower and twitch its pelvic fin
(Fig. 12.10c). At the same time it may beat its tail and flashes of bright
colour may occur on the tail and body. Alternatively, it may face its opponent
head-on and open its gill covers (Fig. 12.10d). Simpson (1968) analysed

these encounters and discovered that a fish's behaviour is influenced by the relative orientation of its opponent. A fish is more likely to turn to a broadside orientation if its opponent is facing it than if it is broadside, so that the two fish often take up a "T" shaped configuration. Also, a fish is more likely to flicker its pelvic fin if the opponent is facing it than if it is broadside.

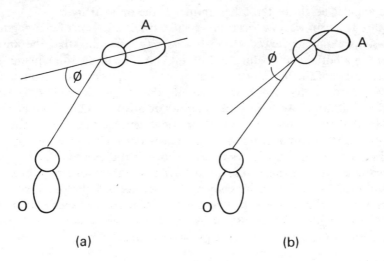

(a)   (b)

FIG.12.9. Orientation of one animal relative to another. (a) φ is the orientation of A relative to O. (b) φ is the orientation of A's head relative to O.

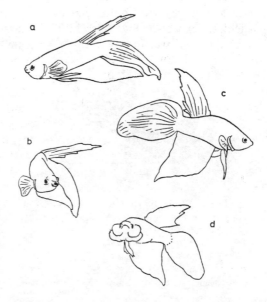

FIG.12.10. (a) and (b) Non-displaying Siamese fighting fish. (c) Display posture with fins spread out and pelvic fin lowered. (d) Display posture with gill covers opened. Reproduced from Simpson (1968) with permission of the author and publishers.

How could a Siamese fighting fish or other animal detect the relative orientation of a conspecific? One simple possibility, which could apply to fighting fish, is that colour markings or other features are visible in one orientation but not in another. This solution would only allow detection of the orientation of one particular kind of animal, however, and a more generally useful solution would be to detect the ratio of the angular length to the angular height of the other animal in the optic array.

Figure 12.11 shows how this ratio specifies the orientation of an imaginary block-shaped animal viewed by an observer O, assuming that the animal remains in a horizontal posture and that it and O lie in the same plane. The angular length of the block depends upon its length, its distance from O and its orientation relative to O, while its angular height depends only upon height and distance. As Figure 12.11 shows, relative orientation is therefore given by the ratio of horizontal angular size to vertical angular size and the ratio of height to length, whatever the animal's distance.

This is a potentially useful result, as it shows that the ratio of two angular sizes specifies another animal's relative orientation without requiring that the size of the other animal is known. All that needs to be predictable are the *proportions* of the target. For an animal of a particular species, the ratio of height to length will be constant over a wide range of sizes, and this will also be true, to some extent, for a particular *type* of animal, such as birds of prey or grazing mammals.

In many cases an animal can detect not only the orientation of another animal's long axis relative to itself, but also the orientation of parts of its body. One example of this is the ability to detect the orientation of another animal's head, eyes or both relative to the observing animal. We would particularly expect to find this ability in those species which have an area centralis in the retina and therefore have acute vision in only a small segment

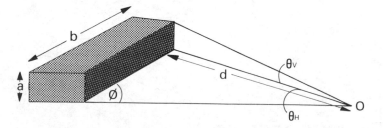

FIG.12.11. A block-shaped "animal" with an orientation relative to the observer O of φ. The block subtends horizontal and vertical angles of θ_H and θ_V at O.

Since d $= a/\tan \theta_V$
and d/sin φ $= b/\sin \theta_H$
Then sin φ $= a/b \cdot \sin \theta_H/\tan \theta_V$
Therefore, if a/b is known, φ can be obtained from θ_H and θ_V.

of the optic array at any instant (Chapter 1). Direction of B's gaze relative to A will specify for A whether B can see what it is doing. We might also expect the prey of such animals to be able to detect the relative orientation of the predator's head; if they are in its line of gaze, they need to take prompt action!

One example of a situation in which animals detect the relative orientation of other animals' heads is given by Bossema and Burgler (1980) in a study of jays. A group of jays adopts a peck order in which each pair of birds has a strict dominant-subordinate relationship. When the group is given food, the dominant eats first while the others mill about near the food. If a subordinate approaches closely, the dominant turns its head to fixate it either binocularly or monocularly. The subordinate hops backwards when this happens, and is more likely to do so if the dominant bird fixates it binocularly than if it fixates monocularly.

How could the direction of another animal's gaze be specified in the optic array? Let us first assume that the other animal has frontally placed eyes and that it fixates by turning its head and eyes together. As Figure 12.12 shows, a simple invariant—the ratio of the two angular distances of the eyes from the nose—specifies direction of gaze. The trigonometry of obtaining the actual angle of gaze is complex, but for many animals the important information will be whether it is zero or not, and if it is zero then the two angles are equal. This equality is invariant with the distance and size of the other animal, and specifies fixation as long as its eyes are symmetrically placed in the head.

Things become more complicated if an animal needs to detect whether another animal is looking sideways at it; fixating it with its eyes while its head faces in another direction. People certainly can detect such fixation, but the ability to do so may not be important to many animals. It would not be important to a small animal needing to detect whether a cat was fixating it. In order to pounce onto its prey a cat needs to align its head towards it, in accordance with Turvey's (1977a) argument, discussed in Chapter 11, that orientation of head and eyes pre-tunes segmental organisation. A mouse would therefore only be in danger from a cat fixating it with head and eyes together.

For animals with laterally placed eyes, detection of gaze will often not be important, as their acuity is more or less constant throughout the visual field. Exceptions are birds with dual foveas, and we have seen that a jay can detect another jay fixating it monocularly. An invariant which would specify such monocular fixation regardless of distance and size of the eye is the ratio of angular height to angular width of the eye. As long as the eye is circular, these angles will be equal if the observer is fixated; as with binocularly placed eyes, it is symmetry which specifies fixation.

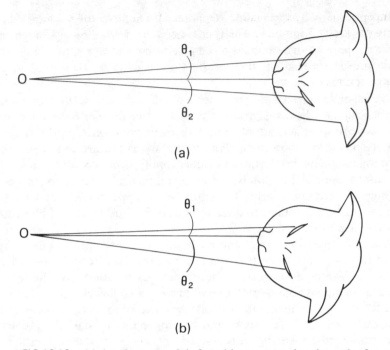

(a)

(b)

FIG.12.12.   (a) An observer at O is fixated by a cat, so that the angles θ_1 and θ_2 between each of the cat's eyes and its nose are equal. (b) A difference between θ_1 and θ_2 indicates that the observer is not fixated.

PERCEPTION AND COMPLEX SOCIAL BEHAVIOUR

So far, we have discussed some relatively simple pieces of information about other animals that an animal needs to organise its predatory, defensive or social actions. These are the other animal's bearing, distance, posture and relative orientation. For each of these, we have looked at examples where animals' behaviour shows that they can detect the information and we have then asked how it could be provided in the optic array. For the housefly and hoverfly, observation and experiment demonstrate how bearing is detected and regulated, but for the other categories we can only make hypotheses.

One direction for future research is to develop and test such hypotheses, using models and artificial optical displays to determine how information about other animals is obtained. Traditionally, much of the study of animal perception has addressed the problem of how other animals are recognised, and we saw examples of such work in Chapter 7. Less research has been devoted to the problems we have discussed in this chapter, although there is ample scope for experiment. We do need to know, for example, how a young chick discriminates its mother from other birds and animals, but we also need to know how it detects her position and posture in order to regulate its distance from her.

In the last section of this chapter, we move on from the social behaviour of relatively simple animals, where it is possible to make and test hypotheses about the detection of information in the optic array, to the more complex social behaviour of mammals. We ask to what extent mammalian social behaviour involves rules for regulating bearing, distance and orientation, and also what further perceptual abilities could be involved.

Regulation of Distance

Are processes of regulation of distance like those we have seen in hoverflies, fish and chickens involved in mammalian social behaviour? In particular, what sort of complexities could arise if two or more animals move about regulating their position relative to the others? We have already seen one simple outcome of such a situation, when two male hoverflies meet and the interaction of their pursuit rules generates increasing oscillations in antiphase, and now we look at a more complex pattern of social behaviour which we think is also an outcome of the interaction of systems regulating relative position.

Some carnivorous mammals are able to capture and kill large and powerful animals because they hunt in packs. A single lion, hunting dog or wolf would have little success in catching zebra, wildebeest or caribou, because it would be outdistanced or injured by a kick from the intended prey. By hunting in packs, however, these predators succeed in capturing large prey. Observations of pack-hunting predators have demonstrated a degree of coordination between individual animals. Lions fan out as they stalk their quarry (Schaller, 1972, Ch. 8), while Mech (1970, Ch. 7) describes wolves surrounding a caribou standing at bay or pursuing a running caribou in single file.

Behaviour of this kind demonstrates that each animal is able to detect the position of the prey and of the other members of the pack relative to itself. We do not intend to argue that no further perceptual and cognitive abilities are involved, but only that rules for regulating position relative to several other animals at once play an important role in the organisation of pack-hunting behaviour. Some evidence for this argument is provided by the behaviour of sheepdogs.

Dogs are closely related to wolves and are descended from pack-hunting ancestors. The ways in which a shepherd and a sheepdog control a group of sheep draw on behavioural predispositions of dogs which evolved as part of pack-hunting behaviour, and Vines (1981) has described how the trainer builds on these predispositions when training a dog to respond to whistled commands.

Our main interest is in the behaviour shown by a naive dog towards a group of sheep; the behaviour on which either pack-hunting skills or co-ordination with a shepherd is built. There are two particularly interesting features of this behaviour. First, an untrained dog tends to "herd" sheep, by circling around them, moving from side to side while keeping a roughly constant distance from them. The sheep draw closer together when a dog is near and move as a group, keeping beyond a minimum distance from the dog.

Second, a naive dog tends to position itself on the opposite side of a group of sheep from its trainer. If the trainer moves either to his right or to his left, the dog matches his move so as to keep the group of sheep directly between them. A shepherd exploits this tendency in training by giving the right or left turn whistle while the dog makes the appropriate turn relative to the sheep.

In these situations, the dog is moving so as to maintain its position relative to both the group of sheep and the trainer. On its own, it moves about a good deal but keeps a roughly constant distance from the sheep, while they keep a constant (and much smaller) distance from each other and a minimum distance from the dog. With the trainer present, the dog keeps the centre of the group of sheep on a line between itself and the trainer.

Are these rules regulating position relative to sheep and trainer part of a pack-hunting strategy? Probably predators such as dogs or wolves stand little chance of taking an animal such as a sheep from a group without risking injury from other prey. They therefore face the problem of splitting off one sheep from its group. Once this is done, they can move between it and the rest of the group and then attack it. To achieve this, however, they must overcome the sheep's strong tendency to keep close to other sheep.

The dog's tendency to keep a position opposite the trainer gives a clue as to how two dogs might be able to break up a group of sheep and split one off. The chances of this happening will be greater if they can make the sheep mill about and increase their distances from neighbouring sheep. Two dogs circling about a group of sheep in an uncoordinated way would not achieve this to any extent, as most of the time the sheep would be able to move as a group away from both dogs at once, maintaining close contact as they did so (Fig. 12.13).

If the dogs maintain positions opposite each other as they circle about, however, there will always be two directions in which each sheep could move to escape from the dogs (Fig. 12.14). The chances of splitting the group of sheep in two, or of splitting one off from the rest, will therefore be greater. All that needs to be added is for the dogs to detect a large gap between one sheep and the others and drive a wedge between them by running into the

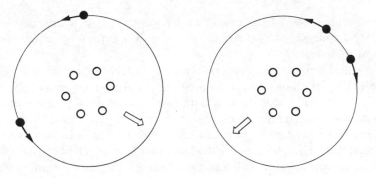

FIG.12.13. Two dogs (closed circles) circling a group of sheep (open circles) in an uncoordinated way. There is always a consistent direction in which the sheep can move to escape from both dogs.

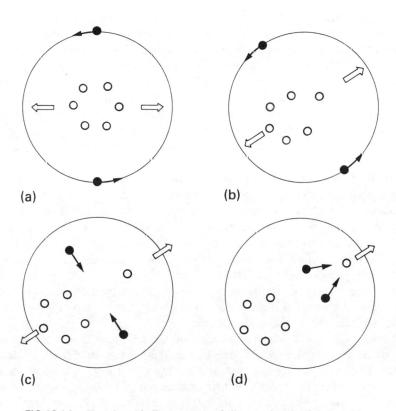

(a)

(b)

(c)

(d)

FIG.12.14. Two dogs circling a group of sheep and maintaining positions diametrically opposite each other (a). As the dogs move, there are two possible escape routes for the sheep. In (b), one sheep moves in the opposite direction to the rest of the flock and is then pursued by the dogs (c,d).

gap. A shepherd "singling" one sheep off from a group works in this way, whistling a command to his dog to run towards him into a gap between one sheep and the rest.

We would not suggest that pack-hunting behaviour requires only rules for regulating position relative to prey and to other members of the pack. Sheep are certainly able to detect the orientation and posture of dogs, keeping closer contact if a dog stares at them fixedly in a tense posture, and dogs and other predators are doubtless able to recognise similar aspects of prey behaviour. Even so, it is worthwhile to ask how much of the complexity of group hunting arises from interactions between the rules of both predators and prey for regulating variables of distance specified in the optic array.

Regulating Relative Orientation

If rules regulating the distance and bearing of other animals are at work in mammalian social interaction, are rules regulating relative orientation of other animals' bodies or parts of their bodies also involved? Earlier, we looked at cases where one animal responds to the relative orientation of another. A fighting fish spreads its gill covers if its opponent is oriented at right angles to it, and a jay hops backwards if a dominant bird looks at it. Are there situations, however, where an animal does not simply *respond* to another's relative orientation but *regulates* it with its own movement, in the same way that a hoverfly regulates the distance and bearing of a potential mate?

Golani (1976) has obtained evidence that play-fighting and courtship in some quadruped mammals involves the regulation of relative orientation. Episodes of mammalian social interaction such as the rough and tumble play of two puppies often do not readily divide into a sequence of static postures and transitions between them in the way that the interaction of two Siamese fighting fish does. Instead, there is a continuous flow of movement, and Golani argues that its description requires the measurement, from single frames of cine records, of the moment-by-moment position of one animal's limbs and head relative to its body, to the body and the limbs of its partner, and to the environment.

Figure 12.15 shows drawings made by Golani from single frames of a film of two Tasmanian devils (dog-like marsupial mammals) play-fighting. In this sequence, the animals roll and tumble about in elaborate ways, but the recording method reveals that through much of the sequence a constant relative orientation of the animals' heads is maintained. Golani terms such a constant relative configuration a "joint," around which the animals move, and says: "The heads of a pair of Tasmanian devils 'wag' their bodies into a multitude of postures and movements. In a context of cheek-to-cheek joint maintenance, the two animals move in unison as one kinetic chain (Golani, 1976, p. 117)."

001

005

033

044

061

070

096

132

147

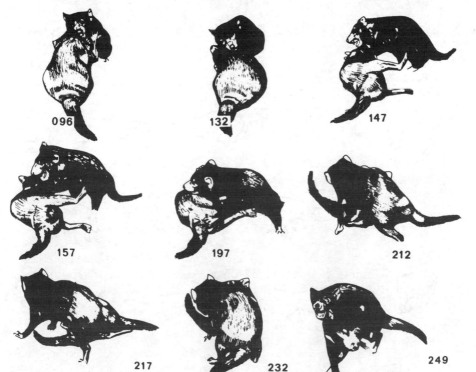

157

197

212

217

232

249

FIG.12.15. Drawings from single frames of a film of two Tasmanian devils in courtship play. Numbers refer to frames of film taken at 16 frames/sec. Until frame 249, the male (in the background until frame 147, in the foreground after frame 212) keeps the female's head adjacent to his right cheek. Reproduced from Golani (1976) with permission of author and publishers.

277

a. CIRCLING

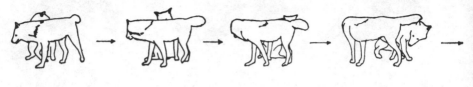

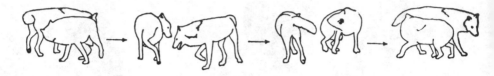

b. FOLLOWING

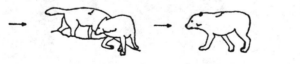

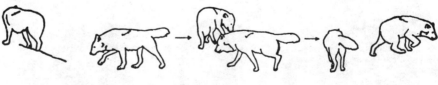

c TWIST-AND-TURN

d. HIP-THRUST

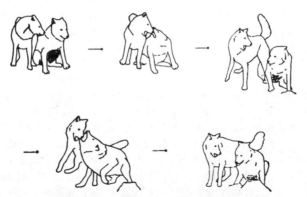

FIG.12.16.   Drawings made from single frames of a film of two wolves. (a) Circling (b) Following (c) Twist and turn (d) Hip-thrust. Reproduced from Moran et al. (1981) with permission of the author and publishers.

Another illustration comes from an analysis of wolf social interaction carried out by Moran, Fentress, and Golani (1981). They filmed "supplanting" interactions, in which a dominant wolf approaches a subordinate one, they interact for a period, and then the subordinate moves away. Moran et al. found that the relative orientations of the two wolves' bodies fell into four main categories. In each of these, as the animals moved, some aspects of their relative orientations remained constant. In *circling,* the dominant's head is maintained at a distance of at least half a wolf-length from the hindquarters of the subordinate, and the two take up an antiparallel orientation (Fig. 12.16a). In *following,* the dominant keeps its head at the same distance from the subordinate's hindquarters, but both animals are oriented in the same direction (Fig. 12.16b).

A more complicated pattern is *twist and turn.* Here, the two animals maintain contact or near contact at the shoulder and a relative orientation of between 45° and 90°. The dominant appears to push the subordinate around in a circular path as this relative configuration is maintained (Fig. 12.16c). Finally, in *hip-thrust,* the wolves maintain a near-parallel orientation and contact at the hips. Periods of no movement are interspersed with sideways pushes of the dominant's hip against the subordinate's, accompanied by snarling and baring of the teeth (Fig. 12.16d).

The crucial thing about these patterns is that they are not static positions of single animals, as displays are. They are descriptions of those aspects of the joint orientation of two animals which remain constant as the animals move. For such stability to occur, each animal must continually monitor the positions of parts of the other's body relative to its own and adjust its own movement to keep the appropriate variables constant.

These examples of regulation of joint orientation in social interaction raise some interesting questions. First, it is interesting to consider them in the light of Maynard Smith and Price's (1973) analysis of the evolution of animal aggression. They argue that ritualised aggression has evolved because those individuals which can best minimise their chances of injury while at the same time maximising their chances of winning a contest will reproduce most successfully. A consequence of this view is that we would expect the evolution among animals of the capacity to detect the fighting ability of an opponent and to adjust their aggressiveness according to their chances of winning a particular encounter (Maynard Smith & Parker, 1976).

There is evidence that animals can detect simple attributes of other animals, such as size, which predict their fighting ability (e.g. Davies & Halliday, 1978). Perhaps during contests between Tasmanian devils or wolves each individual obtains more subtle information about the other which predicts its fighting ability, such as its ability to maintain a particular joint orientation or to force a shift to a new one. The significance of the cheek-to-cheek joint maintained by Tasmanian devils, for example, may be that each animal maintains the best position from which to block any biting move made by the other. As long as some parameter of the opponent's behaviour in the play-fight is a reliable predictor of its chances of winning a real fight, then it pays the reproductive success of both animals to use information from the play-fight to settle a contest.

A second problem raised by these examples is for theories of the control of movement (see Chapter 11). Here, an indefinite number of different patterns of commands are sent to the Tasmanian devil's muscles, all with the effect that its head keeps the same joint orientation with the other animal's head. The concept of "coalitional organisation" which we outlined in Chapter 11 may be relevant to this problem. Thirdly, it is interesting to speculate how widely we might find such processes in social interaction, and particularly whether they occur in primates. Undoubtedly, they are of great importance in many human games and in dancing, and perhaps the play-fighting of dogs provides a bridge between these subtle and elaborate human abilities and simple forms of animal interaction.

More Difficult Problems

We have argued that an important component of pack hunting, play and aggression in mammals is the detection and regulation of the distance, bearing and orientation of one animal and of parts of its body relative to another. We certainly do not want to argue that no perceptual abilities more complex than these are involved in animal social behaviour, and it is time now to look at what other abilities are necessary.

Menzel (1978) has drawn some particularly clear distinctions between different kinds of information one animal might obtain about the path of movement of another, and we will draw on his categories here. How could an animal A obtain information about another animal B's path which would enable it to make contact with B? The simplest possibility is that A regulates B's bearing so as to keep it straight ahead, as a housefly does in pursuing a potential mate. This would result in the approach path shown in Figure 12.17a.

A second possibility is that A could extrapolate from B's path of movement to predict a point at which it could intercept it (Fig. 12.17b), and a third is that it could detect what object in the surroundings is the goal of B's movement (Fig. 12.17c). These abilities are both of a higher order of complexity than regulation of relative bearing. In the second case, A detects not just B's position but B's *path* relative to itself, while in the third case A detects the relationship between B's path and the environment. Is there evidence that animals are capable of detecting such relations?

Observation of dogs hints strongly that they are able to extrapolate the paths of target objects, dogs and people in the kind of way shown in Figure 12.17b. Dogs are strikingly accurate in jumping to intercept a ball and catch it in their jaws; they run to intercept or head off the path of movement of a dog or person; and they will run on ahead of their owner, looking back to check the owner's path of travel and adjust their own accordingly.

Menzel (1978) describes similar observations of chimpanzee behaviour. If a number of chimps are travelling together and there is a clear leader of the group, which determines its direction of travel, other chimps will run on

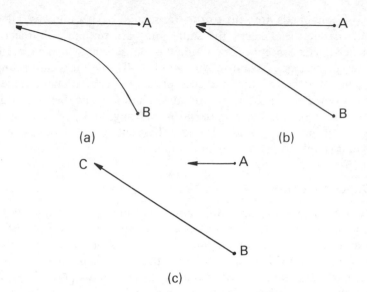

FIG.12.17.   (a) Animal B approaches animal A by keeping its bearing at zero. (b) B extrapolates from A's path of movement and moves straight to an interception point. (c) B detects that A's path is directed towards an object C and moves straight to it. Adapted from Menzel (1978).

ahead and look back from time to time to adjust their direction to keep on the same route as the leader. Further, chimps show evidence of being able to detect the goal of another animal's movement; if a group of chimps approaches a piece of food, all but the one nearest it will turn away, as if each recognises the distance of the others from the goal. A band of chimps hunting a small monkey in a tree spreads out to block its potential routes of escape along branches, suggesting that they are able to detect the layout of branches relative to the quarry as well as to themselves.

More conclusive evidence is available from experiments carried out by Menzel (1978). Chimps show a highly accurate memory for the locations of pieces of fruit scattered around a familiar enclosure. Menzel showed one chimp where a piece of fruit was hidden and then locked it in a hut adjoining the enclosure with its companions. On release, the group emerged from the hut and all the chimps set out together towards the food, some running on ahead to search along the knowledgeable chimp's line of travel. Control procedures showed that the other chimps were not simply finding the fruit by smell or sight, and so they must have been able to extrapolate from the knowledgeable chimp's path of travel.

As well as detecting the orientation of another animal's path relative to the environment, can animals detect the orientation of a part of another animal's body relative to the environment? People can detect what another person is looking or pointing at, but are animals capable of such accomplishments? Dogs can sometimes be ordered to particular places by pointing, although control procedures would be necessary to ensure that they could indeed detect the orientation of a person's arm relative to the goal.

Observation also suggests that monkeys and apes can detect the direction of gaze of another animal relative to the environment. Packer (1977) describes how one male olive baboon will solicit the help of another in attacking a third male and driving him away from a female. This is done by alternately looking at the potential ally and looking at the rival, with a threatening expression. This suggests that the animal whose help is being solicited perceives the orientation of the head relative to the rival as well as to itself. Similarly, a subordinate chimp which knows the location of a piece of food will not approach it directly if a dominant chimp is present but takes a roundabout route so that it approaches the food from a direction out of the dominant's line of sight.

Again, Menzel's (1978) experiments provide more conclusive evidence. In one, Menzel asked whether a chimp could tell where a piece of food was hidden by observing a person either taking a few steps towards it or pointing at it. In both cases, a chimp which had watched the person ran straight to the food. Further, chimps were able to distinguish different kinds of goal according to how far the person had walked towards them. Presumably they are able to pick up information in the same way from the postures and gestures of other chimps.

In another experiment, Menzel and Halperin (1975) showed that other chimps' posture and movement can specify not only where an object is but also how interesting it is to chimpanzees. They hid a piece of fruit and a novel toy in an enclosure; of these two objects, chimps prefer the fruit. One chimp was shown the location of the fruit and another the location of the toy, before both were returned to the group. On release, all the group followed the individual which knew the location of the fruit, demonstrating that some subtle features of the chimps' behaviour must have indicated how desirable a goal they were approaching.

These observations raise interesting questions about the ability of animals to detect other animals' *intentions*, in the sense of the purpose or goal of another animal's actions. A simple form of detection of intention would be one chimp detecting the goal to which another is travelling, but Premack and Woodruff (1978) have argued that chimpanzees are capable of more elaborate perception of intention. They showed chimps videotapes of people attempting to solve various problems. These included trying to open a door or trying to get at bananas just out of reach. The chimp subject was given a set of photographs of various objects such as a key or a pole, and almost always chose the one of the objects which would solve the person's problem.

Premack and Woodruff argue that a chimp's natural mode of perceiving its animate environment is in terms of intentions; not simply the moment-by-moment behaviour of other chimps (or people) but where their behaviour is going in the world. In the next chapter, we will describe how people perceive simple artificial displays in terms of intentions.

CONCLUSIONS

The theme of this chapter has been the usefulness of ecological optics in understanding the perceptual abilities animals need in order to catch prey, avoid predators and interact socially. In Chapters 9 and 10 we described experiments which allowed us to conclude just what parameters of optic flow are detected in order to obtain information about the physical world needed to control movement in it. In this chapter, we have had to be more speculative, drawing attention to processes of regulation of bearing, distance and orientation underlying animal behaviour, and suggesting possible ways in which the information needed about other animals could be provided by invariant properties of optic flow. The value of ecological optics remains to be judged, but it does at least suggest avenues of research.

In our last section, we have come to perceptual abilities of animals which raise more difficult theoretical problems for the ecological approach. We may propose possible invariant properties of optic flow specifying an animal's distance, orientation, or direction of gaze relative to the observer. It is hard, however, to imagine what invariants could specify an interception point or the goal of an animal's travel, and still harder to imagine what invariants could specify a person's intentions for a chimp in Premack and Woodruff's experiments.

At this point, a Gibsonian theorist would assert that there must be "high-level" invariants specifying such things, while a more traditional theorist would argue that ecological optics breaks down and we must turn to more cognitive explanations. These would explain extrapolation in terms of computations based on distance, velocity and bearing, or perception of intention in terms of knowledge held in memory. In the absence of ideas about what invariants could be involved, this is a difficult question to settle. We will return to it in Chapter 14, but first we must consider the usefulness of ecological optics in understanding how people perceive events.

13 Event Perception

In this part of the book we discuss ways in which a variety of animals, including humans, may detect specific patterns of flow or local change in the optic array in order to guide their actions in the world. The kind of perception that we have been discussing is that which demands immediate action—to locomote smoothly, to avoid collision, to steer a straight course or to pursue a mate. However, a great deal of human perception results in comprehension and reflection rather than in immediate action. The film-goer, tennis umpire, the spectator at a football match, the air-traffic controller—all must interpret the complex dynamic visual information in the events they are viewing, although their immediate actions are not necessarily affected. We spent some time in Part II of this book discussing how it is that we recognise significant forms, from the conventional starting point of the static retinal image. In this chapter we will consider how it is that we interpret *dynamic* optical information, and thus consider event perception in terms of analysing transformations in optical flow.

In this chapter we will deal with human perception, since it is not clear to what extent animals contemplate in the way that we do the events in their world, though Humphrey and Keeble (1974) have shown that monkeys will work in order to be shown films, even when the films show events that monkeys find frightening. However, as will become clear later on in the chapter, human perception of events may result in attributional processes which may at least in part be culturally and linguistically mediated. We begin this chapter by describing how human observers interpret patterns of motion in fairly simple and artificial dynamic displays. Here we outline some of the principles which are needed to account for the perception of such displays, principles that we will find useful as we go on to consider the complex patterns of motion given by more natural events.

THE PERCEPTION OF RELATIVE MOTION

People are more sensitive to relative motion than to absolute motion. Suppose a spot of light is moved very slowly in a dark room. There will be a particular threshold velocity at which the point is seen to be moving rather than stationary. Aubert (1866; cited in Kaufman, 1974) found that this threshold velocity was between 10 and 20 mins of arc per second if a luminous dot was moved in the dark. This is the threshold for *observer-relative* motion, which for a static observer corresponds to "absolute" motion. However, if a second spot of light is introduced, the velocity that the first must reach in order for movement to be seen in the display is lower. The threshold for *object-relative* motion is lower than that for observer-relative. Aubert showed that there was a 10-fold decrease in the threshold for motion perception when a dot was moved against a pattern of lines, rather than a uniform field (Kaufman, 1974). In a situation where the velocity of one dot is below the observer-relative threshold, and a second, stationary dot is present, the perception of movement in the display is ambiguous. Either one, or the other, or both dots may appear to be moving.

When motions are above the observer-relative motion threshold, perceptions are rarely ambiguous, but they do seem to be dominated by the relative motions in the display. For example, if a stationary dot is surrounded by a rectangle which moves to and fro around it, the dot may appear to be moving in a direction opposite to that of the rectangle (see Fig. 13.1). This movement of the dot is *induced* by that of the rectangle. Induced motion can be seen in natural situations, when the moon appears to race in a direction opposite to that of the clouds on a windy night. On a cloudless night the moon appears perfectly still (its actual movement is too slow to be detected as it is below the threshold for observer-relative movement). It

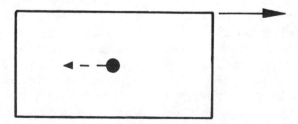

FIG.13.1.   Induced movement. A stationary dot appears to move to the left as the rectangle surrounding it is moved to the right.

is interesting that the moon's movement is seen relative to the clouds even if the stationary buildings nearby could provide an alternative frame of reference. The Gestalt psychologist Duncker (1929) suggested that there was a "separation of systems" in such perception. The movement of any one part of a display is seen relative to its immediate surrounding frame, but is not affected by more remote influences.

A demonstration by Wallach (1959) supports this (see Fig. 13.2). Here a dot is surrounded by a rectangle which is in turn enclosed by a circle. The perceived motion of the dot is influenced only by the actual movement of the rectangle, and little by that of the circle. That of the rectangle in turn is influenced only by the circle.

A further demonstration of how differing perceptions are obtained depending on the relative motions present is given by the "rolling wheel" effect. If a light is placed on the rim of a wheel which is rolled along in an otherwise dark room, the light is seen to trace out its actual, cycloidal path (see Fig. 13.3). It appears to bounce, but no cyclical, wheel-like motion is perceived. If a second light is illuminated on the hub however, the one on

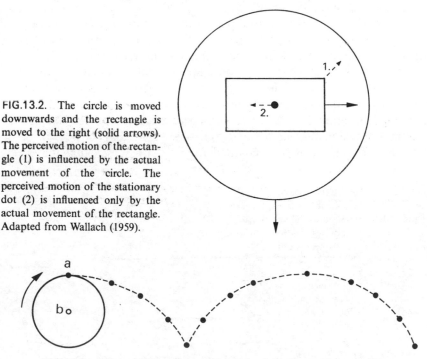

FIG.13.2. The circle is moved downwards and the rectangle is moved to the right (solid arrows). The perceived motion of the rectangle (1) is influenced by the actual movement of the circle. The perceived motion of the stationary dot (2) is influenced only by the actual movement of the rectangle. Adapted from Wallach (1959).

FIG.13.3.   The cycloidal path traced out by a light (a) placed on the rim of a wheel which rolls in the dark. If only (a) is illuminated, this path is perceived. If the hub (b) is also illuminated, then (a) appears to cycle around (b).

the rim now seems to trace out a path which revolves around the hub, and the two lights now form a wheel-like configuration which translates across the field of view. The rolling wheel is one of a number of examples where the perceived configuration of the motion of one element is affected by the presence of another. A final example is shown in Figure 13.4. The central dot which moves on a diagonal path, is flanked by two dots, which move horizontally. The presence of these alters the way in which the central dot is seen to move. It appears to move vertically, between the flanking dots, while all three dots together move horizontally as a unit.

The perception of many such displays seems to conform to a "simplicity" or "minimum" principle. Of many possible interpretations of a display of separately moving elements, the simplest is made; that is, the one in which the motion components seen are minimised (Cutting and Proffitt, 1982). Johansson (1973, 1975) suggests in addition that the preferred perceptual interpretation of dynamic displays is in terms of the motion of *rigid* structures. "Evidently it is obligatory that the spatial relation between two isolated moving stimuli be perceived as the simplest motion that preserves a rigid connection between the stimuli. The general formula is spatial invariance plus motion (Johansson, 1975, p.73)."

This preference for a rigid interpretation is demonstrated in the display in Figure 13.5, where two dots each follow the same rectangular path. Under viewing conditions which minimise the impression that the screen on which the dots appear is flat, observers report the two dots as the end points of a rigid stick which moves rather curiously in depth, rather than seeing them as "chasing" each other around the rectangle.

Such phenomena of relative motion perception have been extensively investigated by Johansson (1973, 1975) who suggests that the perception of many such displays can be accounted for if it is assumed that the visual

FIG.13.4.   (a) Three dots move to and fro on the paths shown. In this situation the perception is as shown at (b). The central dot appears to travel on a vertical path between the two flanking dots, as the entire set of three dots moves from side to side. This perception can be explained in terms of vector analysis (c). The actual motion of the central dot is split into vertical (V) and horizontal (H) vector components. The horizontal component is in the same direction as the actual motion of the flanking dots. Adapted from Johansson (1975).

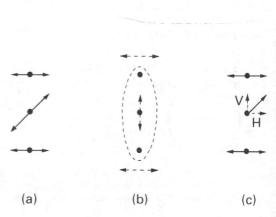

(a)   (b)   (c)

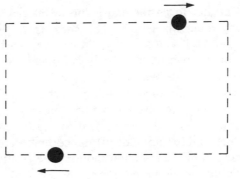

FIG.13.5. Two dots move on a rectangular path in the dark, as shown. The dots appear to form the ends of a stick which moves curiously in depth (Johansson, 1975).

system performs some kind of *perceptual vector analysis*. Let us examine this notion by starting with one of Johansson's own displays. As we have already described, when the display in Figure 13.4 is shown to human observers, they report seeing the central dot moving up and down a vertical path between the two horizontal "flanking" dots. Thus the resulting perception is of the vector which results after the components of *common motion* of the three display elements have been subtracted. To elaborate, the two horizontally moving flanking dots are moving together and therefore share a common horizontal translatory motion, against which other relative motions can be perceived. The diagonal motion of the central dot can be resolved into two vector components (see Fig. 13.4c), one in the direction of the common motion of the flanking dots, and the other perpendicular to this (i.e. vertical). If the common motion component of the whole display is partialled out, the motion which is "left over" (the residual) is a vertical motion of the central dot, which is what people report when shown such a display.

The same kind of analysis can be applied to the perception of the lights attached to a rolling wheel, described above. When a light is placed on the hub in addition to that on the rim, there is a common motion component shared by the two lights which corresponds to the direction in which the wheel is moving. This common motion component completely accounts for the motion of the light on the hub, and when partialled out of the motion of the light on the rim, the residual left to this light is cyclical motion around the hub. This kind of description suggests that common motions are abstracted from a display first, leaving relative motions as the residual, though Cutting and Proffitt (1982) point out that Johansson has not always made such a strong claim.

Cutting and Proffitt (1982) argue that not all perceptions of such displays are consistent with the "common-motion-first" principle. For example, observers occasionally report the rolling wheel display with a single rim and hub light as appearing like a "tumbling stick" (Dunckner, 1929). Here the two lights appear to be the end-points of a stick which rotates about a point halfway along its length. The stick is tumbling because the imaginary midpoint itself traces out a "hobbling" path (see Fig. 13.6). In such a situation relative motion analysis appears to take priority, with common motion left as residual.

There are thus two possible ways in which any given set of absolute motions can be resolved into a perception of relative and common motions. Either common motion can be detected first, in such a way as to minimise (give the simplest account of) the common motion present, and then, after abstraction of the common motion, the relative motions may be perceived as residual. Or relative motion can be detected and its components minimised, and after abstraction of this the common motion will be left as residual. These two possibilities make different predictions about the resulting perceptions of most displays of the "wheel-rolling" kind. As already mentioned, the "common-motion-first" theory predicts that a display with a hub light and a single rim light should appear wheel-like, while the "relative-motion-first" theory predicts that it should appear as a tumbling stick. While the rolling wheel perception is preferred (Duncker,1929; Johansson, 1975; Cutting & Proffitt, 1982), the tumbling stick may be seen, particularly if subjects are not fixating on one of the lights (Duncker, 1929). For other displays the "relative-motion-first" theory gives a much better account of what is perceived. Consider the configuration of lights in Figure 13.7. Here two lights are placed 90° apart on the rim of a wheel. The common motion in the display is again linear translation, and if this were

FIG.13.6.   The path traced out by the midpoint of an imaginary line joining lights on the rim and hub of a wheel. Observers occasionally report this display as like a stick tumbling along this path.

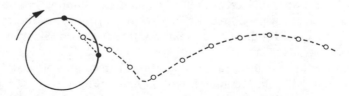

FIG.13.7.   The path traced out by the midpoint of an imaginary line joining two lights placed 90° apart on the rim of a wheel.

abstracted first then we would expect observers to report both lights cycling around the imaginary centre of the wheel. However if the relative motion were minimised, the two lights could be seen revolving around the midpoint of the imaginary line which joins them. After abstraction of this relative motion, the common motion left would be the prolate cycloidal motion of this midpoint—a kind of tumbling stick again. In fact, observers report the latter perception of such a display.

We seem to be left in a dilemma. For some displays it looks as though common motion is minimised and abstracted first, and for others it seems that relative motions are first detected and common motion seen as residual. Cutting and Proffitt suggest that both processes may proceed simultaneously, with the one achieving solution first dominating the perception. That is, the perceptual system may seek to minimise both common and relative motions at the same time. The one which is solved first determines that the other be perceived as residual. This theory seems to give the best account of the perception of this type of display, and certainly reinforces the idea that *absolute* motions are rarely seen as such.

Thus we have seen that the visual system resolves simple dynamic displays into components of common and relative motions. In the next section we will apply these ideas to a more realistic kind of display—that which depicts biological motion.

BIOLOGICAL MOTION

The most dramatic demonstrations of the visual system's application of a "minimum" principle were produced by Johansson (1973) in his biological motion displays. Johansson produced films of people walking, running and dancing in which the only visible features were lights attached to the actors' joints. Lights might be attached to the shoulders, elbows, wrists, hips, knees and ankles, to form a total of 12 moving lights in the dynamic displays (see Fig. 13.8). Such a display is easy to produce by wrapping reflectant tape around the joints and filming with a video camera set up to pick up only high contrast. In the film which results, all information about the contour of the human figure has been removed, and if a still frame of such a film is shown it looks like a meaningless jumble of dots, or, at best, a Christmas tree. However, as soon as the actor is shown moving, the impression is immediately of a human figure. The perception of a moving human can be achieved with as little as 100 msecs of film, or with as few as six lights shown. Not only can the figure be clearly seen (with the invisible contours of arms and legs present in a ghostly way), but the posture, gait and activities of the actor can be clearly described. It is clear from the displays whether the person is walking, running, jumping, limping, doing push-ups, or dancing

FIG.13.8. Lights are attached to the joints of an actor who walks or runs in the dark. The changing pattern of lights is immediately interpreted as a human figure in motion.

with a partner likewise portrayed by a set of moving lights. Runeson and Frykolm (1981) have shown that observers can accurately judge differences in the weight carried by an actor, where both the actor and load together are depicted by a total of 21 points of light.

Johansson considered the perception of biological motion in displays like these to be consistent with perceptual vector analysis, applied hierarchically. Let us take the case of an actor walking across a screen in front of the observer. The entire configuration of moving dots has a common motion component in the horizontal direction in which the actor is moving. Against this, the shoulders and hips make slight undulatory motions. Against this undulatory motion of the hips, the knee describes a pendular motion. Once the pendular motion of the knee has been partialled out, the ankle can be seen to describe a further pendular motion about this. Thus the dynamic configuration can be resolved into a set of hierarchical, relative motions of rigid limb segments. These walking figure displays again show how the visual system apparently "prefers" to interpret moving elements as representing the end-points of *rigid* structures in motion, even if the resulting rigid structures may then appear to have quite complex motions in depth. It should be stressed that Johansson considers the perceptual decoding principles of the vector analytic type, and the preference for rigid motions, to be "hard-wired" rather than derived from experience with real moving objects. We might note at this point a similarity with Ullman's theory (described in Chapter 6), who likewise made use of a rigidity assumption to interpret structure from moving point configurations.

Johansson's moving figures have been subjected to a more rigorous analysis by Cutting and his co-workers. In particular they have investigated how observers may detect subtle differences in gait from these displays. In preliminary work, Cutting and Kozlowski (1977) showed that observers performed well above chance at identifying themselves and their room-mates from such dynamic displays. In a number of subsequent experiments (Kozlowski & Cutting, 1977; Barclay, Cutting, & Kozlowski, 1978; Kozlowski & Cutting, 1978) they have gone on to show that observers are 60–70% accurate on average at detecting the *sex* of a walker from a display. In order to judge sex to this accuracy observers need to see about 2 sec of the display, which corresponds to about two step cycles, suggesting that such judgements rely on some dynamic invariant rather than on static configurational cues. The detection of the sex of a walker does not seem to depend crucially on any particular elements in the display. Above chance level judgements can be made if points on the upper or lower body only are illuminated (but see Kozlowski & Cutting (1978) for a reinterpretation of the lower-body findings), though performance is best when joints on both upper and lower halves of the body are shown. Thus the information on which such judgements are made appears to be given by some *global* invariant, rather than by particular elements in the display.

Barclay, Cutting and Kozlowski (1978) began the search for such an invariant with the observation that male and female bodies differ in the ratio of shoulder width to hip width. Men have broad shoulders and narrow hips compared with women. However, in the kinds of displays typically used, where the actor walks across the line of sight, only a single shoulder light and hip light are visible, so this ratio cannot be detected. Therefore the shoulder to hip width ratio cannot provide the basis for judgements of sex. This ratio does have consequences for other aspects of the relative motion in the display, however (Cutting, Proffitt, & Kozlowski, 1978). During locomotion, the hips and shoulder work in opposition to one another. When the right leg is forward in the step cycle, the right hip is also forward relative to the right shoulder which is back. Likewise, when the left leg is forward, so too is the left hip, with the left shoulder back. The relative widths of the shoulders and hips should thus affect the relative side to side motion of the hip and shoulder joints when viewed from the side. A measure based on this relative swing was found to correlate reasonably well with the consistency with which different walkers were rated as male or female.

However, Cutting et al. (1978) went on to derive a more general invariant from their displays which correlated better with the ratings given to different walkers. This measure was the relative height of the *centre of moment* of the moving walkers. The centre of moment is the reference point around which all movements in all parts of the body have regular geometric relations. It corresponds to the point where the three planes of symmetry for a walker's motion coincide. Its relative location can be determined by knowing only the relative widths (or relative swings) of the hips and shoulders (see Fig. 13.9). The centre of moment for male walkers is lower than that for females, and therefore provides a possible basis for judgements of sex.

Cutting (1978a) was able to show the validity of the centre of moment as a determinant of gait perception by synthesising artificial dynamic dot displays which mimicked the movements of walkers. In this way it was possible to vary *only* the centre of moment in such displays, holding all other variables constant. The synthetic "male" and "female" walkers produced were correctly identified on 82% of trials, though if the lights corresponding to the hips and shoulders were omitted performance dropped to about 59%, still above chance. These results are compatible with those obtained with real walkers, where above chance, but reduced, performance was obtained when some of the lights were removed. Thus it appears that a simple biomechanical invariant, the centre of moment, can be recovered from a display such as this, and could be used to specify reasonably accurately the sex of the walking figure.

We should note here that the centre of moment of a dynamic configuration can serve as the origin for an object-centred coordinate system about which the relative motions of the other elements can be described. We saw in Chapter 7 how Marr and Nishihara (1978) tackled the problem of deriving an object-centred coordinate system from the occluding contours obtained from the image of a static object. The problem was to derive an axis for the figure without prior knowledge of what the shape represented. With the work of Cutting and colleagues we see that the relative motions in a dynamic display, in the absence of contour information, may also be used to derive an object-centred coordinate system about which to describe movement, and the resulting description might then provide the basis for recognising the form depicted.

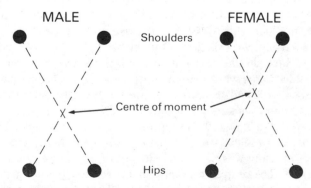

FIG.13.9.   The relative location of the centre of moment for male and female walkers. Adapted from Cutting & Proffitt (1981).

The centre of moment is a general invariant which can be found for other kinds of dynamic display. To return to the rolling wheel configurations (see p.287), the centroid—the centre of the configuration of lights—is directly analogous to the centre of moment. Proffitt and colleagues (Proffitt & Cutting, 1979; Proffitt, Cutting, & Stier, 1979) have shown that the relationship between the centroid, and the centre of the wheel, determines how wheel-like is the motion observed. When the two coincide (as when two lights are placed 180° apart on the rim), "perfect" wheel-like motions are seen. When the centroid and the centre of the wheel are far apart, as when the two lights are placed 90° apart on the rim (see Fig. 13.7), "hobbling" motions are seen.

The centre of a radially expanding optical flow field, which as we have seen (Chapters 8, 9 and 10) is very important in guiding locomotor activity, also comprises the centre of moment for that dynamic display, and Cutting and Proffitt (1981) have also argued that the centre of moment is a useful concept when applied to slow events, such as the ageing of a face (see later) or the movement of stars in the night sky which migratory birds use to steer their course. Recently, Cutting (1982) has demonstrated that viewers may be sensitive to alterations in *second-order* centres of moment (the centres of moment of component structures), when perceiving the bending motions present in "tree" and "bush"-like configurations.

A Grammar for Event Perception

Cutting and Proffitt (1981) argue that it is possible to construct a "grammar" for event perception, like a grammar in language. From the dynamic visual information presented, observers "parse" out different components (see Fig. 13.10). From a total visual scene (used here to refer to information which changes over time, rather than in its more traditional, "static" sense), the first division made is between an event and the ground against which it occurs. For example, an event might consist of a person walking along a crowded shopping precinct. The precinct would be the "ground" for this event, and might itself contain other potential events. Once an event has been parsed, it can then be described as having figural and action components. The action of a figure is its action *relative to the observer*, to be distinguished from the movement of parts of a figure *relative to itself*. In our example, the action of the person consists of their translation across the precinct. The swinging arms and legs constitute the movement of the figure relative to itself. The action of a figure is captured by the dynamics of its centre of moment, while the "static" centre of moment itself serves as a reference point for the description of the motions and locations of the different parts of a figure.

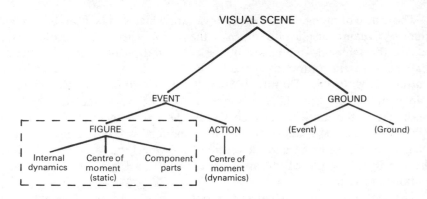

FIG.13.10.   A grammar for event perception. A visual scene can be divided
into event and background. The event consists of a figure and its action.
Adapted from Cutting & Proffitt (1981).

If the figure contains component structures, a hierarchical set of centres
of moment can be abstracted, each serving as the reference point about
which the motion and topography of the component structure can be
described (see Fig. 13.11). For the description of a walking figure, Cutting
and Proffitt's analysis is very similar to Johansson's. After the centre of
moment for the torso is obtained, about which the hip and shoulder
movements are described, the limb movements are described as a nested set
of pendulum actions. The motion of the elbow is described relative to its
"static" centre of moment at the shoulder (which is a second-order centre),
and the motion of the wrist is described relative to its "third-order" centre
of moment at the elbow, and so on. A different example in which there are
component structures to describe would be given by the perception of a tree
swaying in the wind (Cutting, 1982). The centre of moment for a tree is the
point where its trunk meets the ground. Since the tree does not move as a
whole, there is no action component here. Second-order centres are present
where each limb meets the trunk, and third-order centres would be present
at minor branch points along each limb.

This "grammatical" approach to event perception is still highly speculative,
and in places problematical. For example, what should be seen as an "event"
and what should be seen as "ground"? However, it may well provide a useful
framework in which the perception of static scenes can be seen as a special
case of dynamic events, rather than vice versa.

In all the above examples, observers have viewed displays and reported
the *motions* present, or identified the structures (e.g. walking figures) which
give rise to these motions. One aspect of natural event perception which we
have yet to consider is how we go beyond the motions present to attribute
causality to the motions. It is to this topic that we turn next.

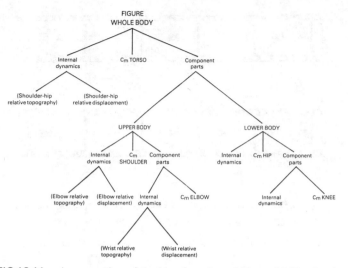

FIG.13.11.   An expansion of the boxed section of Figure 13.10., showing how a moving human figure can be broken down into a hierarchical set of components, each with its centre of moment, internal dynamics and component parts. Adapted from Cutting & Proffitt (1981).

THE PERCEPTION OF CAUSALITY

When we watch a football match we are in no doubt about why the football suddenly speeds up and changes direction—it was kicked. That is, the change in the movement of the ball was *caused by* the action of one of the players' feet. Likewise, in boxing or judo, we see the action of one of the combatants as causing the other to fall to the floor. We might suggest that it is our previous experience of seeing footballs kicked, or opponents thrown, which allows us to make causal *inferences* in new situations. However, Michotte 1946 (translated 1963) made the strong claim that causality was perceived *directly*.

Michotte experimented with simple displays. In one situation (Fig. 13.12a), subjects viewed a display in which a black square (A) moved towards a red square (B) at constant speed. At the moment when A came into contact with B, A stopped and B moved off, either at the same speed or at an appreciably slower one. After a short time B also came to rest. Michotte reports that in this situation observers see the black square bump into the red square and set it into motion. "The impression is clear; it is the blow given by A which *makes* B go, which *produces* B's movement" (p.20). This has been termed the "launching effect." In another demonstration (Fig. 13.12b) A again moves towards B, but continues its course without changing speed. When the two objects contact, B in turn moves off at the same speed

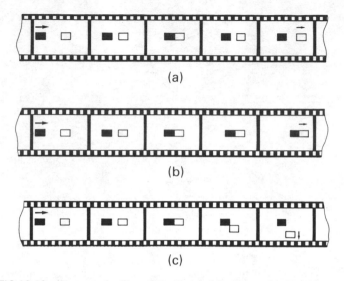

(a)

(b)

(c)

FIG.13.12.   Frames of a film of the kinds of display used by Michotte. ■
Black square A, □ Red square B. (a) Launching; (b) Entraining; (c) A display
where B moves off at 90° and launching is not perceived.

as A until both objects finally come to rest together. In this situation
Michotte describes the impression as of A carrying B along or pushing it
ahead. This effect is known as "entraining."

Michotte backs up his claim that phenomenal causality is directly
apprehended by demonstrating that the impression is critically dependent
on the temporal, spatial and formal properties of the display. In the first
experiment described, if an interval is introduced between A contacting B,
and B moving off, the impression of causing, or launching, B's movement
is eradicated. If B moves off faster than A then the impression is of B being
"triggered" rather than launched, while if B moves off more slowly it appears
to be launched rather than triggered. However, whether launching or
triggering is seen also depends on the length of the path that B subsequently
follows as well as on the ratio of the objects' speeds, an observation which
was confirmed by Boyle (1960).

According to Michotte, the launching effect depended not only on these
spatial and temporal aspects but also on the similarity between the paths of
the motion of the two objects. As object B's path was shifted in angle away
from the direction of A's path so the reported perceptions of launching
declined. If B went off in a direction at right angles to A (Fig. 13.12c),
Michotte claimed that launching was almost never observed. While the
impression of launching is thus crucially dependent on the temporal and
spatial parameters, Michotte claimed that it was unaffected by the *nature* of

the items used. If A was a wooden ball, and B a small, brightly coloured circle, Michotte reported that the launching effect was unchanged. Michotte regards this as important evidence for the "direct" perception of causality, since if previous experiences of cause and effect were responsible there should be no reason to see a causal relationship between two quite dissimilar items.

While few would doubt that such causal impressions can be gained from displays of the types used by Michotte, there has subsequently been some doubt about the universality of observers' impressions. Michotte himself was often vague about the precise numbers of subjects he tested, or the instructions he gave them, and in places based strong claims on the results obtained with a very small number of highly practised subjects. Boyle (1960) reported having to discard 50% of his subjects on the basis of a pre-test in which these subjects failed to report "launching" or "entraining" from standard displays. Beasley (1968) assessed formally the extent of individual differences in the perception of these displays and reported that only 65% and 45% of his subjects responded respectively to "launching" and "entraining" displays in causal terms. Contrary to Michotte's claim, 45% *did* report causal impressions when object B departed at 90° from A in the launching display. In addition, and again contrary to claims made by Michotte, Beasley found that the nature of the objects used—squares, discs or cars—did have an effect on the nature of the responses elicited.

It seems that we should doubt Michotte's claims of the universality of such causal impressions, and hence must doubt that such effects are perceived "directly." It seems as likely that the perception of such displays *is* in line with acquired perceptual and cultural experience of the world. We have learned that certain event sequences imply causal relations between the participants, and the language we use to describe such events reflects, but may also influence, such perceptual learning. Having abandoned the idea that causality is perceived through the direct pick-up of spatial and temporal invariants, it is still interesting to enquire how such causal impressions are obtained through reference to acquired experience.

Weir (1978) has developed a computer model which interprets displays like those of Michotte, in ways similar to human observers. Her approach is a transactionalist one, in which there is a continuous interaction between the stimulus pattern and stored internal representations in the form of action "schemata." It is thus nearer in conception to the kind of framework we presented in Part II of this book. Her computer program accepts a symbolic description of each of a sequence of static images, corresponding to different frames of a film of a Michotte display, so that the movement of each display element has to be computed by comparing elements from one frame to the next. This means that she has to tackle the "correspondence problem" (see Chapter 6) in order to match the objects in each frame: "There will in general be more than one way of pairing the picture regions in two adjacent frames and a way of choosing which of the possible pairings correspond to an *enduring object in motion* must be provided (Weir, 1978, p.249)."

Weir makes use of partial matches between incoming event sequences and stored action schemata to help solve this correspondence process, and so "top-down" processes (see Chapter 4) play a central role in her theory. This is unfortunate for our purposes here, since although we have rejected the hypothesis that causal relations may be directly perceived, we would not want to deny that object motions may be detected in a bottom-up way. Nevertheless some features of Weir's program are worth describing here since a modification of her theory could quite easily be applied to motions which had been computed without involving higher-level concepts.

The object motions are compared with stored "schemata" for different actions, which are dynamic descriptions for actions, rather like the structural descriptions for objects which we considered in Chapter 7. An action schema contains units like "approaches" and "withdraws." The action schema for "Launching" is shown in Figure 13.13a, and that for "Entraining" in Figure 13.13b. For each action there is an *agent*, and an object on which the agent acts (here called the *patient*).

The schema consists of several components. Launching consists of collision followed by withdrawal, and the schema specifies the event sequence that defines a collision. Entraining consists of collision followed by movement together. If the first few frames of the film match the "collision" sequence, then both the launching and entraining schemas are activated. The subsequent actions in the display will allow a decision to be reached about which interpretation is correct.

Weir's simulation allows the possibility of anticipation of expected actions, by the activation of "demons" which look out for expected sequences. It can also incorporate individual differences in perception. For example, some subjects may report launching only if B's speed after impact is substantially below A's before impact. This can be incorporated by restrictions in the definitions of actions like "withdraws from."

We have seen how causal impressions may be obtained from simple displays, and argued that such impressions are likely to be gained by reference to stored experiences, rather than "directly" as Michotte claimed. We now turn to consider how *intentions* and *dispositions* may be perceived in the objects which move in simple dynamic displays.

PERCEPTION AND ATTRIBUTION

Observers who view displays of the type used by Michotte may describe the actions of the objects in animate terms. Thus A may be seen to "kick" or

(a)

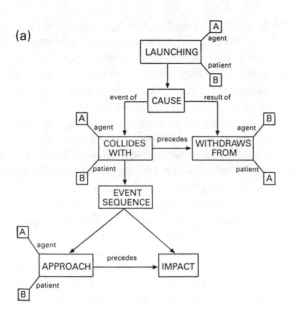

(b)

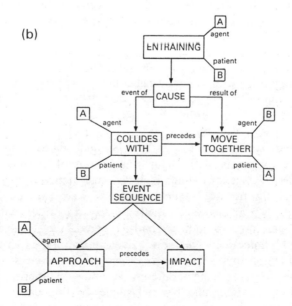

FIG.13.13. Schemas for Launching (a) and Entraining (b). Adapted from Weir (1978).

301

to "shove" B. B may be seen to "escape" from A who is "chasing" it. Therefore, in addition to perceiving causality, we may also perceive intentionality in the action of inanimate objects, just as in everyday life we interpret the actions of animate beings in terms of what they are trying to do. In addition, these momentary intentions which we observe may lead us to attribute enduring dispositional traits to the actors we observe. If person A kicks B, chases him, then kicks him again, A may be seen as a "bully."

The classic study of such attributional processes in perception was conducted by Heider and Simmel (1944), who showed observers a film in which two triangles of different sizes (the larger and smaller hereafter referred to as T and t respectively) and a circle (c) were seen to move in the vicinity of a rectangular frame (the house) with a moveable flap in one side (the door) (see Fig. 13.14). The first few frames of the film sequence depicted the following movements (illustrated roughly in Figure 13.14, and described here, as in the original article, in "anthropomorphic" terms for simplicity): T moved toward the house, opened the door, moved inside and closed the door. t and c appeared and moved around near the door. T moved out of the house towards t; the two fight, with T the winner; during the fight, c moved into the house.

Heider and Simmel showed the entire film to 34 subjects who were simply asked to "write down what happened in the picture." All but one of their subjects described the film in terms of the movements of animate beings. A typical subject's description of the first few frames was:

> A man has planned to meet a girl and the girl comes along with another man. The first man tells the second to go; the second tells the first, and he shakes his head. Then the two men have a fight, and the girl starts to go into the room to get out of the way and hesitates and finally goes in. She apparently does not want to be with the first man. (pp.246–7).

In a second experiment, Heider and Simmel asked their subjects to interpret the movements of the figures as actions of persons and then to answer a series of questions which included such items as "what kind of a person is the big triangle." Such questions were answered with high consistency. Both triangles were usually perceived as male, with the larger one seen as "aggressive," a "bully," "bad-tempered," etc. The circle was seen as "frightened," "meek" or "helpless." Even in the first experiment, where no specific direction to see the objects as people was given, subjects tended to describe the objects as being of different sex and with differing dispositions.

Like Michotte, Heider and Simmel suggested that causal impressions were given by the spatial, temporal and figural aspects of the display. Thus when T is seen to "hit" t, the stimulus parameters are very similar to those in the "launching" experiment of Michotte. T approaches t until it comes

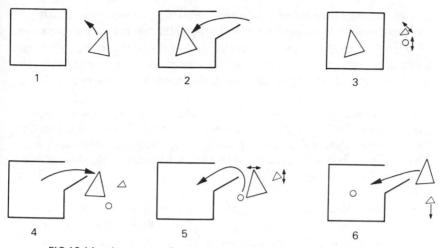

FIG.13.14.   A sequence of events from the early part of Heider and Simmel's (1944) film. The film shows a big triangle, a small triangle, and a small circle moving around near a box with a moveable flap (the door). See text for a description of the event sequence.

into contact with it. Then T stands still while t starts to move in the same direction as T's earlier movement.

> This phenomenal relationship is obviously determined by temporal succession and spatial proximity. The good continuation of the line—the fact that the direction of t's movement continues the direction of T's probably plays a role in the convincing appearance of this apparent energetic movement (p.253).

The movement of T and the door which result in the impression of T "opening" or "closing" the door are similar to Michotte's "entraining" displays, since the movement of T is imparted to the door by prolonged contact rather than sudden impact. The question arises as to why it is always T who appears to push the door (rather than the door pushing T). Heider and Simmel suggest that here the interpretation is influenced by the context in which such movements occur. The door never moves *without* contact from T or one of the other shapes, whereas each of the shapes *is* seen to move in isolation. The shapes are therefore seen as "animate," the door as "inanimate," which resolves the ambiguity in the pushing action.

To resolve ambiguity in the interpretation of the movement in these displays, subjects may use a combination of the stimulus parameters and the personality characteristics which have been attributed to the display members. For example, if two objects move together at the same distance apart, the first may be seen to lead, with the second following, or the second may be seen to chase the first, which is fleeing. The interpretation given depends on the element which is seen as initiating the movement, and also on the power relationships which exist between the "people" who are moving. If T is seen as timid or cowardly, then t may seem to chase him (some such reports were obtained when the original film was shown in reverse). If T is seen as dictatorial or aggressive, then t may seem to follow him.

> If one sees two animals running in file through high grass, one will interpret these movements in accordance with other data. If the one in front is a rabbit and the one behind a dog, he will perceive a dog chasing a rabbit. If the first one is a big rabbit and the second a small one, he will not see "chasing" but "leading" and "following" (p.254).

Thus while Heider and Simmel see some aspects of the interpretation as given by the stimulus parameters, other aspects, while constrained by these features, will additionally be influenced by the total context in which the individual action is embedded. Intention as well as action is involved in the interpretation of their film. If T is hitting t, then T wants to hurt t. If T chases t into the house, then t may be trying to hide from T. Such intentional attributions themselves influence the dispositions which are accorded to the individual elements, and these dispositions may in turn influence how a new action sequence is interpreted.

These examples illustrate that even in the perception of the movements of simple shapes in a relatively neutral context, we see the application of quite complex and subtle attributional processes by humans. What we see happening will depend not only on the momentary motions in the display, but on expectations built up over a sequence of actions, expectations which are derived from our broader social experiences. It would seem to be stretching the Gibsonian line too far to say that all the qualities imparted to these simple objects are specified in the light. The pattern of activity present doubtless constrains the range of possible interpretations, but cannot specify which interpretation will be given (would contemporary women see the circle as female?).

Nevertheless, it is still interesting to explore the ways in which different stimulus parameters influence the perception of such displays. Heider and Simmel's study was limited to a single film. Unlike Michotte, they made no attempt to vary spatial or temporal parameters systematically. Indeed the film which they constructed probably reflected their own intuitions about the phenomenological processes they wished to study. However, Bassili (1976) has conducted a study in which aspects of a Heider and Simmel type of display were systematically varied.

In Bassili's computer-generated displays, a black and a white circle were filmed undergoing various movements. Five different films were produced which ranged from a "chase," in which the temporal and spatial characteristics of the following (black) circle were tightly linked to those of the leading (white) one, down to a film in which both elements moved randomly and independently about the screen. Thus the temporal and spatial linking of the movements were progressively relaxed. Subjects who viewed the films were initially required to "Describe what you saw in one concise sentence" and then asked more specific questions about their perceptions of the film. The effect of temporal contingency was assessed by comparing the responses to two films, in both of which the directions of the motions were random. In one, however, a change in direction of one element was quickly followed by a change in direction of the other. In the other no such temporal contingency held.

It was found that temporal contingency between the changes in direction of the two figures was critical for the perception of an interaction between them, while the motion configuration (the spatial contingencies) were an important factor in the *kind* of interaction and the intentionality attributed to the figures. For example, subjects were much more likely to report that the black circle was chasing or following the white circle, and to ascribe intention to either or both of the circles when the direction of the changes in the black circle's path were tightly linked to those of the white circle. When the directions were random, but temporally linked, subjects saw the circles as interacting in some unspecified way, but were less likely to describe this interaction in intentional terms.

It is interesting to contrast the *interactive* nature of the perception of these displays with the *relative motion* perceptions described earlier in this chapter. For example, Johansson, (p.288) describes the perception of two white dots following one another around a rectangle (Fig. 13.5) as being of the dots forming the end-points of a rigid stick which itself moves in depth, while in the work of Michotte, Heider and Simmel, and Bassili, similar elements are seen as independent elements which influence the actions of each other. It seems likely that the nature of the elements, the viewing conditions and the instructions given to subjects will all influence how such moving displays are interpreted. If the display elements are identical, as in Johansson's displays, they may be more likely to be grouped together as parts of a single object than if they are dissimilar as in Bassili's. If the display is viewed under conditions where the flatness of the screen, and the screen edges, are not apparent, then movement in depth will be more likely to occur. Finally, if subjects are requested to describe the *motions* in the display they may be less likely to respond in terms of animate interactions than if they are asked to state "what happened."

So far we have considered how relatively simple display elements may be perceived in causal interrelationships, and endowed with "human" qualities of intention and personality. These complex attributional processes undoubtedly derive from our everyday social experiences, but the social attributions that we make in everyday life will themselves depend at least in part on information obtained from non-verbal aspects of a perceived interaction or situation (see McArthur & Baron, 1983, for a discussion of an ecological approach to social perception). In the next section we continue to explore aspects of interpersonal perception by turning to the problems associated with the perception and recognition of human faces.

SOCIAL PERCEPTION CONTINUED: THE HUMAN FACE

In the natural world the human face is in almost continuous motion. Some movements of the head involve rigid transformations, as when the head is turned from side to side; but expressive movements of the face are not rigid, as when a person smiles. Such non-rigid motions include stretching and bulging of different parts of the face, produced by complex sets of muscles. Bassili (1978, 1979) has used a technique like Johansson's, in which small illuminated spots are scattered over a face which is then filmed in the dark, to show that observers can identify a "face" from a moving configuration of lights without seeing any structural information about the facial features. Not only can a "face" be identified from such a display, but observers have some success at identifying different emotions portrayed in such displays. Quite specific information about faces can be gleaned simply from the pattern of transformations present, without any need for information about the *form* of the face, just as human walkers can be identified in Johansson's displays, without any detail of the form of their limbs.

The dynamic configuration of the human face is endowed with a number of different kinds of meaning, all of which need to be extracted in the course of social interaction. The extraction of these different kinds of meaning must rely on the abstraction of different invariant and variant information. A face first serves to identify an individual. Individual identity can of course also be determined from other sources of visual information, including gait (as we saw earlier, p.293) and characteristic clothing, and from non-visual information, such as a voice, but the face is probably the most unambiguous "clue" to a person's identity. However, because the face and head are mobile, we must somehow identify structural information from a face which remains invariant despite these transformations in pose and expression.

As well as serving to identify an individual, a person's face also conveys expressive information, which may inform about his or her emotional state, intentions towards or attentiveness to an observer, and which may help to disambiguate verbal information during conversation. Movements of the face may help a listener to know whether a remark is intended seriously or in jest, and whether it is a request or a command. People are reasonably accurate at identifying emotions from facial expressions, and this ability must rely on the detection of a different kind of information from that which subserves face recognition. That is, we must be able to encode from faces both information which specifies an individual's identity (irrespective of pose or expression), and information which specifies a particular expression (irrespective of the identity of the person whose expression it is).

In this section we describe some of the current ideas on how we recognise individuals from their faces, and also consider how we interpret expressive movements.

Identifying Faces

It might seem out of place to include the topic of face recognition in a chapter entitled "event perception." This is because most researchers (including one of the authors of this book! e.g. Bruce, 1983) have chosen to ignore the natural mobility of the human face and treated the problem of how faces are recognised in ways similar to the research on "pattern recognition" described in Chapter 7. The stimuli used in face recognition research have usually been photographs of real faces or composite faces constructed from Photofit or Identi-kit.

In addition to exploring the factors which affect memory for such materials, researchers have enquired whether faces are perceived in a "holistic" manner (like templates) or as sets of independent features (for a comprehensive review see Davies, Ellis, & Shepherd, 1981). The fact that questions about face recognition have been posed in this way serves to illustrate how faces have typically been treated as static visual patterns, rather than as continuously transforming objects.

The use of static faces does not necessarily invalidate research into face recognition, since a photograph of a real face must itself capture structural information about that face which remains invariant across a variety of different views (or photographs). However, the use of such materials has perhaps prevented researchers from thinking carefully about the kind of physical information which could be used to distinguish one face from another in the real world. Many memory experiments for example have confounded picture recognition with face recognition, by presenting identical photographs of faces at study and test. Face recognition can only be seen to have occurred if a face is recognised *despite* changes between presentation and test. Recognition memory for briefly presented unfamiliar faces is significantly impaired if these are tested in a different view (Bruce, 1982), suggesting only a limited ability to abstract invariant information from a single photograph. Therefore even if we learn, from experiments in which the "features" of composite faces are manipulated, that the hair or eyes are preferentially attended to, and/or better remembered, we still have to establish how it is that eyes could be recognised from different angles or when altered as in smiling and frowning.

It is perhaps not surprising that we still know little about the physical information which is extracted from faces and which enables us to recognise them in all their different aspects, since any account must also explain how it is that face recognition is preserved under some sorts of *unnatural* as well as *natural* transformation. For example, faces can be identified from low spatial frequency information (e.g. see Harmon, 1973), or from grossly distorted caricatures and simple cartoons (Fig. 13.15). Despite the robustness of face recognition during quite radical transformations like this, our ability to identify faces is severely impaired if the faces are inverted, even though inversion is a change which preserves the metrical properties of a face (see Fig. 13.15). These are just some of the observations that a theory of face recognition must eventually accommodate.

It is perhaps not too difficult to construct hypotheses about the kinds of structural information about a face which might remain invariant under rigid transformations. For example the ratio of nose length to overall head height could be recovered fairly easily from any viewing angle, and would give a measure of "nose size" which did not depend on viewing angle or distance. However, as yet we have little insight into what information, if any, may remain invariant when a face undergoes *non*-rigid transformations, as when smiling, frowning or grimacing, where there may be little preservation

FIG.13.15. We can recognise familiar faces from simple line drawings or exaggerated caricatures, but we find inverted faces hard to recognise.

of metrical properties. Our nose length measure, for example, might be distorted whenever the nose was wrinkled in disgust.

One way around this problem would be simply to propose that such expressive movements just add "noise" to the process of extracting invariants, and that when we view faces under natural conditions we concentrate on their more passive moments in building up enduring representations which can be used to identify people (e.g. Ekman, 1978). There may even be some kinds of information that we can extract from a face that are affected relatively little by expressive movements. Such information might include (for caucasian faces) hair length, texture and style, overall face shape, age-level, skin tone etc. It is interesting to note that dimensions roughly corresponding to "hair style," "face shape" and "age" have been found by Shepherd et al. to account for similarity judgements made between pairs of unfamiliar faces (Shepherd, Davies, & Ellis, 1981). Therefore we could argue that there are a number of potential sources of information in the face to specify identity, so that expressive movements could simply be regarded as a complicating nuisance.

An alternative approach would be to propose that invariant information about an individual's identity may be given by, and be preserved in, patterns of expressive movement. A strong piece of evidence to support such an idea would be provided if observers could identify their friends from the Bassili displays we described above. Unfortunately we do not know whether this is possible or not. However the kind of approach which could be involved in analysing invariants in changing faces is illustrated by Shaw and Pittenger's work on *ageing*.

Shaw and Pittenger (1977) have looked at the non-rigid transformation which the profile of a human head undergoes while it ages, and have identified information which remains invariant under this transformation. This work might in principle be extended to apply to rapidly changing (as opposed to slowly growing) faces, and hence is of some interest and relevance to the present discussion.

Shaw and Pittenger have shown that people are very consistent at rank ordering profile outlines according to their apparent relative age, suggesting that head shape provides at least one of the sources of information which we use when establishing a person's age. Consider the set of profiles shown in Figure 13.16. You will probably agree that the one on the right looks "young" and the one on the left looks "old." How can we describe the nature of the transformation which relates the older to the younger profiles? Shaw and Pittenger have demonstrated that the growth process transforms the human head in a similar way to that which occurs in dicotyledonous plants. The profile of a human head is very similar in shape to a dicotyledeonous structure (see Fig. 13.17). Ignoring facial detail, the shape is like an inverted heart with a rounded top—a *cardioid*.

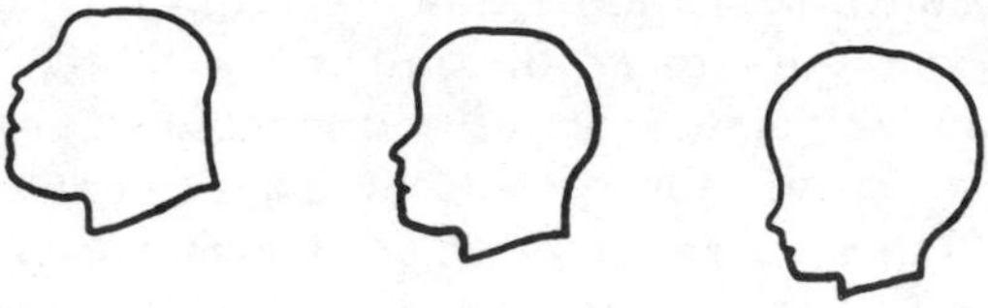

FIG.13.16. The profile on the right looks younger than the one on the left, and the central one appears intermediate in age.

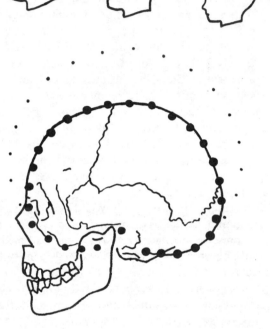

FIG.13.17. The small dots show a regular cardioidal shape lying above a profile of a human skull. Appropriate transformation of this shape gives a good fit to the shape of the skull, as shown by the large black dots. From Shaw, McIntyre, & Mace (1974). Copyright © 1974 by Cornell University. Used by permission of the publishers, Cornell University Press.

Shaw, McIntyre and Mace (1974) demonstrated that a single transformation, if applied to the outline of the skulls of infant, child and adult could map one skull continuously onto the other. They hypothesised that there might be a cardioidal shape invariant for growth space, with ageing representing cardioidal *strain*. Strain is imposed on the bones of the skull by stresses produced by growth of softer, highly elastic tissues. Pittenger and Shaw (1975) tested the extent to which perceived changes in relative age level are captured by a strain transformation as opposed to a shear transformation (which modifies the angle of the facial profile). Subjects were shown a series of profiles produced by modifying a single outline profile over seven levels of strain and five levels of shear (Fig. 13.18). They found that 91% of the relative age judgements made by their subjects were consistent with the hypothesis that a strain transformation was responsible for these perceived age changes, while only 65% of the judgements were consistent with a shear transformation, which confirmed their intuition that it was strain that was the important determinant. In further experimental work they demonstrated that observers were consistent in perceiving a profile

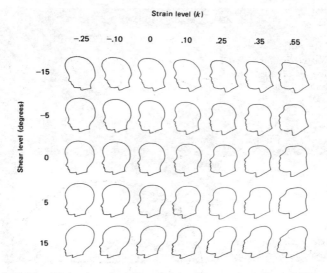

FIG.13.18.   The series of profiles used by Pittenger and Shaw (1975). The profiles were all formed from the same original, which was modified by five different levels of shear (vertical axis) and seven different levels of strain (horizontal axis) to give this set of 35. Reproduced from Shaw & Pittenger (1977) with permission of author and publishers.

with larger strain as "older" than a different one with smaller strain, and that they showed a high sensitivity in these judgements even when the pairs of profiles differed to a very small degree.

Finally they showed that sufficient structural invariants are preserved during growth to permit the identification of heads at different age levels, despite the remodelling produced by ageing. They asked subjects to select the age-transformed skull profile that matched a target profile, from a set of two in which the "foil" was the profile of a different head transformed to the same degree (see Fig. 13.19). Subjects performed this task considerably better than chance. It thus appears that the ageing transformation preserves invariant information which might specify individual identity. We are indeed able to match pictures of people taken at different ages, provided the age spans are not too great (Seamon, 1982), and Shaw and his colleagues have shown how one source of information—skull profile shape—might contribute to these judgements.

We have omitted all the mathematical detail from this account of Shaw and Pittenger's work, and you are referred to their articles for a full discussion of this (see also Todd, Mark, Shaw, & Pittenger, 1980). It is worth pointing out here that the invariant they claim accounts for age transformations is *topological* rather than *metrical*. The former requires a different kind of geometry from the familiar Euclidean geometry we learn

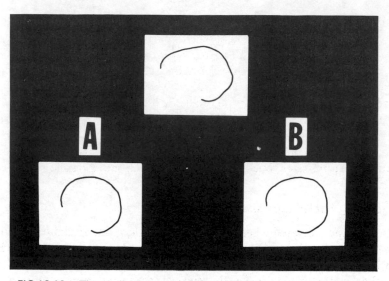

FIG.13.19. The skull outline at the top is the same as B, but age-transformed to a different extent. Skull A is a different individual, at the same transformational level as B. Reproduced from Shaw & Pittenger (1977) with permission of author and publishers.

at school. The concept of "shape" which emerges from a weaker (non-metrical) geometry is qualitative rather than quantitative, but may provide the right way to handle the changes in shape provided by non-rigid transformations.

How might similar kinds of ideas be applied to the everyday problem of recognising faces despite the very rapid non-rigid transformations arising from expressive movements? One possible direction is given by Cutting's (1978b) extension of the work of Shaw and his colleagues, in which he has identified a *centre of moment* for the ageing transformation. Cutting (1978b) manipulated the point within skull profiles around which cardioidal transformations were applied, and had observers make judgements about the "goodness" of the resulting profiles as age-changed versions of a standard skull. The point which yielded the best judgements corresponded to an area within the skull from which age changes are generated during growth.

Now just as Shaw has described the nature of the transformation which occurs when a head ages, and Cutting has found a dynamic "centre" in such growth, so we need to be able to describe the nature of the transformation which occurs when someone smiles, for example, and identify what information is preserved under such a transformation. It might be that centres of moment could be determined for certain expressive movements, centres which might differ in position from person to person, and thus provide one kind of invariant for face recognition. Future work, perhaps making use of dynamic point-light displays, could test the feasibility of these ideas.

Perhaps then we make use of a combination of cues when identifying people from their faces—some of which are affected little by transformation, and some of which (centres of moment for expressive movements) might be given by the pattern of the transformation itself. It certainly seems that the perception of dynamic facial displays should be studied alongside the perception of static photographs to help us to develop the right kinds of ideas about the basis of face recognition. Nevertheless, the importance of dynamic information for the recognition of human faces remains controversial. When we turn to consider the perception of facial expression, transformations over time are likely to be much more crucial.

Perceiving Facial Expression

Good teachers can tell whether their students look interested or bored, and whether they understand or are confused by what is said to them. Blank stares, frowns and head-shaking mean one thing, smiles and nods mean another. Unfortunately, just as the study of face recognition has concentrated on static displays, most studies of the perception of emotion have similarly used photographs of posed expressions to determine how accurately human observers can perceive the different emotions portrayed (for a review see Ekman, 1982). As Ekman has pointed out, posed expressions are not necessarily identical to spontaneous ones, and expressions in natural situations may be altered in line with cultural norms. In this section we will briefly discuss what has been learned of the perception of posed emotions, and then consider to what extent these findings can be generalised to natural situations.

The most important thing to note is that people are fairly accurate at assigning posed emotional expressions to one of a few fairly broad categories, such as happiness, surprise, anger and disgust. There is a good degree of universality in such judgements. People from a variety of literate and some pre-literate cultures judge such displays in similar ways (Ekman & Oster, 1982). While less is known about the accuracy with which observers can judge spontaneous expressive movements, there is evidence that at the very least, positive and negative emotions can be distinguished in natural situations (Ekman, Friesen & Ellsworth, 1982).

What processes might underlie our ability to judge emotional expressions? One possibility is that information about different facial "postures" is encoded and compared to some kind of stored catalogue, just as we suggested in the previous chapter that Marr and Nishihara's scheme could be extended to include postures of animals. A particular emotion might be characterised by the relative dispositions of the component axes of the face (the axis of each eyebrow, each eye, the mouth, etc.) to the major axis of symmetry.

It would be difficult to apply such a scheme in natural situations where there is continuous movement in the face, and a better way to describe the information which underlies expressive judgements might be to make use of dynamic rather than static cues. Ekman and Friesen (1982) have developed a *Facial Action Coding System* (FACS) to describe in detail the movements made by different parts of a face. The FACS consists of an inventory of all the perceptually distinct actions which can be produced by the facial muscles. Using such an inventory, we are in a position to ask whether unique combinations of actions (independent of who the actor is) underly the perception of different emotions.

The kind of analysis is illustrated here for the eyebrows alone (Ekman, 1979). Figure 13.20 shows the distinguishable action units for the brows and forehead together, and the distinguishable combinations of these units. These patterns have been "frozen" for the purposes of illustration, and it is important to emphasise that Ekman and Friesen are concerned to code *actions* rather than configurations. Ekman has shown that different action units are indeed involved in different emotions. For example, action unit 1

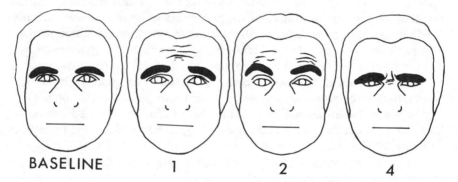

BASELINE   1   2   4

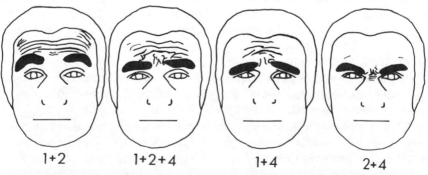

1+2   1+2+4   1+4   2+4

FIG.13.20.   The different action units for the brow and forehead identified by the Facial Action Coding System (Ekman & Friesen, 1978). Action units 1, 2 and 4 may occur alone (top) or in combination (bottom). The drawings were obtained by tracing photographs. Reproduced from P. Ekman (1979) with permission of author and publishers.

alone, or with 4, indicates sadness, 4 alone yields anger or distress, 1 with 2 gives surprise, and $1+2+4$ gives fear.

Ekman has thus shown that distinct patterns of activity are related to changes in emotional state, and it may be these patterns of activity that observers detect in the face. While momentarily frozen expressions might be compared with some stored catalogue of facial postures, it may be more profitable to think of observers matching transformations in expression over time to dynamic emotion "schemata," like the action schemas in Weir's work that we described earlier (p.299). Expressions are never all-or-none, they are graded, and blended. A person's momentary expression of faint surprise may represent a point of increasing or decreasing amazement, so we need to know its relationship both to prior and subsequent expressive movements, and to concurrent events in the world, in order to interpret it properly.

To reinforce this point, consider the following scenario. Suppose someone pulls out a gun, aims it at you, squeezes the trigger, and thereby releases a flag on which is written the word "BANG." Your emotions are likely to swing rapidly through the range from horror and fear to surprise followed by mirth (if you appreciated the joke) or anger (if you didn't). These emotions are likely to be revealed in rapidly changing and blending expressions. A stored catalogue of facial postures would not help an observer decipher your feelings here. Some representational system sensitive to unfolding *events* would be more appropriate.

We have briefly discussed the potential wealth of information available in the human face which can lead us to recognise a person, or decipher their emotional state. A thorough "event" treatment of human face perception remains to be developed, but may provide useful insights not gained through a conventional "pattern recognition" treatment.

CONCLUSIONS

The topics we have discussed in this chapter have been wide-ranging, covering at two extremes the perception of motion in simple displays, to displays of emotion in the human face. These topics have been linked by the common theme that all represent examples of the human apprehension of *events*, in which transformations over time are deemed crucial.

The study of event perception stands in contrast to that of *object* recognition which we described in Chapter 7. Research into object recognition and event perception shares the aim of understanding how humans interpret visual information, but the starting-point for research in object recognition is a static image, rather than a transforming array. Earlier chapters in this section (Chapters 9–12) likewise examined animal and human reactions to transformations in the optic array.

The approach taken in the current section has been broadly Gibsonian, or "ecological," and the questions we asked, and answered, felt very different from those in Part II, which dealt with the processing of the information contained in retinal images. In Chapter 14, our final chapter, we will explore the differences between these two approaches in more detail.

IV
CONCLUSIONS

14 Contrasting Theories of Visual Perception

We have now considered the current state of knowledge of visual perception as it has been built up from research within three traditions. The physiological tradition, which we introduced in the first part of this book, studies the nervous system directly, seeking to establish how the pattern of light falling on receptor cells is transformed by networks of nerve cells into patterns of electrical activity. The second approach, which we described in Part II, moves away from this physiological level and asks what processes operate on the retinal image to yield perceptual experience. The third, "ecological" approach, which we introduced in Part III, also seeks explanation at a more abstract level than physiology, but differs from the second in taking the starting point for vision as the spatiotemporal pattern of light in the optic array.

So far, we have treated these different traditions as frameworks for research and have asked what knowledge has been gained within each. In fact, there is a great deal more to the difference between the second and third approaches than simply whether it is more useful to treat the input for vision as an image or as an optic array. This issue is only one aspect of a much wider theoretical debate concerning the nature of perception and the proper ways to explain it, and it is time now to deal with this debate. For simplicity, we contrast two positions, which we call "traditional" and "ecological," although there is much diversity of opinion within each viewpoint. In Chapters 4 and 8, we introduced these two theoretical positions before going on to describe the research they have each inspired. In this chapter we try to summarise the important differences between them and ask where reconciliation is and is not possible. Our discussion falls under two headings; the nature of the input for vision and the question of whether perception is direct or indirect.

THE NATURE OF THE INPUT

First, we sum up and clarify the issues at stake in choosing the retinal image or the optic array as the starting point for visual perception. Obviously, there is no argument over the facts that a single-chambered eye forms an image on the retina and that the image has to be there for vision to occur. The image is a projection of a segment of the optic array and the spatiotemporal pattern of light is reproduced in it, within limits imposed by the eye's acuity. For many practical purposes, image and optic array are interchangeable. As we saw in Chapter 9, for example, the optical parameter τ can be equally well used to describe a pattern of flow in the optic array or in its projection on a retina.

So, what difference *does* it make to introduce the concept of the optic array? One advantage is in the comparative study of vision, where it helps us to understand that image-forming eyes are not the only light-sensitive structures which can achieve a degree of directional sensitivity (Chapter 1, p.12). A more significant consequence of Gibson's concept of the optic array is that it leads to a quite different conception of the information available in light to a perceiver. The traditional view took the input to be nothing more than a mosaic of point light intensities on the retina, each characterised by its intensity and wavelength. Gibson attacked this belief on several grounds but particularly because it makes the mistake of describing the input for a perceiver in the same terms as the input for a single photoreceptor.

The input for a receptor is a stream of photons, but the input for a perceiver is a *pattern* of light extended over space and time. Gibson therefore argued that ways of describing this pattern should be devised, and examples of the terms he introduced are gradients and rates of flow of optic texture. Although descriptions of spatial structure can be applied equally easily to an optic array or to a retinal image, it is important to avoid artificially "freezing" the retinal image and losing sight of the temporal pattern of light in the changing optic array.

Once the possibility of describing the input for vision in terms of structure is accepted, it becomes possible to ask what relationships hold between a perceiver's environment and the structure of the optic array. Gibson's "ecological optics" sets out to explore these relationships, and we have seen examples of them throughout the third part of this book. In the traditional view, there was simply no place for such questions; input was made up of elements of point intensity, and the intensity of light falling on a single receptor provides no information about the environment.

On these issues, our sympathies are with Gibson's position. He was right, we believe, to argue that the input for vision can be described in terms of the structure of light and not just in terms of point intensities of light. He was right also to argue that there are relationships between the environment surrounding a perceiver and the structure of light in the optic array and that information to specify the structure of the environment is therefore available in the optic array. But this conclusion begs another question; are *all* objects and events in the environment fully specified by the pattern of light in the optic array, or only a limited class of simple properties such as distances, slants and textures of surfaces? We shall see later that Gibson's answer to this question is more difficult to accept.

DIRECT AND INDIRECT THEORIES OF PERCEPTION

As well as defining the nature of the input for vision, a theory of perception must also have something to say about how it is that the structured light reaching a perceiver gives rise to perceptual experience and to visually guided action. The answers given by traditional and ecological theories diverge sharply at this point, and are far less easily reconciled than the differences we have considered so far. The roots of the difference can be found in the history of Gibson's theory.

Gibson's early work was concerned with the perception of the layout and distances of the surfaces surrounding an observer. Since the time of Helmholtz, traditional theory had argued that such perception required processes of *inference* to supplement the supposedly impoverished nature of the flat, static retinal image. These processes of inference were held to *mediate* between retinal image and perception. From his analysis of the structure of the optic array and optic flow, Gibson argued that the problem was wrongly conceived and that processes of inference are required only if a restricted kind of description of the input for vision is adopted.

Gibson therefore argued that, since the structure of light directly specifies surface layout, mediating processes of the kind proposed by Helmholtz are not necessary for perception of "distance." From this conclusion, he went on to argue against *any* role for mediating or inferential processes in perception and to claim that invariant properties of the optic array specifying structures and events in the environment are detected *directly*.

The claim that perception is direct and unmediated has been taken up by "ecological" theorists, but strongly criticised by others, and in the remainder of this chapter we will set out the points at issue between them. First, however, it is worth mentioning the points where there is no disagreement between the two approaches. At a philosophical level, both direct and indirect theorists subscribe to *realism*, maintaining that we are in sensory contact with a real world and that perception reveals this world to us. Both positions also agree that visual perception is mediated by light reflected from surfaces and objects in the world, and both agree that some kind of physiological system is needed to perceive this light. Finally, there is also agreement that perceptual experience can be influenced by learning.

The issue which divides the direct from the indirect accounts of perception is the question of *how* physiological systems must be organised to perceive the world. The traditional approach to visual perception maintains that the world of objects and surfaces that we see must be reconstructed by piecing together more primitive elements such as edges or blobs. To carry out this reconstruction, knowledge of the world is needed, and various kinds of knowledge have been proposed in different "indirect" theories. Examples are knowledge of the sizes of objects in order to detect their distance, or knowledge that natural objects approximate to generalised cones. The process of reconstruction can, the traditional approach maintains, be broken down into stages and analysed both physiologically (as we saw in Part I) and psychologically (as we saw in Part II).

In contrast, the ecological approach maintains that qualities such as surface slant or object shape are perceived directly. An object's shape is not perceived by adding up a set of "features" like edges or blobs, using knowledge of the world to do so. There is information to specify shape in higher-order invariants in the light, and it is not necessary, or even possible, to decompose such processes into more primitive psychological operations or "computations." It may be a task for physiologists to unravel the complexities of how nervous systems are attuned to such higher order invariants, but the ecological psychologist need enquire no further once invariant information has been described.

Now any theory of indirect perception must allow *something* to be detected "directly," and traditionally it is assumed that photoreceptors detect changes in light intensity directly. A biochemist would wish to decompose the process of intensity detection further, but traditional theorists would treat it as an elementary process closed to further analysis, and certainly would not claim that the detection of changes in intensity involved "mediation" by knowledge of the world. They would, however, claim that higher order properties of the world must be reconstructed by making use of those properties which *are* directly detected, and "gluing" them together by making use of knowledge of the world. In contrast, a direct theory of perception maintains that the perception of *all* properties of the world is like the detection of light intensity. The system is attuned to higher-order variables, and the only task for psychology is to discover what these higher-order variables are.

What are the important issues dividing these two positions and is there any possibility of reconciling them? We see two important senses in which perception is regarded as "mediated" in the traditional view, and we will consider the objections of ecological theorists to each in turn. The first is the sense that perception of higher-order variables is mediated by processes of computation from low-level properties, and the second is the sense that perception must involve the formation, matching and storage of representations of the world.

Mediation of Perception by Computational Processes

The first issue between direct and indirect theories of perception concerns the levels at which perception can properly be explained. For a direct theory of perception, there are two, the ecological and the physiological. The ecological level is concerned with the information an animal needs from the environment in order to organise its activities, and with the ways in which the changing optic array can provide the information needed. The physiological level is concerned with how networks of nerve cells are organised so as to detect invariants in the optic array. Gibson was concerned to work at the first of these levels, and had little to say about the second, speaking simply of an animal being "attuned" or "resonating" to invariants. Taking the case of the parameter τ as an example, an explanation at the ecological level would be concerned with how τ specifies time to contact with a surface, and with the evidence showing that the timing of animals' and people's actions relies on detection of τ. A direct theory of perception would say that there is nothing more for psychology to ask about this situation, but would accept as valid a physiological investigation of how nerve cells are organised so as to "resonate" to τ.

We would agree with "direct" theorists that the control of action by information in the structure of light can be studied without reference to physiological processes, but we differ with their assertion that there is no level of explanation lying between the ecological and the physiological. Consider what actually happens when we come to ask how an animal's nervous system is built to detect τ. A physiologist would not simply search for τ-detectors but would ask what sort of model of neural interactions could yield a value of τ as output given a fluctuating pattern of light intensities as input. This model would involve processes computing direction and velocity of movement in different parts of the flow field, and others summing these outputs to yield τ.

This would be an algorithmic level of explanation, to use Marr's terminology discussed in Chapter 3. Ullman (1980) argues that the "direct" theory is mistaken in believing that there are two distinct levels of explanation, the ecological and the physiological, and concurs with Marr in believing that an algorithmic theory must come between the two in order to organise physiological knowledge. We agree with Ullman's position, and feel that "direct" theorists have not paid sufficient attention to the problem of the relationship between ecological and physiological levels of explanation.

Marr (1982) makes a similar argument, accepting the value of ecological optics but asserting the need for algorithmic explanations of how properties of the optic array are detected:

> Gibson's important contribution was to take the debate away from the philosophical consideration of sense-data and the affective qualities of sensation and to note instead that the important thing about the senses is that they are channels for perception of the real world outside, or, in the case of vision, of the visible surfaces. He therefore asked the critically important question. How does one obtain constant perceptions in everyday life on the basis of continually changing sensations? This is exactly the right question, showing that Gibson correctly regarded the problem of perception as that of recovering from sensory information "valid properties of the external world" (Marr, 1982, p.29).

> Although one can criticise certain shortcomings in the quality of Gibson's analysis, its major, and, in my view, fatal shortcoming lies at a deeper level and results from a failure to realize two things. First, the detection of physical invariants, like image surfaces, is exactly and precisely an information-processing problem, in modern terminology. And second, he vastly underrated the sheer difficulty of such detection (Marr, 1982, p.30).

If Ullman's and Marr's arguments are accepted, we can then go on to ask how the variables of optic flow which Gibson and others have identified are computed from a fluctuating pattern of light intensities in a time-varying image. Progress has already been made in devising such algorithms. First, we have already mentioned (Chapter 8, p.202) Clocksin's (1980) work on the extraction of edges from optic flow. Second, Longuet-Higgins and Prazdny (1980) have shown what computations are needed to separate components of optic flow due to the translatory and to the rotatory movement of the observer; a separation which is necessary if optic flow is to provide information about the layout of surfaces.

Third, Buxton and Buxton (1983) have extended Marr and Hildreth's (1980) edge-finding algorithm (Chapter 3, p.73) to consider a time-varying rather than a static image. They propose that the time-varying image is smoothed by a temporal Gaussian filter as well as by a spatial one, and that changes are detected by applying the d'Alembertian operator to the smoothed image. Like the Laplacian, the d'Alembertian is a second differential operator, but it includes changes in intensity over time as well as changes over the two spatial axes. Note that this is an alternative means of measuring change over time to Marr and Ullman's (1981) scheme, and the reader will find a comparison of the two proposals in Buxton and Buxton's paper.

Buxton and Buxton demonstrate a situation in which this algorithm could be important. Recall that Lee (1980b) demonstrated that the optic flow caused by an observer approaching a surface specifies time to contact with the surface. Buxton and Buxton ask how this information could be computed from image data, and show that the d'Alembertian algorithm is a promising candidate. Zero-crossings in the d'Alembertian are obtained at spatial gradients in the image, in just the same way as zero-crossings in the Laplacian, but are also obtained at "depth zeroes." A single gradient in the moving image gives rise to these two zeroes in different places, and Buxton and Buxton show how the relationship between the positions of the two zeroes can yield the distance of the approaching surface, provided that the velocity of approach is known and the surface is far from the focus of expansion of the image. They therefore propose this as a mechanism for depth perception in the periphery of the visual field; a hypothesis which should stimulate physiological and psychophysical research.

We believe that these three examples represent a promising start to the study of how variables of optic flow are computed, and Marr concedes that processes of this kind may form one of the modules which feed information into the 2½D sketch. We cannot agree with the radical Gibsonian argument that analyses of this kind are irrelevant to the explanation of perception, and that matters must be left at the assertion that any information available in light is "directly" perceived. For the purposes of an ecological level of analysis, they can be left at that point, but, if links to a physiological level are to be made, they cannot.

Perhaps some common ground between the two positions can be found by agreeing with the "direct" position that properties of the world can be detected without processes of inference, interpretation and judgement *but* arguing, with "indirect" theorists such as Marr and Ullman, that such processes of detection nonetheless rely on computation. The term *cognitively impenetrable* (Fodor & Pylyshyn, 1981: Pylyshyn, 1981) has been used to refer to perceptual processes which cannot be influenced by beliefs, expectations and the like. Examples of such processes might be the analysis of optic flow, or the elaboration of forms in the primal sketch in Marr's theory (see Chapter 5).

Cognitive impenetrability does not necessarily imply direct detection in the sense that no computational explanation is possible. Fodor and Pylyshyn's (1981) notion of *compiled detectors* is a useful one here, referring to computational processes which run in an autonomous, data-driven way. At a higher level of analysis, compiled detectors can be regarded as detecting properties of the world directly, but at a lower level of analysis their operations can be unpacked. At a behavioural level, it does not matter whether one argues that τ, for example, is perceived directly, or whether it is computed by compiled detectors. What does matter is that its detection need not rely on inferences of the hypothesis-testing variety.

For the purposes of ecological analysis we can proceed simply by saying that τ is detected, and leave others to work out the details of how this detection is accomplished. Much of the research we described in Part II of this book can be seen as attempts by researchers such as Marr to work out these details; while much of that in Part III asks simply what the ecologically relevant variables are, and how they are used, but does not address the issue of how they can be recovered.

Does Perception Require Representations?

We have concluded that the problem of whether perception is mediated by computational processes should be understood in terms of levels of explanation. At an ecological level, structures in light can be regarded as directly detected, and at a physiological level, light intensity can be regarded as directly detected. The two levels are not neatly separable, however, and to explore perception at a physiological level requires theories of algorithms which enable the detection of structures in light and which are implemented by the nervous system.

There is a second sense in which traditional theory regards perception as mediated, however, and this raises issues which extend beyond problems of perception to questions of the nature of our knowledge of the world. The argument is that in order to perceive the world an animal or person must form an internal representation of it. We have seen examples of representations of the world which theories of perception have postulated; Marr's 2½D sketch (see Chapter 6) represents the layout of the surfaces surrounding an observer, while theories of object recognition (Chapter 7) have postulated catalogues of stored descriptions of objects held in memory. The term "representation" is used in a wide variety of senses. It is used to refer to any symbolic description of the world—whether this is the world as it has been in the past (as in stored "memories"), as it is now (the 2½D sketch, or structural descriptions), or as it might be in the future (as in certain kinds of imagery).

Direct theories of perception completely reject *all* such representations as further examples of mediating processes standing between the world and the perceiver. The counter-argument would run as follows. Just as sizes, slants and distances of surfaces surrounding an observer are specified by invariant properties of optic flow patterns, so any object we can recognise, from a pencil to a painting, is specified by as yet unidentified "high-level" invariants. Therefore, just as we can, at an ecological level, regard detection of distance specified by a texture gradient as direct, so we can equally well regard perception of a pencil or painting as direct. There is no need for any processes of constructing or matching representations.

A further argument against a role for representation in perception is that the direct fit between perception and action is broken. The invariants to which an animal is attuned are those specifying the actions it must perform to ensure its survival, and Gibson (1979) devised the term *affordance* to express this point (Chapter 8, p.199). An affordance is an opportunity for action provided by an object, such as support by a firm surface, grasping by a limb of a tree, or mating by an animal of the opposite sex. Gibson claimed that affordances such as these are specified by the structure of the light reflected from objects, and are directly detectable. There is therefore no need to invoke representations of the environment intervening between detection of affordances and action; one automatically leads to the other.

We have already argued in similar terms (Chapter 11, p.250) that an insect's vision does not work to build up a representation of its surroundings, but instead to provide just the information required to modulate its flight. A female fly (or anything resembling one) could be said to afford pursuit, and the fly to detect the information in the optic array specifying this affordance. In these terms, where is the need for a representation of a female fly to which input is matched?

It is clear that if an algorithmic level of explanation is allowed (as we have argued it must be), then "representations" of some sort are inevitably involved, for the purpose of an algorithm is to transform one representation into another. Thus, Marr (1982) states that the algorithms involved in fly vision:

> deliver a representation in which at least three things are specified: 1) whether the visual field is looming sufficiently that the fly should contemplate landing; 2) whether there is a small patch—it could be a black speck or, it turns out, a textured figure in front of a textured ground—having some kind of motion relative to its background; and if there is such a patch, 3) ψ and $\dot{\psi}$ for this patch are delivered to the motor system (Marr, 1982, p.34) [ψ is the angular bearing and $\dot{\psi}$ the angular velocity of the patch; see Chapter 9, p.215].

What Marr is doing here is to analyse the link between the fly's perception and action into a series of algorithms and representations, and we would argue that such an explanation is not only legitimate but necessary if a physiological analysis is to be undertaken. It is not at all the same as saying that a conceptual representation of the world is built up which a "little fly in the head" consults before taking action, although by using the word "contemplate" Marr could mislead us into thinking that this is what he intends. The representations involved are patterns of activity in networks of neurons.

In this situation, it becomes difficult to distinguish the ecological and representational positions. The first states that the tuning of the fly to the invariances in the light reaching it fits it to its environment, while the second states that properties of the fly's environment are represented in the neural networks detecting the structure of light. If the term representation is used in this sense, it seems there is really nothing to argue about. It is only if we wanted to claim that the fly had a "concept" of something to pursue that there should be any dispute. If we allow algorithms we must allow representations, but for many examples of animal vision in particular we should consider these to be patterns of activity in the nervous system rather than "concepts" or "memories."

By choosing the example of a fly's visual perception, however, we have avoided more difficult issues raised by the "representation" debate. In this example, we are dealing with the *direct* control of activity by a known invariant in the light *currently* reaching the fly's eyes. Let us consider an example from animal perception not meeting these criteria; Menzel's demonstration of chimpanzees' memory for the location of pieces of food (Chapter 12, p.282). If a chimp is carried around a familiar field, shown the locations of 20 pieces of food and then released, it will move around the field gathering up all the pieces. Control experiments show that the locations of food cannot be detected by a chimp which has not previously been shown them. What are we to make of this phenomenon?

The first difference from the fly example is that control of activity is not direct; information obtained from light specifying where food is hidden is used later to guide travel around the field. The second is that there is no information in the light reaching the chimpanzee while it is gathering up the food to specify where food is. In an indirect theory of perception, these facts are accommodated by saying that the chimp forms a representation of the information specifying the locations of food, and this representation is later used to guide travel around the field.

A direct theorist would reply that the representational explanation makes the mistake of putting over-narrow bounds on the sample of light in which information can be detected. If we take the sample of light to be that stretching over both sessions of the experiment, then there are invariants specifying the locations of food and there is no need to invoke representations. There is no difference in principle, to a "direct" theorist, between this situation and one in which a chimpanzee's view of a piece of food while approaching it is briefly interrupted by an obstacle. In both cases, activities extended over time are guided by directly detected invariants in a sample of light extended over time. The difficulties many have in accepting this formulation are typified by Menzel's comment that: "I am an ardent admirer of Gibson, and I don't doubt that his theory could explain much of the data cited in this chapter; but when he starts talking about how animals can 'see' things that are hidden from sight or even located in a different room he loses me (Menzel, 1978, p.417)."

The disagreements become sharper when we move to human perception. The Gibsonian position is that anything we perceive must be specified by invariant properties of stimulation, directly detected without any need for representation of information. There are invariants specifying a friend's face, a performance of *Hamlet,* or the sinking of the *Titanic,* and no knowledge of the friend, of the play or of maritime history is required to perceive these things. Gibson also applied the concept of affordance to human perception; a pen, he argued, affords writing and a mailbox the posting of a letter. No knowledge of writing or of the postal system needs to be represented in memory, as invariants specifying these affordances are directly detected.

An important difference between these examples and those we used earlier is that we are now dealing with situations where no invariants specifying objects, events or affordances have been demonstrated or seem likely to be demonstrated. The calm with which some Gibsonian theorists contemplate this difficulty is captured in Michaels and Carello's (1981) reply to the question: "How can the ecological approach account for experiential dimensions of hedonic tone (humor, pleasure, amusement) that appear to have no physical stimulus referent?" with the answer: "The invariants must be very higher-order indeed" (Michaels & Carello, 1981, p. 178).

Critics of the Gibsonian position do not accept that this answer is adequate, and we will outline the objections made to it by Fodor and Pylyshyn (1981). Their principal criticism is that the terms "invariant" and "directly detected" are left so unconstrained in their meanings in Gibsonian theory as to be meaningless. They take the example of an art expert detecting the fact that a painting was executed by da Vinci and not by an imitator. To explain this by stating that the expert has directly detected the invariant property "having been painted by da Vinci" is, they argue, to use the term "invariant" in a trivial way. For any percept, if a sufficiently large sample of available light is considered, there can in principle be some invariant to specify a property of this sort; here, a sample including the light reflected from all da Vincis, imitations of da Vincis, books on da Vinci, and so on.

Fodor and Pylyshyn argue that the notions of invariant and direct detection can be constrained by what they term a "sufficiency criterion." The pattern of light reflected from a looming surface is sufficient to cause the perception of impending collision, as shown by experiments with artificial simulations of such a pattern. Therefore, it makes sense to speak of an invariant property of this pattern being detected directly. In contrast, we have no reason to believe that a sample of light reflected from a da Vinci is sufficient to cause recognition of it. Rather, Fodor and Pylyshyn argue, further information beyond that in the light is necessary, and this must be information about the properties of da Vinci's paintings represented in memory.

This sufficiency criterion therefore restricts the notion of direct perception to situations where structured patterns of light with particular invariant properties can be shown to be sufficient to explain perception and behaviour (although, as we argued earlier, the processes involved in detecting them can be analysed at an algorithmic level). On this criterion, perception of other people, familiar objects and almost everything we perceive falls on the da

Vinci rather than the looming surface side of the boundary, and therefore requires additional kinds of representation of the perceived object.

Thus for most of human perception we must advocate that information in light is compared with stored knowledge of the world. There are some compelling demonstrations to testify to this, such as the "hollow face" illusion (Chapter 6, Fig. 6.8). There is sufficient information here to see the mask as hollow, but we stubbornly fail to do so. If we move our head from side to side the face appears to follow us, an unlikely solution of the actual motion perspective present. The hollow face is not an example of an illusion which involves static observers or monocular viewing, and is a difficult one for the ardent Gibsonian to dismiss as a laboratory trick. We must invoke a memory of some sort here to explain why we see what we are used to seeing despite useful information to the contrary.

However, we do feel that the ecological psychologists make some very pertinent criticisms of current conceptions of memory, and it is worth examining these here. Firstly, the kinds of representational schemes used in research into object recognition, which we discussed in Chapter 7, are not easy to adapt to the recognition of dynamic configurations like moving human figures. Marr and Nishihara's axis-based representations are derived from the occluding contours in static images, and it may be that different representational schemes could be constructed which are based on information in a transforming optic array. Two rather different approaches to this problem were introduced briefly in Chapter 13, where we talked about Cutting's analysis of the centres of moment in moving displays, and Weir's action "schemas," in which temporal relations such as "approach" and "withdrawal" were specified. These kinds of ideas are worth pursuing.

Secondly, and more generally, ecological psychologists (e.g. Bransford, McCarrell, Franks, & Nitsch, 1977) object to the notion of memory as a set of associated locations which must be searched through. This particular metaphor for memory is ingrained in our everyday language (we talk of trying to "find" a name that we've forgotten) and entrenched in almost all contemporary models of memory (Roediger, 1980). Ecological psychologists object that such conceptions of memory often imply that we must search exhaustively through our memories to discover that something is novel, and make it difficult to articulate the nature of the novelty once this is discovered.

They point instead to the subtle interactions between the context in which something is perceived and the meaning attributed to it. To take one of Bransford et al.'s examples, consider an outstretched hand. This could mean "come with me", "I have five children", "read my palm", etc, and Bransford et al. consider it absurd that every possible meaning for this configuration should be stored as a different potential association, yet this is precisely how many models of memory are described. We feel that these are important points, and that it is well worth seeking alternative formulations for memory.

However, while the criticisms made by direct theorists are valid, they have yet to present any adequate alternative.

We have so far considered two senses of the term "representation"; a momentary pattern of activity in a neural network, and a relatively long term "memory" which allows us to know the meanings of things. There is also an intermediate kind of memory that we should discuss. In Chapter 6 we discussed representations such as Hochberg's "schematic maps" and Marr's 2½D sketch, which have been postulated to allow a representation of the immediate visual world to be established. We would agree with ecological theorists (e.g. Turvey, 1977b) that at least some such "short term" visual memories may be wrongly conceived, because they are built up from static "snapshots" of the world. If we place more emphasis on the recovery of structure from optic flow, some kinds of "store" may become unnecessary.

However, there is interesting recent evidence suggesting that the visual guidance of human locomotion does not involve a direct meshing of optic flow and activity but a time-limited storage process of some kind. Thomson (1983) asked subjects to view a target, then close their eyes and walk or run to the target "blind." He found they could locate a target at a distance greater than 5 metres, provided it took them less than 8 seconds to get to it. If it took longer than that, either because it was too far, or because of a delay before they started, then they got lost. To explain results like this, it seems reasonable to propose that there is some "representation" or "memory" for the location of the target which can be used in the formulation and control of motor programs for journeys of short duration, but which cannot be maintained for longer ones. It may be this kind of representation which allows us to "see" that part of the visual world we are not currently looking at as we pursue our daily activities.

CONCLUDING COMMENTS

Our aim in this chapter has not been to review thoroughly the debate between Gibsonian and traditional theories, or to offer new insights, but rather to organise and sift the issues, and to offer our own resolution of them. The debate is a furious one, and the reader is referred to the papers by Ullman (1980), Fodor and Pylyshyn (1981), Turvey (1977b) and Turvey, Shaw, Reed, and Mace (1981) for further detail of it. Some points of argument are, we feel, relatively easily settled, particularly by recognising the different levels at which perception can be explained and the relationships between them. We have argued that Gibson's early insights into the nature of the input for vision, and the ecological optics he formulated, have been of enormous value, and the insights into perception we have discussed in the third part of the book testify to their productivity.

On the other hand, we find that the Gibsonian approach is not helpful in dealing with the relationship between ecological optics and physiological levels of explanation. Gibson's concern to avoid mediation and inference led him to shy away from these problems, and we find their clearest treatment in discussions such as Ullman's (1980) and Marr's (1982). We must stress that Marr's work shares a good deal with Gibson's views. He places great emphasis on understanding the relationship between the structures in the world which a perceiver needs to detect and the ways in which they structure light, just as Gibson's ecological optics does. In Marr's approach, assumptions about the world are built into algorithms for perceiving it, and explicit forms of "inference" avoided wherever possible. In comparison, Marr's use of an image, rather than optic flow, as a starting point is no important barrier between them.

In addition, we find it difficult to accept that Gibson's formulation does away with any role for memory in understanding perception. We find it unconvincing to explain a person returning after ten years to their grandparents' home and seeing that a tree has been cut down as having detected directly an event specified by a transformation in the optic array. At this point, we concur with Fodor and Pylyshyn (1981) that the terms of Gibson's theory are being extended to the point of becoming empty. Even so, we believe that Gibsonian criticisms of traditional views will be valuable in forcing a re-examination of the models of the role of memory in perception.

A further comment we have on the debate between direct and indirect theorists is that the examples in which their arguments carry most force are quite different. The Gibsonian concept of affordance, for example, is at its most powerful in the context of simple visually-guided behaviour such as that of insects. Here it does indeed make sense to speak of the animal detecting the information available in light which is needed to organise its activities, and the notion of a conceptual representation of the environment seems redundant.

For more intelligent creatures, and for people, we can make the same kinds of argument about detection of distance, falling-off places and so on in the guidance of locomotion. It is in these contexts where Gibsonian arguments carry most conviction. Indeed, some "direct" theorists, such as Turvey et al. (1981), seem to claim that it is only these kinds of activities which fall within the scope of an "ecological" theory of perception, and with this we would have no argument. It is only if they wished to argue that these activities alone constitute perception that we would be unhappy.

Exponents of the representational view, however, challenge Gibsonian theory by invoking human abilities to perceive objects, events and meanings which are bound up in a rich cultural context. Fodor and Pylyshyn's (1981) discussion of the recognition of a genuine da Vinci is an example. Here, two aspects of Gibsonian ideas become a good deal less convincing. First, the mere assertion that there are high-level invariants in the structure of light which allow the direct perception of such objects dilutes the concept of invariant away. Secondly, the argument of animal-environment mutuality, which was so useful when we considered the classes of information a fly might need to survive and reproduce, becomes vague and even trivial when we consider human beings perceiving and acting in a cultural rather than a physical environment.

We feel that a distinction made by Fodor and Pylyshyn (1981) between "seeing" and "seeing as" captures the difference between the two kinds of situation:

> What you see when you see a thing depends upon what the thing you see *is*. But what you see the thing *as* depends upon what you know about what you are seeing . . . Here is Smith at sea on a foggy evening, and as lost as ever he can be. Suddenly the skies clear, and Smith sees the Pole Star. What happens next? In particular, what are the consequences of what Smith perceives for what he comes to believe and do? Patently, that depends upon what he sees the Pole Star *as*. If, for example, he sees the Pole Star as the star that is at the Celestial North Pole (plus or minus a degree or two), then Smith will know, to that extent, where he is; and we may confidently expect that he will utter "Saved!" and make for port. Whereas, if he sees the Pole Star but takes it to be a firefly, or takes it to be Alpha Centauri, or—knowing no astronomy at all—takes it to be just some star or other, then seeing the Pole Star may have no particular consequences for his behaviour or his further cognitive states. Smith will be just as lost after he sees it as he was before (Fodor & Pylyshyn, 1981, p. 189).

We believe that the ecological approach has little useful to say about *seeing as*, although it has given us useful insights into *seeing*. For animals, we can be fairly specific about the information needed from the environment to guide activity, because we can refer to their requirements for survival and reproduction. For people, we cannot do this, apart from simple requirements such as avoiding cliffs, walking upright and dodging or catching flying objects. Most human activity takes place within a cultural environment, and we see no alternative to the assumption that people see objects and events *as* what they are in terms of a culturally given conceptual representation of the world.

In these pages we have set down our own reasons for rejecting the strong claim that perception is *direct*, as ecological psychologists would have it. We have argued that perception involves computations and that it involves representations, and that it is a legitimate task of psychology to enquire into the nature of these computations and representations. Having said this, we would stress that the nature of the computations performed may seem different once one considers the transforming optic array as the input to visual processing, rather than the retinal image. Different kinds of computations require different sorts of representation, and many of the traditional ideas may need re-thinking in the light of the findings of ecological psychologists.

The importance of describing what animals and people *do* in their worlds and *how* they do it cannot be overstated, and this is the greatest strength of the ecological level of analysis. This demands that we study real behaviour in real situations. We should never assume that by stripping down real world activities into tractable laboratory tasks we will find out the right things. Consider an experiment by Ebbeson, Parker, and Konëcni (1977). They examined how drivers decided whether to cross an intersection depending on the speed and distance of an oncoming car. They did this in two ways; in the laboratory, using model cars, and in the field, with real cars, and real risks. In the laboratory it appeared that "drivers" were making a complex decision about when to cross, based on the estimation of the distance and velocity of the approaching car. These subjects made 9% errors. In the field, it seemed that drivers simply made use of temporal headway (time to contact) with the approaching car, which does not require the separate computation of distance and velocity (though we would argue it does require computation). These drivers made no errors.

By studying drivers, long-jumpers or gannets carrying out visually guided activities in a natural setting, we can gain rich insights into the optic variables which are used to guide activity, and it is this kind of research that we have considered in Part III of this book. Once the important variables have been discovered, however, we still need to know *how* they are detected, and this is the role of the kind of research described in Part II. Although the theories inspiring the two kinds of research differ strongly on fundamental issues, we feel that there is considerable scope for using the insights of both to solve smaller, more defined problems in visual perception.

It is in understanding how simple animals such as flies perceive their surroundings that a combination of the two approaches has achieved most success, specifying the ecological problems vision must solve for the animal, devising appropriate algorithms and unravelling their implementation by nervous systems. In human beings, this enterprise is vastly more difficult, particularly because human perception operates in a cultural as well as a physical environment. The formulation and testing of algorithmic theories, and the investigation of their physiological bases, is therefore a difficult task, but nonetheless a fascinating one.

References

Alderson, G. H. K., Sully, D. J., & Sully, H. G. (1974) An operational analysis of a one-handed catching task using high speed photography. *Journal of Motor Behaviour, 6,* 217–26.

Attneave, F. (1971) Multistability in perception. *Scientific American, 225,* December, 63–71.

Ball, W., & Tronick, E. (1971) Infant responses to impending collision: optical and real. *Science, 171,* 818–820.

Barclay, C. D., Cutting, J. E., & Kozlowski, L. T. (1978) Temporal and spatial factors in gait perception that influence gender recognition. *Perception and Psychophysics, 23,* 145–52.

Barlow, H. B. (1972) Single units and sensation: a neuron doctrine for perceptual psychology? *Perception, 1,* 371–94.

Barlow, H. B., & Hill, R. M. (1963) Selective sensitivity to direction of motion in ganglion cells of the rabbit's retina. *Science, 139,* 412–14.

Barlow, H. B., & Levick, W. R. (1965) The mechanism of directionally selective units in rabbit's retina. *Journal of Physiology, 178,* 477–504.

Barnes, R. D. (1968) *Invertebrate zoology,* second edition. Philadelphia: W. B. Saunders.

Bassili, J. N. (1976) Temporal and spatial contingencies in the perception of social events. *Journal of Personality and Social Psychology, 33,* 680–5.

Bassili, J. N. (1978) Facial motion in the perception of faces and of emotional expression. *Journal of Experimental Psychology: Human Perception and Performance, 4,* 373–9.

Bassili, J. N. (1979) Emotion recognition: The role of facial movement and the relative importance of upper and lower areas of the face. *Journal of Personality and Social Psychology, 37,* 2049–58.

Bateson, P. P. G. (1966) The characteristics and context of imprinting. *Biological Review, 41,* 177–220.

Bateson, P. P. G., & Jaeckel, J. B. (1974) Imprinting: Correlations between activities of chicks during training and testing. *Animal Behaviour, 22,* 899–906.

Beasley, N. A. (1968) The extent of individual differences in the perception of causality. *Canadian Journal of Psychology, 22,* 399–407.

Beck, J. (1972) Similarity grouping and peripheral discriminability under uncertainty. *American Journal of Psychology, 85,* 1–20.

Beck, J., & Gibson, J. J. (1955) The relation of apparent shape to apparent slant in the perception of objects. *Journal of Experimental Psychology*, *50*, 125–33.

Berkeley, G. (1709) An essay towards a new theory of vision. In *A new theory of vision and other writings*, Introduction by A. D. Lindsay. London: J. M. Dent & Sons Ltd (1910).

Bernstein, N. (1967) *The coordination and regulation of movements*. Oxford: Pergamon Press.

Blakemore, C. (1970) The representation of three-dimensional visual space in the cat's striate cortex. *Journal of Physiology*, *209*, 155–78.

Blondeau, J., & Heisenberg, M. (1982) The three-dimensional optomotor torque system of *Drosophila melanogaster*. *Journal of Comparative Physiology*, *145*, 321–9.

Boden, M. (1977) *Artificial intelligence and natural man*. Hassocks: Harvester Press.

Boring, E. G. (1942) *Sensation and perception in the history of experimental psychology*. New York: Appleton-Century-Crofts.

Bossema, I., & Burgler, R. R. (1980) Communication during monocular and binocular looking in European jays (*Garrulus garrulus glandarius*). *Behaviour*, *74*, 274–83.

Bower, T. G. R. (1966) The visual world of infants. *Scientific American*, *215*, December, 80–92.

Bower, T. G. R. (1971) The object in the world of the infant. *Scientific American*, *225*, October, 30–8.

Bower, T. G. R., Broughton, J. M., & Moore, M. K. (1970) Infant responses to approaching objects: An indicator of response to distal variables. *Perception and Psychophysics*, *9*, 193–6.

Boyle, D. G. (1960) A contribution to the study of phenomenal causation. *Quarterly Journal of Experimental Psychology*, *12*, 171–9.

Braddick, O. J. (1973) The masking of apparent motion in random-dot patterns. *Vision Research*, *13*, 355–69.

Braddick, O. J. (1980) Low-level and high-level processes in apparent motion. *Philosophical Transactions of the Royal Society of London, Series B*, *209*, 137–51.

Braddick, O.J. (1981) Spatial frequency analysis in vision. *Nature*, *291*, 9–11.

Braitenberg, V., & Ferretti, C. L. (1966) Landing reaction of *Musca domestica* induced by visual stimuli. *Naturwissenschaften*, *53*, 155.

Bransford, J. D., McCarrell, N. S., Franks, J. J., & Nitsch, K. E. (1977) Toward unexplaining memory. In R. Shaw, & J. Bransford (Eds.), *Perceiving, acting and knowing: Toward an ecological psychology*. Hillsdale, New Jersey: Lawrence Erlbaum Associates Inc.

Brindley, G. S., & Merton, P. A. (1960) The absence of position sense in the human eye. *Journal of Physiology*, *153*, 127–30.

Bruce, V. (1982) Changing faces: visual and non-visual coding processes in face recognition. *British Journal of Psychology*, *73*, 105–16.

Bruce, V. (1983) Recognizing faces. *Philosophical Transactions of the Royal Society of London, Series B*, *302*, 423–36.

Bruce, V., & Morgan, M. J. (1975) Violations of symmetry and repetition in visual patterns. *Perception*, *4*, 239–49.

Bruner, J. S., & Goodman, C. C. (1947) Value and need as organising factors in perception. *Journal of Abnormal and Social Psychology*, *42*, 33–44.

Buxton, B. F., & Buxton H. (1983) Monocular depth perception from optical flow by space-time signal processing. *Proceedings of the Royal Society of London, Series B*, *218*, 27–47.

Camhi, J. M. (1970) Yaw-correcting postural changes in locusts. *Journal of Experimental Biology*, *52*, 519–31.

Campbell, F. W., & Robson, J. G. (1968) Application of Fourier analysis to the visibility of gratings. *Journal of Physiology*, *197*, 551–66.

Carpenter, R. H. S. (1977) *Movements of the eyes*. London: Pion Press.

Cartwright, B. A., & Collett, T. S. (1979) How honey-bees know their distance from a nearby visual landmark. *Journal of Experimental Biology*, *82*, 367–72.

Clarke, P. G. H., & Whitteridge, D. (1973) The basis of stereoscopic vision in sheep. *Journal of Physiology*, *229*, 22–23P.

Cleland, B. G., & Levick, W. R. (1974) Properties of rarely encountered types of ganglion cells in the cat's retina and an overall classification. *Journal of Physiology*, *240*, 457–92.

Clocksin, W. F. (1980) Perception of surface slant and edge labels from optical flow: a computational approach. *Perception*, *9*, 253–71.

Clowes, M. B. (1971) On seeing things. *Artificial Intelligence*, *2*, 79–112.

Collett, T. S. (1977) Stereopsis in toads. *Nature*, *267*, 349–51.

Collett, T. S. (1980) Some operating rules for the optomotor system of a housefly during voluntary flight. *Journal of Comparative Physiology*, *138*, 271–82.

Collett, T. S., & Land, M. F. (1975) Visual control of flight behaviour in the hoverfly *Syritta pipiens*. *Journal of Comparative Physiology*, *99*, 1–66.

Cooper, G. F., & Robson, J. G. (1966) Directionally selective movement detectors in the retina of the grey squirrel. *Journal of Physiology*, *186*, 116–17P.

Cornsweet, T. N. (1970) *Visual perception*. New York: Academic Press.

Cott, H. B. (1940) *Adaptive coloration in animals*. London: Methuen.

Croze, H. (1970) Searching image in carrion crows. *Zeitschrift für Tierpsychologie, Supplement 5*, cited in Edmunds, M. (1974) *Defence in animals*. New York: Longman.

Cutting, J. E. (1978a) Generation of synthetic male and female walkers through manipulation of a biomechanical invariant. *Perception*, *7*, 393–405.

Cutting, J. E. (1978b) Perceiving the geometry of age in a human face. *Perception and Psychophysics*, *24*, 566–8.

Cutting, J. E. (1982) Blowing in the wind: Perceiving structure in trees and bushes. *Cognition*, *12*, 25–44.

Cutting, J. E., & Kozlowski, L. T. (1977) Recognizing friends by their walk: Gait perception without familiarity cues. *Bulletin of the Psychonomic Society*, *9*, 353–6.

Cutting, J. E., & Proffitt, D. R. (1981) Gait perception as an example of how we may perceive events. In R. D. Walk, & H. L. Pick, Jr. (Eds.) *Intersensory perception and sensory integration*. New York: Plenum.

Cutting, J. E., & Proffitt, D. R. (1982) The minimum principle and the perception of absolute and relative motions. *Cognitive Psychology*, *14*, 211–46.

Cutting, J. E., Proffitt, D. R., & Kozlowski, L. T. (1978) A biomechanical invariant for gait perception. *Journal of Experimental Psychology: Human Perception and Performance*, *4*, 357–72.

Davies, G., Ellis, H., & Shepherd, J. (1981). *Perceiving and remembering faces*. London: Academic Press.

Davies, N. B., & Halliday, T. R. (1978) Deep croaks and fighting assessment in toads *Bufo bufo*. *Nature*, *274*, 683–5.

Davson, H. (1977) *The eye, Volume 2B. The photobiology of vision*. London: Academic Press.

Daw, N. W. (1968) Colour-coded ganglion cells in the goldfish retina: extension of their receptive fields by means of new stimuli. *Journal of Physiology*, *197*, 567–92.

de Monasterio, F. M. (1978a) Properties of concentrically organized X and Y ganglion cells of macaque retina. *Journal of Neurophysiology*, *41*, 1394–417.

de Monasterio, F. M. (1978b) Properties of ganglion cells with atypical receptive-field organization in retina of macaques. *Journal of Neurophysiology*, *41*, 1435–49.

Dethier, V. G. (1955) The physiology and histology of the contact chemoreceptors of the blowfly. *Quarterly Review of Biology*, *30*, 348–71.

De Valois, R. L., Abramov, I., & Jacobs, G. H. (1966) Analysis of response patterns of LGN cells, *Journal of the Optical Society of America*, *56*, 966–77.

De Valois, R. L., Albrecht, D. G., & Thorell, L. G. (1982) Spatial frequency selectivity of cells in macaque visual cortex. *Vision Research*, *22*, 545–59.

Dow, B. M., & Gouras, P. (1973) Colour and spatial specificity of single units in rhesus monkey foveal striate cortex. *Journal of Neurophysiology*, *36*, 79–100.

Dowling, J. E. (1968) Synaptic organization of the frog retina: An electron microscopic analysis comparing the retinas of frogs and primates. *Proceedings of the Royal Society of London, Series B*, *170*, 205–28.

Dowling, J. E., & Werblin, F. S. (1969) Organization of retina in the mudpuppy *Necturus maculosus*. II. Intracellular recording. *Journal of Neurophysiology*, *32*, 339–55.

Duncker, K. (1929) Über induzierte Bewegung (Ein Beitrag zur Theorie optische wahrgenommener Bewegung). *Psychologische Forschung*, *12*, 180–259. Translated and abridged as "Induced Motion" in W.D. Ellis (Ed.), *A source book of Gestalt Psychology*. London: Routledge & Kegan Paul (1955).

Ebbesen, E. B., Parker, S., & Konečni, V. J. (1977). Laboratory and field analyses of decisions involving risk. *Journal of Experimental Psychology: Human Perception and Performance*, *3*, 576–89.

Edwards, A. S. (1946) Body sway and vision. *Journal of Experimental Psychology*, *36*, 526–35.

Eisner, T., Silberglied, R. E., Aneshansley, D., Carrel, J. E., & Howland, H. C. (1969) Ultraviolet video-viewing: The television camera as an insect eye. *Science*, *146*, 1172–4.

Ekman, P. (1978) Facial signs: facts, fantasies and possibilities. In T. Sebeok (Ed.), *Sight, sound and sense*. Bloomington: Indiana University Press.

Ekman, P. (1979) About brows: emotional and conversational signals. In M. von Cranach, K. Foppa, W. Lepenies, & D. Ploog (Eds.), *Human ethology*. Cambridge: Cambridge University Press.

Ekman, P. (1982) *Emotion in the human face*, second edition. Cambridge: Cambridge University Press.

Ekman, P., & Friesen, W. V. (1982) Measuring facial movement with the Facial Action Coding System. In P. Ekman (Ed.), *Emotion in the human face*, second edition. Cambridge: Cambridge University Press.

Ekman, P., Friesen, W. V., & Ellsworth, P. (1982) Does the face provide accurate information? In P. Ekman (Ed.), *Emotion in the human face*, second edition. Cambridge: Cambridge University Press.

Ekman, P., & Oster, H. (1982) Review of research, 1970–1980. In P. Ekman (Ed.), *Emotion in the human face*, second edition. Cambridge: Cambridge University Press.

Ellis, H. D. (1975) Recognising faces. *British Journal of Psychology*, *66*, 409–26.

Enroth-Cugell, C., & Robson, J. G. (1966) The contrast sensitivity of retinal ganglion cells of the cat. *Journal of Physiology*, *187*, 517–52.

Ewert, J. P. (1974) The neural basis of visually guided behaviour. *Scientific American*, *230*, March, 34–49.

Fantz, R. L. (1961) The origin of form perception. *Scientific American*, *204*, May, 66–72.

Fechner, G. T. (1860) *Elemente der Psychophysik*. Leipzig, Germany: Brectkopf and Härtel.

Fender, D. H., & Julesz, B. (1967) Extension of Panum's fusional area in binocularly stabilized vision. *Journal of the Optical Society of America*, *57*, 819–30.

Fishman, M. C. & Michael, C. R. (1973) Integration of auditory information in the cat's visual cortex. *Vision Research*, *13*, 1415–19.

Fitch, H. L., Tuller, B., & Turvey, M. T. (1982) The Bernstein Perspective III. Timing of coordinative structures with special reference to perception. In J. A. S. Kelso (Ed.), *Human motor behaviour: An introduction*. Hillsdale, New Jersey: Lawrence Erlbaum Associates.

Fodor, J. A., & Pylyshyn, Z. W. (1981) How direct is visual perception? Some reflections on Gibson's "Ecological Approach". *Cognition*, *9*, 139–96.

Fox, R., Lehmkuhle, S. W., & Westendorff, D. H. (1976) Falcon visual acuity. *Science*, *192*, 263–5.

Frisby, J. P. (1979) *Seeing: Mind, brain and illusion.* Oxford: Oxford University Press.

Frisby, J. P., & Mayhew, J. E. W. (1980) Spatial frequency tuned channels: implications for structure and function from psychophysical and computational studies of stereopsis. *Philosophical Transactions of the Royal Society of London, Series B, 290,* 95–116.

Frisch, H. L., & Julesz, B. (1966) Figure-ground perception and random geometry. *Perception and Psychophysics, 1,* 389–98.

Galton, F. (1907) *Inquiries into human faculty and its development.* London: J. M. Dent & Sons Ltd.

Gaze, R. M., & Jacobson, M. (1963) "Convexity detectors" in the frog's visual system. *Journal of Physiology, 169,* 1–3P.

Gibson, E. J., Gibson, J. J., Smith, O. W., & Flock, H. R. (1959) Motion parallax as a determinant of perceived depth. *Journal of Experimental Psychology, 58,* 40–51.

Gibson, E. J. & Walk, R. D. (1960) The "visual cliff". *Scientific American, 202,* April, 64–71.

Gibson, J. J. (1947) *Motion picture testing and research.* AAF Aviation Psychology Research Report No. 7. Washington, D. C. Government Printing Office.

Gibson, J. J. (1950a) *The perception of the visual world.* Boston: Houghton Mifflin.

Gibson, J. J. (1950b) The perception of visual surfaces. *American Journal of Psychology, 63,* 367–84.

Gibson, J. J. (1961) Ecological optics. *Vision Research, 1,* 253–62.

Gibson, J. J. (1966) *The senses considered as perceptual systems.* Boston: Houghton Mifflin.

Gibson, J. J. (1968) What gives rise to the perception of motion? *Psychological Review, 75,* 335–46.

Gibson, J. J. (1975) *The implications of experiments on the perception of space and motion.* Final Report to Office of Naval Research, Arlington, Va.

Gibson, J. J. (1979) *The ecological approach to visual perception.* Boston: Houghton Mifflin.

Gibson, J. J., & Cornsweet, J. (1952) The perceived slant of visual surfaces—optical and geographical. *Journal of Experimental Psychology, 44,* 11–15.

Gibson, J. J., & Dibble, F. N. (1952) Exploratory experiments on the stimulus conditions for the perception of a visual surface. *Journal of Experimental Psychology, 43,* 414–19.

Gibson, J. J., & Waddell, D. (1952) Homogeneous retinal stimulation and visual perception. *American Journal of Psychology, 65,* 263–70.

Gilbert, C. D. (1977) Laminar differences in receptive field properties of cells in cat primary visual cortex. *Journal of Physiology, 268,* 391–421.

Golani, I. (1976) Homeostatic motor processes in mammalian interactions: A choreography of display. In P. P. G. Bateson, & P. H. Klopfer (Eds.), *Perspectives in ethology,* Vol. II. New York: Plenum, pp. 69–134.

Goodman, L. J. (1965) The role of certain optomotor reactions in regulating stability in the rolling plane during flight in the desert locust *Schistocerca gregaria. Journal of Experimental Biology, 42,* 385–407.

Götz, K. G. (1975) The optomotor equilibrium of the *Drosophila* navigation system. *Journal of Comparative Physiology, 99,* 187–210.

Götz, K. G., Hengstenberg, B., & Biesinger, R. (1979) Optomotor control of wingbeat and body posture in *Drosophila. Biological Cybernetics, 35,* 101–12.

Graham, N., & Nachmias, J. (1971) Detection of grating patterns containing two spatial freqencies: a comparison of single-channel and multiple-channel models. *Vision Research, 11,* 251–59.

Gregory, R. L. (1972) *Eye and brain,* second edition. London: World University Library.

Gregory, R. L. (1973) The confounded eye. In R. L. Gregory, & E. H. Gombrich (Eds.), *Illusion in nature and art.* London: Duckworth.

Gregory, R. L. (1980) Perceptions as hypotheses. *Philosophical Transactions of the Royal Society of London, Series B, 290,* 181–97.

Griffin, D. R. (1958) *Listening in the dark*. New Haven, Connecticut: Yale University Press.

Gross, C. G., Rocha-Miranda, E. E., & Bender, D. B. (1972) Visual properties of neurons in inferotemporal cortex of the macaque. *Journal of Neurophysiology, 35,* 96–111.

Gulick, W. L., & Lawson, R. B. (1976) *Human stereopsis: A psychophysical analysis*. New York: Oxford University Press.

Gurfinkel, V. S., Kots, Ya. M., Krinsky, V. I., Pal'tsev, Ye. I., Feldman, A. G., Tsetlin, M. L., & Shik, M. L. (1971) Concerning tuning before movement. In I. M. Gelfand, V. S. Gurfinkel, S. E. Fomin, & M. L. Tsetlin (Eds.), *Models of the structural–functional organisation of certain biological systems*. Cambridge, Massachusetts.: M.I.T. Press.

Guzman, A. (1968) Decomposition of a visual scene into three-dimensional bodies. *AFIPS Proceedings of the Fall Joint Computer Conference, 33,* 291–304.

Hailman, J. P. (1977) *Optical signals: Animal communication and light*. Bloomington: Indiana University Press.

Harkness, L. (1977) Chameleons use accommodation cues to judge distance. *Nature, 267,* 346–9.

Harmon, L. D. (1973) The recognition of faces. *Scientific American, 229,* November, 71–82.

Harris, J. P., & Gregory, R. L. (1973) Fusion and rivalry of illusory contours. *Perception, 2,* 235–47.

Hartline, H. K., & Graham, C. H. (1932) Nerve impulses from single receptors in the eye. *Journal of Cellular and Comparative Physiology, 1,* 227–95.

Hartline, H. K., Wagner, H. G., & Ratliff, F. (1956) Inhibition in the eye of *Limulus. Journal of General Physiology, 39,* 651–73.

Hausen, K. (1976) Functional characterization and anatomical identification of motion sensitive neurons in the lobula plate of the blowfly *Calliphora erythrocephala. Zeitschrift für Naturforschung, 31C,* 629–33.

Heckenmuller, E. G. (1965) Stabilization of the retinal image: A review of method, effects and theory. *Psychological Bulletin, 63,* 157–69.

Heider, F., & Simmel, M. (1944) An experimental study of apparent behaviour. *American Journal of Psychology, 57,* 243–59.

Heiligenberg, W. (1973) Electrolocation of objects in the electric fish *Eigenmannia. Journal of Comparative Physiology, 87,* 137–64.

Helmholtz, H. von (1866) *Treatise on physiological optics*, Vol. III (trans. 1925 from the third German edition, Ed. J. P. C. Southall). New York: Dover (1962).

Hertz, M. (1928) Figural perception in the jay bird. *Zeitschrift für vergleichende Physiologie, 7,* 144–94. Trans. and abridged in W. D. Ellis (1955) *A source book of Gestalt Psychology*. London: Routledge & Kegan Paul.

Hertz, M. (1929) Figural perception in bees. *Zeitschrift für vergleichende Physiologie, 8,* 693–748. Trans. and abridged in W. D. Ellis (1955) *A source book of Gestalt Psychology*. London: Routledge & Kegan Paul.

Hochberg, J. (1950) Figure-ground reversal as a function of visual satiation. *Journal of Experimental Psychology, 40,* 682–86.

Hochberg, J. (1968) In the mind's eye. In R. N. Haber (Ed.), *Contemporary theory and research in visual perception*. London: Holt, Rinehart & Winston Inc.

Hochberg, J. (1978) *Perception*, second edition. Englewood Cliffs, New Jersey: Prentice Hall.

Hochberg, J., & Brooks, V. (1960) The psychophysics of form: reversible perspective drawings of spatial objects. *American Journal of Psychology, 73,* 337–54.

Hochstein, S., & Shapley, R. M. (1976) Linear and nonlinear spatial subunits in Y cat retinal ganglion cells. *Journal of Physiology, 262,* 265–84.

Holden, A. L. (1977) Responses of directional ganglion cells in the pigeon retina. *Journal of Physiology, 270,* 253–69.

Horn, G., & Hill, R. M. (1969) Modification of receptive fields of cells in the visual cortex occurring spontaneously and associated with bodily tilt. *Nature, 221,* 186–98.

Hubbard, A. W., & Seng, C. N. (1954) Visual movements of batters. *Research Quarterly, 25,* 42–57.

Hubel, D. H., & Wiesel, T. N. (1959) Receptive fields of single neurons in the cat's striate cortex. *Journal of Physiology, 148,* 574–91.

Hubel, D. H., & Wiesel, T. N. (1962) Receptive fields, binocular interaction and functional architecture in the cat's visual cortex. *Journal of Physiology, 160,* 106–54.

Hubel, D. H., & Wiesel, T. N. (1968) Receptive fields and functional architecture of monkey striate cortex. *Journal of Physiology, 195,* 215–43.

Hubel, D. H., & Wiesel, T. N. (1970) Stereopsis vision in the macaque monkey. *Nature , 225,* 41–2.

Hubel, D. H., & Wiesel, T. N. (1977) Functional architecture of macaque monkey visual cortex. *Proceedings of the Royal Society of London, series B, 198,* 1–59.

Hubel, D. H., Wiesel, T. N., & Stryker, M. P. (1977). Orientation columns in macaque monkey visual cortex demonstrated by the 2-deoxyglucose autoradiographic technique. *Nature, 269,* 328–30.

Hubel, D. H., Wiesel, T. N., & Stryker, M. P. (1978) Anatomical demonstration of orientation columns in macaque monkey. *Journal of Comparative Neurology, 177,* 361–80.

Huffman, D. A. (1971) Impossible objects as nonsense sentences. In B. Meltzer, & D. Michie (Eds.), *Machine Intelligence 6.* Edinburgh: Edinburgh University Press.

Humphrey, N. K., & Keeble, G. R. (1974) The reactions of monkeys to "fearsome" pictures. *Nature, 251,* 500–2.

Ittelson, W. H. (1952) *The Ames demonstrations in perception.* Princeton, New Jersey: Princeton University Press.

Jackson, J. F., Ingram, W., & Campbell, H. W. (1976) The dorsal pigmentation pattern of snakes as an antipredator strategy: a multivariate approach. *American Naturalist, 110,* 1029–53.

Johansson, G. (1973) Visual perception of biological motion and a model for its analysis. *Perception and Psychophysics, 14,* 201–11.

Johansson, G. (1975) Visual motion perception. *Scientific American, 232,* June, 76–89.

Julesz, B. (1965) Texture and visual perception. *Scientific American, 212,* February, 38–48.

Julesz, B. (1971) *Foundations of cyclopean perception.* Chicago: University of Chicago Press.

Julesz, B. (1975) Experiments in the visual perception of texture. *Scientific American, 232,* April, 34–43.

Julesz, B., Frisch, H. L., Gilbert, E. N., & Shepp, L. A. (1973) Inability of humans to discriminate between visual textures that agree in second-order statistics—revisited. *Perception, 2,* 391–405.

Julesz, B., & Miller, J. (1975) Independent spatial-frequency-tuned channels in binocular fusion and rivalry. *Perception, 4,* 125–43.

Kalmus, H. (1949) Optomotor responses in *Drosophila* and *Musca. Physiologia Comparata et Oecologia, 1,* 127–47.

Kaufman, L. (1974) *Sight and mind: An introduction to visual perception.* New York: Oxford University Press.

Kelso, J. A. S., Putnam, C. A., & Goodman, D. (1983) On the space–time structure of human inter-limb coordination. *Quarterly Journal of Experimental Psychology, 35A,* 347–75.

Kettlewell, B. (1973) *The evolution of melanism.* Oxford: Oxford University Press.

Kilpatrick, F. P. (1952) (Ed.) *Human behaviour from the transactionalist point of view.* Princeton, New Jersey: Princeton University Press.

Kirschfeld, K. (1976) The resolution of lens and compound eyes. In F. Zettler, & R. Weiler (Eds.), *Neural principles in vision.* Berlin: Springer.

Kirschfeld, K. (1982) Carotenoid pigments: their possible role in protecting against photooxidation in eyes and photoreceptor cells. *Proceedings of the Royal Society of London, Series B, 216,* 71–85.

Klopfer, P. H. (1967) Stimulus preferences and imprinting. *Science, 156,* 1394–6.

Koffka, K. (1935) *Principles of Gestalt Psychology.* New York: Harcourt Brace.

Köhler, W. (1947) *Gestalt psychology: An introduction to new concepts in modern psychology.* New York: Liveright Publishing Corporation.

Kolers, P. A. (1963) Some differences between real and apparent visual movement. *Vision Research, 3,* 191–206.

Kovach, J. K. (1971) Interaction of innate and acquired: Colour preferences and early exposure learning in chicks. *Journal of Comparative and Physiological Psychology, 75,* 386–98.

Kozlowski, L. T., & Cutting, J. E. (1977) Recognizing the sex of a walker from a dynamic point-light display. *Perception and Psychophysics, 21,* 575–80.

Kozlowski, L. T., & Cutting, J. E. (1978) Recognizing the gender of walkers from point-lights mounted on ankles: Some second thoughts. *Perception and Psychophysics, 23,* 459.

Kuffler, S. W. (1953) Discharge patterns and functional organization of mammalian retina. *Journal of Neurophysiology, 16,* 37–68.

Land, M. F. (1968) Functional aspects of the optical and retinal organization of the mollusc eye. *Symposia of the Zoological Society of London, 23,* 75–96.

Land, M. F. (1980) Compound eyes: Old and new optical mechanisms. *Nature, 287,* 681–6.

Land, M. F. (1981) Optics and vision in invertebrates. In H. Autrum (Ed.), *Comparative physiology and evolution of vision in invertebrates. B: Invertebrate visual centres and behaviour I.* Berlin: Springer-Verlag.

Land, M. F., & Collett, T. S. (1974) Chasing behaviour of houseflies (*Fannia canicularis*): A description and analysis. *Journal of Comparative Physiology, 89,* 331–57.

Lee, D. N. (1976). A theory of visual control of braking based on information about time-to-collision. *Perception, 5,* 437–59.

Lee, D. N. (1977). The functions of vision. In H. L. Pick, & E. Saltzman (Eds.), *Modes of perceiving and processing information.* Hillsdale, New Jersey: Lawrence Erlbaum Associates.

Lee, D. N. (1980a). Visuo-motor coordination in space-time. In G. E. Stelmach, & J. Requin (Eds.), *Tutorials in motor behaviour.* North-Holland Publishing Company.

Lee, D. N. (1980b) The optic flow field: the foundation of vision. *Philosophical Transactions of the Royal Society of London, Series B, 290,* 169–79.

Lee, D. N. & Aronson, E. (1974) Visual proprioceptive control of standing in infants. *Perception and Psychophysics, 15,* 529–32.

Lee, D. N., & Lishman, J. R. (1975) Visual proprioceptive control of stance. *Journal of Human Movement Studies, 1,* 87–95.

Lee, D. N., & Lishman, J. R. (1977) Visual control of locomotion. *Scandinavian Journal of Psychology, 18,* 224–30.

Lee, D. N., Lishman, J. R., & Thomson, J. A. (1982) Regulation of gait in long-jumping. *Journal of Experimental Psychology: Human Perception and Performance, 8,* 448–59.

Lee, D. N., & Reddish, P. E. (1981) Plummeting gannets: A paradigm of ecological optics. *Nature, 293,* 293–4.

Lee, D. N., Young, D. S., Reddish, P. E., Lough, S., & Clayton, T. M. H. (1983) Visual timing in hitting an accelerating ball. *Quarterly Journal of Experimental Psychology, 35A,* 333–46.

Lettvin, J. Y., Maturana, H. R., McCulloch, W. S., & Pitts, W. H. (1959) What the frog's eye tells the frog's brain. *Proceedings of the Institute of Radio Engineers, 47,* 1940–51.

LeVay, S., Hubel, D. H., & Wiesel, T. N. (1975) The pattern of ocular dominance columns in macaque visual cortex revealed by a reduced silver stain. *Journal of Comparative Neurology, 159,* 559–76.

Levick, W. R. (1967) Receptive fields and trigger features of ganglion cells in the visual streak of the rabbit's retina. *Journal of Physiology, 188,* 285–307.

Lindsay, P. H., & Norman, D. A. (1972) *Human information processing.* New York: Academic Press.

Lishman, J. R., & Lee, D. N. (1973) The autonomy of visual kinaesthesis. *Perception*, *2*, 287–94.

Lock, A., & Collett, T. (1979) A toad's devious approach to its prey: A study of some complex uses of depth vision. *Journal of Comparative Physiology*, *131*, 179–89.

Lock, A., & Collett, T. (1980) The three-dimensional world of a toad. *Proceedings of the Royal Society of London, Series B*, *206*, 481–7.

Locke, J. (1690) *An essay concerning human understanding*. Edited from the fourth (1700) and fifth (1706) Editions by P. H. Nidditch. Oxford: Oxford University Press (1975).

Longuet-Higgins, H. C., & Prazdny, K. (1980) The interpretation of moving retinal images. *Proceedings of the Royal Society of London, Series B*, *208*, 385–97.

McArthur, L. Z., & Baron, R. M. (1983) Toward an ecological theory of social perception. *Psychological Review*, *90*, 215–38.

McCleod, R. W., & Ross, H. E. (1983) Optic-flow and cognitive factors in time-to-collision estimates. *Perception*, *12*, 417–23.

Mach, E. (1914) *The analysis of sensations*. Republished, 1959, Dover Publications.

Maffei, L., & Fiorentini, A. (1977) Spatial frequency rows in the striate visual cortex. *Vision Research*, *17*, 257–64.

Manning, A. (1978) *An introduction to animal behaviour*, third edition. London: Edward Arnold.

Mariani, A. P. (1982) Association amacrine cells could mediate directional selectivity in pigeon retina. *Nature*, *298*, 654–55.

Marks, W. B., Dobelle, W. H., & MacNichol, E. F. (1964) Visual pigments of single primate cones. *Science*, *143*, 1181–3.

Marr, D. (1976) Early processing of visual information. *Philosophical Transactions of the Royal society of London, Series B*, *275*, 483–524.

Marr, D. (1977) Analysis of occluding contour. *Proceedings of the Royal Society of London, Series B*, *197*, 441–75.

Marr, D. (1982) *Vision: A computational investigation into the human representation and processing of visual information*. San Francisco: W. H. Freeman & Co.

Marr, D., & Hildreth, E. (1980) Theory of edge detection. *Proceedings of the Royal Society of London, Series B*, *207*, 187–217.

Marr, D., & Nishihara, H. K. (1978) Representation and recognition of the spatial organisation of three-dimensional shapes. *Proceedings of the Royal Society of London, Series B*, *200*, 269–94.

Marr, D., & Poggio, T. (1976) Cooperative computation of stereo disparity. *Science*, *194*, 283–7.

Marr, D., & Poggio, T. (1979) A computational theory of human stereo vision. *Proceedings of the Royal Society of London, Series B*, *204*, 301–28.

Marr, D., & Ullman, S. (1981) Directional selectivity and its use in early visual processing. *Proceedings of the Royal Society of London, Series B*, *211*, 151–80.

Maturana, H. R., & Frenk, S. (1963) Directional movement and horizontal edge detectors in the pigeon retina. *Science*, *142*, 977–9.

Mayhew, J. E. W., & Frisby, J. P. (1981) Psychophysical and computational studies towards a theory of human stereopsis. *Artificial Intelligence*, *17*, 349–85.

Maynard Smith, J., & Parker, G. A. (1976) The logic of asymmetric contests. *Animal Behaviour*, *24*, 159–75.

Maynard Smith, J., & Price, G. R. (1973) The logic of animal conflict. *Nature*, *246*, 15–18.

Mech, L. D. (1970) *The wolf: The ecology and behavior of an endangered species*. Garden City, New York: The Natural History Press.

Menzel, E. W. (1978) Cognitive mapping in chimpanzees. In S. H. Hulse, F. Fowler, & W. K. Honig (Eds.), *Cognitive processes in animal behavior*. Hillsdale, New Jersey: Lawrence Erlbaum Associates.

Menzel, E. W., & Halperin, S. (1975) Purposive behaviour as a basis for objective communication between chimpanzees. *Science*, *189*, 652–4.

Metzger, W. (1930) Optische Untersuchungen in Ganzfeld II. *Psychologische Forschung*, *13*, 6–29.

Michael, C. R. (1968a) Receptive fields of single optic nerve fibres in a mammal with an all-cone retina. I. Contrast-sensitive units. *Journal of Neurophysiology*, *31*, 249–56.

Michael, C. R. (1968b) Receptive fields of single optic nerve fibres in a mammal with an all-cone retina. II. Directionally sensitive units. *Journal of Neurophysiology*, *31*, 257–67.

Michael, C. R. (1968c) Receptive fields of single optic nerve fibres in a mammal with an all-cone retina. III. Opponent colour units. *Journal of Neurophysiology*, *31*, 268–82.

Michael, C. R. (1978) Colour vision mechanisms in monkey striate cortex: Dual-opponent cells with concentric receptive fields. *Journal of Neurophysiology*, *41*, 572–88.

Michaels, C. F. (1978) The information for direct binocular stereopsis. Unpublished manuscript (cited in Michaels and Carello, 1981).

Michaels, C. F., & Carello, C. (1981) *Direct perception*. Englewood Cliffs, New Jersey: Prentice Hall.

Michotte, A. (1963) *The perception of causality*. Translated by T. and E. Miles from French (1946) edition. London: Methuen.

Millott, N. (1968) The dermal light sense. *Symposia of the Zoological Society of London*, *23*, 1–36.

Minsky, M. (1977) Frame-system theory. In P. N. Johnson-Laird and P. C. Wason (Eds.), *Thinking: Readings in cognitive science*. Cambridge: Cambridge University Press.

Mittelstaedt, H. (1962) Control systems of orientation in insects. *Annual Review of Entomology*, *7*, 177–98.

Mollon, J. D. (1982) Color vision. *Annual Review of Psychology*, *33*, 41–85.

Moran, G., Fentress, J. C., & Golani, I. (1981) A description of relational patterns of movement during "ritualized fighting" in wolves. *Animal Behaviour*, *29*, 1146–65.

Morton, J. (1969) The interaction of information in word recognition. *Psychological Review*, *76*, 165–78.

Movshon, J. A., Thompson, I. D., & Tolhurst, D. J. (1978) Spatial and temporal contrast sensitivity of neurones in areas 17 and 18 of the cat's visual cortex. *Journal of Physiology*, *283*, 101–20.

Neisser, U. (1967) *Cognitive psychology*. New York: Appleton-Century-Crofts.

Nelson, B. (1978) *The Gannet*. Berkhamsted: T. & A. D. Poyser.

Neuhaus, W. (1930) Experimentelle Untersuchung der Scheinbewegung. *Archiv für die gesamte Psychologie*, *75*, 315–458.

Normann, R. A., & Werblin, F. S. (1974) Control of retinal sensitivity. I. Light and dark adaptation of vertebrate rods and cones *Journal of General Physiology*, *63*, 37–61.

Olson, R. K., & Attneave, F. (1970) What variables produce similarity grouping? *American Journal of Psychology*, *83*, 1–21.

Packer, C. (1977) Reciprocal altruism in *Papio anubis*. *Nature*, *265*, 441–3.

Pantle, A., & Picciano, L. (1976) A multistable movement display: evidence for two separate motion systems in human vision. *Science*, *193*, 500–2.

Partridge, B. L, & Pitcher, T. J. (1980) The sensory basis of fish schools: relative roles of lateral line and vision. *Journal of Comparative Physiology*, *135*, 315–25.

Peichl, L., & Wässle, H. (1979) Size, scatter and coverage of ganglion cell receptive field centres in the cat retina. *Journal of Physiology*, *291*, 117–41.

Pheiffer, C. H., Eure, S. B., & Hamilton, C. B. (1956) Reversible figures and eye movements. *American Journal of Psychology*, *69*, 452–55.

Phillips, W. A. (1974) On the distinction between sensory storage and short term visual memory. *Perception and Psychophysics*, *16*, 283–90.

Phillips, W. A., & Baddeley, A. D. (1971) Reaction time and short term visual memory. *Psychonomic Science*, *22*, 73–4

Pietrewicz. A. T., & Kamil, A. C. (1977) Visual detection of cryptic prey by blue jays. *Science*, *195*, 580–2.

Pittenger, J. B., & Shaw, R. E. (1975) Aging faces as viscal–elastic events: implications for a theory of non-rigid shape perception. *Journal of Experimental Psychology: Human Perception and Performance*, *1*, 374–82.

Posner, M. I., & Keele, S. W. (1967) Decay of information from a single letter. *Science*, *158*, 137–9.

Premack, D., & Woodruff, G. (1978) Does the chimpanzee have a theory of mind? *Behavioural and Brain Sciences*, *4*, 515–26.

Pringle, J. W. S. (1974) Locomotion: flight. In M. Rockstein (Ed.), *The Physiology of Insecta*, Vol. III, second edition. London: Academic Press, pp. 433–76.

Pritchard, R. M. (1961) Stabilized images on the retina. *Scientific American*, *204*, June, 72–8.

Proffitt, D. R., & Cutting, J. E. (1979) Perceiving the centroid of configurations on a rolling wheel. *Perception and Psychophysics*, *25*, 389–98.

Proffitt, D. R., Cutting, J. E., & Stier, D. M. (1979) Perception of wheel-generated motions. *Journal of Experimental Psychology*, *5*, 289–302.

Purple, R. L., & Dodge, F. A. (1965) Interaction of excitation and inhibition in the eccentric cell in the eye of *Limulus*. *Cold Spring Harbor Symposia on Quantitative Biology*, Vol. 30.

Pylyshyn, Z. W. (1981) The imagery debate: Analog media versus tacit knowledge. *Psychological Review*, *88*, 16–45.

Ratliff, F., Hartline, H. K., & Lange, D. (1966) The dynamics of lateral inhibition in the compound eye of *Limulus*. In C. G. Bernhard (Ed.), *The functional organisation of the compound eye*. Oxford: Pergamon.

Reed, E., & Jones, R. (Eds.) (1982) *Reasons for realism. Selected essays of J. J. Gibson*. Hillsdale, New Jersey: Lawrence Erlbaum Associates Inc.

Reichardt, W. (1969) Movement perception in insects. In W. Reichardt (Ed.), *Processing of optical data by organisms and by machines*. New York: Academic Press.

Reichardt, W., & Poggio, T. (1976) Visual control of orientation behaviour in the fly. Part I. A quantitative analysis. *Quarterly Review of Biophysics*, *9*, 311–75.

Reichardt, W., & Poggio, T. (1979) Figure-ground discrimination by relative movement in the visual system of the fly. *Biological Cybernetics*, *35*, 81–100.

Roberts, L. G. (1965) Machine perception of three-dimensional solids. In J. T. Tippett, D. A. Berkowitz, L. C. Clapp, C.J. Koester and A. Vanderburgh (Eds), *Optical and electro-optical information processing*. Cambridge, Massachusetts: M.I.T. Press.

Roediger, H. L. (1980) Memory metaphors in cognitive psychology. *Memory and Cognition*, *8*, 231–46.

Rosenfeld, S. A., & Van Hoesen, G. W. (1979) Face recognition in the rhesus monkey. *Neuropsychologia*, *17*, 503–9.

Ross, J. (1976) The resources of binocular perception. *Scientific American*, *234*, March, 80–6.

Rossel, S. (1983) Binocular stereopsis in an insect. *Nature*, *302*, 821–2.

Runeson, S., & Frykolm, G. (1981) Visual perception of lifted weights. *Journal of Experimental Psychology: Human Perception and Performance*, *7*, 733–40.

Ryan, C. M. E. (1982) Concept formation and individual recognition in the domestic chicken (*Gallus gallus*). *Behaviour Analysis Letters*, *2*, 213–20.

Saye, A., & Frisby, J. P. (1975) The role of monocularly conspicuous features in facilitating stereopsis from random-dot stereograms. *Perception*, *4*, 159–71.

Schaller, G. B. (1972) *The Serengeti lion: A study of predator-prey relations*. Chicago: Chicago University Press.

Schiff, W., Caviness, J. A., & Gibson, J. J. (1962) Persistent fear responses in rhesus monkeys to the optical stimulus of "looming". *Science*, *136*, 982–3.

Schiff, W., & Detwiler, M. L. (1979) Information used in judging impending collision. *Perception*, *8*, 647–58.

Schmidt, R. A. (1969) Movement time as a determiner of timing accuracy. *Journal of Experimental Psychology*, 79, 43–7.

Seamon, J. G. (1982) Dynamic facial recognition: Examination of a natural phenomenon. *American Journal of Psychology*, 95, 363–81.

Sedgwick, H. A. (1973) *The visible horizon*. Ph.D. thesis, Cornell University.

Selfridge, O. G. (1959) Pandemonium: a paradigm for learning. In *The mechanisation of thought processes*. London: HMSO.

Shaw, R. E., & Bransford, J. (1977) Introduction: Psychological approaches to the problem of knowledge. In R. E. Shaw, & J. Bransford (Eds.), *Perceiving, acting and knowing: Toward an ecological psychology*. Hillsdale, New Jersey: Lawrence Erlbaum Associates Inc.

Shaw, R. E., McIntyre, M., & Mace, W. (1974) The role of symmetry in event perception. In R. B. MacCleod, & H. L. Pick (Eds.), *Perception: Essays in honour of James J Gibson*. Ithaca, New York: Cornell University Press.

Shaw, R. E., & Pittenger, J. B. (1977) Perceiving the face of change in changing faces: implications for a theory of object recognition. In R. E. Shaw, & J. Bransford (Eds.), *Perceiving, acting and knowing: Toward an ecological psychology*. Hillsdale, New Jersey: Lawrence Erlbaum Associates Inc.

Shepherd, J., Davies, G., & Ellis, H. (1981) Studies of cue saliency. In G. Davies, H. Ellis, & J. Shepherd (Eds.), *Perceiving and remembering faces*. London: Academic Press.

Sherrington, C. S. (1906) *Integrative action of the nervous system*. New Haven: Yale University Press (reset edition, 1947).

Shirai, Y. (1973) A context sensitive line finder for recognition of polyhedra. *Artificial Intelligence*, 4, 95–120.

Simpson, M. J. A. (1968) The display of the Siamese fighting fish *Betta splendens*. *Animal Behaviour Monographs*, 1, 1–73.

Sivak, J. G. (1978) A survey of vertebrate strategies for vision in air and water. In Ali, M. A. (Ed.), *Sensory ecology: Review and perspectives*. New York: Plenum.

Sperling, G. (1960) The information available in brief visual presentations. *Psychological Monographs*, 74, whole no. 498.

Sperling, G. (1970) Binocular vision: A physical and neural theory. *American Journal of Psychology*, 83, 461–534.

Spurr, R. T. (1969) Subjective aspects of braking. *Automobile Engineer*, 59, 58–61.

Stevens, J. K., Emerson, R. C., Gerstein, G. L., Kallos, T., Neufield, G. R., Nichols, C. W., & Rosenquist, A. C. (1976) Paralysis of the awake human: visual perceptions. *Vision Research*, 16, 93–8.

Stone, J. (1972) Morphology and physiology of the geniculocortical synapse in the cat: The question of parallel input to the striate cortex. *Investigative Ophthalmology*, 11, 338–46.

Stone, J., & Fukuda, Y. (1974) Properties of cat retinal ganglion cells: A comparison of W cells with X and Y cells. *Journal of Neurophysiology*, 37, 722–48.

Sumner, F. B, (1934) Does "protective coloration" protect? Results of some experiments with fishes and birds. *Proceedings of the National Academy of Science*, 10, 559–64.

Sutherland, N. S. (1973) Object recognition. In E. C. Carterette and M. P. Friedman (Eds.), *Handbook of perception*, Volume III: *Biology of perceptual systems*. London: Academic Press.

Sutherland, N. S., & Williams, C. (1969) Discrimination of checkerboard patterns by rats. *Quarterly Journal of Experimental Psychology*, 21, 77–84.

Ternus, J. (1926) Experimentelle Untersuchung über phänomenale Identität. *Psychologische Forschung*, 7, 81–136. Trans. as "The problem of phenomenal identity" in W. D. Ellis (1955) *A source book of Gestalt psychology*. London: Routledge & Kegan Paul.

Thayer, G. H. (1918) *Concealing coloration in the animal kingdom*. New York: Macmillan.

Thomson, J. A. (1983) Is continuous visual monitoring necessary in visually guided locomotion? *Journal of Experimental Psychology: Human Perception and Performance*, 9, 427–43.

Tinbergen, N. (1951) *The study of instinct.* Oxford: Clarendon Press.
Todd, J. T., Mark, L. S., Shaw, R. E., & Pittenger, J. B. (1980) The perception of human growth. *Scientific American, 242,* February, 106–14.
Tuller, B., Turvey, M. T., & Fitch, H. L. (1982) The Bernstein Perspective II. The concept of muscle linkage or coordinative structure. In J. A. S. Kelso (Ed.), *Human motor behaviour: An introduction.* Hillsdale, New Jersey, Lawrence Erlbaum Associates Inc.
Turner, E. R. A. (1964) Social feeding in birds. *Behaviour, 24,* 1–46.
Turvey, M. T. (1977a) Preliminaries to a theory of action with reference to seeing. In R. Shaw and J. Bransford (Eds.), *Perceiving, acting and knowing: Toward an ecological psychology.* Hillsdale, New Jersey: Lawrence Erlbaum Associates Inc.
Turvey, M. T. (1977b) Contrasting orientations to the processing of visual information. *Psychological Review, 84,* 67–89.
Turvey, M. T., Fitch, H. L., & Tuller, B. (1982) The Bernstein Perspective I. The problems of degrees of freedom and context–conditioned variability. In J. A. S. Kelso (Ed.), *Human motor behaviour: An introduction.* Hillsdale, New Jersey. Lawrence Erlbaum Associates Inc.
Turvey, M. T., Shaw, R. E. and Mace, W. (1978) Issues in the theory of action: Degrees of freedom, coordinative structures and coalitions. In J. Requin (Ed.), *Attention and performance VII.* Hillsdale, New Jersey: Lawrence Erlbaum Associates Inc.
Turvey, M. T., Shaw, R. E., Reed, E. S., & Mace, W. M. (1981) Ecological laws of perceiving and acting: In reply to Fodor and Pylyshyn (1981). *Cognition, 9,* 237–304.
Ullman, S. (1979) *The interpretation of visual motion.* Cambridge, Massachusetts: M. I. T. Press.
Ullman, S. (1980) Against direct perception. *Behavioural and Brain Sciences, 3,* 373–415.
Uttal, W. R. (1981) *Taxonomy of visual processes.* Hillsdale, New Jersey: Lawrence Erlbaum Associates Inc.
Van Essen, D. C. (1979) Visual areas of the mammalian cerebral cortex. *Annual Review of Neuroscience, 2,* 227–63.
Victor, J. D., & Shapley, R. M. (1979) The nonlinear pathway of Y ganglion cells in the cat retina. *Journal of General Physiology, 74,* 671–89.
Vines, G. (1981) Wolves in dogs' clothing. *New Scientist,* 10th Sept., 1981.
Volkmann, F. C. (1976) Saccadic suppression: A brief review. In R. A. Monty and J. W. Senders (Eds.), *Eye movements and psychological processes.* Hillsdale, New Jersey: Lawrence Erlbaum Associates Inc.
Von Hofsten, C. (1980) Predictive reaching for moving objects by human infants. *Journal of Experimental Child Psychology, 30,* 369–82.
Von Hofsten, C., & Lindhagen, K. (1979) Observations of the development of reaching for moving objects. *Journal of Experimental Child Psychology, 28,* 158–73.
Von Holst, E. (1954) Relation between the central nervous system and the peripheral organs. *British Journal of Animal Behaviour, 2,* 89–94.
Von Wright, J. M. (1968) Selection in visual immediate memory. *Quarterly Journal of Experimental Psychology, 20,* 62–8.
Von Wright, J. M. (1970) On selection in immediate visual memory. *Acta Psychologica, 33,* 280–92.
Wagner, H. (1982) Flow-field variables trigger landing in flies. *Nature, 297,* 147–8.
Wallach, H., & O'Connell, D. N. (1953) The kinetic depth effect. *Journal of Experimental Psychology, 45,* 205–17.
Wallach, H. (1959) The perception of motion. *Scientific American, 201,* July, 56–60.
Walls, G. L. (1942) *The vertebrate eye and it adaptive radiation.* New York: Hafner.
Waltz, D. L. (1975) Generating semantic descriptions from scenes with shadows. In P. H. Winston (Ed.), *The psychology of computer vision.* New York: McGraw-Hill.
Watson, J. B. (1913) Psychology as the behaviourist views it. *Psychological Review, 20,* 158–77.

Watson, J. B. (1924) *Psychology from the standpoint of a behaviourist.* Philadelphia: Lippincott.

Wehrhahn, C., & Reichardt, W. (1973) Visual orientation of the fly *Musca domestica* towards a horizontal slope. *Naturwissenschaften, 60,* 203–4.

Weir, S. (1978) The perception of motion: Michotte revisited. *Perception, 7,* 247–60.

Wertheimer, M. (1912) Experimentelle Studien über das Sehen von Bewegung. *Zeitschrift für Psychologie, 61,* 161–265. Translated in T. Shipley (Ed.), *Classics in psychology.* New York, Philosophical Library, 1961.

Wertheimer, M. (1923) Untersuchungen zur Lehre von der Gestalt, II. *Psychologische Forschung, 4,* 301–50. Translated as "Laws of organisation in perceptual forms" in W. D. Ellis (1955) *A source book of Gestalt Psychology.* London: Routledge & Kegan Paul.

Wheatstone, C. (1838) Contributions to the physiology of vision. Part I: On some remarkable and hitherto unobserved phenomena of binocular vision. *Philosophical Transactions of the Royal Society of London, 128,* 371–94.

Whiting, H. T. A., & Sharp, R. H. (1974) Visual occlusion factors in a discrete ball-catching task. *Journal of Motor Behaviour, 6,* 11–16.

Wiesel, T. N., & Hubel, D. H. (1966) Spatial and chromatic interactions in the lateral geniculate body of the rhesus monkey. *Journal of Neurophysiology, 29,* 1115–56.

Wigglesworth, V. B. (1964) *The life of insects.* London: Weidenfeld & Nicolson.

Wilson, H. R., & Bergen, J. R. (1979) A four mechanism model for threshold spatial vision. *Vision Research, 19,* 19–32.

Winston, P. H. (1973) Learning to identify toy block structures. In R. L. Solso (Ed.), *Contemporary issues in cognitive psychology: The Loyola symposium.* Washington D. C.: Hemisphere Publishing Corp.

Winston, P. H. (1975) Learning structural descriptions from examples. In P. H. Winston (Ed.), *The psychology of computer vision.* New York: McGraw-Hill.

Wittreich, W. J. (1959) Visual perception and personality. *Scientific American, 200,* April, 56–75.

Wood, D. C. (1976) Action spectrum and electrophysiological responses correlated with the photophobic response of *Stentor coeruleus. Photochemistry and Photobiology, 24,* 261–6.

Wundt, W. (1896) *Grundriss der Psychologie.* Translated by C. H. Judd (1907) as *Outlines of psychology.* New York: G. E. Stechart and Co.

Zeki, S. M. (1978) Uniformity and diversity of structure and function in rhesus monkey prestriate visual cortex. *Journal of Physiology, 277,* 273–90.

Glossary and Indices

Glossary

This glossary gives definitions of technical terms, particularly physiological and mathematical ones, not defined in the text, and also of terms used in sections of the book distant from those in which they are explained. Terms in italics are defined elsewhere in the glossary.

Absorption spectrum The relationship between the wavelength of light striking a *pigment* and how strongly the light is absorbed.

Accommodation Adjustment of the optics of an eye to keep an object in focus on the retina as its distance from the eye varies. In the human eye this is achieved by varying the thickness of the lens.

Action potential The interior of a nerve cell has a negative electrical charge relative to the exterior. If the *axon* of a nerve cell is stimulated electrically, the membrane allows current to cross it and the charge is momentarily reversed. This change in membrane behaviour spreads rapidly down the axon and the wave of change in voltage across the membrane which it causes is called an action potential.

Acuity See *Visual acuity*.

Adaptation A change in the sensitivity to light of either a *photoreceptor* or of the visual system as a whole, so as to match the current average light intensity. Adaptation to bright light (e.g., when you wake up and switch on a light) occurs rapidly, while dark adaptation (e.g., when you walk from daylight into a dark cinema) is a slower process.

Affordance A term introduced by Gibson, which refers to a possibility for action afforded to a perceiver by an object. The affordances of an object depend upon the perceiver as well as upon the characteristics of the object. For example, a stream affords such actions as jumping and paddling to a person, but to a frog it affords swimming.

Aggregate field The area within which the *receptive fields* of cells in a single *hypercolumn* of the *visual cortex* fall.

Algorithm A specified procedure for solving a problem.

Amacrine cell A type of cell in the vertebrate retina (see Fig. 2.5).

Ambient optic array See *Optic array*.

Area centralis Area in a vertebrate retina rich in *cones*, with little pooling of receptor outputs. In the human eye, the area centralis corresponds to the *fovea*, but this is not so in all species.

Axon The long, slender process of a nerve cell leading away from the cell body and ending at *synapses* with other cells.

Bipolar cell A type of cell in the vertebrate retina (see Fig. 2.5).

Bottom-up process See *Data-driven process*.

Centre-off response A cell with a *concentric receptive field* that responds to a reduction of light intensity in the centre of its field relative to that in the surround is said to have a centre-off response.

Centre-on response A cell with a *concentric receptive field* which responds to an increase in light intensity in the centre of its field relative to that in the surround is said to have a centre-on response.

Closed-loop control A control system in which the output is continuously modified by feedback from the environment. An example is a person maintaining balance on a surfboard; their posture (the output) is continually adjusted in response to movement of the board (feedback).

Complex cell Cell in the *visual cortex* responding either to an edge, a bar or a slit stimulus of a particular orientation falling anywhere within its *receptive field*.

Computational theory A term introduced by Marr. Computational theories of vision are concerned with how, in principle, particular kinds of information such as the shapes of objects or distances of surfaces can be extracted from images. Solutions to such problems involve consideration of the constraints which apply to the structures of natural objects and surfaces and the ways in which they reflect light. An example is the demonstration that the shape of an object can be recovered from its silhouette if the shape approximates to a *generalised cone*.

Concentric field A *receptive field* divided into an inner circular region and an outer ring-shaped region. Light falling in each of the two regions has opposite effects on the response of the cell.

Conceptually driven process A process of extraction of information from sensory input which relies for its operation on prior knowledge of the properties of objects or events to be detected. For example, a conceptually driven process for recovering the structures of solid objects represented in an image would require prior information about the geometrical properties of any objects (such as the nature of cubes and cylinders) which could be present.

Cone Vertebrate *photoreceptor* with short outer segment, which does not respond to light of low intensity.

Contrast Difference between maximum and minimum intensities in a pattern of light.

Data driven process A process of extraction of information from sensory input which relies only on information available in the input. For example, a data driven process for recovering the structures of solid objects represented in an image would require no knowledge of the geometrical properties of particular kinds of object.

Dendrites The processes of nerve cells which carry *slow potentials* from *synapses* to the cell body.

Depolarisation A change in the *membrane potential* of a nerve cell such that the interior becomes less negatively charged relative to the exterior. If the membrane of an *axon* is depolarised, *action potentials* are generated with increased frequency.

Derivative The result of differentiating a function. A time derivative is obtained if a function relating some quantity to time is differentiated with respect to time. For example, the time derivative of a function relating the volume of water in a bath to time expresses how the rate of emptying or filling of the bath varies with time.

Diffraction The scattering of rays of light by collision with particles of matter as they pass through a medium such as air or water.

Direction preference An alternative term to *direction selectivity*.

Direction selectivity A difference in the response of a cell to a pattern of light moving through its *receptive field* according to the direction of movement.

Directional sensitivity A single *photoreceptor* is stimulated by light arriving through a segment of the *optic array*. In this book, we have used the term directional sensitivity to refer to the size of this segment. The smaller it is, the greater the directional sensitivity of the photoreceptor. In order to achieve a high degree of directional sensitivity, some means of forming an image is required. The term is used by some authors as a synonym of *directional selectivity*.

Eccentric cell Type of *photoreceptor* in the eye of the horseshoe crab (see Fig. 2.1).

Eccentricity Angular distance of a point on the retina from the centre of the *fovea*.

Edge segment In Marr's theory of early visual processing, a token in the *raw primal sketch* formed where *zero-crossing segments* from $\nabla^2 G$ *filters* of adjacent sizes coincide.

Electrotonic spread The spread of a *slow potential* over the membrane of a *dendrite* or nerve cell body.

End-inhibition A property of some cells in the *visual cortex* causing them to respond strongly to either an edge, a bar or a slit which ends within the *receptive field*.

Exproprioceptive information Information about the position of a perceiver's body, or parts of the body, relative to the environment. Lee (1977) introduced this term to give a three-fold classification of types of sensory information, along with the traditional classes of *exteroceptive* and *proprioceptive* information.

Exteroceptive information Information about surfaces, objects and events in a perceiver's environment.

Fibre See *Axon*.

Filter, $\nabla^2 G$ An *algorithm* which smooths an array of light intensity values in an image with a *Gaussian filter* and then applies a *Laplacian* operator to each region of the smoothed image. The wider the filter, the greater the degree of smoothing of the image by the Gaussian part of the filter.

Firing rate The frequency at which *action potentials* pass down the *axon* of a nerve cell.

Fixation In the case of an animal with mobile eyes, alignment of the eyes so that the image of the fixated target falls on the *area centralis*. Otherwise, alignment of the head to point towards the fixated target.

Fourier analysis Fourier's theorem proves that any one-dimensional pattern can be fully described as the sum of a number of sine-waves of different frequencies and amplitudes. The same is true of a two-dimensional pattern provided that the horizontal and vertical components of each sinusoid are analysed. Fourier analysis is a procedure for breaking down a pattern into its sinusoidal components.

Fourier transform The description of a pattern in terms of the frequencies and amplitudes of its sinusoidal components which is obtained by applying *Fourier analysis*.

Fovea Pit-shaped depression in a vertebrate retina, usually in an *area centralis*.

Ganglion cell A type of cell in the vertebrate retina (see Fig. 2.5). The *axons* of ganglion cells are packed together in the *optic nerve* and carry information from retina to brain.

Gaussian filter Algorithm smoothing spatial or temporal variation in an image by averaging neighbouring values of light intensity, the contribution of values to the average being weighted according to a Gaussian (normal) function.

Generalised cone The surface created by moving a cross-section of constant shape but variable size along an axis (see Fig. 7.15).

Grating A pattern of parallel dark and bright stripes of equal widths. In a sinusoidal (or sine-wave) grating, brightness varies sinusoidally across the pattern, so that the stripes are blurred (see Fig. 2.7).

Horizontal cell A type of cell in the vertebrate retina (see Fig. 2.5).

Hypercolumn A block of the *visual cortex* in which all cells have *receptive fields* falling in a single area of the retina.

Hypercomplex cell A *complex cell* with the property of *end-inhibition*.

Hyperpolarisation A change in the *membrane potential* of a nerve cell such that the interior becomes more negatively charged relative to the exterior. If the membrane of an *axon* is hyperpolarised, *action potentials* are generated with lower frequency.

Impulse See *Action potential*.

Interneuron Nerve cell in the central nervous system which is neither a *receptor* nor a *motor neuron*.

Intracellular recording Recording the *membrane potential* of a nerve cell by means of an electrode penetrating the membrane.

Invariant In Gibson's use of the term, some measure of the pattern of light reflected from an object, event or scene which remains constant as other measures of the pattern vary. An invariant therefore provides information for a perceiver about some aspect of their surroundings. For example, the size of elements of optic texture in the light reflected from a surface varies with the nature of the surface and with its distance from the perceiver, and therefore does not provide information to specify the slant of the surface relative to the perceiver. For a particular slant, however, the rate of change of the size of texture elements is invariant for different surfaces and different distances.

LGN (lateral geniculate nucleus) The part of the mammalian brain where the *axons* of retinal *ganglion cells* terminate, and from which axons run to the *visual cortex* (see Fig. 2.13).

Laplacian (∇^2) If a quantity such as light intensity varies along one dimension, then the second derivative of that quantity describes the rate at which its gradient is changing at any point. For example, a positive value of the second derivative would indicate that the gradient of light intensity is becoming more positive. If light intensity varies along two dimensions (as it does in an image), the Laplacian is a means of obtaining the net rate of change of the intensity gradients in all orientations around a point. A positive value of the Laplacian would indicate that the gradient of light intensity around a point was becoming more positive, but would not specify along which axis this change was occurring.

Lateral lines Organs on each side of a fish's body which contain *receptor cells* sensitive to vibration in water.

Membrane potential The difference in electrical potential between the interior and the exterior of a nerve cell. In the resting state, the interior is always negative relative to the exterior.

Motion parallax Movement of the image of an object over the retina. The rate of movement depends upon both the velocity of the object relative to the eye, and its distance from the eye.

Motor neuron A nerve cell which *synapses* with a muscle cell. *Action potentials* passing down the *axon* of the motor neuron cause the muscle to contract.

Neuron Nerve cell.

Ocular preference Cells in the *visual cortex* which respond more strongly to a stimulus presented to one eye than to the other are said to show ocular preference.

Off-centre cell Cell in the visual pathway with a *centre-off response*.

On-centre cell Cell in the visual pathway with a *centre-on response*.

Ommatidium Unit of the compound eye containing a light-sensitive rhabdom (see Fig. 1.8).

Open-loop control Control system in which the output is not continuously modified by feedback from the environment. An example is a person swatting a fly; once the swing of the arm begins, it is completed whatever the fly does.

Operant conditioning A term introduced by Skinner. In an operant conditioning procedure, an animal's behaviour is changed by pairing a piece of behaviour (the operant) with reinforcement. For example, if a rat receives food each time it presses a bar, it will come to press the bar more frequently. Such methods can be used to determine whether an animal can discriminate two stimuli. For example, if a rat can learn to press a bar when it hears a tone of one pitch and not to press when it hears one of another pitch, then it must be able to discriminate the tones.

Opponent-colour response If light of one wavelength falling in its *receptive field* causes a cell to fire more frequently than its resting rate, and light of a different wavelength causes it to fire less frequently, the cell is said to have an opponent-colour response.

Opsins A group of *pigments* found in *photoreceptor cells.*

Optic array Term introduced by Gibson, to refer to the instantaneous pattern of light reaching a point in space from all directions. In different regions of the optic array, the spatial pattern of light will differ, according to the nature of the surface from which it has been reflected.

Optic flow field The fluctuating pattern of light intensity reaching an observer caused by any relative movement between observer and environment.

Optic nerve Nerve running from retina to brain.

Optic texture The spatial pattern of light reflected from a textured surface.

Optomotor response The turning response of an animal presented with uniform flow of *optic texture*, in the direction which minimises rate of flow relative to the animal.

Orientation preference Variation in the response of a cell in the *visual cortex* with the orientation of an edge, bar or slit. The preferred orientation is that giving the greatest response.

Peak spectral sensitivity The wavelength of light to which a *photoreceptor* responds most strongly.

Photon Unit of energy in electromagnetic radiation.

Photopic vision Vision in light sufficiently bright to excite *cones.*

Photoreceptor cell A *receptor cell* sensitive to light.

Pigment A chemical substance which absorbs light. Pigment molecules change in shape as they absorb light and, in a *photoreceptor*, this change begins a series of biochemical processes which lead to the *receptor potential.*

Pitch Rotation of a flying insect or bird in a "head-up" or "head-down" manner (see Fig. 9.1).

Plexiform layer Layer of nerve cell processes and *synapses* in the vertebrate retina (see Fig. 2.5).

Poles (of optic flow field) These are the two points in the *optic flow field* surrounding an observer moving through the environment at which there is no flow of *optic texture*. One is the point towards which the observer is moving (see Fig. 8.7) and the other is the point away from which the observer is moving.

Projection Light rays are said to be projected to the image plane when an image is formed. The word also has a quite different meaning in neurophysiology, to refer to the region where the *axons* of a group of nerve cells in the brain terminate and make *synaptic* contact.

Proprioceptive information In Lee's use of the term, information about the positions of parts of the body relative to one another.

Psychophysics The analysis of perceptual processes by studying the effect on a subject's experience or behaviour of systematically varying the properties of a stimulus along one or more physical dimensions.

Raw primal sketch In Marr's theory of vision, a rich representation of the intensity changes present in the original image.

Receptive field The area of the retina in which light causes a response in a particular nerve cell.

Receptor cell A nerve cell sensitive to external energy.

Receptor potential The change in *membrane potential* of a receptor cell caused by external energy impinging on it.

Refraction The bending of rays of light as they cross a boundary between two transparent media of different optical densities.

Retinal ganglion cell See *Ganglion cell.*

Retinotopic map An array of nerve cells which have the same positions relative to one another as their *receptive fields* have on the surface of the retina.

Retinula cell A *photoreceptor* in the eye of an insect or other arthropod (see Figs. 1.8 and 2.1).

Rod Vertebrate *photoreceptor* with long outer segment, sensitive to light of low intensity.

Roll Rotation of a flying insect or bird around the long axis of the body (see Fig. 9.1).

Saccade Rapid movement of the eye to fixate a target.

Scalar A quantity which has magnitude only.

Scotopic vision Vision in dim light, sufficiently bright to excite *rods* but not *cones.*

Sensitivity spectrum The relationship between the wavelength of light striking a *photoreceptor* and the size of the *receptor potential.*

Simple cell Cell in the visual cortex showing linear *spatial summation* of light intensities in parts of its *receptive field* separated by straight line boundaries.

Sinusoidal grating See *Grating.*

Slow potential A small change in the *membrane potential* of a nerve cell, such as a *receptor potential*, which decays as it spreads passively over the membrane. In contrast, an *action potential* is propagated by an active change in membrane properties and does not decay in amplitude as it is transmitted.

Spatial frequency The frequency, expressed as cycles per unit of visual angle, of a sinusoidal pattern of light such as a *grating*. At a particular viewing distance, the spatial frequency of a grating depends upon the width of its stripes; the narrower these are, the higher the frequency.

Spatial frequency tuning A nerve cell in a visual pathway which responds more strongly to sinusoidal *gratings* which have *spatial frequencies* in a particular range than to gratings of other frequencies is said to show spatial frequency tuning.

Spatial summation If the response of a cell to a pattern of light is determined only by the difference in the amounts of light falling in different regions of its *receptive field*, then it is said to show linear spatial summation.

Stereopsis Perception of depth dependent upon disparity in the images projected on the retinas of the two eyes.

Stereoscopic fusion The process whereby the two disparate retinal images are combined to yield a single percept in depth.

Striate cortex See *Visual cortex.*

Synapse A point where the membranes of two nerve cells nearly touch and where electrical activity in one cell influences the *membrane potential* of the other cell.

3-D model representation An object-centred representation of shape, organised hierarchically (see Fig. 7.16).

Top-down process See *Conceptually driven process.*

Topology A branch of geometry describing the properties of forms which are unaffected by continuous distortion such as stretching. For example, a doughnut and a record have the same topology.

Torque Turning force, equal to force applied multiplied by the distance of its point of application from the centre of rotation.

Transduction The process by which external energy impinging on a *receptor cell* causes a change in its *membrane potential.*

$2\frac{1}{2}$D sketch A viewer-centred representation of the depths and orientations of visible surfaces (see Fig. 6.21).

Vector A quantity which has both magnitude and direction.

Vergence movements Movements of the eyes making them either more or less convergent.

Vestibular system The organ in the inner ear involved in the *transduction* of angular acceleration of the body into nerve impulses.

Visual acuity An observer's visual acuity is measured by the angle between the stripes in the highest frequency *grating* which they can distinguish from a plain field of the same average brightness as the grating.

Visual angle The angle which an object subtends at the eye (see Fig. 1.13).

Visual cortex, primary Region of the mammalian cortex in the occipital lobe receiving input from the *LGN*. Cells in the primary visual cortex respond to light falling on the retina and are arranged in a *retinotopic map*. In primates, this region is also known as the striate cortex.

W cells The *ganglion cells* of the mammalian retina which do not have *concentric fields*.

X cells The *ganglion cells* of the mammalian retina with *concentric fields* which show linear *spatial summation* of light intensities in the centre and surround areas of the *receptive field*.

Y cells The *ganglion cells* of the mammalian retina with *concentric fields* which show non-linear responses to changes in light intensity.

Yaw Rotation of a flying insect or bird around the vertical axis (see Fig. 9.1).

Zero-crossing A point where values of a function change sign (see Fig. 3.9).

Zero-crossing segment A series of *zero-crossings* obtained from an image which share the same orientation (see Fig. 3.12).

Subject Index

Accommodation:
  as cue to depth, 130, 218
  of vertebrate eye, 21, 22
Acuity—see Visual acuity
Adaptation, 26, 35, 36, 48
Affordance, 199, 200, 326, 327, 329, 332, 333
Ageing of head profiles, 309–312
Algorithmic level of theory, 62, 90, 323–325, 327, 328
Amacrine cells, 39, 40, 50, 51
Ambient optic array—see Optic array
Ambiguous pictures, 98–101, 200
Ames' demonstrations, 92, 93
Anaglyph, 131, 132
Apparent motion, 152, 202
Artificial intelligence, 93
  (see also Computer models)
Attribution, 302–304
Balance, 231–234
Bandwidth, 70, 71
Behaviourism, 91, 92, 94, 203
Binocular depth cells, 131
Binocular disparity—see Stereopsis
Bipolar cells, 39, 40, 49
Bottom-up processing, 94, 96, 176
  (see also Data driven processing)
Braking, 239–241
Camera analogy, 31, 90, 129
Camouflage—see Colouration of animals

Cardioidal strain, 310–312
Catching, 243–245
Causality, perception of, 297–300
Centre of moment, 293–296, 312
Centre-off response, 41, 79, 80, 81–84
Centre-on response, 41, 65, 79, 80, 81–84
Children, vision in, 230–234, 242, 243
Chimpanzees, 281–284, 328
Ciliary muscles, 22
Closure, grouping by, 104, 124
Cognitive impenetrability, 325
Colour vision, 29–31
  (see also Opponent-colour responses)
Colouration of animals, 111–117
  background picturing, 112
  countershading, 114, 115
  disruptive colouration, 112
  outlining, 113
  signal patches, 114, 116
Common fate, grouping by, 102, 103, 114, 115
Compiled detectors, 325
Complex cells, 55, 70
  as feature detectors, 63, 64
Compound eye, 13–15
  of *Limulus*, 33, 34
Computational theory, 62, 89, 95, 136, 137, 154, 155
Computer models:
  of early visual processing, 121–127

Author Index